THE FORCES IN AMERICAN ECONOMIC GROWTH SERIES

*Under the General Editorship of* Alfred D. Chandler, Jr.

# Cotton and the Growth of the American Economy: 1790–1860

# Cotton and the Growth of the American Economy: 1790–1860



## *Sources and Readings*

COMPILED AND EDITED BY

Stuart Bruchey

MICHIGAN STATE UNIVERSITY

Harcourt, Brace & World, Inc.

NEW YORK · CHICAGO · SAN FRANCISCO · ATLANTA

*Library of Congress Catalog Card Number: 67–16825*

PRINTED IN THE UNITED STATES OF AMERICA

For Mary Louise, William, and Asa

# THE FORCES IN AMERICAN ECONOMIC GROWTH SERIES

THE *Forces in American Economic Growth series provides a documentary record of the building of the American economy. Each book in the series concentrates on the economic force or forces that generated the most compelling pressure for change at key junctures in American history. In each volume the men responsible for change speak for themselves. By presenting such a record the editors hope to enhance the reader's sense of economic reality, his awareness of underlying historic currents, and his ability to investigate and interpret business and economic change and growth.*

*The series attempts to achieve this goal by providing illustration and by permitting analysis. The documents presented are intended to show how new patterns of economic action occurred and how American entrepreneurs, managers, engineers, financiers, business analysts, workers, and labor-union leaders carried on their various activities at different periods of history. The record provides more than mere illustration. The documents have been collected and presented in a way to encourage analysis and interpretation. They raise questions of why and what as well as how. Why did new ways come when they did and in the way they did? What stimulated and what hindered change? What was the role of personality in producing innovation and bringing economic growth?*

*The series, in short, supplies the record, the source materials, that a reader can use to form his own judgment about the nature of economic and historical change. It will allow him to be his own historian and his own interpreter of the changing American business and economic scene.*

ALFRED D. CHANDLER, JR.

# CONTENTS

## PART II

## The Opening of the West



## PART III

## Production

## PART IV

## Financing and Marketing the Cotton Crop

# A GENERAL INTRODUCTION TO THE READINGS

THE PROCESS of economic growth is a phenomenon in which numerous factors interact in complex ways. Some of these factors are economic, but others are political, social, psychological, and technological. They consist in part of actions and in part of frameworks—habits and traditions, institutions and values—in which actions are taken. The actions themselves are public as well as private: in any developing country the behavior of governments as well as of businessmen, workers, teachers, inventors, investors, and a host of other private individuals and groups must be taken into account. How to deal with so many factors constitutes one of the most puzzling problems known to students of the social sciences; the importance of any one factor depends upon the way in which it is combined with other factors in the process of development, and each shifts its position from time to time as the process goes on! In a word, there is no single key that will unlock all the doors to the mysteries of growth.

It is nevertheless true that particular factors loom as particularly important at particular times. Why this should be so will be clear on a moment's reflection. If one looks at an economy as a whole—certainly any economy that has passed beyond the subsistence level of development—one sees that it is composed of a number of geographical regions, economic sectors (such as agriculture, trade, and manufacturing), industries, and business firms. But, even if the economy is undergoing growth, not all its components are growing at the same rate; indeed, some are declining or simply holding their own. If overall growth is taking place, it is only because the growth of some components is more than compensating for the failure of others to grow or to grow at the same rate. Some, in a word, are exercising leadership in the growth process; they are "key" regions, sectors, industries, or firms. So, while economic growth always involves a multiplicity of interacting factors, it is possible to focus on the areas where some of them are most effectively at work.

A few examples will clarify the point. Were one to examine the American economy of the mid-twentieth century one might well focus upon the contributions of the electronics industry to rising productivity in both production and administration. Earlier in the twentieth century another new industry—automobiles—created an impact which also radiated both backward and forward into other areas of the economy—backward into those industries whose products the manufacture of automobiles consumed (rubber, glass, iron, and steel) and forward into new kinds of enterprises which the automobile created (for example, highway construction and outdoor advertising).

The longer the chain of "linkages," of course, the greater the effect on incomes and employment. In the late nineteenth century it was railroad expansion that widened and deepened national markets, and in the years before the Civil War it was cotton that did so.

Cotton is an excellent example of the leadership provided by a new "industry." Of negligible importance prior to the last two decades of the eighteenth century, its rise, as we shall see in Part I, coincided with the mounting tempo of the English industrial revolution. Throughout the eighteenth century English population and trade had been experiencing generally rapid growth, creating a situation that encouraged entrepreneurs to undertake a series of technical improvements in spinning and weaving and in the application of steam power to the new textile machinery that would make it possible to provide first England and then a large part of the world with good, cheap cotton cloth. Innovation in the United States also helped in the achievement of this result, for the invention of the cotton gin cheapened the cost of processing long-staple Upland, the only kind of cotton that could be extensively cultivated in the American South, and allowed American supply to respond with amazing alacrity to the increasing British demands. Amounting to 2 million pounds in 1791, the crop underwent an almost 25 fold expansion in the decade before 1801. By 1860 the crop was in the neighborhood of a billion pounds—a 500 fold increase in 70 years.

In his stimulating pioneer study, *The Economic Growth of the United States,*[1] Douglass C. North emphasizes the fact that no other product approached cotton in importance during these years. For the period 1815–60 as a whole cotton alone constituted more than half the total value of domestic exports. It had two early rivals, wheat and flour (counting as one) and unmanufactured tobacco, which made up 16 per cent and 15 per cent, respectively, of the value of domestic exports for the years 1816–20. But these were the high points for both during the antebellum years. The role of tobacco in relation to total American exports was thus a declining one. Once it had been the leading colonial staple—and in that respect comparable to cotton—but the vast demand created by the continual interplay between industrialization and population increase dwarfed the role of the forerunner on an altered scale of magnitudes.

America thus provides an instance of the principle that young nations in possession of rich resources may accelerate their rates of economic growth via exports of their leading staples. Earnings from cotton provided a main means of paying for imports, amounting to 60 per cent of total expenditure on imports for consumption in 1860. But manufactured goods, sugar, coffee, and other articles for consumption were by no means the only kinds of import financed by exports of cotton. So, too, were imports of railroad iron and other kinds of capital goods. Foreign investments in the United States were also important. As North has shown, these two forms of capital import

[1] Englewood Cliffs, N.J.: Prentice-Hall, 1961.

were particularly significant during the years 1815–18, 1832–39, and 1850–57, although exports of western grain and California gold also helped finance imports of capital goods in the last-named period.

Foreign capital played an important role in American economic growth, just as it often has in more recent cases of underdeveloped countries. English and other European investors purchased large quantities of bonds floated by numerous state governments in order to raise capital to finance canals and other "internal improvements." They also purchased the securities of "plantation banks"—set up in Mississippi and Louisiana—and these banks then used the funds to make long-term loans to planters for the purpose of buying land and slaves. And in the expansive 1830's, foreign capital entered the country in part in the form of specie.

Imported specie, serving as the basis upon which commercial banks made loans, contributed more importantly to industrial development than is sometimes realized. Loans were typically for short periods but were often renewed and thus converted into credits of up to a year or more in length. Such loans often financed purchases of machinery, a large amount of which was made of wood and was relatively inexpensive. Most of the funds needed by industrialists were required for wage payments and inventory maintenance, and these could be met by short-term loans. The 1850's, however, ushered in a new technological age in which sums required for machinery were increasingly large in relation to those needed for wages and inventories. And, because commercial banks were unable to tie up *large* sums in long-term loans, the need for them was increasingly met by the formation of corporations to finance industrial capital via sales of stocks and bonds. This is the reason for the mushrooming growth of the corporation that occurred in the 1850's. Yet one must not overstress the capital-intensive nature of industry before the Civil War. On the eve of that conflict partnerships and proprietorships, assisted by bank loans, were able to provide most of the capital required by industry.

While the foreign demand for cotton provided capital to bolster domestic credit institutions, it also acted in other ways to encourage American growth. Detailed accounts of these effects are presented in the following readings and in the introductions to them, and therefore only their general outline need be indicated here. Most important of all the consequences of that demand—most important because of its own potent ability to generate subsequent effects—was the rise and spread of specialized economic activity. It is worth repeating and bearing in mind a fundamental precept emphasized by Adam Smith—that the degree of specialization depends upon the width of the market (quantity of demand). Unless the demand for a commodity or service is sufficient to enable a person to devote his full time to producing it he will have to spend part of his time doing whatever else helps him make a living. He cannot afford to specialize as a cobbler but will have to accept employment as a carpenter and perhaps as a farmer too. But the more he is required to diversify his occupations the more difficult it will be for him to acquire a high degree of skill in any of them. His productivity, that is, his output per unit of labor input, will be low in comparison with that of a specialist doing one thing alone and depending upon exchange with other specialists for the goods he needs but does not himself produce. The greater the degree of specialization, then, the greater will be the volume of trade. These things are true not only for individuals but also for the economic sectors and regions that make up an economy. Specialized agriculture is more productive than diversified agriculture. If a region tends to concentrate its resources on a particular kind of production and depends upon other specialized regions for what it needs but does not itself produce in sufficient quantities, not only its own productivity but also that of the whole economy will tend to rise.

Precisely this kind of specialized regional activity tended to develop in the United States during the antebellum decades, and so too did both sectoral and occupational specialization. As we shall see, the demand for cotton does not alone suffice to explain these occurrences; yet it was a necessary condition for them. The foreign demand for cotton enabled the South—the Southwest in particular—to concentrate its resources to a significant degree on the production of that staple, using the earnings from its sale to pay the East for manufactured goods and financial and shipping services and the West for food supplies and livestock. The internal market for the goods and services of each of the regions, in sum, widened in part because of the foreign market for cotton. Both the growth of specialized commercial agriculture in the West and the development of industry in the East thus partly depended upon the demand for cotton created by the English industrial revolution.

They also depended upon the provision of improved forms of internal transport to knit the separate regions into an interdependent, and hence national, economy. But transportation improvements themselves owed much to the movement of cotton culture from its original coastal base into the uplands and then into the Southwest. In ways that will be explained, the spread of cotton culture helped pave the way for the economic rise of the West, and it was the ensuing rivalry of coastal cities for the trade of the West that induced state governments themselves to build roads, canals, bridges, and railroads, or to charter and aid numerous quasi-public business corporations for that purpose. New York, the great port that won out in the competition in the Northeast, however, owed as much to the enterprising foresight of her private businessmen who established both Atlantic and coastal packet lines to serve the needs of the cotton trade as it did to the state government that built the Erie Canal.

The settlement of the West, both cause and consequence of these developments in transportation facilities, in turn generated massive speculations in western lands and put pressure upon commercial and other banks in the region to make credit available on easy terms to finance those speculations. The Panics of 1819, 1837, and 1857 were all preceded by speculative paroxysms associated with land. But they were also associated with developments in the British sector of the Atlantic community and cannot be meaningfully separated from the more intricate causal complex thereby implied.

The cotton fiber is thus a causal thread of surprising strength and deviousness. While it helps explain many of the important economic—and also social and political—developments of the pre-Civil War period, it cannot completely explain any of them; no single factor is capable of doing so. Much else besides cotton would have to be placed upon a crowded stage in order to explain the movements for internal improvements, commercial and central banking, land speculation, and other important economic phenomena of the antebellum period. Obviously, no single book of readings can display all these interrelated factors at work. But it may display one of them, and it is for this reason that the following readings—like the planters of the antebellum South—tend to concentrate on cotton.

Immediately following this introduction is a section of statistical tables, divided into two groups. The first group begins with the few available statistics on world production and consumption of raw cotton; these show the importance of the United States as a producer and of Great Britain as a consumer relative to other countries. Other tables give details of British consumption and of United States production and consumption, especially the changing contribution of the individual states. The second group contains tables that show the vigorous rise of internal commerce that owed so much to regional specialization and the demand for cotton.

After the statistical section, Part I ("Demand and Supply") contains selections that help explain the first group of statistical tables by telling the story of British and American invention. Part II describes the role of cotton and of transportation improvements in the opening of the West and shows the significance of those developments from the point of view of the emerging national economy. Part III focuses on problems of plantation management and other aspects of production, and Part IV follows the intricate channels of supply and finance involved in the marketing of the cotton crop. The selections in this group are largely from previously unpublished manuscript sources.

# STATISTICS OF COTTON AND INTERNAL COMMERCE

## 1] Production and Consumption

TABLES 1 A–C. WORLDWIDE PRODUCTION AND CONSUMPTION OF RAW COTTON

A. COTTON PRODUCTION BY AREAS: 1791–1860
[In millions of pounds.]

| Area | 1791 | 1801 | 1811 | 1821 | 1831 | 1840 | 1850 | 1860 |
|---|---|---|---|---|---|---|---|---|
| Brazil | 22 | 26 | 35 | 32 | 38 | 30 | 40 | 36 |
| West Indies | 12 | 10 | 12 | 10 | 9 | 8 | 3 | 6 |
| Egypt | — | — | 1 | 6 | 18 | 25 | 30 | 34 |
| Rest of Africa | 45 | 46 | 44 | 40 | 36 | 34 | 34 | 35 |
| India | 130 | 160 | 170 | 175 | 180 | 185 | 210 | 450 |
| Rest of Asia | 190 | 160 | 146 | 135 | 115 | 110 | 120 | 132 |
| Mexico and South America | 68 | 56 | 57 | 44 | 35 | 35 | 40 | 57 |
| Other Areas | — | 15 | 11 | 8 | 4 | 13 | 15 | 100 |
| United States | 2 | 48 | 80 | 180 | 385 | 654 | 990 | 1650 |
| Total | 469 | 531 | 556 | 630 | 820 | 1044 | 1482 | 2500 |
| Percentile share of United States | 0.4 | 9.0 | 16.3 | 28.6 | 49.6 | 62.6 | 67.8 | 66.0 |

## B. Cotton Consumption by Areas: 1840–60

[In millions of pounds.]

| Area | 1840 | 1850 | 1860 |
|---|---|---|---|
| Russia | 14 | 48 | 87 |
| France | 116 | 140 | 226 |
| Germany | 26 | 46 | 140 |
| Austria | 34 | 58 | 94 |
| Switzerland | 18 | 24 | 30 |
| Sweden | 2 | 8 | 16 |
| Holland | 4 | 5 | 6 |
| Belgium | 16 | 22 | 29 |
| Spain | 14 | 34 | 52 |
| Italy | 8 | 16 | 26 |
| Great Britain | 459 | 588 | 1084 |
| United States | 146 | 297 | 387 |
| India | — | — | 220 |

## C. Capital and Labor Employed in the Cultivation of Cotton and Value of Crop, United States and Other Areas, Various Years: 1791–1835

| Year | Capital employed in growing (millions of dollars) | | | Persons employed in growing, and dependent (millions) | | Value of crop (millions of dollars) | |
|---|---|---|---|---|---|---|---|
| | United States | Egypt | Brazil | United States | Elsewhere | United States | Elsewhere |
| 1791 | 3 1/3 | — | 33 | 1/20 | 1 | 1/3 | 40 1/2 |
| 1801 | 80 | — | 50 | 1/10 | 7/8 | 8 | 39 1/3 |
| 1811 | 134 | 1/10 | 58 | 1/7 | 7/8 | 12 1/2 | 37 |
| 1821 | 300 | 3 1/3 | 83 | 1/3 | 7/8 | 29 3/4 | 37 |
| 1831 | 650 | 30 | 58 | 3/4 | 4/5 | 38 1/2 | 29 1/4 |
| 1834 | — | — | — | — | — | 76 | 36 1/3 |
| 1835 | 800 | 31 | 50 | 1 | 4/5 to 1 | — | — |

## Tables 2 A–E. The Rise of the British Cotton Textile Industry

### A. Imports of Raw Cotton by Great Britain: 1700–1860

[In pounds. By major areas of origin and showing reexports, 1700–80.]

| Year | Imports | | | Reexports |
|---|---|---|---|---|
| | Levant | West Indies | Total | |
| 1700 | 659,406 | 722,290 | 1,395,751 | 313,090 |
| 1725 | 718,552 | 1,100,667 | 1,841,499 | 103,108 |
| 1750 | 1,085,383 | 1,125,936 | 2,317,972 | 64,405 |
| 1775 | 2,762,679 | 2,726,298 | 6,693,734 | 616,681 |
| 1780 | 338,743 | 4,166,122 | 6,877,369 | 324,407 |

| Year | Total | Year | Total |
|---|---|---|---|
| 1781 | 5,198,778 | 1821 | 132,537,000 |
| 1782 | 11,828,039 | 1822 | 142,838,000 |
| 1783 | 9,735,663 | 1823 | 191,403,000 |
| 1784 | 11,482,083 | 1824 | 149,380,000 |
| 1785 | 18,400,384 | 1825 | 228,005,000 |
| 1786 | 19,475,020 | 1826 | 177,607,000 |
| 1787 | 23,250,268 | 1827 | 272,449,000 |
| 1788 | 20,467,436 | 1828 | 227,761,000 |
| 1789 | 32,576,023 | 1829 | 222,767,000 |
| 1790 | 31,447,605 | 1830 | 263,961,000 |
| 1791 | 28,706,675 | 1831 | 288,675,000 |
| 1792 | 34,907,497 | 1832 | 286,833,000 |
| 1793 | 19,040,929 | 1833 | 303,657,000 |
| 1794 | 24,358,567 | 1834 | 326,875,000 |
| 1795 | 26,401,340 | 1835 | 363,703,000 |
| 1796 | 32,126,357 | 1836 | 406,959,000 |
| 1797 | 23,354,371 | 1837 | 407,287,000 |
| 1798 | 31,880,641 | 1838 | 507,851,000 |
| 1799 | 43,379,278 | 1839 | 389,397,000 |
| 1800 | 56,010,732 | 1840 | 592,488,000 |
| 1801 | 56,004,305 | 1841 | 487,992,000 |
| 1802 | 60,345,600 | 1842 | 531,750,000 |
| 1803 | 53,812,284 | 1843 | 673,193,000 |
| 1804 | 61,867,329 | 1844 | 646,111,000 |
| 1805 | 59,682,406 | 1845 | 721,980,000 |
| 1806 | 58,176,283 | 1846 | 467,856,000 |
| 1807 | 74,925,306 | 1847 | 474,708,000 |
| 1808 | 43,605,982 | 1848 | 713,020,000 |
| 1809 | 92,812,282 | 1849 | 755,469,000 |
| 1810 | 132,488,935 | 1850 | 663,577,000 |
| 1811 | 91,576,535 | 1851 | 757,380,000 |
| 1812 | 63,025,936 | 1852 | 929,782,000 |
| 1813 | 50,966,000 | 1853 | 895,279,000 |
| 1814 | 60,060,239 | 1854 | 887,333,000 |
| 1815 | 100,709,000 | 1855 | 891,752,000 |
| 1816 | 95,281,000 | 1856 | 023,886,000 |
| 1817 | 126,304,000 | 1857 | 969,319,000 |
| 1818 | 178,746,000 | 1858 | 1,034,342,000 |
| 1819 | 151,153,000 | 1859 | 1,225,989,000 |
| 1820 | 151,673,000 | 1860 | 1,390,939,000 |

## B. Imports of Cotton by Area of Origin, United Kingdom: 1840–60

[In thousands of pounds.]

| Years | United States | Brazil | The Mediterranean including Egypt and Turkey |
|---|---|---|---|
| 1840 | 487,857 | 14,779 | 8,325 |
| 1841 | 358,241 | 16,671 | 9,097 |
| 1842 | 414,031 | 15,223 | 4,489 |
| 1843 | 574,739 | 18,675 | 9,674 |
| 1844 | 517,219 | 21,085 | 12,406 |
| 1845 | 626,650 | 20,158 | 14,615 |
| 1846 | 401,949 | 14,746 | 14,278 |
| 1847 | 364,599 | 19,967 | 4,814 |
| 1848 | 600,247 | 19,971 | 7,232 |
| 1849 | 634,504 | 30,738 | 17,370 |
| 1850 | 493,153 | 30,300 | 18,931 |
| 1851 | 596,639 | 19,339 | 16,951 |
| 1852 | 765,631 | 26,506 | 48,059 |
| 1853 | 658,452 | 24,191 | — |
| 1854 | 722,151 | 19,704 | — |
| 1855 | 681,629 | 24,578 | — |
| 1856 | 780,040 | 21,831 | — |
| 1857 | 654,758 | 29,911 | — |
| 1858 | 833,238 | 18,618 | — |
| 1859 | 961,707 | 22,479 | — |
| 1860 | 1,115,891 | 12,287 | — |

## C. Cotton Consumption, Cotton Yarn Exports, and Cotton Piece Goods Exports, United Kingdom: 1800–60

[In millions of pounds.]

| Year | Consumption | Yarn exports | Piece goods exports | Year | Consumption | Yarn exports | Piece goods exports |
|---|---|---|---|---|---|---|---|
| 1800 | 52 | 5.0 | 12.0 | 1831 | 263 | 61.6 | 76.9 |
| 1801 | 54 | 5.0 | 14.4 | 1832 | 277 | 75.7 | 84.1 |
| 1802 | 56 | 4.8 | 15.6 | 1833 | 287 | 70.6 | 90.6 |
| 1803 | 52 | 7.2 | 14.5 | 1834 | 303 | 76.5 | 101.4 |
| 1804 | 61 | 10.2 | 15.2 | 1835 | 318 | 83.2 | 101.8 |
| 1805 | 59 | 10.3 | 19.5 | 1836 | 347 | 88.2 | 116.4 |
| 1806 | 57 | 8.3 | 21.4 | 1837 | 366 | 103.5 | 97.0 |
| 1807 | 73 | 6.8 | 21.1 | 1838 | 417 | 114.6 | 126.0 |
| 1808 | 42 | 5.3 | 26.5 | 1839 | 382 | 105.7 | 133.5 |
| 1809 | 88 | 11.5 | 39.7 | 1840 | 459 | 118.5 | 144.3 |
| 1810 | 124 | 11.9 | 38.7 | 1841 | 438 | 123.2 | 137.1 |
| 1811 | 89 | 5.4 | 24.5 | 1842 | 435 | 137.5 | 134.0 |
| 1812 | 73 | 9.0 | 33.7 | 1843 | 518 | 140.3 | 167.7 |
| 1813 | 78 | 10.9 | 34.4 | 1844 | 544 | 138.5 | 191.0 |
| 1814 | 74 | 12.8 | 35.1 | 1845 | 607 | 135.2 | 199.3 |
| 1815 | 81 | 9.2 | 46.2 | 1846 | 614 | 161.9 | 194.5 |
| 1816 | 89 | 15.7 | 34.6 | 1847 | 441 | 120.3 | 172.0 |
| 1817 | 107 | 12.7 | 43.3 | 1848 | 577 | 135.8 | 200.2 |
| 1818 | 110 | 14.7 | 46.6 | 1849 | 630 | 149.5 | 244.1 |
| 1819 | 109 | 18.1 | 37.0 | 1850 | 588 | 131.4 | 247.9 |
| 1820 | 120 | 23.0 | 45.7 | 1851 | 659 | 144.0 | 281.7 |
| 1821 | 129 | 21.5 | 48.6 | 1852 | 740 | 145.5 | 278.2 |
| 1822 | 145 | 26.6 | 55.6 | 1853 | 761 | 147.5 | 291.0 |
| 1823 | 154 | 27.4 | 55.1 | 1854 | 776 | 147.1 | 309.0 |
| 1824 | 165 | 34.6 | 62.9 | 1855 | 839 | 165.5 | 353.7 |
| 1825 | 167 | 32.6 | 61.4 | 1856 | 891 | 181.5 | 371.5 |
| 1826 | 150 | 42.2 | 48.7 | 1857 | 826 | 176.8 | 361.3 |
| 1827 | 197 | 43.3 | 66.7 | 1858 | 906 | 200.0 | 424.2 |
| 1828 | 218 | 43.2 | 66.3 | 1859 | 977 | 192.2 | 467.7 |
| 1829 | 219 | 60.6 | 73.5 | 1860 | 1084 | 197.3 | 506.7 |
| 1830 | 248 | 63.7 | 80.6 | | | | |

## D. Exports of Cotton Manufactures and Total Exports: 1814–60, Produce and Manufactures of the United Kingdom

[Million £]

| Year | (A) Cotton manu-factures | (B) All exports | (A) as a percentage of (B) | Year | (A) Cotton manu-factures | (B) All exports | (A) as a percentage of (B) |
|---|---|---|---|---|---|---|---|
| 1814 | 20.0 | 45.5 | 43.9 | 1838 | 24.1 | 50.1 | 48.1 |
| 1815 | 20.6 | 51.6 | 39.9 | 1839 | 24.6 | 53.2 | 46.2 |
| 1816 | 15.6 | 41.7 | 37.4 | 1840 | 24.7 | 51.3 | 48.1 |
| 1817 | 16.0 | 41.8 | 38.3 | 1841 | 23.5 | 51.5 | 45.6 |
| 1818 | 18.8 | 46.6 | 40.3 | 1842 | 21.7 | 47.3 | 45.9 |
| 1819 | 14.7 | 35.2 | 41.8 | 1843 | 23.5 | 52.2 | 45.0 |
| 1820 | 16.5 | 36.4 | 45.3 | 1844 | 25.8 | 58.5 | 44.1 |
| 1821 | 16.1 | 36.7 | 43.9 | 1845 | 26.2 | 60.1 | 43.6 |
| 1822 | 17.2 | 37.0 | 46.5 | 1846 | 25.6 | 57.8 | 44.3 |
| 1823 | 16.3 | 35.5 | 45.9 | 1847 | 23.7 | 58.8 | 40.3 |
| 1824 | 18.5 | 38.4 | 48.2 | 1848 | 22.7 | 52.9 | 42.9 |
| 1825 | 18.4 | 38.9 | 47.3 | 1849 | 26.8 | 63.6 | 42.1 |
| 1826 | 14.1 | 31.5 | 44.8 | 1850 | 28.3 | 71.4 | 39.6 |
| 1827 | 17.6 | 37.2 | 47.3 | 1851 | 30.1 | 74.4 | 40.5 |
| 1828 | 17.2 | 36.8 | 46.7 | 1852 | 29.9 | 78.1 | 38.3 |
| 1829 | 17.5 | 35.8 | 48.9 | 1853 | 32.7 | 98.9 | 33.1 |
| 1830 | 19.4 | 38.3 | 50.7 | 1854 | 31.8 | 97.2 | 32.7 |
| 1831 | 17.3 | 37.2 | 46.5 | 1855 | 34.8 | 95.7 | 36.4 |
| 1832 | 17.4 | 36.5 | 47.7 | 1856 | 38.2 | 115.8 | 33.0 |
| 1833 | 18.5 | 39.7 | 46.6 | 1857 | 39.1 | 122.1 | 32.0 |
| 1834 | 20.5 | 41.6 | 49.3 | 1858 | 43.0 | 116.6 | 36.9 |
| 1835 | 22.1 | 47.4 | 46.6 | 1859 | 48.2 | 130.4 | 36.9 |
| 1836 | 24.6 | 53.4 | 46.1 | 1860 | 52.0 | 135.9 | 38.3 |
| 1837 | 20.6 | 42.1 | 48.9 | | | | |

E. Consumption of Cotton and Other Textile Raw Materials, Annual Averages, Great Britain: 1798–1861

| Years (averaged) | Cotton | Wool | Flax | Total |
|---|---|---|---|---|
| Total, millions of pounds: | | | | |
| 1798-1800 | 41.8 | 109.6 | 108.6 | 260.0 |
| 1829-1831 | 243.2 | 149.4 | 193.8 | 586.4 |
| 1859-1861 | 1,022.5 | 260.4 | 212.0 | 1,494.9 |
| Each material as per cent of total: | | | | |
| 1798-1800 | 16.0 | 42.2 | 41.8 | 100.0 |
| 1829-1831 | 41.5 | 25.5 | 33.0 | 100.0 |
| 1859-1861 | 68.4 | 17.4 | 14.2 | 100.0 |
| Average annual increase, per cent: | | | | |
| 1798-1831 | 15.5 | 1.2 | 2.5 | 4.0 |
| 1831-1861 | 10.9 | 2.5 | 0.3 | 5.1 |
| Per capita, pounds:[a] | | | | |
| 1798-1800 | 2.8 | 7.3 | 7.2 | 17.3 |
| 1829-1831 | 9.9 | 6.1 | 7.9 | 24.0 |
| 1859-1861 | 35.3 | 9.0 | 7.3 | 51.6 |

[a] Erroneously given as percentages in the source cited.—S.B.

## Tables 3 A–R. United States Production, Consumption, Prices, and Exports of Raw Cotton

### A. The Cotton Production and Trade of the United States: 1784–1860

| Year ending Aug. 31 | Total production | | Total exports | | Total exports to Great Britain |
|---|---|---|---|---|---|
| | Thousands of bales | Thousands of pounds | Thousands of bales | Thousands of pounds | Thousands of bales |
| 1784 | No data | No data | .01 | 1 | .01 |
| 1785 | " " | " " | .01 | 2 | .01 |
| 1786 | " " | " " | .01 | 1 | .01 |
| 1787 | " " | " " | .11 | 16 | .11 |
| 1788 | " " | " " | .39 | 58 | .39 |
| 1789 | " " | 1,000 | .84 | 126 | .84 |
| 1790 | " " | 1,500 | .08 | 12 | .08 |
| 1791 | 9 | 2,000 | .89 | 189 | .89 |
| 1792 | 13 | 3,000 | .63 | 138 | .63 |
| 1793 | 22 | 5,000 | 2.00 | 488 | 2.00 |
| 1794 | 35 | 8,000 | 7.00 | 1,602 | 7.00 |
| 1795 | 36 | 8,000 | 28.00 | 6,276 | 28.00 |
| 1796 | 44 | 10,000 | 27.00 | 6,107 | 27.00 |
| 1797 | 49 | 11,000 | 17.00 | 3,788 | 17.00 |
| 1798 | 67 | 15,000 | 42.00 | 9,360 | 42.00 |
| 1799 | 89 | 20,000 | 42.00 | 9,532 | 42.00 |
| 1800 | 156 | 35,000 | 79.00 | 17,790 | 71.00 |
| 1801 | 211 | 48,000 | 92.00 | 20,911 | 84.00 |
| 1802 | 241 | 55,000 | 121.00 | 27,501 | 103.00 |
| 1803 | 251 | 60,000 | 158.00 | 41,106 | 115.00 |
| 1804 | 241 | 65,000 | 130.00 | 38,118 | 95.00 |
| 1805 | 281 | 70,000 | 154.00 | 40,383 | 131.00 |
| 1806 | 348 | 80,000 | 155.00 | 37,491 | 105.00 |
| 1807 | 286 | 80,000 | 228.00 | 66,213 | 190.00 |
| 1808 | 272 | 75,000 | 39.00 | 12,064 | 29.00 |
| 1809 | 366 | 82,000 | 228.00 | 53,210 | 60.00 |
| 1810 | 340 | 85,000 | 373.00 | 93,874 | 145.00 |
| 1811 | 269 | 80,000 | 209.00 | 62,186 | 128.00 |
| 1812 | 305 | 75,000 | 117.00 | 28,953 | 95.00 |
| 1813 | 305 | 75,000 | 78.00 | 19,400 | 38.00 |
| 1814 | 285 | 70,000 | 72.00 | 17,806 | 49.00 |
| 1815 | 364 | 100,000 | 302.00 | 82,999 | 203.00 |
| 1816 | 458 | 124,000 | 302.00 | 81,747 | 166.00 |
| 1817 | 461 | 130,000 | 304.00 | 85,649 | 200.00 |
| 1818 | 448 | 125,000 | 331.00 | 92,471 | 208.00 |
| 1819 | 596 | 167,000 | 314.00 | 87,997 | 205.00 |
| 1820 | 606 | 160,000 | 484.00 | 127,860 | 302.00 |
| 1821 | 647 | 180,000 | 449.00 | 124,893 | 300.00 |
| 1822 | 742 | 210,000 | 511.00 | 144,675 | 330.00 |

A. The Cotton Production and Trade of the United States: 1784–1860 (*cont'd*)

| Total exports to Great Britain | Total consumption | | Percentage of crop exported | Average New York prices for middling Uplands (cents) | Average Liverpool prices for middling Uplands (pence) |
|---|---|---|---|---|---|
| Thousands of pounds | Thousands of bales | Thousands of pounds | | | |
| 1 | No data | No data | No data | No data | No data |
| 2 | " " | " " | " " | " " | " " |
| 1 | " " | " " | " " | " " | " " |
| 16 | " " | " " | " " | " " | " " |
| 58 | " " | " " | " " | " " | " " |
| 126 | " " | " " | 12.60 | " " | " " |
| 12 | " " | 5,000 | .80 | 14.50 | " " |
| 189 | " " | No data | 9.45 | 26.0 | 13-30 |
| 138 | " " | " " | 4.60 | 29.0 | 20-30 |
| 487 | " " | " " | 9.60 | 32.0 | 13-22 |
| 1,602 | " " | " " | 20.02 | 33.0 | 12-18 |
| 6,276 | " " | " " | 78.45 | 36.0 | 15-27 |
| 6,106 | " " | " " | 61.07 | 36.5 | 12-29 |
| 3,788 | " " | " " | 34.44 | 34.5 | 12-37 |
| 9,360 | " " | " " | 62.40 | 39.0 | 22-45 |
| 9,532 | " " | " " | 47.66 | 44.0 | 17-60 |
| 16,180 | 36 | 8,000 | 55.08 | 24.0 | 16-36 |
| 18,953 | 39 | No data | 43.57 | 44.0 | 18.00 |
| 23,474 | No data | " " | 50.00 | 19.0 | 16.00 |
| 27,757 | " " | " " | 68.51 | 19.0 | 12.50 |
| 25,771 | " " | " " | 58.64 | 20.0 | 14.00 |
| 32,571 | 44 | " " | 57.69 | 23.0 | 16.50 |
| 24,256 | No data | " " | 46.86 | 22.0 | 18.20 |
| 53,180 | " " | " " | 82.76 | 21.50 | 14.50 |
| 7,993 | " " | " " | 16.08 | 19.00 | 22.00 |
| 13,366 | " " | " " | 64.89 | 16.00 | 20.00 |
| 36,172 | 64 | 16,000 | 111.02 | 16.00 | 15.50 |
| 38,073 | 57 | No data | 77.73 | 15.50 | 12.50 |
| 23,461 | No data | " " | 38.60 | 10.50 | 16.70 |
| 9,279 | " " | " " | 25.87 | 12.50 | 23.00 |
| 12,008 | " " | " " | 25.44 | 15.00 | 29.50 |
| 55,839 | 90 | 31,500 | 82.99 | 21.00 | 20.70 |
| 45,007 | No data | No data | 65.92 | 29.50 | 18.25 |
| 54,327 | " " | " " | 65.85 | 26.50 | 20.12 |
| 57,915 | " " | " " | 73.97 | 24.00 | 20.00 |
| 57,445 | " " | " " | 52.69 | 24.00 | 13.50 |
| 79,832 | " " | " " | 79.25 | 17.00 | 11.50 |
| 83,419 | " " | " " | 69.33 | 14.32 | 8.23 |
| 93,363 | " " | " " | 68.86 | 14.32 | 6.95 |

A. THE COTTON PRODUCTION AND TRADE OF THE UNITED STATES: 1784–1860 (*cont'd*)

| Year ending Aug. 31 | Total production | | Total exports | | Total exports to Great Britain |
|---|---|---|---|---|---|
| | Thousands of bales | Thousands of pounds | Thousands of bales | Thousands of pounds | Thousands of bales |
| 1823 | 621 | 185,000 | 583.00 | 173,723 | 453.00 |
| 1824 | 762 | 215,000 | 505.00 | 142,370 | 282.00 |
| 1825 | 892 | 255,000 | 617.00 | 176,440 | 424.00 |
| 1826 | 1,121 | 350,000 | 656.00 | 204,535 | 396.00 |
| 1827 | 957 | 316,860 | 854.00 | 294,310 | 446.00 |
| 1828 | 721 | 241,400 | 600.00 | 210,590 | 425.00 |
| 1829 | 870 | 296,812 | 749.00 | 264,847 | 498.00 |
| 1830 | 976 | 331,150 | 839.00 | 298,459 | 596.00 |
| 1831 | 1,038 | 354,547 | 773.00 | 270,980 | 619.00 |
| 1832 | 987 | 355,492 | 892.00 | 322,215 | 638.00 |
| 1833 | 1,070 | 374,653 | 867.00 | 303,609 | 630.00 |
| 1834 | 1,205 | 437,558 | 1,028.00 | 372,946 | 756.00 |
| 1835 | 1,254 | 460,358 | 1,023.00 | 375,638 | 723.00 |
| 1836 | 1,361 | 507,550 | 1,117.00 | 415,493 | 771.00 |
| 1837 | 1,424 | 539,669 | 1,168.00 | 442,833 | 851.00 |
| 1838 | 1,801 | 682,757 | 1,576.00 | 597,063 | 1,165.00 |
| 1839 | 1,361 | 522,444 | 1,075.00 | 412,681 | 798.00 |
| 1840 | 2,178 | 834,111 | 1,876.00 | 718,509 | 1,247.00 |
| 1841 | 1,635 | 644,172 | 1,313.00 | 517,628 | 859.00 |
| 1842 | 1,684 | 668,389 | 1,465.00 | 581,703 | 936.00 |
| 1843 | 2,379 | 972,960 | 2,010.00 | 822,146 | 1,470.00 |
| 1844 | 2,030 | 836,529 | 1,629.00 | 671,350 | 1,202.00 |
| 1845 | 2,395 | 992,719 | 2,084.00 | 864,759 | 1,439.00 |
| 1846 | 2,101 | 863,321 | 1,667.00 | 685,042 | 1,102.00 |
| 1847 | 1,779 | 766,599 | 1,241.00 | 534,967 | 831.00 |
| 1848 | 2,440 | 1,017,391 | 1,858.00 | 774,895 | 1,324.00 |
| 1849 | 2,867 | 1,249,976 | 2,228.00 | 971,340 | 1,540.00 |
| 1850 | 2,334 | 1,001,165 | 1,590.00 | 681,176 | 1,107.00 |
| 1851 | 2,454 | 1,021,048 | 1,989.00 | 827,303 | 1,418.00 |
| 1852 | 3,126 | 1,338,061 | 2,444.00 | 1,045,880 | 1,669.00 |
| 1853 | 3,416 | 1,496,302 | 2,528.00 | 1,107,439 | 1,737.00 |
| 1854 | 3,075 | 1,322,241 | 2,319.00 | 997,234 | 1,604.00 |
| 1855 | 2,983 | 1,294,462 | 2,244.00 | 973,987 | 1,550.00 |
| 1856 | 3,656 | 1,622,908 | 2,955.00 | 1,240,935 | 1,921.00 |
| 1857 | 3,094 | 1,438,520 | 2,253.00 | 1,000,180 | 1,429.00 |
| 1858 | 3,257 | 1,517,518 | 3,590.00 | 1,586,981 | 1,810.00 |
| 1859 | 4,019 | 1,892,665 | 3,021.00 | 1,350,567 | 2,019.00 |
| 1860 | 4,861 | 2,275,372 | 3,774.00 | 1,739,893 | 2,669.00 |

A. The Cotton Production and Trade of the United States: 1784–1860 (*cont'd*)

| Total exports to Great Britain | Total consumption | | Percentage of crop exported | New York prices for middling Uplands (cents) | Liverpool prices for middling Uplands (pence) |
|---|---|---|---|---|---|
| Thousands of pounds | Thousands of bales | Thousands of pounds | | | |
| 134,436 | No data | No data | 83.89 | 11.40 | 7.21 |
| 79,629 | " " | " " | 66.22 | 14.75 | 7.66 |
| 125,452 | " " | " " | 69.15 | 18.59 | 10.10 |
| 123,506 | " " | " " | 58.43 | 12.19 | 5.85 |
| 213,883 | 149 | 49,489 | 92.22 | 9.26 | 5.79 |
| 142,278 | 121 | 40,397 | 87.19 | 10.32 | 5.84 |
| 169,918 | 119 | 40,328 | 89.24 | 9.88 | 5.32 |
| 201,947 | 127 | 42,888 | 89.22 | 10.04 | 6.44 |
| 210,875 | 182 | 62,110 | 76.44 | 9.71 | 5.38 |
| 229,733 | 174 | 72,568 | 90.63 | 9.38 | 6.22 |
| 220,551 | 194 | 68,044 | 81.03 | 12.32 | 7.87 |
| 274,537 | 196 | 71,298 | 85.22 | 12.90 | 8.10 |
| 265,238 | 217 | 79,598 | 81.59 | 17.45 | 9.13 |
| 287,630 | 237 | 73,391 | 81.86 | 16.50 | 8.79 |
| 322,448 | 223 | 84,343 | 82.05 | 13.25 | 6.09 |
| 441,614 | 246 | 93,258 | 67.83 | 10.14 | 6.28 |
| 306,951 | 276 | 105,980 | 79.18 | 13.36 | 7.19 |
| 477,521 | 295 | 113,059 | 86.15 | 8.92 | 5.42 |
| 338,344 | 297 | 117,331 | 80.35 | 9.50 | 5.73 |
| 371,446 | 268 | 106,326 | 87.02 | 7.85 | 4.86 |
| 601,312 | 325 | 132,978 | 88.75 | 7.25 | 4.37 |
| 495,429 | 347 | 142,861 | 80.25 | 7.73 | 4.71 |
| 597,212 | 389 | 161,435 | 87.11 | 5.63 | 3.92 |
| 453,074 | 423 | 173,689 | 79.12 | 7.87 | 4.80 |
| 358,122 | 428 | 184,468 | 69.78 | 11.21 | 6.03 |
| 552,227 | 616 | 256,890 | 76.16 | 8.03 | 3.93 |
| 670,527 | 642 | 280,124 | 53.70 | 7.55 | 4.09 |
| 474,705 | 613 | 263,191 | 68.03 | 12.34 | 7.10 |
| 789,998 | 486 | 202,015 | 81.03 | 12.14 | 5.51 |
| 714,235 | 690 | 295,150 | 78.16 | 9.50 | 5.05 |
| 760,740 | 804 | 352,032 | 74.01 | 11.02 | 5.54 |
| 666,378 | 737 | 317,011 | 75.42 | 10.97 | 5.31 |
| 672,577 | 706 | 306,585 | 75.24 | 10.39 | 5.60 |
| 806,982 | 778 | 326,650 | 76.53 | 10.30 | 6.22 |
| 634,418 | 820 | 364,054 | 69.53 | 13.51 | 7.73 |
| 799,994 | 596 | 263,238 | 104.51 | 12.23 | 6.91 |
| 902,608 | 928 | 414,660 | 71.30 | 12.08 | 6.68 |
| 1,230,607 | 978 | 470,278 | 76.47 | 11.00 | 5.97 |

### B. Percentage Increases in United States Production of Cotton, Five-Year Periods: 1791–95 to 1856–60

| Years | Percentage of Increase |
|---|---|
| 1791-1795 | |
| 1796-1800 | 250 |
| 1801-1805 | 221 |
| 1806-1810 | 35 |
| 1811-1815 | -1 |
| 1816-1820 | 77 |
| 1821-1825 | 50 |
| 1826-1830 | 47 |
| 1831-1835 | 37 |
| 1836-1840 | 47 |
| 1841-1845 | 35 |
| 1846-1850 | 13 |
| 1851-1855 | 31 |
| 1856-1860 | 35 |

### C. Cotton Production by Individual States: 1791–1859

[In millions of pounds.]

| State | 1791 | 1801 | 1811 | 1821 | 1826 | 1833 | 1834 | 1839 | 1849 | 1859 |
|---|---|---|---|---|---|---|---|---|---|---|
| North Carolina | — | 4.0 | 7.0 | 10.0 | 10.0 | 10.0 | 9.5 | 51.9 | 29.5 | 64.6 |
| South Carolina | 1.5 | 20.0 | 40.0 | 50.0 | 70.0 | 73.0 | 65.5 | 61.7 | 120.0 | 141.0 |
| Georgia | 0.5 | 10.0 | 20.0 | 45.0 | 75.0 | 88.0 | 75.0 | 163.4 | 199.6 | 312.3 |
| Florida | — | — | — | — | 2.0 | 15.0 | 20.0 | 12.1 | 18.0 | 29.9 |
| Alabama | — | — | — | 20.0 | 45.0 | 65.0 | 85.0 | 117.1 | 225.8 | 440.5 |
| Mississippi | — | — | — | 10.0 | 20.0 | 70.0 | 85.0 | 193.2 | 194.0 | 535.1 |
| Louisiana | — | — | 2.0 | 10.0 | 38.0 | 55.0 | 62.0 | 153.9 | 71.5 | 311.0 |
| Texas | — | — | — | — | — | — | — | — | 23.2 | 193.1 |
| Arkansas | — | — | — | — | 0.5 | 0.8 | 0.5 | 6.0 | 26.1 | 163.0 |
| Tennessee | — | 1.0 | 3.0 | 20.0 | 45.0 | 50.0 | 45.0 | 27.7 | 77.8 | 132.0 |
| All other states | — | 5.0 | 8.0 | 12.0 | 25.0 | 13.0 | 10.0 | 4.5 | 1.6 | 24.7 |

D. United States Cotton Production, Percentage Share of Individual States: 1791–1859

| State | 1791 | 1801 | 1811 | 1821 | 1826 | 1833 | 1834 | 1839 | 1849 | 1859 |
|---|---|---|---|---|---|---|---|---|---|---|
| North Carolina | — | 10.0 | 8.7 | 5.7 | 3.1 | 2.3 | 2.1 | 6.5 | 3.0 | 3.2 |
| South Carolina | 75.0 | 50.0 | 50.0 | 28.2 | 21.2 | 16.7 | 14.3 | 7.8 | 12.2 | 6.9 |
| Georgia | 25.0 | 25.0 | 25.0 | 25.4 | 22.7 | 20.0 | 16.4 | 20.7 | 20.2 | 15.4 |
| Florida | — | — | — | — | 0.6 | 3.4 | 4.4 | 1.6 | 1.8 | 1.5 |
| Alabama | — | — | — | 11.3 | 13.6 | 14.8 | 18.6 | 14.8 | 22.9 | 21.7 |
| Mississippi | — | — | — | 5.7 | 6.0 | 15.9 | 18.6 | 24.3 | 19.7 | 26.4 |
| Louisiana | — | — | 2.5 | 5.7 | 11.5 | 12.5 | 13.5 | 19.5 | 7.2 | 15.4 |
| Texas | — | — | — | — | — | — | — | — | 2.3 | 1.0 |
| Arkansas | — | — | — | — | 0.1 | 0.1 | 0.1 | 0.8 | 2.6 | 0.8 |
| Tennessee | — | 2.5 | 3.8 | 11.3 | 13.6 | 11.3 | 9.8 | 3.5 | 7.8 | 6.5 |
| All other states | — | 12.5 | 10.0 | 6.7 | 7.6 | 3.0 | 2.2 | 0.5 | 0.2 | 1.2 |

E. Percentage Increases in the Cotton Production of Individual States, Selected Years: 1791–1859

| State | 1791 | 1801 | 1811 | 1821 | 1826 | 1833 | 1834 | 1839 | 1849 | 1859 |
|---|---|---|---|---|---|---|---|---|---|---|
| North Carolina | — | — | 75.0 | 42.8 | 0.0 | 0.0 | -5.0 | 446.3 | -43.2 | 119.0 |
| South Carolina | — | 1233.3 | 100.0 | 25.0 | 40.0 | 4.3 | -10.3 | -5.8 | 94.5 | 17.5 |
| Georgia | — | 200.0 | 100.0 | 125.0 | 66.7 | 17.3 | -17.3 | 117.9 | 22.1 | 56.5 |
| Florida | — | — | — | — | — | 650.0 | -33.3 | -39.5 | 48.8 | 66.1 |
| Alabama | — | — | — | — | 125.0 | 44.4 | 30.8 | 37.8 | 92.4 | 65.3 |
| Mississippi | — | — | — | — | 100.0 | 250.0 | 21.4 | 127.3 | 0.4 | 175.8 |
| Louisiana | — | — | — | 400.0 | 250.0 | 44.7 | 12.7 | 148.2 | -53.6 | 335.5 |
| Texas | — | — | — | — | — | — | — | — | — | 727.5 |
| Arkansas | — | — | — | — | — | 60.0 | -37.5 | 1100.0 | 330.0 | 524.5 |
| Tennessee | — | — | 200.0 | 566.6 | 125.0 | 11.1 | -10.0 | 38.5 | 180.9 | 69.6 |
| All other States | — | — | 60.0 | 50.0 | 108.5 | -48.0 | -23.1 | -55.0 | -64.5 | 1443.8 |

## F. Relative Rank of Individual States in Total United States Cotton Production: 1791–1859

| State | 1791 | 1801 | 1811 | 1821 | 1826 | 1833 | 1834 | 1839 | 1849 | 1859 |
|---|---|---|---|---|---|---|---|---|---|---|
| North Carolina | — | 4 | 4 | 5 | 7 | 9 | 9 | 6 | 7 | 9 |
| South Carolina | 1 | 1 | 1 | 1 | 2 | 2 | 4 | 5 | 4 | 7 |
| Georgia | 2 | 2 | 2 | 2 | 1 | 1 | 3 | 2 | 2 | 3 |
| Florida | — | — | — | — | 8 | 7 | 7 | 8 | 10 | 10 |
| Alabama | — | — | — | 3 | 3 | 4 | 1(2)* | 4 | 1 | 2 |
| Mississippi | — | — | — | 5 | 6 | 3 | 1(2)* | 1 | 3 | 1 |
| Louisiana | — | — | 6 | 5 | 4 | 5 | 5 | 3 | 6 | 4 |
| Texas | — | — | — | — | — | — | — | — | 9 | 5 |
| Arkansas | — | — | — | — | 9 | 10 | 10 | 9 | 8 | 6 |
| Tennessee | — | 5 | 5 | 3 | 3 | 6 | 6 | 7 | 5 | 8 |
| All other states | — | 3 | 3 | 4 | 5 | 8 | 8 | 10 | 11 | 11 |

* Presumably indicates uncertainty as to relative rank of Alabama and Mississippi in 1834.—S.B.

## G. Cotton Production Per Capita by Individual States, Census Years: 1790–1860

[In pounds.]

| State | 1790 | 1800 | 1810 | 1820 | 1830 | 1840 | 1850 | 1860 |
|---|---|---|---|---|---|---|---|---|
| North Carolina | — | 8.4 | 12.6 | 16.4 | 13.5 | 69.0 | 33.9 | 65.0 |
| South Carolina | 6.1 | 57.8 | 96.4 | 99.4 | 123.9 | 103.8 | 179.4 | 200.3 |
| Georgia | 6.0 | 61.3 | 79.4 | 131.4 | 158.6 | 236.5 | 220.3 | 300.0 |
| Florida | — | — | — | — | 242.9 | 224.1 | 207.0 | 213.5 |
| Alabama | — | — | — | 156.2 | 177.4 | 198.1 | 292.5 | 456.9 |
| Mississippi | — | — | — | 133.3 | 328.4 | 513.8 | 319.6 | 676.5 |
| Lousiana | — | — | 26.0 | 65.4 | 212.5 | 437.2 | 137.8 | 439.3 |
| Texas | — | — | — | — | — | — | 108.9 | 319.6 |
| Arkansas | — | — | — | — | 21.1 | 61.2 | 124.3 | 374.7 |
| Tennessee | — | 9.4 | 11.4 | 47.2 | 69.6 | 33.4 | 77.5 | 119.0 |

## H. Cotton Production Per Capita by Relative Rank of Individual States, Census Years: 1790–1860

| State | 1790 | 1800 | 1810 | 1820 | 1830 | 1840 | 1850 | 1860 |
|---|---|---|---|---|---|---|---|---|
| North Carolina | — | 3 | 4 | 7 | 9 | 7 | 10 | 10 |
| South Carolina | 1 | 1 | 1 | 4 | 6 | 6 | 5 | 8 |
| Georgia | 2 | 2 | 2 | 3 | 4 | 3 | 3 | 6 |
| Florida | — | — | — | — | 2 | 4 | 4 | 7 |
| Alabama | — | — | — | 1 | 5 | 5 | 2 | 2 |
| Mississippi | — | — | — | 2 | 1 | 1 | 1 | 1 |
| Louisiana | — | — | 3 | 5 | 3 | 2 | 6 | 3 |
| Texas | — | — | — | — | — | — | 8 | 5 |
| Arkansas | — | — | — | — | 8 | 8 | 7 | 4 |
| Tennessee | — | — | 5 | 6 | 7 | 9 | 9 | 9 |

## I. Number of Plantations Raising Five or More Bales of Cotton: 1849–50

| State | Number of plantations |
|---|---|
| Alabama | 16,100 |
| Arkansas | 2,175 |
| Florida | 990 |
| Georgia | 14,578 |
| Kentucky | 21 |
| Louisiana | 4,205 |
| Mississippi | 15,110 |
| North Carolina | 2,827 |
| South Carolina | 11,522 |
| Tennessee | 4,043 |
| Texas | 2,262 |
| Virginia | 198 |
| Total | 74,031 |

## J. Quantity, Value, and Destination of Cotton Exported from the United States During the Year Ending September 30, 1832

| Export destination | Kinds of Cotton | | Value (dollars) |
|---|---|---|---|
| | Sea Island (pounds) | Other (pounds) | |
| Russia | — | 838,951 | 87,973 |
| Sweden and Norway | — | 699,002 | 75,711 |
| Denmark | — | 305,450 | 27,812 |
| Holland | — | 3,920,016 | 392,430 |
| England | 7,011,235 | 210,196,428 | 21,262,900 |
| Scotland | 319,994 | 10,674,457 | 1,088,344 |
| Ireland | — | 805,158 | 77,807 |
| Gibraltar | — | 492,778 | 42,537 |
| British East Indies | 136,140 | — | 20,420 |
| British West Indies | — | 376 | 41 |
| British American Colonies | — | 36,171 | 4,298 |
| Hanse Towns, etc. | — | 4,075,122 | 403,099 |
| France on the Atlantic | 1,276,004 | 67,722,972 | 6,931,564 |
| France on the Mediterranean | — | 8,468,831 | 791,311 |
| Spain on the Atlantic | — | 1,296,474 | 142,924 |
| Spain on the Mediterranean | — | 987,401 | 93,491 |
| Cuba | — | 335,900 | 17,660 |
| Italy and Malta | — | 580,974 | 51,606 |
| Trieste and other Austrian ports | — | 1,654,775 | 179,402 |
| Europe generally | — | 380,513 | 33,353 |
| Total | 8,743,373 | 313,471,749 | 31,724,682 |

## K. Value of Total Exports and Cotton Exports: United States: 1815–60

[In dollars.]

| Year | Total exports | Cotton exports | Year | Total exports | Cotton exports |
|---|---|---|---|---|---|
| 1815 | 52,557,753 | 17,529,000 | 1838 | 104,979,000 | 61,556,811 |
| 1816 | 81,920,452 | 24,106,000 | 1839 | 112,252,000 | 61,238,982 |
| 1817 | 87,671,569 | 22,627,614 | 1840 | 123,669,000 | 63,870,307 |
| 1818 | 93,281,133 | 31,334,258 | 1841 | 111,817,000 | 54,330,341 |
| 1819 | 70,142,521 | 21,081,760 | 1842 | 99,878,000 | 47,593,464 |
| 1820 | 69,692,000 | 22,308,667 | 1843 | 82,826,000 | 49,119,806 |
| 1821 | 54,596,000 | 20,157,484 | 1844 | 105,746,000 | 54,063,501 |
| 1822 | 61,350,000 | 24,035,058 | 1845 | 106,040,000 | 51,739,643 |
| 1823 | 68,326,000 | 20,445,520 | 1846 | 109,583,000 | 42,767,341 |
| 1824 | 68,972,000 | 21,947,401 | 1847 | 156,742,000 | 53,415,848 |
| 1825 | 90,738,000 | 36,846,649 | 1848 | 138,191,000 | 61,998,294 |
| 1826 | 72,891,000 | 25,025,214 | 1849 | 140,351,000 | 66,396,967 |
| 1827 | 74,310,000 | 29,359,545 | 1850 | 144,376,000 | 71,984,616 |
| 1828 | 64,021,000 | 22,487,229 | 1851 | 188,915,000 | 112,315,317 |
| 1829 | 67,435,000 | 26,575,311 | 1852 | 166,984,000 | 87,965,732 |
| 1830 | 71,671,000 | 29,674,883 | 1853 | 203,489,000 | 109,456,404 |
| 1831 | 72,296,000 | 25,289,492 | 1854 | 237,044,000 | 93,596,220 |
| 1832 | 81,521,000 | 31,724,682 | 1855 | 218,910,000 | 88,143,844 |
| 1833 | 87,529,000 | 36,191,105 | 1856 | 281,219,000 | 128,382,351 |
| 1834 | 102,260,000 | 49,448,402 | 1857 | 293,824,000 | 131,575,859 |
| 1835 | 115,216,000 | 64,961,302 | 1858 | 272,011,000 | 131,386,661 |
| 1836 | 124,339,000 | 71,284,925 | 1859 | 292,902,000 | 161,434,923 |
| 1837 | 111,443,000 | 63,240,102 | 1860 | 333,576,000 | 191,806,555 |

| Year | Cotton [a] unmanufactured | | Tobacco [a] unmanufactured | | Wheat [a] and flour | | Corn and [a] corn meal | | Rice [a] | |
|---|---|---|---|---|---|---|---|---|---|---|
| | Value | Per cent of total | Value | Per cent of total | Value | Per cent of total | Value | Per cent of total | Value | Per cent of total |
| 1816-20 | $ 121.5 | 39 | $ 47.5 | 15 | $ 50.6 | 16 | $ 7.6 | 2 | $ 13.1 | 4 |
| 1821-25 | 123.4 | 48 | 28.1 | 11 | 25.4 | 10 | 4.1 | 2 | 8.7 | 3 |
| 1826-30 | 133.1 | 49 | 27.8 | 10 | 25.6 | 9 | 4.4 | 2 | 11.4 | 4 |
| 1831-35 | 207.6 | 56 | 31.5 | 8 | 30.1 | 8 | 4.5 | 1 | 11.2 | 3 |
| 1836-40 | 321.2 | 63 | 43.0 | 8 | 29.0 | 6 | 4.3 | 1 | 11.0 | 2 |
| 1841-45 | 256.8 | 55 | 42.6 | 9 | 33.9 | 7 | 4.8 | 1 | 9.9 | 2 |
| 1846-50 | 296.6 | 46 | 39.0 | 6 | 82.2 | 13 | 40.3 | 6 | 13.7 | 2 |
| 1851-55 | 491.5 | 53 | 55.3 | 6 | 97.5 | 10 | 21.9 | 2 | 10.7 | 1 |
| 1856-60 | 744.6 | 54 | 86.5 | 6 | 157.7 | 11 | 24.7 | 2 | 11.3 | 1 |

| Year | Beef, [a] tallow, hides, and horned cattle | | Pork (pickled), [a] bacon, lard, and live hogs | | Dried, [a] smoked, or pickled fish | | Staves, shingles, [a] boards, and hewn timber | | Domestic [b] manu-factures | |
|---|---|---|---|---|---|---|---|---|---|---|
| | Value | Per cent of total | Value | Per cent of total | Value | Per cent of total | Value | Per cent of total | Value | Per cent of total |
| 1816-20 | $ 3.7 | 1 | $ 4.2 | 1 | $ 6.8 | 2.0 | $ 15.5 | 5 | $ 21.1 | 7 |
| 1821-25 | 3.9 | 2 | 7.3 | 3 | 5.1 | 2.0 | 7.6 | 3 | 27.9 | 11 |
| 1826-30 | 3.6 | 1 | 7.8 | 3 | 4.7 | 2.0 | 8.7 | 3 | 32.3 | 12 |
| 1831-35 | 4.0 | 1 | 9.2 | 2 | 4.8 | 1.0 | 9.5 | 3 | 36.2 | 10 |
| 1836-40 | 2.8 | 1 | 7.7 | 2 | 4.1 | 1.0 | 10.7 | 2 | 46.4 | 9 |
| 1841-45 | 6.9 | 1 | 13.6 | 3 | 3.9 | 1.0 | 9.4 | 2 | 50.9 | 11 |
| 1846-50 | 10.5 | 2 | 36.3 | 6 | 3.4 | 1.0 | 10.8 | 2 | 70.1 | 11 |
| 1851-55 | 12.6 | 1 | 37.1 | 4 | 2.4 | 0.3 | 17.6 | 2 | 126.4 | 14 |
| 1856-60 | 21.8 | 2 | 53.9 | 4 | 3.9 | 0.3 | 29.3 | 2 | 167.3 | 12 |

[a] *House Miscellaneous Document* No. 49, Pt. 2, 48 Cong., 1 Sess., Vol. XXIV.
[b] *House Document* No. 15, Pt. 10, 57 Cong., 2 Sess., XLII, 3242.

## M. EXPORTS OF PRINCIPAL STATES: 1815–60

[In millions of dollars.]

| Year | Total United States | Chief general ports: New York (N. Y. City) | Massachusetts (Boston) | Pennsylvania (Philadelphia) | Maryland (Baltimore) | Cotton ports: Lousiana (New Orleans) |
|---|---|---|---|---|---|---|
| 1815 | 52 | 10 | 5 | 4 | 5 | 5 |
| 1816 | 81 | 19 | 10 | 7 | 7 | 5 |
| 1817 | 87 | 18 | 11 | 8 | 8 | 9 |
| 1818 | 93 | 17 | 11 | 8 | 7 | 12 |
| 1819 | 70 | 13 | 11 | 6 | 5 | 9 |
| 1820 | 69 | 13 | 11 | 5 | 6 | 7 |
| 1821 | 64 | 13 | 12 | 7 | 3 | 7 |
| 1822 | 72 | 17 | 12 | 9 | 4 | 7 |
| 1823 | 74 | 19 | 13 | 9 | 6 | 7 |
| 1824 | 75 | 22 | 10 | 9 | 4 | 7 |
| 1825 | 99 | 35 | 11 | 11 | 4 | 12 |
| 1826 | 77 | 21 | 10 | 8 | 4 | 10 |
| 1827 | 82 | 23 | 10 | 7 | 4 | 11 |
| 1828 | 72 | 22 | 9 | 6 | 4 | 11 |
| 1829 | 72 | 20 | 8 | 4 | 4 | 12 |
| 1830 | 73 | 19 | 7 | 4 | 3 | 15 |
| 1831 | 81 | 25 | 7 | 5 | 4 | 16 |
| 1832 | 87 | 26 | 11 | 3 | 4 | 16 |
| 1833 | 90 | 25 | 9 | 4 | 4 | 18 |
| 1834 | 104 | 25 | 10 | 3 | 4 | 26 |
| 1835 | 121 | 30 | 10 | 3 | 3 | 36 |
| 1836 | 128 | 28 | 10 | 3 | 3 | 37 |
| 1837 | 117 | 27 | 9 | 3 | 3 | 35 |
| 1838 | 108 | 23 | 9 | 3 | 4 | 31 |
| 1839 | 121 | 33 | 9 | 5 | 4 | 33 |
| 1840 | 132 | 34 | 10 | 6 | 5 | 34 |
| 1841 | 121 | 33 | 11 | 5 | 4 | 34 |
| 1842 | 104 | 27 | 9 | 3 | 4 | 28 |
| 1843[a] | 84 | 16 | 6 | 2 | 2 | 27 |
| 1844 | 111 | 32 | 9 | 3 | 5 | 30 |
| 1845 | 114 | 36 | 10 | 3 | 5 | 27 |
| 1846 | 113 | 36 | 10 | 4 | 6 | 31 |
| 1847 | 158 | 49 | 11 | 8 | 9 | 42 |
| 1848 | 154 | 53 | 13 | 5 | 7 | 40 |
| 1849 | 145 | 45 | 10 | 5 | 8 | 37 |
| 1850 | 151 | 52 | 10 | 4 | 6 | 38 |
| 1851 | 218 | 86 | 12 | 5 | 5 | 54 |
| 1852 | 209 | 87 | 16 | 5 | 6 | 49 |
| 1853 | 230 | 78 | 19 | 6 | 7 | 68 |
| 1854 | 275 | 122 | 21 | 10 | 11 | 60 |
| 1855 | 275 | 113 | 28 | 6 | 10 | 55 |
| 1856 | 326 | 119 | 29 | 7 | 11 | 80 |
| 1857 | 362 | 134 | 30 | 7 | 13 | 91 |
| 1858 | 324 | 108 | 22 | 6 | 10 | 88 |
| 1859 | 356 | 117 | 18 | 5 | 9 | 101 |
| 1860 | 400 | 145 | 17 | 5 | 9 | 107 |

[a] Nine-month period; shift from Sept. 30 to June 30 as end of fiscal year. No satisfactory figures for individual ports exist before 1856; a few such lists which have been published contain obvious discrepancies. The figures for the first eight major states, except Massachusetts, are virtually those of

## M. Exports of Principal States: 1815–60 (*cont'd*)

[In millions of dollars.]

| Cotton ports | | | Other states | | | | | |
|---|---|---|---|---|---|---|---|---|
| South Carolina (Charleston) | Georgia (Savannah) | Alabama (Mobile) | Maine (Portland, Quoddy) | Virgina (Richmond, Norfolk) | Florida | Texas | California (San Francisco) | Year |
| 6 | 4 | | | 6 | | | | 1815 |
| 10 | 7 | | | 8 | | | | 1816 |
| 10 | 8 | | | 5 | | | | 1817 |
| 11 | 11 | — | | 7 | | | | 1818 |
| 8 | 6 | — | | 4 | | | | 1819 |
| 8 | 6 | — | 1 | 4 | | | | 1820 |
| 7 | 6 | — | 1 | 3 | | | | 1821 |
| 7 | 5 | — | 1 | 3 | — | | | 1822 |
| 6 | 4 | — | — | 4 | — | | | 1823 |
| 8 | 4 | — | — | 3 | — | | | 1824 |
| 11 | 4 | — | 1 | 4 | — | | | 1825 |
| 7 | 4 | 1 | 1 | 4 | — | | | 1826 |
| 8 | 4 | 1 | 1 | 4 | — | | | 1827 |
| 6 | 3 | 1 | 1 | 3 | — | | | 1828 |
| 8 | 4 | 1 | — | 3 | — | | | 1829 |
| 7 | 5 | 2 | — | 4 | — | | | 1830 |
| 6 | 3 | 2 | — | 4 | — | | | 1831 |
| 7 | 5 | 2 | — | 4 | — | | | 1832 |
| 8 | 6 | 4 | 1 | 4 | — | | | 1833 |
| 11 | 7 | 5 | — | 5 | — | | | 1834 |
| 11 | 8 | 7 | 1 | 6 | — | | | 1835 |
| 13 | 10 | 11 | — | 6 | — | | | 1836 |
| 11 | 8 | 9 | — | 3 | — | | | 1837 |
| 11 | 8 | 9 | — | 3 | — | | | 1838 |
| 10 | 5 | 10 | — | 5 | — | | | 1839 |
| 10 | 6 | 12 | 1 | 4 | 1 | | | 1840 |
| 8 | 3 | 10 | 1 | 5 | — | | | 1841 |
| 7 | 4 | 9 | 1 | 3 | — | | | 1842 |
| 7 | 4 | 11 | — | 1 | — | | | 1843[a] |
| 7 | 4 | 9 | 1 | 2 | 1 | | | 1844 |
| 8 | 4 | 10 | 1 | 2 | 1 | | | 1845 |
| 6 | 2 | 5 | 1 | 3 | — | | | 1846 |
| 10 | 5 | 9 | 1 | 5 | 1 | | | 1847 |
| 8 | 3 | 11 | 1 | 3 | 1 | — | | 1848 |
| 9 | 6 | 12 | 1 | 3 | 2 | — | | 1849 |
| 11 | 7 | 10 | 1 | 3 | 2 | — | | 1850 |
| 15 | 9 | 18 | 1 | 3 | 3 | — | | 1851 |
| 11 | 4 | 17 | 1 | 2 | 2 | — | | 1852 |
| 15 | 7 | 16 | 2 | 3 | 1 | 1 | — | 1853 |
| 11 | 4 | 13 | 2 | 4 | 3 | 1 | 3 | 1854 |
| 12 | 7 | 14 | 4 | 4 | 1 | — | 8 | 1855 |
| 17 | 8 | 23 | 2 | 5 | 1 | 1 | 10 | 1856 |
| 16 | 10 | 20 | 3 | 7 | 3 | 1 | 12 | 1857 |
| 16 | 9 | 21 | 2 | 7 | 1 | 2 | 15 | 1858 |
| 17 | 15 | 28 | 3 | 6 | 3 | 3 | 15 | 1859 |
| 21 | 18 | 38 | 3 | 5 | 1 | 6 | 10 | 1860 |

their chief port. The Massachusetts figures include Maine to 1820, as well as Salem and other ports in addition to Boston, which had about 85% to 90% of the total. About 10% of the later New York figures represent the lake trade with Canada.

## N. Imports of Principal States: 1815–60

[In millions of dollars.]

| Year | Total United States | Chief general ports | | | |
|---|---|---|---|---|---|
| | | New York (N. Y. City) | Massachusetts (Boston) | Pennsylvania (Philadelphia) | Maryland (Baltimore) |
| 1815 | 113 | | | | |
| 1816 | 147 | | | | |
| 1817 | 99 | | | | |
| 1818 | 121 | | | | |
| 1819 | 87 | | | | |
| 1820 | 74 | | | | |
| 1821 | 62 | 23 | 14 | 8 | 4 |
| 1822 | 83 | 35 | 18 | 11 | 4 |
| 1823 | 77 | 29 | 17 | 13 | 4 |
| 1824 | 80 | 36 | 15 | 11 | 4 |
| 1825 | 96 | 49 | 15 | 15 | 4 |
| 1826 | 84 | 38 | 17 | 13 | 4 |
| 1827 | 79 | 38 | 13 | 11 | 4 |
| 1828 | 88 | 41 | 15 | 12 | 5 |
| 1829 | 74 | 34 | 12 | 10 | 4 |
| 1830 | 70 | 35 | 10 | 8 | 4 |
| 1831 | 103 | 57 | 14 | 12 | 4 |
| 1832 | 101 | 53 | 18 | 10 | 4 |
| 1833 | 108 | 55 | 19 | 10 | 5 |
| 1834 | 126 | 73 | 17 | 10 | 4 |
| 1835 | 149 | 88 | 19 | 12 | 5 |
| 1836 | 189 | 118 | 25 | 15 | 7 |
| 1837 | 140 | 79 | 19 | 11 | 7 |
| 1838 | 113 | 68 | 13 | 9 | 5 |
| 1839 | 162 | 99 | 19 | 15 | 6 |
| 1840 | 107 | 60 | 16 | 8 | 4 |
| 1841 | 127 | 75 | 20 | 10 | 6 |
| 1842 | 100 | 57 | 17 | 7 | 4 |
| 1843[a] | 64 | 31 | 16 | 2 | 2 |
| 1844 | 108 | 65 | 20 | 7 | 3 |
| 1845 | 117 | 70 | 22 | 8 | 3 |
| 1846 | 121 | 74 | 24 | 7 | 4 |
| 1847 | 146 | 84 | 34 | 9 | 4 |
| 1848 | 154 | 94 | 28 | 12 | 5 |
| 1849 | 147 | 92 | 24 | 10 | 4 |
| 1850 | 178 | 111 | 30 | 12 | 6 |
| 1851 | 220 | 111 | 32 | 14 | 6 |
| 1852 | 212 | 132 | 33 | 14 | 6 |
| 1853 | 267 | 178 | 41 | 18 | 6 |
| 1854 | 304 | 195 | 48 | 21 | 6 |
| 1855 | 261 | 164 | 45 | 15 | 7 |
| 1856 | 314 | 210 | 43 | 16 | 9 |
| 1857 | 360 | 236 | 47 | 17 | 10 |
| 1858 | 282 | 178 | 42 | 12 | 8 |
| 1859 | 338 | 229 | 43 | 14 | 9 |
| 1860 | 362 | 248 | 41 | 14 | 9 |

[a] Nine-month period. In this, as in other tables, the figures have been reduced to millions or thousands by omitting the final digits rather than by giving the nearest million. Thus, 7,900,000 would appear as "7" rather than "8." A dash (—) indicates an amount less than a single unit of measure-

## N. Imports of Principal States: 1815–60 (*cont'd*)

[In millions of dollars.]

| Cotton ports | | | | Other states | | |
|---|---|---|---|---|---|---|
| Lousiana (New Orleans) | South Carolina (Charleston) | Georgia (Savannah) | Alabama (Mobile) | Maine (Portland, Quoddy) | California (San Francisco) | Year |
| | | | | | | 1815 |
| | | | | | | 1816 |
| | | | | | | 1817 |
| | | | | | | 1818 |
| | | | | | | 1819 |
| | | | | | | 1820 |
| 3 | 3 | 1 | — | — | | 1821 |
| 3 | 2 | — | — | — | | 1822 |
| 4 | 2 | — | — | — | | 1823 |
| 4 | 2 | — | — | — | | 1824 |
| 4 | 1 | — | — | 1 | | 1825 |
| 4 | 1 | — | — | 1 | | 1826 |
| 4 | 1 | — | — | 1 | | 1827 |
| 6 | 1 | — | — | 1 | | 1828 |
| 6 | 1 | — | — | — | | 1829 |
| 7 | 1 | — | — | — | | 1830 |
| 9 | 1 | — | — | — | | 1831 |
| 8 | 1 | — | — | 1 | | 1832 |
| 9 | 1 | — | — | 1 | | 1833 |
| 13 | 1 | — | — | 1 | | 1834 |
| 17 | 1 | — | — | — | | 1835 |
| 15 | 2 | — | — | — | | 1836 |
| 14 | 2 | — | — | — | | 1837 |
| 9 | 2 | — | — | — | | 1838 |
| 12 | 3 | — | — | — | | 1839 |
| 10 | 2 | — | — | — | | 1840 |
| 10 | 1 | — | — | — | | 1841 |
| 8 | 1 | — | — | — | | 1842 |
| 8 | 1 | — | — | — | | 1843[a] |
| 7 | 1 | — | — | — | | 1844 |
| 7 | 1 | — | — | — | | 1845 |
| 7 | — | — | — | — | | 1846 |
| 9 | 1 | — | — | — | | 1847 |
| 9 | 1 | — | — | — | | 1848 |
| 10 | 1 | — | — | — | | 1849 |
| 10 | 1 | — | — | — | — | 1850 |
| 12 | 2 | — | — | 1 | 6 | 1851 |
| 12 | 2 | — | — | 1 | — | 1852 |
| 13 | 1 | — | — | 1 | 8 | 1853 |
| 14 | 1 | — | — | 2 | 5 | 1854 |
| 12 | 1 | — | — | 2 | | 1855 |
| 16 | 1 | — | — | 1 | 7 | 1856 |
| 24 | 2 | — | — | 2 | 9 | 1857 |
| 19 | 2 | — | — | 1 | 8 | 1858 |
| 18 | 1 | — | — | 2 | 11 | 1859 |
| 22 | 1 | — | 1 | 1 | 9 | 1860 |

ment. Import figures by states are not available for years before 1821 but can be estimated approximately on the basis of customs duties.

### O. Sea Island Cotton Exported from the United States: 1805–60

[In millions of pounds.]

| Year | Quantity | Year | Quantity | Year | Quantity |
|---|---|---|---|---|---|
| 1805 | 8.8 | 1824 | 9.5 | 1843 | 7.5 |
| 1806 | 6.1 | 1825 | 9.7 | 1844 | 6.1 |
| 1807 | 8.9 | 1826 | 6.0 | 1845 | 9.4 |
| 1808 | 0.9 | 1827 | 15.1 | 1846 | 9.4 |
| 1809 | 8.7 | 1828 | 11.3 | 1847 | 6.3 |
| 1810 | 8.6 | 1829 | 12.8 | 1848 | 7.7 |
| 1811 | 8.0 | 1830 | 8.1 | 1849 | 12.0 |
| 1812 | 4.4 | 1831 | 8.3 | 1850 | 8.2 |
| 1813 | 4.1 | 1832 | 8.7 | 1851 | 8.3 |
| 1814 | 2.5 | 1833 | 11.1 | 1852 | 11.7 |
| 1815 | 8.4 | 1834 | 8.1 | 1853 | 11.2 |
| 1816 | 9.9 | 1835 | 7.8 | 1854 | 10.5 |
| 1817 | 8.1 | 1836 | 7.8 | 1855 | 13.1 |
| 1818 | 6.5 | 1837 | 5.3 | 1856 | 12.8 |
| 1819 | 7.5 | 1838 | 7.3 | 1857 | 12.9 |
| 1820 | 11.6 | 1839 | 5.1 | 1858 | 12.1 |
| 1821 | 11.3 | 1840 | 8.8 | 1859 | 13.7 |
| 1822 | 11.3 | 1841 | 6.2 | 1860 | 15.6 |
| 1823 | 12.1 | 1842 | 7.3 | | |

## P. Weighted Yearly Averages and Monthly Prices of Short-Staple Cotton at New Orleans: 1802–60

[In cents per pound.]

| Crop Year | September | October | November | December | January | February | March | April | May | June | July | August | Weighted average |
|---|---|---|---|---|---|---|---|---|---|---|---|---|---|
| 1802 | — | — | — | — | — | 14.0 | — | 16.0 | 14.0 | 13.0 | — | — | 14.7 |
| 1803 | — | — | — | 15.5 | 15.8 | 16.0 | 14.5 | 14.5 | 13.5 | 14.5 | 14.5 | 16.5 | 15.0 |
| 1804 | — | — | 17.5 | 17.5 | 17.8 | 18.5 | 18.5 | 20.5 | 24.5 | 26.0 | 22.7 | 25.5 | 19.6 |
| 1805 | 24.0 | 21.8 | 21.5 | 23.0 | 23.5 | 24.5 | 22.7 | 24.5 | 21.5 | 22.5 | 22.5 | 22.0 | 23.3 |
| 1806 | 22.0 | 22.0 | 22.5 | 22.5 | 22.5 | 22.5 | 20.5 | 21.5 | 21.5 | 21.5 | 22.0 | 22.0 | 21.8 |
| 1807 | 22.0 | 22.0 | 21.3 | 19.0 | 19.0 | 15.5 | 13.7 | 15.3 | 14.4 | 13.9 | 13.4 | 13.7 | 16.4 |
| 1808 | 13.7 | 13.9 | 15.0 | 15.0 | 15.0 | 12.3 | 12.3 | 13.4 | 13.2 | 13.4 | 12.7 | 11.6 | 13.6 |
| 1809 | 11.6 | 11.6 | 11.6 | 13.2 | 13.4 | 13.4 | 13.4 | 14.5 | 14.5 | 14.0 | 14.8 | 14.8 | 13.6 |
| 1810 | 14.8 | 15.8 | 16.0 | 16.0 | 16.3 | 16.0 | 13.5 | 13.5 | 13.5 | 12.0 | 12.0 | 12.0 | 14.7 |
| 1811 | 13.8 | 10.0 | 10.0 | 08.5 | 08.5 | 09.3 | — | 08.8 | — | — | 07.9 | — | 08.9 |
| 1812 | — | — | — | — | — | — | — | — | — | — | — | — | — |
| 1813 | — | — | — | — | — | — | — | — | 15.5 | — | — | — | 15.5 |
| 1814 | — | — | — | — | — | 16.0 | 18.0 | — | — | 16.0 | 18.0 | 20.5 | 16.9 |
| 1815 | 21.5 | 25.5 | 25.0 | 27.5 | 27.0 | — | — | — | — | 32.5 | — | — | 27.3 |
| 1816 | — | — | — | 24.5 | 24.0 | 25.0 | 26.0 | 25.0 | 28.0 | 28.0 | 28.0 | 26.5 | 25.4 |
| 1817 | 25.5 | 26.5 | 26.5 | 31.0 | 30.5 | 30.0 | — | — | — | 29.0 | 31.5 | 33.0 | 29.8 |
| 1818 | 32.5 | 28.0 | — | 25.0 | 23.5 | — | 22.0 | 21.0 | 17.0 | 14.5 | 17.0 | 13.5 | 21.5 |
| 1819 | 13.5 | 13.5 | 17.0 | 14.5 | 14.5 | 14.5 | — | 13.0 | — | 15.5 | 16.0 | — | 14.3 |
| 1820 | — | — | — | 15.0 | — | 14.8 | — | — | 15.5 | 16.0 | 16.5 | — | 15.2 |
| 1821 | — | — | 16.8 | 16.8 | — | 18.0 | — | 18.3 | 16.5 | 15.5 | 15.5 | 14.3 | 17.4 |
| 1822 | 12.8 | 12.8 | 13.5 | 12.8 | 11.0 | 11.3 | 11.3 | 11.0 | 11.0 | 12.3 | — | 11.3 | 11.5 |
| 1823 | 12.3 | 14.5 | 17.5 | 14.8 | 15.5 | 13.8 | 13.8 | 13.8 | 14.3 | 15.8 | 15.8 | 15.8 | 14.5 |
| 1824 | 15.8 | — | 12.3 | 12.5 | 12.5 | 13.5 | 17.0 | 18.5 | 29.0 | 29.5 | 29.0 | — | 17.9 |
| 1825 | — | — | 15.0 | 13.3 | 12.5 | 12.5 | 11.8 | 10.5 | 11.0 | 10.0 | 09.5 | 09.5 | 11.9 |
| 1826 | — | 09.3 | 10.5 | 09.8 | 09.5 | 09.4 | 09.4 | 08.8 | 08.8 | 08.8 | 08.8 | 08.8 | 09.3 |
| 1827 | 10.0 | 10.3 | 10.3 | 09.3 | 09.0 | 09.3 | 09.4 | 10.0 | 10.4 | 10.8 | 10.8 | 10.3 | 09.7 |
| 1828 | 10.3 | — | 09.5 | 10.3 | 10.3 | 09.6 | 09.6 | 10.3 | 09.3 | 08.8 | 08.5 | 08.6 | 09.8 |
| 1829 | — | — | 09.3 | 08.3 | 08.8 | 08.8 | 09.1 | 08.8 | 09.1 | 09.1 | 09.4 | — | 08.9 |
| 1830 | 08.8 | — | 09.5 | 09.4 | 08.9 | 08.4 | 07.8 | 07.5 | 07.8 | 08.0 | 08.1 | 08.1 | 08.4 |
| 1831 | 08.1 | 08.1 | 08.4 | 08.5 | 09.0 | 09.0 | 09.4 | 09.4 | 09.4 | 08.1 | 08.3 | 08.5 | 09.0 |

P. Weighted Yearly Averages and Monthly Prices of Short-Staple Cotton at New Orleans: 1802–60 (*cont'd*)

| Crop Year | September | October | November | December | January | February | March | April | May | June | July | August | Weighted average |
|---|---|---|---|---|---|---|---|---|---|---|---|---|---|
| 1832 | 09.4 | 10.5 | 10.3 | 10.3 | 09.4 | 09.4 | 09.8 | 09.8 | 10.9 | 11.6 | 11.8 | — | 10.0 |
| 1833 | — | 18.0 | 13.8 | 12.3 | 10.3 | 09.8 | 10.0 | 10.8 | 11.3 | 11.3 | 11.8 | 11.8 | 11.2 |
| 1834 | 11.8 | 14.3 | 13.3 | 15.8 | 15.3 | 14.8 | 15.8 | 16.0 | 17.0 | 17.0 | 18.5 | 18.5 | 15.5 |
| 1835 | — | 15.3 | 14.3 | 14.6 | 14.5 | 14.5 | 15.5 | 16.8 | 15.5 | 15.5 | 14.8 | 14.8 | 15.2 |
| 1836 | — | 15.0 | 15.3 | 14.3 | 14.1 | 12.8 | 13.8 | 11.5 | 11.5 | — | — | 11.3 | 13.3 |
| 1837 | 09.4 | 09.8 | 09.3 | 09.1 | 09.1 | 09.1 | 08.1 | 08.8 | 09.3 | 09.3 | 08.4 | 09.3 | 09.0 |
| 1838 | 08.8 | 10.4 | 10.5 | 11.5 | 12.3 | 12.9 | 13.8 | 14.6 | 14.4 | 14.3 | 12.5 | 10.3 | 12.4 |
| 1839 | 09.3 | 10.3 | 09.3 | 07.5 | 07.9 | 07.3 | 06.5 | 06.8 | 06.9 | 07.5 | 07.8 | 08.3 | 07.9 |
| 1840 | 08.3 | 08.4 | 08.3 | 08.4 | 08.5 | 09.6 | 09.6 | 10.0 | 10.1 | 09.8 | 09.3 | 09.0 | 09.1 |
| 1841 | 08.5 | 08.6 | 08.6 | 08.3 | 07.9 | 07.3 | 07.4 | 07.5 | 06.6 | 06.6 | 07.6 | 06.3 | 07.8 |
| 1842 | 07.4 | 06.1 | 06.0 | 05.6 | 05.8 | 05.2 | 04.9 | 05.4 | 06.0 | 06.0 | 06.0 | 06.0 | 05.7 |
| 1843 | 06.6 | 07.1 | 07.1 | 09.0 | 07.7 | 07.7 | 07.8 | 07.1 | 07.2 | 07.1 | 07.0 | 07.0 | 07.5 |
| 1844 | 05.8 | 05.8 | 05.3 | 05.3 | 04.7 | 05.4 | 05.3 | 06.1 | 06.1 | 06.1 | 06.1 | 06.3 | 05.5 |
| 1845 | 06.6 | 07.3 | 06.8 | 06.8 | 06.6 | 06.7 | 06.7 | 06.8 | 06.3 | 06.6 | 06.8 | 07.0 | 06.8 |
| 1846 | 08.1 | 09.4 | 09.2 | 09.1 | 10.1 | 10.1 | 10.5 | 10.7 | 11.4 | 09.3 | 09.9 | 10.6 | 09.9 |
| 1847 | 10.4 | 09.2 | 07.1 | 06.7 | 06.7 | 06.7 | 07.0 | 05.9 | 05.1 | 05.5 | 05.6 | 06.0 | 07.0 |
| 1848 | 05.5 | 05.3 | 04.9 | 05.4 | 05.8 | 06.1 | 06.3 | 06.1 | 06.6 | 06.9 | 07.1 | 09.3 | 05.8 |
| 1849 | 09.3 | 09.9 | 10.3 | 10.3 | 11.2 | 11.2 | 10.6 | 11.1 | 12.1 | 11.7 | 12.1 | 12.2 | 10.8 |
| 1850 | 12.4 | 13.1 | 13.1 | 13.3 | 12.9 | 11.3 | 10.0 | 10.7 | 08.6 | 08.1 | 07.8 | 06.6 | 11.7 |
| 1851 | 08.4 | 06.9 | 07.0 | 07.6 | 07.3 | 07.4 | 07.3 | 07.1 | 08.3 | 09.1 | 08.9 | 09.1 | 07.4 |
| 1852 | 09.8 | 09.6 | 09.6 | 07.9 | 08.9 | 08.5 | 09.0 | 10.0 | 09.3 | 09.6 | 10.0 | 10.3 | 09.1 |
| 1853 | 10.9 | 09.3 | 08.5 | 09.0 | 09.0 | 08.4 | 08.9 | 08.0 | 07.5 | 07.6 | 08.0 | 08.0 | 08.8 |
| 1854 | 07.9 | 08.1 | 08.1 | 07.5 | 08.4 | 08.5 | 08.6 | 09.5 | 10.3 | 11.9 | 10.5 | 09.6 | 08.4 |
| 1855 | 09.2 | 09.1 | 08.5 | 08.8 | 08.6 | 09.1 | 09.2 | 10.0 | 10.3 | 10.6 | 10.6 | 10.6 | 09.1 |
| 1856 | 11.4 | 11.9 | 11.4 | 11.9 | 12.3 | 12.6 | 13.1 | 13.8 | 13.6 | 13.6 | 14.6 | 14.9 | 12.4 |
| 1857 | 15.1 | 12.0 | 11.6 | 10.6 | 09.4 | 11.4 | 11.1 | 11.1 | 11.4 | 11.1 | 11.9 | 11.1 | 11.2 |
| 1858 | 11.9 | 11.9 | 11.1 | 11.5 | 11.5 | 10.9 | 11.4 | 12.3 | 11.0 | 11.4 | 11.4 | 11.6 | 11.5 |
| 1859 | 11.1 | 10.8 | 11.0 | 10.9 | 10.8 | 10.7 | 10.7 | 10.8 | 10.8 | 11.0 | 10.5 | 10.6 | 10.8 |
| 1860 | 10.3 | 10.6 | 10.9 | 11.1 | 11.1 | 10.8 | 11.8 | 12.5 | 11.3 | 10.6 | 10.5 | 11.0 | 11.1 |

## Q. Annual Averages of Monthly Prices of Sea Island Cotton at Charleston, South Carolina: 1800–60

[In cents per pound.]

| Year | Price | Year | Price | Year | Price | Year | Price |
|---|---|---|---|---|---|---|---|
| 1800 | 44.9 | 1816 | 44.8 | 1831 | 20.0 | 1846 | 26.6 |
| 1801 | 46.4 | 1817 | 43.5 | 1832 | 18.2 | 1847 | 31.4 |
| 1802 | 44.2 | 1818 | 63.2 | 1833 | 20.2 | 1848 | 19.0 |
| 1803 | 51.5 | 1819 | 42.1 | 1834 | 25.1 | 1849 | 23.2 |
| 1804 | 38.6 | 1820 | 32.8 | 1835 | 34.8 | 1850 | 27.8 |
| 1805 | 51.6 | 1821 | 26.7 | 1836 | 39.5 | 1851 | 29.3 |
| 1806 | 36.7 | 1822 | 24.8 | 1837 | 46.0 | 1852 | 37.2 |
| 1807 | 34.3 | 1823 | 24.5 | 1838 | 35.3 | 1853 | 41.2 |
| 1808 | 24.7 | 1824 | 24.6 | 1839 | 38.7 | 1854 | 33.4 |
| 1809 | 25.4 | 1825 | 54.3 | 1840 | 22.5 | 1855 | 31.6 |
| 1810 | 28.4 | 1826 | 32.7 | 1841 | 26.8 | 1856 | 39.8 |
| 1811 | 22.5 | 1827 | 21.1 | 1842 | 18.1 | 1857 | 38.1 |
| 1812 | 17.5 | 1828 | 25.6 | 1843 | 16.6 | 1858 | 29.3 |
| 1813 | 19.0 | 1829 | 22.9 | 1844 | 18.8 | 1859 | 35.2 |
| 1814 | 25.3 | 1830 | 24.8 | 1845 | 26.6 | 1860 | 47.0 |
| 1815 | 37.9 | | | | | | |

## R. Monthly Range of Short-Staple Cotton Prices in the Charleston Market: 1815–20

[In cents per pound.]

| | 1815 | 1816 | 1817 | 1818 | 1819 | 1820 |
|---|---|---|---|---|---|---|
| January | | 24–28 | 24 1/2–25 1/2 | 33–35 | 25–27 | 15–17 |
| February | | 25 1/2–28 | 25–26 1/2 | 30–33 | 23–25 1/2 | 15–16 1/2 |
| March | | 25–28 | 25–29 | 29–33 | 17–25 | 13–16 1/2 |
| April | 17–18 | 26–28 | 27–29 | 29 1/2–33 | 14–18 | 14–17 1/2 |
| May | 16–18 | 28–31 1/4 | 27–30 | 29–34 | 13–18 | 15–17 1/2 |
| June | 17–20 | 30–32 | 27–30 | 31–34 | 12 1/2–17 1/2 | 16–20 |
| July | 20–22 | 30–32 | 27–30 | 31–33 | 14–18 | 18–20 |
| August | 20–22 | 30–32 | 26–30 | 30–33 | 14–18 | 18–20 |
| September | 21–25 | 25–28 | 26–30 | 30–33 | 14–18 | 18–19 |
| October | 25–28 | 23–27 | 26–31 1/2 | 30–32 | 15–18 1/2 | 15 1/2–20 |
| November | 26–28 | 21–24 | 30–33 1/2 | 26–32 | 15–18 1/2 | 15–16 |
| December | 26–28 | 24–26 | 32 1/2–35 | 24–27 | 15–16 | 15 1/2–16 1/2 |

# 2] Specialization

TABLES 4 A–H. SELECTED STATISTICS OF UNITED STATES INTERNAL COMMERCE

A. NUMBER AND TONNAGE OF STEAMBOATS OPERATING ON THE WESTERN RIVERS: 1817–60

| (A) Official figures of steamboats licensed and enrolled | | | (B) Corrected figures | | (C) Merchant steam vessels of British Empire | | |
|---|---|---|---|---|---|---|---|
| | | | Western rivers | | | | |
| Year | United States tonnage | Western rivers tonnage | Number | Tonnage | Year | Number | Tonnage |
| 1817 | – | – | 17 | 3,290 | 1817 | 19 | 3,950 |
| 1820 | – | – | 69 | 13,890 | 1820 | 43 | 7,243 |
| 1823 | 24,879 | 15,478 | 75 | 12,501 | 1823 | 111 | 14,153 |
| 1825 | 23,061 | 9,140 | 73 | 9,992 | 1825 | 168 | 20,287 |
| 1830 | 63,052 | 30,124 | 187 | 29,481 | 1830 | 315 | 33,444 |
| 1836[a] | 145,102 | 79,981 | 381 | 57,090 | 1836 | 600 | 67,969 |
| 1840 | 198,184 | 98,851 | 536 | 83,592 | 1839 | 770 | 86,731 |
| 1845 | 319,527 | 156,739 | 557 | 98,246 | 1844 | 988 | 125,675 |
| 1850 | 481,004 | 251,019 | 740 | 141,834 | 1849 | 1,296 | 167,310 |
| 1855 | 655,239 | 268,799 | 727 | 173,068 | 1854 | 1,708 | 326,452 |
| 1860 | 770,641 | 292,470 | 735 | 162,735 | 1860 | 2,337 | 500,144 |

[a] Figures through 1834 are for the calendar year; beginning with 1836 they are for the twelve months ending September 30. No district tonnage figures were published from December 31, 1834, to September 30, 1836.

## B. Western States Terms of Trade

[Base: 1824–46 *]

| Year | Index numbers | Year | Index numbers | Year | Index Numbers |
|---|---|---|---|---|---|
| 1816 | 57 | 1831 | 103 | 1846 | 118 |
| 1817 | 64 | 1832 | 105 | 1847 | 134 |
| 1818 | 61 | 1833 | 99 | 1848 | 128 |
| 1819 | 62 | 1834 | 96 | 1849 | 134 |
| 1820 | 47 | 1835 | 122 | 1850 | 136 |
| 1821 | 42 | 1836 | 131 | 1851 | 158 |
| 1822 | 47 | 1837 | 126 | 1852 | 165 |
| 1823 | 67 | 1838 | 119 | 1853 | 140 |
| 1824 | 70 | 1839 | 130 | 1854 | 150 |
| 1825 | 67 | 1840 | 121 | 1855 | 189 |
| 1826 | 70 | 1841 | 105 | 1856 | 151 |
| 1827 | 69 | 1842 | 92 | 1857 | 163 |
| 1828 | 71 | 1843 | 105 | 1858 | 156 |
| 1829 | 82 | 1844 | 113 | 1859 | 176 |
| 1830 | 82 | 1845 | 142 | 1860 | 167 |

* 1824–46 = 100 [S.B.]

## C. River Trade of New Orleans: 1813–60

| Years | Arrivals of steamboats | Freight received (tons) | Value of produce | Years | Arrivals of steamboats | Freight received (tons) | Value of produce |
|---|---|---|---|---|---|---|---|
| 1813-14 | 21 | 67,560 | — | 1837-38 | 1,549 | 449,600 | $ 45,627,720 |
| 1814-15 | 40 | 77,220 | — | 1838-39 | 1,551 | 399,500 | 42,263,880 |
| 1815-16 | — | 94,560 | $ 9,749,253 | 1839-40 | 1,573 | 537,400 | 49,763,825 |
| 1816-17 | — | 80,820 | 8,773,379 | 1840-41 | 1,958 | 542,500 | 49,822,115 |
| 1817-18 | — | 100,880 | 13,501,036 | 1841-42 | 2,132 | 566,500 | 45,716,045 |
| 1818-19 | 191 | 136,300 | 16,771,711 | 1842-43 | 2,324 | 782,600 | 53,782,054 |
| 1819-20 | 198 | 106,706 | 12,637,079 | 1843-44 | 2,570 | 652,000 | 60,094,716 |
| 1820-21 | 202 | 99,320 | 11,967,067 | 1844-45 | 2,530 | 868,000 | 57,199,122 |
| 1821-22 | 287 | 136,400 | 15,126,420 | 1845-46 | 2,770 | 971,700 | 77,193,464 |
| 1822-23 | 392 | 129,500 | 14,473,725 | 1846-47 | 4,024 | 937,600 | 90,033,256 |
| 1823-24 | 436 | 136,240 | 15,063,820 | 1847-48 | 2,917 | 1,025,900 | 79,779,151 |
| 1824-25 | 502 | 176,420 | 19,044,640 | 1848-49 | 2,873 | 1,009,900 | 81,989,692 |
| 1825-26 | 608 | 193,300 | 20,446,320 | 1849-50 | 2,784 | 886,000 | 96,897,873 |
| 1826-27 | 715 | 235,200 | 21,730,887 | 1850-51 | 2,918 | 1,058,200 | 196,924,083 |
| 1827-28 | 698 | 257,300 | 22,886,420 | 1851-52 | 2,778 | 1,160,500 | 108,051,708 |
| 1828-29 | 756 | 245,700 | 20,757,265 | 1852-53 | 3,252 | 1,328,800 | 134,233,735 |
| 1829-30 | 989 | 260,900 | 22,065,518 | 1853-54 | 3,076 | 1,286,300 | 115,336,798 |
| 1830-31 | 778 | 307,300 | 26,044,820 | 1854-55 | 2,763 | 1,247,200 | 117,106,823 |
| 1831-32 | 813 | 244,600 | 21,806,763 | 1855-56 | 2,956 | 1,500,200 | 144,256,081 |
| 1832-33 | 1,280 | 291,700 | 28,238,432 | 1856-57 | 2,745 | 1,431,800 | 158,161,369 |
| 1833-34 | 1,081 | 327,800 | 29,820,817 | 1857-58 | 3,264 | 1,572,700 | 167,155,546 |
| 1834-35 | 1,005 | 399,900 | 37,566,842 | 1858-59 | 3,259 | 1,803,400 | 172,952,664 |
| 1835-36 | 1,272 | 437,100 | 39,237,762 | 1859-60 | 3,566 | 2,187,560 | 185,211,254 |
| 1836-37 | 1,372 | 401,500 | 43,515,402 | | | | |

[a] This does not include articles rafted down of which no record was kept.
[b] This includes the small amount of produce received by Lake Pontchartrain, from 1 to 6 per cent of total. It is impossible to separate it from the receipts by river, since no separate account was kept, except for cotton and a few other articles.

D. DESTINATION OF SPECIFIED ARTICLES EXPORTED FROM THE PORT OF CINCINNATI: 1850–51

| Commodities | To New Orleans | To other downriver ports | To upriver ports | By canals and railways | By flatboats |
|---|---|---|---|---|---|
| Beef, barrels | 19,319 | 68 | 314 | 236 | 1,611 |
| Beef, tierces | 8,677 | 8 | 657 | 14 | 96 |
| Butter, barrels | 1,850 | 867 | 2 | 539 | — |
| Butter, firkins and kegs | 35,200 | 959 | 15 | 8 | 315 |
| Corn, sacks | 15,672 | 3,519 | 156 | 790 | — |
| Cheese | 69,258 | 48,432 | 2,165 | 1,900 | 920 |
| Candles, boxes | 76,245 | 20,272 | 10,695 | 6,195 | 522 |
| Cotton, bales | — | 10 | 3,182 | 1,940 | — |
| Coffee, sacks | 10 | 12,439 | 7,853 | 17,856 | — |
| Flour, barrels | 281,609 | 95,943 | 7,719 | 4,859 | 95,877 |
| Iron, pieces | 6,608 | 54,894 | 6,634 | 40,119 | — |
| Iron, bundles | 1,503 | 25,281 | 2,182 | 15,144 | — |
| Iron, tons | 64 | 1,341 | 219 | 8,152 | 117 |
| Lard, barrels | 22,854 | 117 | 3,277 | 4,143 | 1,821 |
| Lard, kegs | 56,380 | 5,358 | 5,739 | 2,823 | 1,587 |
| Lard oil, barrels | 13,617 | 1,547 | 3,726 | 7,220 | — |
| Linseed oil | 4,443 | 1,362 | 1,042 | 974 | — |
| Molasses | 33 | 2,665 | 12,711 | 9,589 | — |
| Pork, hogsheads | 19,044 | 1,313 | 8,809 | 1,054 | 1,312 |
| Pork, tierces | 11,341 | 18 | 8,759 | 644 | 42 |
| Pork, barrels | 112,622 | 1,055 | 3,801 | 4,608 | 3,781 |
| Pork, pounds | 1,345,860 | 755,860 | 1,559,280 | 1,092,953 | 525,820 |
| Soap, boxes | 9,425 | 6,440 | 3,600 | 2,068 | 375 |
| Sugar, hogsheads | — | 1,426 | 4,378 | 7,196 | — |
| Whiskey, barrels | 140,661 | 56,164 | 31,231 | 3,268 | 17,980 |

### E. Tonnage over Erie Canal to Tidewater from Western States and from New York: 1836–60

| Year | From Western states | From New York |
|---|---|---|
| 1836 | 54,219 | 364,906 |
| 1837 | 56,255 | 331,251 |
| 1838 | 83,233 | 336,016 |
| 1839 | 121,761 | 264,596 |
| 1840 | 158,148 | 309,167 |
| 1841 | 224,176 | 308,344 |
| 1842 | 221,477 | 258,672 |
| 1843 | 256,376 | 378,969 |
| 1844 | 308,025 | 491,791 |
| 1845 | 304,551 | 655,039 |
| 1846 | 506,830 | 600,440 |
| 1847 | 812,840 | 618,412 |
| 1848 | 650,154 | 534,183 |
| 1849 | 768,659 | 498,065 |
| 1850 | 841,501 | 530,358 |
| 1851 | 1,045,820 | 462,857 |
| 1852 | 1,151,978 | 492,726 |
| 1853 | 1,213,690 | 637,748 |
| 1854 | 1,094,391 | 602,167 |
| 1855 | 1,092,876 | 327,839 |
| 1856 | 1,212,550 | 374,580 |
| 1857 | 1,019,998 | 197,201 |
| 1858 | 1,273,099 | 223,588 |
| 1859 | 1,036,634 | 414,699 |
| 1860 | 1,896,975 | 379,086 |

### F. Receipts of Flour and Grain at Buffalo from the West: 1836–60

| Year | Flour (barrels) | Grain (bushels)[a] | Year | Flour (barrels) | Grain (bushels)[a] |
|---|---|---|---|---|---|
| 1836 | 139,178 | 543,461 | 1849 | 1,207,435 | 8,628,013 |
| 1837 | 126,805 | 550,660 | 1850 | 1,103,039 | 6,635,905 |
| 1838 | 277,620 | 974,751 | 1851 | 1,258,224 | 11,449,661 |
| 1839 | 294,125 | 1,117,262 | 1852 | 1,299,513 | 13,892,919 |
| 1840 | 597,142 | 1,075,888 | 1853 | 975,557 | 15,574,741 |
| 1841 | 730,040 | 1,852,325 | 1854 | 739,756 | 18,512,465 |
| 1842 | 734,308 | 2,015,928 | 1855 | 936,761 | 20,788,673 |
| 1843 | 917,517 | 2,055,025 | 1856 | 1,126,048 | 20,129,467 |
| 1844 | 915,030 | 2,335,568 | 1857 | 845,953 | 15,348,930 |
| 1845 | 746,750 | 1,848,040 | 1858 | 1,536,109 | 20,005,044 |
| 1846 | 1,374,529 | 6,493,342 | 1859 | 1,420,333 | 15,229,060 |
| 1847 | 1,857,000 | 9,868,187 | 1860 | 1,122,335 | 31,441,440 |
| 1848 | 1,249,000 | 7,396,012 | | | |

[a] Includes wheat, corn, oats, barley, and rye.

## G. Tonnage Going to Western States by Erie Canal: 1836–60

| Year | Merchandise (tons) | Year | Merchandise (tons) |
|---|---|---|---|
| 1836 | 38,893 | 1849 | 87,899 |
| 1837 | 25,291 | 1850 | 115,045 |
| 1838 | 34,629 | 1851 | 177,623 |
| 1839 | 34,197 | 1852 | 219,799 |
| 1840 | 22,055 | 1853 | 261,752 |
| 1841 | 31,040 | 1854 | 331,879 |
| 1842 | 24,063 | 1855 | 220,466 |
| 1843 | 37,335 | 1856 | 183,513 |
| 1844 | 42,415 | 1857 | 108,125 |
| 1845 | 49,618 | 1858 | 76,890 |
| 1846 | 58,330 | 1859 | 98,876 |
| 1847 | 75,883 | 1860 | 119,682 |
| 1848 | 84,872 | | |

## H. Receipts on All Ohio Canals: 1827–60

| Year | Receipts (dollars) | Year | Receipts (dollars) |
|---|---|---|---|
| 1827 | 1,500 | 1844 | 490,818 |
| 1828 | 12,043 | 1845 | 452,394 |
| 1829 | 47,941 | 1846 | 576,409 |
| 1830 | 60,576 | 1847 | 754,196 |
| 1831 | 101,508 | 1848 | 754,508 |
| 1832 | 116,830 | 1849 | 694,824 |
| 1833 | 187,026 | 1850 | 711,022 |
| 1834 | 214,530 | 1851 | 799,025 |
| 1835 | 237,581 | 1852 | 629,758 |
| 1836 | 261,940 | 1853 | 595,539 |
| 1837 | 356,262 | 1854 | 485,774 |
| 1838 | 464,999 | 1855 | 442,192 |
| 1839 | 506,201 | 1856 | 321,074 |
| 1840 | 532,689 | 1857 | 327,819 |
| 1841 | 495,439 | 1858 | 279,866 |
| 1842 | 463,728 | 1859 | 234,679 |
| 1843 | 433,582 | 1860 | 267,729 |

## SOURCES

TABLES 1 A–B. Ernst von Halle, *Baumwollproduktion und Pflanzungswirtschaft in den Nordamerikan Südstaaten I: Die Skalvenzeit* (Leipzig: Duncker & Humblot, 1897), pp. 175 and 182.

TABLE 1C. U.S. Congress, House, Treasury Department Report [by Levi Woodbury] on *Cotton, Cultivation, Manufacture and Foreign Trade of,* House Document No. 146. 24th Congress, 1st Session (1836).

TABLE 2A. 1697–98 to 1780: Alfred P. Wadsworth and Julia DeLacy Mann, *The Cotton Trade and Industrial Lancashire* (Manchester, England: Manchester University Press, 1931), pp. 520–22; figures for "Misc. Europe and Africa" and for "Prize" omitted. 1781–1814: Edward Baines, *History of the Cotton Manufacture in Great Britain* (London: H. Fisher, R. Fisher, and P. Jackson, 1835), pp. 215 and 347. 1815–60: William Page, ed., *Commerce and Industry: Tables of Statistics for the British Empire from 1815,* 2 vols. (London: Constable, 1919), vol. II, p. 140. Reprinted by permission of the publishers.
The figures from Wadsworth and Mann and from Baines relate to Great Britain; those from Page relate to the United Kingdom.

TABLE 2B. Page, *op. cit.,* p. 145.

TABLE 2C. *Ibid.,* pp. 331–32.

TABLE 2D. R. Robson, *The Cotton Industry in Britain* (London: Macmillan, 1957), pp. 331–32.

TABLE 2E. Von Halle, *op. cit.,* p. 183.

TABLE 3A. Matthew B. Hammond, *The Cotton Industry: an Essay in American Economic History. Part I: The Cotton Culture and the Cotton Trade* (New York: Macmillan, 1897), p. 357.

TABLE 3B. Von Halle, *op. cit.,* p. 162.

TABLES 3 C–D. *Ibid.,* p. 169.

TABLES 3 E–F. *Ibid.,* p. 170.

TABLE 3G. *Ibid.,* p. 172.

TABLE 3H. *Ibid.,* p. 173.

TABLE 3I. J. D. B. DeBow, *Statistical View of the United States . . . Being a Compendium of the Seventh Census* (Washington, D.C.: Beverly Tucker, 1854), p. 178.

TABLE 3J. Baines, *op. cit.,* p. 303.

TABLE 3K. Douglass C. North, "Balance of Payments," *Trends in the American Economy in the Nineteenth Century* (Princeton: Princeton University Press, 1960), Table 1 and Table B-1, Appendix B. Reprinted by permission of the Princeton University Press.

TABLE 3L. George Rogers Taylor, *The Transportation Revolution, 1815–1860* (New York: Holt, Rinehart and Winston, 1951), p. 451. Reprinted by permission of the publisher.

TABLE 3M. Robert G. Albion, *The Rise of New York Port, 1815–1860* (New York: Scribner's, 1939), p. 390. Reprinted by permission of Charles Scribner's Sons.

TABLE 3N. *Ibid.,* p. 391.

TABLE 3O. Lewis C. Gray, *History of Agriculture in the Southern United States to 1860,* 2 vols. (Washington, D.C.: Carnegie Institution of Washington, 1933), vol. II, p. 1032. Reprinted by permission of the publisher.

TABLE 3P. *Ibid.,* p. 1027.

TABLE 3Q. *Ibid.,* p. 1031.

TABLE 3R. Alfred G. Smith, Jr., *Economic Readjustment of an Old Cotton State; South Carolina, 1820–1860* (Columbia: University of South Carolina Press, 1958). Reprinted by permission of the publisher.

TABLE 4A. Louis C. Hunter, *Steamboats on the Western Rivers* (Cambridge, Mass.: Harvard University Press, 1949), p. 33. Reprinted by permission of the publisher.

TABLE 4B. Thomas S. Berry, *Western Prices Before 1861; a Study of the Cincinnati Market* (Cambridge, Mass.: Harvard University Press, 1943), Appendix B, Table 19. Reprinted by permission of the publisher.

TABLE 4C. Guy Stevens Callender, *Selections from the Economic History of the United States, 1765–1860* (Boston: Ginn, 1909), p. 315.

TABLE 4D. J. D. B. DeBow, *Industrial Resources of the Western and Southern States*, 3 vols. (New Orleans: DeBow's Review, 1852), vol. I, pp. 253–54.

TABLE 4E. North, *op. cit.*, p. 251.

TABLE 4F. *Ibid.*, p. 253.

TABLE 4G. *Ibid.*, p. 254.

TABLE 4H. Ernest L. Bogart, *Internal Improvements and State Debt in Ohio; an Essay in Economic History* (London: Longmans, Green and Co., 1924), p. 146. Reprinted by permission of David McKay Company, Inc.

# PART I

# Demand and Supply

# INTRODUCTION

WHILE THE story of the rise of the Cotton Kingdom touches the industrial history of a number of nations, it is central to the history of two of them and can be told very largely in terms of American response to British demand. The beginnings of the cotton-textile industry in Great Britain date from the early eighteenth century, particularly from the enactment of legislation by Parliament in 1700 that was designed to protect the native woolen industry from the competition of printed cotton fabrics imported from the Far East. So fashionable were cottons that the effect of the ban was to encourage their manufacture in Britain itself, and while Parliament tried to stop that too in 1719 the effort was unavailing. The fustian industry—the manufacture of textiles with a linen warp and a cotton woof—gradually developed in Manchester, Lancashire; as it grew so too did imports of raw cotton from the Levant, the West Indies, and other sources, as shown in Table 2A in the statistical section. As the first of the following readings points out, in 1751 imports rose to 2,976,610 pounds, in 1764 to 3,870,392 pounds, and in 1781 to 5,198,778 pounds. After this they "took a sudden rise," increasing to 19 million pounds annually in the next five years, and to 29 millions in the following five, "thus making a more rapid progress in five years than in the proceeding hundred." The cotton industry's subsequent dwarfing of rival textiles is shown in Table 2E in the statistical section.

Behind this rapid rise was the remarkable series of inventions described in the first two readings that follow. These inventions not only form a chapter in the history of the rise of Great Britain to technological and industrial leadership in the eighteenth and nineteenth centuries but also belong to the larger story of worldwide industrial revolution—a story that is even now continuing to be written.

The significance of the inventions will be more readily understood if we realize that spinning and weaving are the two chief processes in the manufacture of textiles and that a state of imbalance between the two tended to encourage efforts to restore equilibrium. Before the stream of inventiveness began its flow a single loom provided work for five or six spinning wheels. Kay's flying shuttle (1733), a manual device that speeded weaving operations, aggravated the disparity still more by enabling the weaver to double his output. The stage was thus set for the improvements in spinning machinery introduced by Arkwright, Hargreaves, and Crompton.

Arkwright's water frame, patented in 1769, fed the roving—a loosely twisted strand of fibers—through a series of rollers operating at different rates of speed and wound it on vertical spindles. In this manner the fiber was drawn out and twisted in a single, continuous operation. The water frame, however, spun only coarse yarns. Hargreaves' spinning jenny, patented in 1770, made a finer product. The machine was a kind of multiplied spinning wheel in which at first 8 spindles and later as many as 100 were set in motion by the operation of a single wheel. As the spindles were rotated the roving was fed to them from a clasp bar that was moved by hand first away from the spindles and then toward them. An intermittent rather than a continuous process, this technique for drawing out and twisting the fibers produced a yarn that was both fine and strong. Crompton's "mule" combined features of the water frame and the jenny. Invented in 1779 as a manually operated machine, it was subsequently enlarged and by 1790 made automatic. Its yarns were finer than the product of the most skilled handworkers of India.

These improvements in spinning once more created a disequilibrium and set the stage for further change, this time for mechanization of the weaving process. However, although Cartwright's power loom was patented in 1785, its widespread adoption was delayed until a number of needed improvements were made after the beginning of the nineteenth century. Before that time an enlarged number of hand-loom weavers enjoyed the unusual opportunity for good earnings stemming from the lack of technological equilibrium between spinning and weaving.

Cartwright's loom, Arkwright's water frame, and Crompton's mule together formed a formidable array of power-driven textile machines. The power to run them was provided at first by water wheels, but after the beginning of the nineteenth century water yielded increasingly to improved models of the steam engine invented by Watt in 1769. It would be difficult to overemphasize the importance of the steam engine to the rise of the Cotton Kingdom. By means of it, we are reminded in the second of the following readings, cotton manufacture was extended "far beyond the limit which it could otherwise have reached." The steam engine figured prominently in the enlargement of demand for raw cotton, and also, as we shall see, it played no less a part—in the form first of the steamboat and then of the railroad—in the enlargement of supply.

The effect of the steam engine on demand will be evident on a moment's reflection. The invention of power-driven machinery increasingly transferred the spinning of cotton yarn from the cottage to the mill. Mill production, in turn, often became factory production once the perfecting of the power loom made it possible to bring both power spinning and power weaving under the same roof. The scale of output of both yarn and cloth greatly increased, and this was the source of the vast rise in British consumption of raw cotton that is shown in Table 2C in the statistical section. To sum up in the words of Paul Mantoux, whose indispensable study of the English industrial revolution of the eighteenth century was the first comprehensive one to be undertaken, "The rapid transformation in the cotton industry, wrought by a succession of technical inventions, made it the earliest and also the classical example of modern large-scale industry."[1] The advantages of scale make vitally important contributions to economic growth, and they helped Great Britain to move into a position of world leadership in the nineteenth century.

How interesting it is that the supply response of the American South to the British demand for raw cotton should have played a key role in the more rapid economic growth of the United States!

[1] Paul Joseph Mantoux, *The Industrial Revolution in the Eighteenth Century* (London: J. Cape, 1961), p. 191.

While not unknown to the colonial period, cotton had been cultivated on a comparatively small scale before the final decades of the eighteenth century. The extent to which it figured among American exports as late as 1784 may be gauged by the reputed seizure of eight bags of American cotton by the customs officers in Liverpool on the ground that so much cotton could not possibly be the produce of the United States. (The customs officers were sure it must have originated in the West Indies, the produce of which was forbidden by the Navigation Act to be imported into England under a foreign flag.) How dramatically this situation was to change in the course of a few years is clearly revealed by the figures for cotton exports during and after the 1790's (see Table 3A in the statistical section).

First to respond to the British demand was the production of Sea Island cotton. Of the two varieties of cotton grown in the United States, Upland and Sea Island, the second was a late-comer. Not until about 1786 did some planters, after having acquired seed from the Bahama Islands, introduce its culture along the Georgia-Carolina coast. The English market promptly placed a high premium on the silky, long-fibered but strong cotton from America. Before the end of the century prices in Liverpool rose to a high of 5 shillings per pound, and American production responded accordingly. By 1805 exports of the Sea Island staple amounted to nearly 9 million pounds. Unlike the "Uplands", Sea Island fibers were easily detachable from the seed by squeezing it between a pair of simple rollers. Climatic requirements, however, confined the culture of Sea Island to within a strip 30 or 40 miles wide along the coast of South Carolina and Georgia, and in consequence exports never amounted to as much as 16 million pounds in any year prior to 1860 (see Table 3O in the statistical section). How small this figure is in relation to annual national cotton exports will be made clear by a glance at Table 3A. In sum, a pound of Sea Island was worth a good deal more than a pound of "middling Uplands" (which was second-grade cotton), but the overwhelming bulk of the cotton exported by the United States during the period was nevertheless of the latter variety.

What made possible the massive export of Upland cotton was the invention by Eli Whitney of the cotton gin. Rarely, if ever, does an invention so clearly appear to have been the child of economic necessity. Confronted by rising British demand and a supply response that was potentially vast, provided only that some mechanical way was found to abridge the labor cost of separating the sticky short fibers from the green seeds, Whitney was by no means the only American trying to solve the problem. As the following readings make clear, his gin was a simple device—so simple as to lend credence to the belief that someone else would surely have soon developed it if Whitney had not. The gin consisted of a cylinder fitted with wire teeth. The latter drew the seed cotton through a wire screen that separated the seed from the lint, and a revolving brush then removed the lint from the teeth of the cylinder. Before its invention, a good hand took a day to clean one pound of cotton. The gin enabled him to increase his output by 50 times. Because it was easily imitable—particularly after the shed in which Whitney had stored his model was broken into and the machine stolen—a number of models soon appeared in the South, with the result that Whitney and his partner, Miller, found themselves entangled in a maze of virtually fruitless litigation. Had they been able to secure their patent and the monopoly prices this would have made possible, the spread of cotton culture would surely have been delayed. Their inability to do so meant that the gin became available at a competitive price.

Whitney's gin removed the last great obstacle to the spread of cotton culture throughout the South. In possession of a favorable climate, abundant supplies of cheap and richly productive land, and an expandable plantation-labor system with which to work it, the South soon saw cotton establish a comparative advantage over most alternative crops in the regions suited to its growth. Sugar, tobacco, and rice continued to be important crops in local areas on the fringes of the Cotton Kingdom, but neither they nor any other staple succeeded in challenging the sway of the ruling house. The cultivation of rice could not be greatly expanded because it was confined to marsh lands that could be drained, diked, and flooded. Requirements of soil and climate confined sugar to a small area. Wheat did not do well in the lower South. The indigo industry of the Carolinas and Georgia all but died out when the Revolution ended the bounty of 6 pence per pound that the British had paid. As for tobacco, according to Ulrich B. Phillips, that industry was entering in 1783 "upon a half century of such wellnigh constant low prices that the opening of each new tract for its culture was offset by the abandonment of an old one, and the export remained stationary at a little less than half a million hogsheads." [2]

The larger truth of the matter is that increasing world demand provided a great stimulus to the growing of cotton wherever it could be profitably produced. The British demand was far larger than that of any other country, but it must not be overlooked that in the period 1830–60 the textile industries of France, Prussia and the Zollverein, Russia, Austria, Holland, Spain, and a number of Italian states were also growing. Table 3J in the statistical section shows exports from the United States to a number of these countries during the year ending September 30, 1832. The growing textile industry of the United States itself must not be overlooked as a factor in world demand for raw cotton. Prior to the years of natural protection afforded by Jefferson's Embargo (1807), the Nonintercourse Act, the various nonimportation policies immediately preceding the War of 1812, and especially the war itself, American textile manufacturing was of little consequence. By mid-century the Andrews Report of 1853 to the United States Senate could remark that "our manufacturing establishments already use about *one-third* of the entire crop of raw cotton of the United States," and "supply more than *three-fourths* of the cotton manufactures *consumed* in the United States."

Table 1A in the statistical section shows the effect of world demand upon the principal cotton producing areas of the world. By 1821, as the table makes clear, cotton production in the United States exceeded that of any other area, and in the years between 1840 and 1860 it accounted for roughly two-thirds of the world supply. The following readings include two interesting contemporary explanations for the dominant position of the United States. A thorough explanation would require a type of investigation apparently not previously undertaken—namely, a detailed comparison of production costs for each area contributing to the total world supply. Cost advantages must explain the predominance of the American South, and the

[2] Ulrich B. Phillips, *American Negro Slavery* (Gloucester, Mass.: Peter Smith, 1959), p. 150.

problem would be to explain these cost advantages year in and year out throughout the period. It is altogether likely that the output of marginal suppliers around the world increased from time to time when unusual rises in cotton prices made it possible to expand production in areas of relatively higher cost.

The following readings open with a series of brief accounts of the leading English and American inventions affecting the demand for cotton. The first of these is a description, written in the 1860's by Professor C. F. McCay of the University of Georgia, of the textile inventions. McCay, a frequent contributor of learned articles on cotton to *DeBow's Review,* was a respected authority. The next selection is an account of Watt's invention of the steam engine, written in the 1830's by Edward Baines, an early historian of the rise of the British cotton-textile industry. Note in particular Baines' emphasis on the importance of the steam engine to the *expansion* of manufacturing. The story of Whitney's invention of the cotton gin is then related, in part in an article written for the *New England Magazine* in 1890 and in part by Whitney's letters to his father. Also included is Whitney's own brief description of the gin. Next come excerpts from an early history of South Carolina by David Ramsay, medical practitioner and dependable historian, who discusses the great early staples of South Carolina and the effect of cotton upon them. Note that Ramsay did not approve a single-minded devotion to the growing of cotton. Also note his implied judgment that the planters, in contrast with former merchants and military men who took up planting, were not "regular and methodical in business." In Part IV we shall hear again of this charge, which is frequently encountered in the social and economic literature of the South.

The next group of readings concerns the preeminent contribution by the United States to the world's supply of cotton. The first selection is from a scholarly report on cotton made in 1836 by Secretary of the Treasury Levi Woodbury. In it Secretary Woodbury presents one possible explanation of American leadership. Before reading this selection the student should review Table 1C in the statistical section. The second selection gives the views of Israel D. Andrews, author of the justly celebrated Andrews Report, on the same question of American dominance. The last selection, also by Andrews, assesses the importance of cotton by showing the effect of earnings from cotton sales in foreign markets on the United States' balance of payments.

In considering the reasons for the comparatively small supply of cotton provided by other parts of the world, one might well ask what known agricultural conditions in India may help explain the difficulty with which poor farmers increased their output there. Also, what was the probable effect of Great Britain's abolition of slavery in her West Indian possessions in 1833 upon labor costs and the ability of that area to contribute to the world supply of cotton? In British Guiana (which was acquired from the Dutch in 1805) the culture of cotton had almost ceased by 1830. Would the fact that the price of cotton declined more rapidly than that of sugar have anything to do with this development? What other conditions in other areas of supply conceivably affected production costs? How "elastic" in general was the supply of cotton—that is, to what extent did world production respond to increases in the price of cotton?

THE READINGS

# 1] The Great Inventions

## a] An American Professor Sketches the Principal English Inventions Affecting Textiles

. . . . . . . . . . . . . . . .

COTTON has been employed as a material for clothing from the earliest times, and at the beginning of the eighteenth century nearly two millions of pounds were imported into England to supply their spinning wheels and looms, and to be used for the other purposes to which it was applied. In 1751 the imports rose to 2,976,610 pounds, in 1764 they were 3,870,392 pounds, and in 1781 they had increased to 5,198,778. At this period they took a sudden rise, and in the next five years increased to nineteen millions, and in the next five to twenty-nine millions of pounds, thus making a more rapid progress in five years than in the preceding hundred.

The cause of this rapid advance was the introduction of machinery for the spinning of cotton. This reduced the price and increased the demand, and led to the exclusion of linen, silk, and wool, and the substitution of cotton in their place.

As early as 1738 Wyatt had taken out a patent for the spinning of cotton by machinery. He was assisted by Paul, who afterward took out a patent for carding the cotton by machinery. But so complex and imperfect were the details of this machinery of Wyatt and Paul that these projects failed. The principle was discovered, but important practical improvements were wanting before it could be made successful.

In 1769, Arkwright took out a patent for his water-frame and throstle, and in 1770, Hargreaves invented his spinning-jenny, both of which were on the same principle as Wyatt's machine, but led to a very different result. Between 1770 and 1780 these machines were fairly tested, and in the next ten years they were rapidly introduced. The patent of Arkwright was broken down in the courts of law in 1785, by the persevering opposition of those who had wrongfully appropriated his discoveries; and the expiration of the other patents in a short time opened the whole manufacture to the free use of the people. In 1800 the imports of cotton had risen to fifty-six millions, an increase of eleven fold in twenty years. In the first eighty years of the

---

FROM C. F. McCay, "Cultivation of Cotton" in L. Stebbins, ed., *Eighty Years' Progress of the United States* (Hartford, Conn.: L. Stebbins, 1868), pp. 108–09.

eighteenth century the increase had been one hundred and fifty per cent.; in the last twenty years it had been a thousand.

These improvements of Arkwright and Hargreaves were not the end and perfection of the inventions for spinning. These machines were not adapted for the finer numbers, and in 1779 Samuel Crompton invented the mule, which combined the excellences of the two former inventions. No patent was taken out for it, and it was worked for a while in secret. But the high prices Crompton obtained for his yarn soon attracted such attention that he could no longer keep it concealed. For number forty, he received three dollars and a half a pound; and for number sixty, six dollars. These prices were commanded by the superiority of his yarn, and the mule was, therefore, a great improvement on the old machines. At first the invention was quite imperfect, but it was soon improved and brought nearly to its present perfection. In the course of ten years it was everywhere introduced. Under its influence the demand for labor rapidly increased.

The next important invention was the power-loom, first proposed and patented by Cartwright. The patent was issued in 1787, but all efforts failed to introduce it successfully until after the beginning of the present century. The improvements in dressing the warp, which were indispensable to the success of the power-loom, were made in 1803. In 1813 there were twenty-four hundred of these in use in England. In 1820 these had increased to fifty-five thousand, and in 1833 to a hundred thousand.

The steam engine of Watt was not less important to the manufacture of cotton than these improvements in spinning and weaving. The water power of England was limited, irregular, and entirely insufficient for the numerous machines that were soon introduced, and the new motive power was especially adapted to their work. Being cheap on account of the abundance of coal, regular in its operations so as to give a uniform stroke to the loom, not liable to interruptions and strikes as human labor had been, it has contributed very much to the progress of the cotton manufacture. Watt's first patent was taken out in 1769, but it was not until 1785 that steam was applied to the driving of a cotton mill. In 1800 there were thirty engines employed at Manchester, and in 1859 the number in the whole kingdom had risen to twenty-two hundred.

Under the influence of these improvements, the progress in the manufacture of cotton has been of the most rapid description.

It was under the influence of those great inventions that the importations of cotton rose in twenty years—from 1781 to 1801—from five to fifty-six millions of pounds, and the English exports of cottons from two millions of dollars to twenty-seven millions. In all this time the price of the raw material rather advanced than decreased. According to Tooke's "History of Prices," the range for different qualities of West India and Surinam from 1780 to 1785 was from 13 pence per pound to 40; while from 1795 to 1800 it was from 15 to 55 pence. But the cost of yarns was very different. In 1786 and 1787 the price of No. 100 was nine and a half dollars a pound; in 1790, seven and a half dollars; in 1795, four dollars and three quarters; and in 1800, two dollars and thirty-five cents.

We thus see that the effect of the introduction of machinery was to give an immense increase to the consumption of cotton, a large reduction in the price of cotton goods, and a substitution of cotton for wool, silk, and flax, and an increase in the demand for labor.

. . . . . . . . . . . . . . . .

## b] AN EARLY NINETEENTH-CENTURY HISTORIAN OF THE COTTON INDUSTRY ASSESSES THE STEAM ENGINE

. . . . . . . . . . . . . . . .

AMAZING as is the progress which had taken place in the cotton manufacture prior to 1790, it would soon have found a check upon its further extension, if a power more efficient than water had not been discovered to move the machinery. The building of mills in Lancashire must have ceased, when all the available fall of the streams had been appropriated. The manufacture might indeed have spread to other counties, as it has done to some extent; but it could not have flourished in any district where coal as well as water was not to be found; and the diffusion of the mills over a wide space would have been unfavourable to the division of labour, the perfection of machine-making, and the cheapness of conveyance.

At this period a power was happily discovered, of almost universal application and unlimited extent, adapted to every locality where fuel was cheap, and available both to make machines and to work them, both to produce goods, and to convey them by land and water. This power was the *steam-engine,* which, though not an invention of that age, was first made of great and extensive utility by the genius of James Watt.

The first thought of employing the expansive force of steam as a mechanical power is believed to have been entertained by Solomon de Caus, engineer to Louis XIII., who proposed the raising of water by steam as a philosophical principle, in a book written in 1615, after he had been in England, in the suite of the Elector Palatine, who married the daughter of James I. In 1630, Charles I. granted a patent to David Ramseye, a groom of the privy chamber, for nine articles of invention, two of which seem to indicate the origin of the steam-engine, viz.: "To raise water from low pitts, by fire;" and "To raise water from low places, and mynes, and coal pits, by a new waie never yet in use." These facts take away from the ingenious Marquis of Worcester the honour which has generally been ascribed to him, of having first applied steam as a mechanical power. In the *"Century of Inventions,"* published by that eccentric nobleman in 1663, there is the most distinct statement of the immense power of steam, which he had proved by its bursting a cannon, and which he had applied to the producing of

---

FROM Edward Baines, *History of the Cotton Manufacture in Great Britain* (London: H. Fisher, R. Fisher, and P. Jackson, 1835), pp. 220–27.

fountains forty feet high. The first person who constructed a machine in which steam was successfully turned to purposes of usefulness, was Captain Savery, who obtained a patent on the 25th July, 1698, for his invention. This engine was thought of so much importance, that an Act of Parliament was passed, 10 and 11 William III. c. 31, "for the encouragement of a new invention, by Thomas Savery, for raising water, and occasioning motion to all sorts of mill-work, by the impellent force of fire." Before he obtained his patent, Savery had erected several steam-engines to pump water out of the Cornish mines, and had published a description of the machine in a book, entitled *"The Miner's Friend,"* in 1696. This engine, though very ingenious, had many defects, the principal of which were, that it occasioned a great waste of steam and fuel, and, from its limited powers, could only be applied in certain situations. A material improvement was made in it by Thomas Newcomen, an ingenious ironmonger at Dartmouth, in Devonshire, who came to an agreement with Savery, and obtained a joint patent with him for the new engine in 1705. Mr. Beighton, in 1717, simplified the movements of the machine, without changing its principle; and, after his time, no considerable improvement was made till 1769.

James Watt, a native of Greenock, was brought up as a maker of philosophical instruments in Glasgow and London, and settled in Glasgow in 1757. He was appointed instrument maker to the university, and thus became acquainted with Dr. Black, professor of medicine and lecturer on chemistry in that institution, who, about this time, published his important and beautiful discovery of latent heat. The knowledge of this doctrine led Watt to reflect on the prodigious waste of heat in the steam-engine, where steam was used merely for the purpose of creating a vacuum in the cylinder under the piston, and for that end was condensed in the cylinder itself,—the piston being then forced down solely by atmospheric pressure. The cylinder was therefore alternately warmed by the steam, and cooled by the admission of cold water to condense the steam; and when the steam was readmitted after the cooling process, much of it was instantly condensed by the cold cylinder, and a great waste of the steam took place: of course, there was an equal waste of the fuel which produced the steam, and this rendered the use of the machine very costly.

It happened that Watt was employed, in the year 1763, to repair a small working model of Newcomen's steam-engine for Professor Anderson. He saw its defects, and studied how to remedy them. He perceived the vast capabilities of an engine, moved by so powerful an agent as steam, if that agent could be properly applied. His scientific knowledge, as well as his mechanical ingenuity, was called forth; all the resources of his sagacious and philosophical mind were devoted to the task; and after years of patient labour and costly experiments, which nearly exhausted his means, he succeeded in removing every difficulty, and making the steam-engine the most valuable instrument for the application of power, which the world has ever known.

It is not a little remarkable that his patent, "for lessening the consumption of steam and fuel in fire engines," should have been taken out in the same year as Arkwright's patent for spinning with rollers, namely, 1769—one of the most brilliant eras in the annals of British genius;—when Black and Priestley were making their great discoveries in science; when Hargreaves, Arkwright, and Watt revolutionized the processes of manufactures; when Smeaton and Brindley executed prodigies of engineering art; when the senate was illuminated by Burke and Fox, Chatham and Mansfield; when Johnson and Goldsmith, Reid and Beattie, Hume, Gibbon, and Adam Smith, adorned the walks of philosophy and letters.

The patent of 1769 did not include all Watt's improvements. He connected himself in 1775 with Mr. Boulton, of Soho, Birmingham, a gentleman of wealth, enterprise, and mechanical talent; and, having made still further improvements in the steam-engine, an Act of Parliament was passed the same year, vesting in him "the sole use and property of certain steam-engines (or fire-engines) of his invention, throughout his majesty's dominions," for the extraordinary term of twenty-five years. So comprehensive was the Act, that it prevented others from making steam-engines which contained improvements of their own, if their engines condensed the steam in a separate vessel: this was the foundation of Watt's improvements, and it was so great an improvement, that no person could without immense disadvantage dispense with it. Watt, therefore, took up his position in a narrow pass, which he was able to defend against a host; and he kept the whole business of making steam-engines to himself, deterring all invaders of his privilege by instantly commencing prosecutions. He enjoyed his patent for more than thirty years, from 1769 to 1800: and, though it was probably unproductive for the first ten years, it afterwards produced him a large fortune, so that he retired from business a wealthy man, on the expiration of the exclusive privilege. The monopoly was much more extended than any legislature ought to have granted; but it must be allowed that no man could have better deserved or better used it.

Watt laboured incessantly to perfect this important and complicated engine, and took out three other patents in 1781, 1782, and 1784, for great and essential improvements. The three great improvements which he made in the steam-engine are thus briefly described: 1st. The condensation of the steam in a separate vessel: this increased the original powers of the engine, giving to the atmospheric pressure, and to the counter-weight, their full energy, while, at the same time, the waste of steam was greatly diminished. 2d. The employment of steam pressure, instead of that of the atmosphere: this accomplished a still further diminution of the waste, and was fertile in advantages, as it rendered the machine more manageable, particularly by enabling the operator at all times, and without trouble, to suit the power of the engine to its load of work, however variable and increasing. The third improvement was the double impulse, which may be considered as the finishing touch given to the engine, by which its action is rendered nearly as uniform as the water-wheel.

Up to the time of Watt, and indeed up to the year 1782, the steam-engine had been almost exclusively used to pump water out of mines. He perfected its mechanism, so as to adapt it to the production of rotative motion and the working of machinery; and the first engine of that kind was erected by Boulton and Watt at Bradley iron-works, in that year. The first engine which they made for a cotton mill was in the works of Messrs. Robinsons, of Papplewick, in Nottinghamshire, in the year 1785. An atmospheric engine had been put up by Messrs. Arkwright and Simpson for their cotton mill on Shude-hill, Manchester, in 1783: but it was not till 1789 that a steam-engine was erected by Boulton and Watt in that town for cotton spinning, when they made one for Mr. Drinkwater: nor did Sir Richard Arkwright adopt the new invention till 1790, when he had one of Boulton and Watt's engines put up in a cotton mill at Nottingham. In Glasgow, the first steam-engine for cotton spinning was set up for Messrs. Scott and Stevenson, in 1792. So truly had it been predicted in the Act of 1775, that "several years, and repeated proofs, would be required before the public would be fully convinced of their interest to adopt the invention." But when the unrivalled advantages of the steam-engine, as a moving force for all kinds of machinery, came to be generally known, it was rapidly adopted throughout the kingdom, and for every purpose requiring great and steady power. The number of engines in use in Manchester, before the year 1800, was probably 32, and their power 430 horse; and at Leeds there were 20 engines, of 270 horse-power.

By some writers, who have not remarked the wonderful spring which had been given to the cotton manufacture before the steam-engine was applied to spinning machinery, too great stress has been laid upon this engine, as if it had almost created the manufacture. This was not the case. The *spinning machinery* created the cotton manufacture. But this branch of industry has unquestionably been extended by means of the steam-engine far beyond the limit which it could otherwise have reached; and now the steam-engine stands in the same relation to the spinning machines, as the heart does to the arms, hands, and fingers, in the human frame; the latter perform every task of dexterity and labour, the former supplies them with all their vital energy. Without the steam-engine, Manchester and Glasgow would not have approached to their present greatness.

. . . . . . . . . . . . . . .

## c] Eli Whitney and the Cotton Gin

### [1] The Invention

. . . . . . . . . . . . . . .

The genius who unlocked the imprisoned resources of the South was Eli Whitney. The home of his early years was far from the scene of his great triumph. In the little town of Westborough, about thirty miles west of Boston, he was born, December 8, 1765. His father was a farmer, but combined with his knowledge of farming considerable mechanical skill. In a little workshop near his house he had collected a variety of tools for making chairs and wheels, and for such odd jobs of repairing as he and his neighbor

---

FROM Edward C. Bates, "The Story of the Cotton Gin," *New England Magazine*, New Series, vol. 2 (May, 1890), pp. 288–92.

farmers constantly desired. In the use of tools the son showed early aptitude. "He lost no time," says his sister, "but as soon as he could handle tools he was always making something in the shop, and seemed not to like working on the farm." At the age of twelve he made a fiddle that excited much admiration, and the ingenuity which he thus showed brought him many delicate jobs of repairing. To the boy's inquiring mind, his father's watch, as the most delicate mechanism within his reach, was of fascinating interest. During the family's absence at church, it is related, having feigned illness as an excuse for remaining at home, he took the watch to pieces, but, unlike other boys who have attempted the same feat, he put the parts together again so nicely that the deed was undiscovered. When his step-mother lamented the breaking of a table-knife belonging to a valuable set, the ingenious boy made one exactly like it excepting the stamp on the blade; "and this he would likewise have executed," says Professor Olmstead in his memoir, "had not the tools required been too expensive for his slender means."

Not only did Whitney manifest inventive and mechanical skill at an early age, but his energy and perseverance became likewise apparent. During the Revolutionary War, when the price of nails was high, he engaged in their manufacture. Needing an assistant in his work, he obtained permission from his father to go to the neighboring village. Not finding a man to suit him, he mounted his horse and traveled forty miles before he was successful. When, with the close of war, the nail business was no longer profitable, Whitney turned his hand to a new industry—making hat-pins for women and walking-sticks for men. In these anecdotes of his youth appears the germ of the inventive faculty which afterwards, in a wider field, attained such grand development; and not less clearly appear the industry, energy, and perseverance which afterwards enabled him both to fight for his rights against overwhelming odds and, after the failure of his first great enterprise, to amass a fortune in new pursuits.

It was natural that a young man of Whitney's active mind and ambition should be dissatisfied with the limited education which his native village afforded. At the age of nineteen he decided to prepare for college. In May, 1789, after five years of hard work in earning his living and carrying on his studies, notwithstanding his step-mother's opposition and the protest of an "intelligent friend" that "it was a pity such a fine mechanical genius as his should be wasted," he succeeded in entering the freshman class at Yale. There he showed great proficiency in mathematics, and his written exercises which have been preserved are evidence of a clear, logical, and vigorous mind. In the repairing of apparatus, and other ways, he had several opportunities for astonishing his instructors and friends with his skill in using tools.

A few months after his graduation, in the autumn of 1792, Whitney was engaged as tutor by a gentleman in Georgia. During the journey from New York to Savannah, he enjoyed the company of Mrs. Greene, the widow of the famous Revolutionary general, and her family. Their friendship proved to be of inestimable value. On arriving in Georgia, he found the position for which he had been engaged already filled.[1] Without resources or employ-

[1] But compare Whitney's own account, page 60.—S.B.

ment, he gladly accepted the invitation of Mrs. Greene to remain at her house while he was carrying out his project of studying law. Under her hospitable roof he remained for several months.

The first opportunity for employing his peculiar skill was in making a tambour frame. Mrs. Greene complained that the one she was using was imperfect, and tore the thread of her embroidery. Anxious to please his kind benefactor, Whitney quickly constructed a frame so superior to the one in use as to excite the wonder and delight of the whole family.

This exhibition of skill was still in the mind of Mrs. Greene, when a party of Revolutionary officers who had served under her husband came to pay their respects. Many of them, if not all, were planters. In discussing the state of agriculture and their needs, they lamented the lack of a machine for separating cotton-fibre from the seeds. With the pressing demand in England for raw cotton, this was the only obstacle to their prosperity. By a happy inspiration, Mrs. Greene remarked, "Gentlemen, apply to my young friend, Mr. Whitney,—he can make anything." Whitney, protesting against the praises of his friend, removed what hopeful expectations the most ardent may have had, by calmly replying that he had never seen either cotton or cotton-seed.

Mrs. Greene's object in her friendly introduction was to attract the attention of her influential visitors to the promising young man whom she was befriending. The conversation, however, had an unexpected result. The young law student threw aside his books, and soon set off for Savannah. There he wandered about the wharves, in and around the storehouses, seeking a sample of cotton. After a long search he returned with a small parcel. A workroom in the basement of the house was set apart for his use. He made the tools necessary for his task, drew his own wire, and proceeded to construct a gin ("engine" is the full form) for separating cotton-fibre from the seeds. His purpose was divulged to no one save Mrs. Greene. The winter of 1792–93 was nearly over when his mysterious task was fully and satisfactorily completed. Early in the spring the cotton-gin was set up in a shed, and prominent planters from all over the state were invited to see it work. It was successful from the start. The machine for which there had been such clamoring for many years was at last provided by the ingenuity of a Yankee student.

I have referred to the cotton-gin as "a machine for separating the cotton-fibres from the seeds." A more definite understanding of the operation demands a few words on the nature of cotton and the mechanism of the gin.

The cotton which is used for spinning cloth is "the down, or fine cellular hair, attached to the seeds of the plants belonging to the genus *Gossypium*, natural order *Malvaceæ*." This genus has many species, some botanists giving as many as twenty; but the two important species known to commerce are the Indian and the American cottons. The American cottons are of two varieties: "the *Barbadensian*, or black-seeded cottons, bearing pure yellow blossoms, with a reddish purple spot at the base of the petals; and the *Hirsute*, or hairy cotton, more or less covered with a distinct coating of hairs, bearing white or faintly primrose-colored blossoms." The *Barbadensian*, known as "Sea Island cotton," grows on the islands off the coast of the

Carolinas, and surpasses all other varieties in the length, strength, and beauty of its staples. The great bulk of American cotton known as "upland" cotton, is of the other variety. Its fibres are shorter than in the Sea Island cotton, and cling most persistently to the green seeds in every lobe.

The low shrub on which the balls of cotton grow is planted in this country during April or May, and matures in August and September. Visitors to Southern states extol the beauty of the long rows of shrubs, with their glossy, dark green leaves, and balls of snowy whiteness.

As soon as the cotton is gathered, the process of ginning begins. The most primitive method was by the *churka,* used by the Chinese and Hindoos. It is a rude machine, consisting chiefly of two wooden rollers fixed in a frame. The rollers revolve in contact, drawing the cotton between them and excluding the seeds. Although the machine has undergone only slight improvement in the course of centuries, it is still used to some extent in India. This method, at best, is slow, clumsy, and imperfect.

In America, the little cotton that was raised before Whitney's gin made extensive production possible was ginned by hand. When the day's work in the fields was over, the slaves were set to work picking out the seeds. An overseer stood by to urge on the indolent and rouse the sleepy. It was a day's work for a man to cleanse a pound of cotton by hand.

The gin invented by Whitney is simple in its construction, and rapid and thorough in its work. The cotton is placed in a large hopper on an iron bed with many interstices. Through these project the teeth of a series of circular "saws." As the saws revolve, their sharp points catch the fibers of cotton and draw them through. The seeds are excluded by their size. The cotton is detached from the saws, and carried from the machine, by an arrangement of brushes. By the use of the gin, a thousand pounds of clean cotton, instead of one pound, are the result of a man's daily work. Another gin, known as Macarthy's roller gin, is used to some extent, especially for Sea Island cotton, but Whitney's is still in most general use. Many slight changes have been made in its construction, but so thoroughly did the young inventor do his work, that no better principle for making gins has yet been discovered.

No sooner had the fact of Eli Whitney's wonderful discovery become known, than planters from all parts of the state came to see the machine upon which their fortunes depended. Their impatience could not be restrained. The shed which contained the cotton-gin was forcibly entered, and in the morning the machine was gone. The principle of its construction—as yet unpatented—was discovered. New machines, with slight and unimportant variations, were manufactured and set up in various parts of the state. The owners of the original gin (Mr. Whitney had taken as a partner Mr. Phineas Miller, who had married his friend, Mrs. Greene) were involved, after the issue of their patent in the fall of 1793, in almost endless litigation. Their rights, moral and legal, were shamefully disregarded.

In spite of the loss of their only model, and the infringement of their patent, Whitney and Miller still had hopes of securing a share of the wealth which their machine was sure to create. Their plan was to sell no machines, but to gin cotton for the planters on shares, the owners of the gin retaining one pound in every three. This turned out to be an unfortunate plan.

Whitney, who went North for the purpose, was unable to supply the needed machines. The scarcity of money, due to the wild speculations in land, crippled his operations. Scarlet fever broke out among his workmen; and, to cap a long series of misfortunes, just as Whitney was recovering from a serious illness, he arrived at New Haven to find his factory and half-finished machines in ashes. This was a serious blow. Not only was the financial loss large, but the impatient planters, who had raised an immense quantity of cotton, the value of which depended on its being ginned, were given extra inducements to make machines for themselves in spite of the patent.

The owners of the cotton-gin were not disheartened by their misfortunes. They raised money at ruinous rates of interest, and proceeded with their enterprise. But no sooner had their prospects brightened a little than a new calamity came upon them. The report became current that their gin injured the fibre of the cotton, and decreased its value. The rumor, which seems to have been founded solely on prejudice, came at a critical period in the affairs of the struggling concern, and for a time—until it was shown to be without adequate foundation—completely crippled their business. Their gins stood still, in the midst of a cotton-growing country, for lack of cotton to keep them busy.

It is apparent, I think, that the misfortunes of Whitney and Miller would have been only temporary, had it not been for the general infringement of their patent. Their rights were entirely disregarded throughout the cotton-growing district. The first case which they could bring to trial, in 1797, was decided against them. Such was the importance of the machine, the extent of the infringement, and the wealth and influence of the guilty parties, that no jury could be found to return a verdict on the merits of the case. No one now denies that justice was on the side of the patentees; but, nevertheless, sixty cases were tried before a verdict was secured against those who had infringed the patent. This decision was in 1808. The patent had only one year more to run; and justice, coming at so late a date, brought little recompense to the inventor. "The want of a disposition in mankind to do justice," was the philosophic reason for all his trouble, given by Whitney in a letter to Robert Fulton; "and I have always believed," he adds, "that I should have had no difficulty in causing my right to be respected, if it had been less valuable, and been used only by a small portion of the community." Whitney was, with good reason, disgusted at his treatment, and never afterwards, though he made several ingenious and valuable inventions, did he apply for a patent. The rewards which he received for his invention of the cotton-gin were disheartening misfortunes, the loss of a lucrative and honorable profession, costly and troublesome law-suits, health shattered by worry and travel, a paltry grant from South Carolina,—and imperishable fame as one of the foremost figures in the history of industrial development.

It would be impossible to enumerate the results of a great mechanical invention. Its influence extends to all ranks of society and to every region of the world. Like the telegraph, the steamboat, and other great inventions, the cotton-gin has had a striking influence upon modern civilization. It changed the occupations and modes of life of great multitudes in both America and England; it demanded, and brought about, new inventions to

The first cotton gin. After *Harper's Weekly,* December 18, 1869.

supplement its work; it transformed the sluggish life of the South into a life of activity, power, and wealth; and, perhaps more important than all, it caused a change in the political development of the United States, which reached its climax in a great civil war.

. . . . . . . . . . . . . . . . . . . .

## [2] Whitney's Short Description of the Gin

. . . . . . . . . . . . . . . . . . . .

THE PRINCIPAL parts of this machine are 1. The Frame. 2. the Cylinder. 3. the Breastwork. 4. the Clearer and 5. the Hopper.

I. The frame, by which the whole work is supported and kept together, is of a square or parallelogramic form, and proportioned to the other parts as may be most convenient.

II. The Cylinder is of wood: Its form is perfectly described by its name, and its dimention may be from six to nine inches in Diameter and from two to five feet in length. This Cylinder is placed horizontally across the

---

FROM Jeanette Mirsky and Allan Nevins, *The World of Eli Whitney* (New York: Macmillan, 1952), pp. 303–04. Reprinted by permission of the publisher.

frame, leaving room for the clearer on one side and the hopper on the other. In the Cylinder is fixed an iron axis which may pass quite thro', or consist only of gudgeons driven into each end. There are shoulders on this axis to prevent any horizontal variation and it extends so far without the form as to admit a winch at one end, by which it is put in motion and so far at the other end as to receive the whirl by which the clearer is turned. The surface of the Cylinder is filled with teeth set in annular rows which are at such a distance from each other as to admit a cotton seed to play freely in the space between them. The space between each tooth in the same row is so small as not to admit a seed nor half a seed to enter it. These teeth are made of stiff Iron wire, driven into the wood of the Cylinder. ["Steel wire would perhaps be best if it were not too expensive," say the specifications in the Long Description.] The teeth are all inclined the same way and in such a manner that the angle included between the tooth and a tangent drawn from the point into which the tooth is driven, will be about 55° or 60° Degrees. The gudgeons of the Cylinder run in brass boxes which are in two parts one of which is fixed in the wood of the frame and the other is confined down upon the axis with screws.

III. The Breastwork is fixed above the cylinder parallel and contiguant to the same. It has transverse grooves or openings thro' which the rows of teeth pass as the cylinder revolves, and its use is to obstruct the seeds while the Cotton is carried forward thro' the grooves by the teeth. The thickness of the breastwork is two and half or three inches and the under side of it is made of iron or brass.

IV. The Clearer is placed horizontal with and parallel to the Cylinder. Its length is the same as that of the Cylinder, and its diameter is proportioned by convenience. There are two four or more Brushes or rows of Bristles fixed in the surface of the clearer in such a manner that the ends of the bristles will sweep the surface of the Cylinder. Its axis and boxes are similar to those of the Cylinder. It is turned by means of a band and whirls; moves in a contrary direction from the Cylinder by which it is put in motion and so far outruns it as to sweep the cotton from the teeth as fast as it is carried thro' the Breastwork. The periphery of the whirls is spiral and the band a broad strap of Leather.

V. One side of the Hopper is formed by the Breastwork, the two ends by the frame and the other side is movable from and towards the Breastwork so as to make the hopper more or less capacious.

The cotton is put into the Hopper, carried thro' the Breastwork by the teeth, brushed off from the teeth by the Clearer and flies off from the Clearer with the assistance of the air, by its own centrifugal force. The machine is turned by water, horses, or in any other way as is most convenient.

There are several modes of making the various parts of this machine, which together with their particular shape and formation, are pointed out and explained in a description with Drawings.

## [3] Whitney Tells his Father About the Invention

ELI WHITNEY TO ELI WHITNEY, SEN'R.

NEW HAVEN, Sept. 11th, 1793

DEAR PARENT,

I received your letter of the 16th of August with peculiar satisfaction and delight. It gave me no small pleasure to hear of your health and was very happy to be informed that your health and that of the family has been so good since I saw you. I have fortunately just heard from you by Mr. Robbinson who says you were well when he left Westboro'. When I wrote you last I expected to have been able to come to Westboro' sooner than I now fear will be in my power. I presume, sir, you are desirous to hear how I have spent my time since I left College. This I conceive you have a right to know and that it is my duty to inform you and should have done it before this time; but I thought I could do it better by verbal communication than by writing, and expecting to see you soon, I omitted it. As I now have a safe and direct opportunity to send by Mr. Robbinson, I will give you a summary account of my southern expedition.

I went from N. York with the family of the late Major General Greene to Georgia. I went immediately with the family to their Plantation about twelve miles from Savannah with an expectation of spending four or five days and then proceed into Carolina to take the school as I have mentioned in former letters. During this time I heard much said of the extreme difficulty of ginning Cotton, that is, seperating it from its seeds. There were a number of very respectable Gentlemen at Mrs. Greene's who all agreed that if a machine could be invented which would clean the cotton with expedition, it would be a great thing both to the Country and to the inventor. I involuntarily happened to be thinking on the subject and struck out a plan of a Machine in my mind, which I communicated to Miller, (who is agent to the Executors of Genl. Greene and resides in the family, a man of respectibility and property) he was pleased with the Plan and said if I would pursue it and try an experiment to see if it would answer, he would be at the whole expense, I should loose nothing but my time, and if I succeeded we would share the profits. Previous to this I found I was like to be disappointed in my school, that is, instead of a hundred, I found I could get only fifty Guineas a year. I however held the refusal of the school untill I tried some experiments. In about ten Days I made a little model, for which I was offered, if I would give up all right and title to it, a Hundred Guineas. I concluded to relinquish my school and turn my attention to perfecting the Machine. I made one before I came away which required the labor of one man to turn it and with which one man will clean ten times as much cotton as he can in any other way before known and also cleanse it much

FROM Matthew B. Hammond, "Correspondence of Eli Whitney relative to the Invention of the Cotton Gin," *American Historical Review*, vol. III, no. 1 (October, 1897), pp. 99–101.

better than in the usual mode.[1] This machine may be turned by water or with a horse, with the greatest ease, and one man and a horse will do more than fifty men with the old machines. It makes the labor fifty times less, without throwing any class of People out of business.

I returned to the Northward for the purpose of having a machine made on a large scale and obtaining a Patent for the invintion. I went to Philadelphia soon after I arrived, made myself acquainted with the steps necessary to obtain a Patent, took several of the steps and the Secretary of State Mr. Jefferson agreed to send the Pattent to me as soon it could be made out—so that I apprehended no difficulty in obtaining the Patent—Since I have been here I have employed several workmen in making machines and as soon as my business is such that I can leave it a few days, I shall come to Westboro'. I think it is probable I shall go to Philadelphia again before I come to Westboro', and when I do come I shall be able to stay but few days. I am certain I can obtain a patent in England. As soon as I have got a Patent in America I shall go with the machine which I am now making, to Georgia, where I shall stay a few weeks to see it at work. From thence I expect to go to England, where I shall probably continue two or three years. How advantageous this business will eventually prove to me, I cannot say. It is generally said by those who know anything about it, that I shall make a Fortune by it. I have no expectation that I shall make an independent fortune by it, but think I had better pursue it than any other business into which I can enter. Something which cannot be foreseen may frustrate my expectations and defeat my Plan; but I am now so sure of success that ten thousand dollars, if I saw the money counted out to me, would not tempt me to give up my right and relinquish the object. I wish you, sir, not to show this letter nor communicate anything of its contents to any body except My Brothers and Sister, *enjoining* it on them to keep the whole a *profound secret*.

Mr. Robbinson came into town yesterday and goes out tomorrow, this has been such a bustling time that I have not had oportunity to say six words to him. I have told him nothing of my business—perhaps he will hear something about it from some body else in town. But only two or three of my friends know what I am about tho' there are many surmises in town—if Mr. Robbinson says anything about it, you can tell him I wrote you concerning it, but wished not to have it mentioned. I have been considerably out of health since I wrote you last; but now feel tollerably well. I should write to my Brothers and Sister but fear I shall not have time—hope they will accept my good wishes for their happiness and excuse me.

With respects to Mama I am,

kind Parent, your most obt. Son

ELI WHITNEY, Junr.

Mr. Eli Whitney.

[1] In a letter to Jefferson, dated Nov. 24, 1793, Whitney stated that with this machine "it is the stated task of one negro to clean fifty weight (I mean fifty pounds after it is separated from the seed), of the green seed cotton per day." Olmsted, *Memoir of Eli Whitney, Esq.*, p. 17.

ELI WHITNEY TO ELI WHITNEY, SEN'R.

NEW HAVEN, August 17th 1794.

HON'D SIR,—

It gives me pleasure that I have it in my power to inform you that I am in perfect health. I left Savannah just three weeks ago. We had a passage of Eight Days to New York, where I spent several days and have been here about a week. I was taken sick with the Georgia fever about the middle of June and confined to my bed ten or twelve days, but had got quite well before I left the Country. There were several very hot Days preceeding my sickness during which I fatigued myself considerable and which was probaply [sic] the cause of my illness.

My Machinery was in opperation before I came from Georgia. It answers the purpose well, and is likely to succeed beyond our expectations. My greatest apprehensions at present are, that we shall not be able to get machines made as fast as we shall want them. We have now Eight Hundred Thousand weight of Cotton on hand and the next crop will begin to come in very soon. It will require Machines enough to clean 5 or 6 thousand wt. of clean cotton pr Day to satisfy the demand for next Year. I mean for the crop which comes in this fall. And I expect the crop will be double another year.

. . . . . . . . . . . . . . . . . . .

## 2] The Impact of Cotton upon the Older Staples of South Carolina

. . . . . . . . . . . . . . . . . . .

SUCH IS the grain [rice] which was introduced into Carolina about 115 years ago, and has ever since been in high demand. With several in Charlestown and the adjacent country, it is the principal vegetable aliment they use for the greatest part of their lives. They experience nothing of that blindness which ignorance attributes to its constant use. The variation in the amount of the crops of this useful commodity is an important document in the history of Carolina; for it has been materially affected not only by the introduction of other staples, but by the political revolutions of the country. When it was introduced there were few negros in the province, the government was unsettled, and the soil and other circumstances most favorable to its growth were unknown. For the first twenty years after it began to be planted, the ravages of pirates on the coast made its exportation so hazardous as to discourage the cultivation of it. In the year 1724,

FROM David Ramsay, *Ramsay's History of South Carolina, from its First Settlement in 1670 to the Year 1809* (Newberry, S.C.: W. J. Duffie, 1858; first published Charleston, 1809), pp. 115–16, 119–23, and 125.

about six years after the pirates were entirely suppressed, 18,000 barrels of rice were exported. Our knowledge of what was previously made or exported is conjectural; but each succeeding crop brought an additional quantity to market. In the year 1740, the amount exported was 91,110 barrels; in 1754 it had reached to 104,682 barrels. Till the middle of the eighteenth century the chief article of export was rice; but about that time much of the attention and force of the planters was transferred from it to indigo. Nevertheless the culture of this grain continued to advance, though slowly, till the commencement of the American revolution; when the average quantity annually exported was about 142,000 barrels. In the course of the revolutionary war, the small crops of rice were consumed in the country; and so many of the negroes were either destroyed or carried off that the crop of 1783, the first after the evacuation of Charlestown, amounted only to 61,974 barrels. With the return of peace the cultivation of rice was resumed, and continued to increase till the year 1792; when the crop exported amounted to 106,419 barrels. About this time cotton began to employ so much of the agricultural force of the State, that the crops of rice since that period have rarely exceeded what they were about the middle of the eighteenth century.

. . . . . . . . . . . . . . .

. . . It proved more really beneficial to Carolina than the mines of Mexico or Peru are or ever have been either to old or new Spain. In the year 1754, the export of indigo from the province amounted to 216,924 lbs. And shortly before the American Revolution, it had arisen to 1,107,660 lbs. In the Revolutionary war it was less attended to than rice. In the year 1783, it again began to be more cultivated: 2,051 casks of indigo was exported, and it continued to form a valuable export for some years, but large importations of it from the East Indies into England so lowered the price as to make it less profitable. Near the close of the eighteenth century, it gave place to the cultivation of cotton. The same grounds being generally suitable for both, were for the most part planted with the new staple; and indigo has been ever since comparatively neglected. Its culture was at all times in a great measure confined to the low and middle country.

Cotton has been known to the world as an useful commodity ever since the days of Herodotus, who upwards of two thousand years ago wrote that "Gossypium grew in India which instead of seed produced wool." As rice feeds more of the human race than any other grain, so cotton clothes more of mankind than either wool, flax, hemp, or silk. Both of these articles have grown for many centuries in the East Indies in a country similar to Carolina. Though the same reasoning and analogy, and the same information that led to the introduction of rice might have pointed out the propriety of attempting the culture of cotton in Carolina, yet the latter was not planted to any considerable extent for one hundred years after the introduction of the former. It had been declared by Dr. Hewat in his valuable historical account of South Carolina, printed in 1719, "that the climate and soil of the province were favorable to the culture of cotton." The first Provincial Congress in South Carolina, held in January, 1775, recommended to the inhabitants "to raise cotton," yet very little practical attention was paid to their recommendation. A small quantity only was raised for domestic manufactures. This neglect cannot solely be referred to the confusion of the times, for agriculture had been successfully prosecuted for ten years after the termination of the Revolutionary war before the Carolinians began to cultivate it to any considerable extent. In this culture the Georgians took the lead. They began to raise it as an article of export soon after the peace of 1783. Their success recommended it to their neighbors. The whole quantity exported from Carolina in any one year prior to 1795 was inconsiderable, but in that year it amounted to £1,109,653. The cultivation of it has been ever since increasing, and on the first year of the present century eight million of pounds were exported from South Carolina. The uncertainty of this crop has disgusted a few planters, and brought them back to the less hazardous culture of rice. These two staples have so monopolized the agricultural force of the State, that for several years past other articles of export and even provisions have been greatly neglected. In the great eagerness to get money, the planters have brought themselves into a state of dependence on their neighbors for many of the necessaries of life which formerly were raised at home. So much cotton is now made in Carolina and Georgia, that if the whole was manufactured in the United States, it would go far in clothing a great proportion of the inhabitants of the Union; for one laborer can raise as much of this commodity in one season as will afford the raw material for fifteen hundred yards of common cloth, or a sufficiency for covering one hundred and fifty persons. That part of it which is now manufactured in Europe, and brought back in an improved state, sometimes pays more, and on a general average nearly as much in duties to the United States, as the planter gets for the raw material. The duty, being in proportion to the value, on a pound weight of fine cotton goods is much more than the cultivator of the commodity gets for the same weight of cotton in its merchantable state. This staple is of immense value to the public, and still more so to individuals. It has trebled the price of land suitable to its growth, and when the crop succeeds and the market is favorable, the annual income of those who plant it is double to what it was before the introduction of cotton.

The cotton chiefly cultivated on the sea-coast is denominated the black seed or long staple cotton, which is of the best quality and admirably adapted to the finest manufactures. The wool is easily separated from the seed by roller-gins which do not injure the staple. A pair of rollers worked by one laborer give about twenty-five pounds of clean cotton daily. The cotton universally cultivated in the middle and upper country is called the green seed kind. It is less silky and more wooly, and adheres so tenaciously to the seed that it requires the action of a saw-gin to separate the wool from the seed. This cuts the staple exceedingly; but as the staple of this kind of cotton is not fit for the finer fabrics it is not considered injurious. The quality of these two kinds is very different. The wool of the green seed is considerably the cheapest; but that species is much more productive than the other. An acre of good cotton land will usually produce one hundred and fifty pounds of clean wool of the long staple kind. An acre of land of equal quality will usually produce two hundred pounds of the green seed or short staple kind. Besides these, yellow or nankeen cotton is also cultivated in the upper country for domestic use. Two ingenius artists, Miller and Whiteney of Connecticut, invented a saw-gin for the separation of the wool from the seed which has facilitated that operation in the highest degree. The Legislature of South Carolina purchased their patent-right for 50,000 dollars, and then munificently threw open its use and benefits to all its citizens.

Such have been the profits of the planters of cotton, and so great has been their partiality for raising it, to the exclusion of other valuable commodities, that the history of the agriculture of Carolina, in its present state, comprehends little more than has been already given: but it is proper to bring into view what this has been and what it might and would be now if rice and cotton, especially the latter, did not absorb almost the whole energies of the planting interest.

Wheat, next to rice, is of most extensive use as an aliment. The culture of it was introduced and encouraged by Joseph Kershaw, who, more than forty years ago, erected mills at Pinetree, now Camden, for manufacturing it into flour. . . .

. . . There was every prospect that flour would soon make an important addition to the exports of Carolina. These prospects have been, for some years, obscured; for, by nice calculations, the planters found that they could make more money by cotton than wheat. Considerable quantities of flour are now imported, and though much is made in the interior country, very little, or none, is exported.

The next great article derived from the cultivation of the earth is maize, or Indian corn; for its production the swamps, when perfectly drained, and the highlands are both well adapted. The crop varies with the soil and seasons on highland from ten to twenty-five bushels, and in the swamps from twenty-five to seventy-five bushels. The aliment derived from this grain is considered as more strengthening and better adapted to laborers than either rice or wheat. The negroes of Carolina give it a decided preference, and are said to be better able to perform their labor when fed on corn than on any other grain. From the year 1739 nearly to the end of the eighteenth century it has been an article of export, but on a moderate scale; for rice and indigo were always deemed more profitable. With the new staple, cotton, it cannot bear any competition. In the year 1792, when cotton was beginning to be extensively cultivated, 99,985 bushels of corn were exported; which exceeded any amount that can be recollected, either before or since. As the former advanced the latter declined. Corn, no longer an article of export, is now largely imported for domestic use on the sea-coast.

Though Carolina, by her rice, cotton and lumber, contributed largely to the food, clothing and shelter of man, yet these were not the only rewards conferred on the cultivators of its soil. It produced another commodity which, though not to be numbered among the necessaries, is by its votaries placed high in the list of the comforts of life. Tobacco is an indigenous plant of America. It had been successfully cultivated in Virginia before Carolina was settled. Little doubt could have existed that it might be made to grow in a more southern latitude; but it does not appear among the articles of export from Carolina till 1783, and then only six hundred and forty-three hogsheads are stated as the amount. In the following it had reached to 2,680, and in the year 1799 to 9,646 hogsheads. In the rich lands of the back country it was found to answer well; but the expense of bringing so bulky an article so great a distance to market, left little clear profits. It could not stand in competition with cotton.

. . . . . . . . . . . . . . . .

Though the demand for cotton should cease, or the price fall, there would be no ground for serious regret. Many other profitable objects of culture are within the grasp of the planters. When their industry and ingenuity is turned to these and other projects which might be mentioned, there is good reason to believe that the result will console them for their loss of a valuable staple by finding others which will add more to their comforts and real enjoyments than they ever have derived from the proceeds of their cotton crops.

Planters are the most independent and influential men in Carolina, especially when they are out of debt and have money remaining from their last crop to meet with cash in hand the expenses of the current year. Such of them as commence planting with both land and slaves bought on credit, often fail. Where either is inherited or acquired without debt, the other may be purchased by an industrious prudent man with a fair prospect of advantage. When crops are anticipated by engagements founded on them before they are made, ruin is often the consequence, and much oftener since the revolution than before; for the indulgence formerly granted to subjects in Carolina has seldom been extended to citizen planters. The failure of a single pre-engaged crop may break up a promising agriculturist driven to extremities by a pressing creditor.

Merchants and military men, when they have devoted themselves to agriculture in Carolina, have generally made good planters. Their former habits have a tendency to make them regular and methodical in business—to keep up strict discipline—and to count the cost of every undertaking. Professional men who attempt agriculture, seldom succeed in both as well as when they devote themselves diligently and exclusively to one pursuit. In no business do the random habits of desultory men more certainly lead to ruin than in planting.

The education of the sons of planters in distant countries is often injurious to such of them as are destined to follow the same line of business as their fathers. They frequently return with sentiments and habits very unsuitable to their future prospects. In consequence of their foreign education they may be better scholars but they are generally worse planters.

. . . . . . . . . . . . . . . .

# 3] The Contribution of the United States to the World Supply of Cotton

## a] Secretary of the Treasury Levi Woodbury Explains Some Difficulties in Estimating World Supply

[SEE TABLE 1C IN STATISTICAL SECTION]

. . . . . . . . . . . . . . .

IN FORMING an estimate of the whole crop of cotton grown in the world in any particular year, I have found no precedent to aid me except for the single year of 1834, when evidence was given before the Chamber of Peers, in France, that it probably amounted to about 460 millions of pounds. But this computation was so deficient, assigning none to Mexico, and none to S. America, or Africa, except to Brazil 24 millions of pounds, and to Egypt 20 millions of pounds, and only 60 millions of pounds to India, and 350 millions of pounds to the United States, and the balance of 6 millions of pounds to the West Indies, that no safe reliance could be placed on it as correct for the whole known world. My own course has been to ascertain from all attainable sources the exports in raw cotton of each country; to add to those the probable amount consumed at home and not exported, looking to the climate of the place, the habits of its population, and the scattered facts on this point found in respectable authors, and then to compute therefrom the whole quantity grown. Another general test of the correctness of one of my conclusions, viz: that the whole crop in the world has quite doubled in the last half century, and now equals quite 900 millions of pounds, though the estimate before named is only 460 millions of pounds, exists in the fact that a greater increase than this has happened in the crop of the United States alone; and though, in some other countries, a diminution has occurred in the exports of cotton from various causes, which need not here be detailed, yet the use of it has probably been reduced in no country, and in many, within that period, it has, from greater cheapness, by improvements in machinery and steam, with its healthfulness, compared with other clothing, largely increased, and in some been for the first time introduced. Supposing that in warm climates, and in a population not highly civilized as in Turkey, two pounds of cotton per head for each person are yearly consumed, and in the south of China and India,

---

FROM U.S. Congress, House, Treasury Department Report [by Levi Woodbury] *Cotton, Cultivation, Manufacture and Foreign Trade of,* House Document No. 146. 24th Congress, 1st Session, pp. 8–12. [Authorities cited in the text have been deleted.]

not over one and a half pounds to each person, and in the places near or under the equator still less; and that in more civilized countries where cotton is used, as in England, France, and the United States, from eight to twelve pounds per head are consumed; and supposing that only a little more than half the population of the globe, estimated at four hundred and fifty millions, use cotton, the consumption would, on an average, at only two pounds per head, be quite equal to the estimated crop for the whole world. For some years past it is supposed that the consumption of cotton has been greater than the crop, and hence, that the old stocks on hands have been more exhausted, and a larger portion of the new crop called for early. This has sustained the price and required an augmented crop of at least 20 millions of pounds per annum.

. . . . . . . . . . . . . . . . . . . .

The crop of Brazil is computed on its ascertained exports at different periods to England and elsewhere, and a home consumption in a small ratio to its population. It has been diminished of late years by importing cotton manufactures for home consumption, as in 1833 and '4, from England largely. Cotton was first planted or cultivated in Brazil in 1781, for exportation.

The crop of the West Indies is estimated in a similar manner; after deducting from their exports the probable portion of cotton brought there from the Spanish Main, and thence re-exported. In 1812, it is said, that the crop of all the West Indies did not exceed 5½ millions, and chiefly in Barbadoes, Bahama islands, Dominico, and Granada. But this is believed to have been underrated. England now exports there largely of cotton manufactures, and the United States export there some of them yearly, as well as France. All this tends to diminish the crop raised for home consumption, and probably that for export. Cotton was grown first in 1776, at St. Domingo, for export. But earlier in other islands, and they furnished a large part of English wants before 1785. In 1789, Hayti, alone, exported over 7 millions of pounds; about 2½ millions of pounds in 1801, and since that, less than 1 million of pounds yearly. In 1824, a little over 1 million of pounds, and in 1832 about 1½ million.

The supposed crop of Egypt, in former years, is predicated on the authority of the Dictionary of Spanish Commerce and Finance, vol. 3, page 29. On her exports, and for 1834, the New Monthly Magazine for September, 1835. She imported cotton from Smyrna and Greece till within twenty years. By the last advices her crop grown, in 1835, is said to be short, not exceeding 18 or 20 millions of pounds.

The crop of the rest of Africa is computed from her exports from Morocco, Gambia, &c. and the habits and number of her population, and her soil and climate, where cotton is indigenous, and has always been grown in many sections since first discovered. Of late she imports on the eastern side fewer cotton goods from India, and more there and on the western side from England and the United States. In the island of Mauritius, in 1806, nearly two millions of pounds of cotton were raised, but it fell off gradually till in 1831, little or none was produced.

In India, the estimate rests on her exports and vast population, long clothed chiefly in cotton of her own growth. The Isle of Bourbon produced it of a quality almost equal to the Sea Island. But of late years her exports of manufactured goods have declined, and her importations of them from England alone, exceed $10,000,000 yearly. . . . It is believed, that the cultivation of cotton for export is on the increase; labor is so low, and the trade of India having become more free. The estimates for the crop in India are probably not high enough, rather than being too large.

The rest of Asia, including China, Japan, Persia, Arabia and Turkey, from the mildness of its climate, great population, and customary clothing, is supposed not to be computed too high. In 1766, it was grown much about Smyrna. Only about 6 millions of pounds in 1834, near Smyrna, and most of that was shipped to Marseilles and Trieste.

The cultivation of cotton, in China, began about the 13th century, for purposes of manufacture, though before raised in gardens for ornament. The crop increased rapidly, and was very large, probably much beyond the amount assigned in [Table 1C], till 1785 to 1790, when it began to be considerably discontinued for the purpose of raising grain, during and in consequence of famine. Much has since been imported from India, though now in the small statistical knowledge attainable on this point as to China, she may raise more cotton than the large amount computed for her, in connection with Japan, Cochin-China, &c. Travellers and merchants see but little of China usually, except the south parts and the sea board; and if in the great use of silk, furs, &c. in the colder portions, it is considered that 100 millions of her population use cotton, and from their poverty only 1½ pounds each, the whole amount would be 150 millions of pounds yearly in China alone.

This crop in South America and Mexico rests on similar principles, as the chief clothing was cotton when the country was first discovered by the Spaniards. It is now often of superior quality. The exports since have been considerable. But of late years the crop must be less, as Mexico, as well as Peru and Chili imports now from England yearly many cottons, besides what they get from the United States and elsewhere. Cotton began to be cultivated for export in Caraccas in 1782. The saw gin is not yet used, but wooden rollers. The plant is found indigenous. In Hall's Columbia, page 27, it is said only about 4 millions of pounds are grown in that Government yearly. This is too small an amount. Cultivated in Surinam since 1735.

[The column for "Elsewhere" in Table 1C in the statistical section] includes some remote islands, and the south of Spain, Italy and Greece, and their islands, with the Canaries, where cotton was formerly more raised, and still is considerably. From Italy and Egypt, in 1825, when cotton was very high, over 23¾ millions of pounds were exported. Some has been raised in New South Wales, and the cultivation is said to be resumed in Italy. Though some exports were formerly described as from Portugal, little or no cotton grew there; and the exports of it thence came chiefly from Brazil.

Some confusion has arisen from the different use or application of the word "cotton." It is said to be a word of Arabic origin; but the application sometimes of the word "linen," and at others of the word "woollen," to the vegetable of three or four general varieties, and which produces the wool or down now called "cotton," has led to some mistakes about its growth and use formerly in certain countries, which it is now difficult to correct. But it was probably grown and used largely in ancient times in Arabia, as well as India, America, and Africa, except perhaps in Egypt, where linen, it is supposed, chiefly superseded it, and can now be detected, but no cotton, in the clothing of the mummies, by the joints in the fibres of the stalk of the flax, being visible with a microscope, whereas the fibres of cotton from the pod have no joints. The kind of cotton chiefly cultivated now, and especially in the United States, is not the tree or shrub, but the annual and herbaceous varieties.

. . . . . . . . . . . . . . . .

## b] SECRETARY WOODBURY'S EXPLANATION OF AMERICAN PREEMINENCE IN WORLD CHANNELS OF SUPPLY (1836)

. . . . . . . . . . . . . . . .

. . . It will be seen that, in producing the whole cotton crop of the United States, only about two millions of acres of land are cultivated. . . . it appears that all the foreign exports of cotton in the world do not probably exceed 535 millions of pounds, and of which the United States now [1836] export about 384 millions of pounds; a large portion of the residue is from the remotest parts of Asia, very little of it now coming to Europe. But if necessary or profitable, we could raise the whole of the other 150 millions, by putting into cultivation only about 500,000 acres more cotton land, and employing less than 100,000 more field hands in this branch of industry.

But supposing that Asia, from her distance and habits, continues to use chiefly her own raw cotton, that the increase of population in the United States should continue much as heretofore, and that the countries in Europe and elsewhere, now supplied with cotton manufactures made chiefly from our crops, should increase in population, or in the use of cotton, as fast as the United States does in population alone, and there would be required to supply the increased annual demand only about 21 millions of pounds more of raw cotton, or the product in the United States of less than 70,000 acres more each year. This has been clearly our average increase of crops in the last ten years. It has required about 11,000 more field laborers a year, or only 1/40 the annual increase of our whole population. But we probably have now, not in cultivation, more acres of land suitable for cotton, than would be sufficient to raise all the cotton now grown in the world; as that would require only three to five millions of acres. Hence it must be obvious, that there is good cotton land enough in the United States, and at low

FROM U.S. Congress, House, Treasury Department Report [by Levi Woodbury] *Cotton, Cultivation, Manufacture and Foreign Trade of,* House Document No. 146. 24th Congress, 1st Session, pp. 14–15.

prices, easily to grow, not only all the cotton wanted for foreign export in the world, but to supply the increased demand for it, probably, for ages. The only preventive, of which there is much likelihood, seems to be in the augmented price of such labor as is usually devoted to this culture; so that it may not be possible to raise the crop at so low a rate as to keep possession of the European market against all competition.

In getting possession of that market so fully and rapidly heretofore, (as shown in the extracts from the last annual report) the United States have been much aided by the good quality of their cotton, the low price of land, and the great improvements in cleaning cotton by Whitney's cotton gin since 1793. One person is able to perform with it in a day the work of 1,000 without it. Besides these advantages, the unusual industry and enterprise of our population, and its freedom from taxation compared with the people of most other countries, and the wide extent of our commerce, have promoted our unprecedented progress.

The old mode of cleaning it by wooden rollers, and with the bow by hand, is still used in India and Colombia, and it is there sown broad cast instead of in drills, and much neglected afterwards.

The great vibrations in the prices per pound of raw cotton grown in the United States, are very striking. . . . The influence of these on the sales of public land and our revenue, from both them and the imports of foreign merchandise, has been briefly examined in the last annual report, extracts from which are annexed. The further influence of these on the prosperity of the south, on the rise in the value of their slave property, and on the great profits yielded by all their capital invested in growing cotton, must be very apparent to every careful observer. The single fact, that in no year has the price been but a fraction below 10 cents per pound, or a rate sufficient to yield a fair profit, while it has, at times, been as high as 29, 34, and even 44, and been, on an average, over 16 cents per pound since 1802, and over 21 since 1790, is probably without a parallel, in showing a large and continued profit.

. . . . . . . . . . . . . . .

## c] Israel D. Andrews' Explanation of the Same Phenomenon (1853)

. . . . . . . . . . . . . . .

There is not now any serious cause for apprehension by the agricultural, commercial, or manufacturing interests of the United States, of successful competition with the southern States of this confederacy, by any other country, in the production of cotton.

FROM U.S. Congress, Senate, *Report of Israel D. Andrews . . . on the Trade and Commerce of the British North American Colonies . . .* , Senate Executive Document No. 112. 32nd Congress, 1st Session, 1853 (Washington: Robert Armstrong, Printer, 1853), pp. 818–21.

From the day our independence was recognised by Great Britain, till within a few years past, her leading statesmen, with but few exceptions, used every effort and devoted every faculty and power to diminish and prevent all necessity for dependence, in any degree, by her capitalists, (having large and increasing investments in manufactures and commerce) *upon any of the products of the United States. . . .* Until within a few years past, Great Britain has not relaxed her illiberal and selfish policy; and the cotton interests of the United States have seemed to be especial objects of her unceasing hostility.[1] She has used every exertion, and availed herself of every means she possessed, to create competition and rivals to the southern States of this confederacy in the cultivation of cotton, and to relieve herself from any dependence upon those States for the means of employment for her working classes, in the manufacture of cotton, and in auxiliary avocations. She experimented in its cultivation, at great cost in her West India colonies, with the advantage of slave labor, until she abolished the institution of "domestic servitude" in those colonies, as to those who had been held as "slaves." She then tried "apprentice" labor, with still more unfavorable success. She tried the cultivation of cotton in every one of her numerous possessions in the different quarters of the globe, where the climate and soil allowed any expectation of a favorable result. She encouraged its cultivation in different countries, not politically connected with her. Every kind of labor has been employed in these experiments: free labor; Irish, Scotch, Anglo-Saxon, and African; colonists, apprentices, coolies, Chinese, convicts, and slaves; Christians and Pagans, civilized and savage. Of her efforts to induce its cultivation elsewhere than in this country, we had no right to complain. But of her illiberal restrictions and wrongs done to us, we had; and they engendered no little ill feeling towards her in this country. . . . The futility of warring against the natural laws governing trade and commerce, and against advantages given by the superior adaptation of climate and soil, and experienced and effective (because united) labor for the production of an article like cotton, and the folly and presumption of any nation striving to establish for itself an exclusive and selfish monopoly or control of all things, is fully demonstrated in the former course of the British people towards us. It is, perhaps, best for her that her experiments in making cotton, to "root the Yankees out," have so signally failed; for the cotton crop of the United States is the main link connecting the two countries commercially; and if it is broken, the entire trade between them will soon become comparatively valueless to both.

And the efforts to induce to the production of cotton, to compete with the United States, have not been confined to Great Britain. France attempted it in Algeria, without favorable success. It has been tried by the Turkish Sultan, and a superintendent and intelligent and experienced slave laborers procured from the State of South Carolina, but the trial did

[1] A member of the English Parliament—ex-Lord-Chancellor Brougham, who was considered somewhat famous—in a speech respecting our cotton manufactories, soon after the war which ended in 1815, said: "It was well worth while to incur a loss upon the first exportation, in order, by the *glut,* to *stifle,* in the *cradle,* those rising manufactures in the United States which the war had *forced* into existence, contrary to the natural course of things."

not succeed profitably. It has been tried in different places, on the extensive shores of the Euxine, opened to the commerce of Christendom by the cannon of the allies at Navarino, in 1827; it has been tried in Mexico, in Central America, in the different republics of South America, and in the empire of Brazil; it has been tried in different parts of the East Indies, and in Africa; and the fact has been fully and conclusively tested and established, that the soils, seasons, climate, and labor of no country can successfully compete with those of that vast region of this confederacy which has been appropriately styled the "COTTON ZONE," in the raising of this product. It is proper, however, to state that many of the most intelligent cotton planters of that region insist that their now generally conceded superiority is not so much attributable to any radical difference of the soil or dissimilarity of the climate in that region, from those of several other countries in like latitudes, as it is to the advantages afforded by the aggregated and combined, and cheap, and reliable labor they derive from that patriarchal system of domestic servitude existing throughout the "Cotton Zone," and to the superior intelligence, and greater experience, and skill, and energy, of the American planter; and to the improved and constantly improving *systems* of cultivation pursued by them—the most affluent attending personally to his own crop.

. . . . . . . . . . . . . . .

## 4] The Importance of Cotton to the United States: Israel D. Andrews on Exports of Cotton in Relation to the Balance of Trade

. . . Some political economists contend that what is called the "balance of trade" being in favor of or against the United States, as shown by the importation or exportation of bullion and specie, is the best evidence of the prosperous or unprosperous condition of our trade and commerce. On the other hand, others insist that such importation or exportation is no true test on either side; and that when any country has a surplus of bullion and specie, it is best to export a portion of the redundant supply; and that then those articles, besides fulfilling their proper functions of being the media and regulators and equalizers of trade and commerce, become themselves legitimate subjects of trade and commerce like other products; and that this rule especially applies to a country *producing* the precious metals.

The sole object, however, of the reference now made to the importation

---

FROM U.S. Congress, Senate, *Report of Israel D. Andrews . . . on the Trade and Commerce of the British North American Colonies . . .* , Senate Executive Document No. 112. 32nd Congress, 1st Session, 1853 (Washington: Robert Armstrong, Printer, 1853), pp. 825–27.

and exportation of bullion and specie is to notice the fact, equally forcible as respects both of these theories, that but for exportations of raw cotton, according to the treasury statistics, more than forty-eight millions of bullion and specie would have been required annually, since 1821, to have been exported (in addition to all that was exported) to meet the balances of trade against us that would have existed but for those exportations of raw cotton. It is true the treasury accounts of *exports* are not safe criteria as to values, they being in the United States, as in other countries, generally undervalued; but without the exportations of cotton from the United States, the balance-sheet would be a sorry exhibit of our condition as a commercial people, and of general prosperity. Our other exports, and especially of other agricultural products, are, when separately estimated, really insignificant in comparison with cotton.

. . . . . . . . . . . . . . .

The relative importance and value of the cotton crop of the United States to the other leading agricultural products of this country, and other principal articles of our domestic and foreign commerce, is more striking when the circumstances attendant upon the progress of each crop, and the others respectively, are considered. The augmentation of our population—the vast extension of our territory—the great increase of the area of our lands in tillage—the immense additions to our agricultural labor in our native population and in foreign emigrants—have given us consequent vastly increased resources and ability for greater production. As before shown, however, the greater portions of most of the agricultural products of the United States, and of the manufactures of them, except cotton, *are consumed in the United States.* The fact that the *exportations* from the United States of many of its most important products have not increased in proportion to our increase of population, resources, and ability, and that the article of *raw cotton* is a signal exception, surely is some evidence of its value and of the real position and actual increase of the wealth and prosperity of the cotton region. When it is recollected that very little of the additional labor given by *foreign emigration* inures to the cultivation of cotton, (and it is estimated that not more than one in 600 of the agricultural emigrants go to the cotton region;) and when the extent of internal improvements in the States where cotton is not grown, to transport their produce to market, is considered, it will be seen that this advancement of the cotton region is solely the result of steady industry, regulated by the intelligence to make it advantageous. The increased labor of that region has been almost exclusively derived from those contiguous States that do not cultivate cotton. The disparity between the increase of cotton and that of other agricultural products appears much greater when these facts are considered; and the doctrine that labor advantageously applied, and not population merely, is the true foundation of a country's wealth and prosperity, is fully verified.

The treasury accounts before referred to show that the aggregate increase of our foreign *importations* of merchandise has not equalled our increased exportations of raw cotton, and that it, as before stated, has most of all other articles enabled us to keep down the balance against us created by such importations. And it should be noticed, also, that the increase of importations is mainly for the use and consumption of those portions of the country that do not produce cotton. The consumption of imported merchandise and products in the cotton region may be greater than the proportion of its white population to that of other sections, but in the aggregate it is much less, and it is also much less than the proportion of its whole population to that of the other States.

Adding the increase of the *exportations* of our domestic manufactures of cotton to the exportations of raw cotton, the comparison between it and other agricultural products is still more favorable to it. Prior to 1826, such *exportations,* if any were made, were not specified in the treasury returns, and all our importations of cotton goods specified in those returns are exclusively those of *foreign* manufacture that had been imported hither. And the nearly total decrease of the importation of foreign raw cotton, and the manufactures thereof, and the substitution therefor of our own product, and manufactures thereof, should also be estimated.

Nor is the supply furnished from the cotton crop for the numerous "household" or "home-made" manufactures used in the United States an unimportant item constituting its value. The aggregate of the value of all these manufactures was, in 1849, upwards of $27,540,000, and it is estimated, as before stated, that the cotton consumed in them is worth annually upwards of $7,500,000. But for our own crop, this would have to be imported.

. . . . . . . . . . . . . . .

# PART II

# The Opening of the West

# INTRODUCTION

SOME 60 years ago Guy Stevens Callender, one of the most thoughtful economic historians thus far produced in the United States, characterized the opening of the West as the most important event in American economic history during the first 40 or 50 years of the nineteenth century. By the opening of the West Callender meant far more than the pushing of the frontier into the area west of the Appalachian mountains. That process went on with especial rapidity in the years after 1800, when the census had recorded fewer than 400,000 inhabitants of the Western States and Territories. By 1810 there were a million, and by 1820, 2,600,000. This impressive early growth in western population, however, was of limited economic significance to the rest of the nation. Large numbers of settlers lived at the level of subsistence or close to it, and their cash incomes were either nonexistent or too low to enable them to serve as a market for goods from other parts of the country. The value of produce received at New Orleans in 1807 was only $5,370,000; by 1816 it had risen only to $8,773,000. And those other evidences of flourishing trade—flourishing towns and cities—were conspicuously few. In 1810, New Orleans—with a population of 24,562—was the only city of any considerable size in the West. Pittsburgh had 4,768 inhabitants, Lexington, 4,326, and Cincinnati, 2,540. Louisville, St. Louis, Nashville, and Natchez each had fewer than 1,000.

Besides the menace from the Indians, a principal deterrent to the growth of the West before the end of the War of 1812 was the high cost of transportation for the commodities of the region. The wheat, flour, butter, pork, tobacco, hemp, lead, and other products of the Ohio Valley were of low value in relation to their bulk. Because of this, it was cheaper to ship them more than 3,000 miles by water—down the Ohio and Mississippi rivers to New Orleans, then up the Atlantic coast to Philadelphia, New York, or Boston—than 300 miles overland across the Appalachian highlands to Philadelphia or Baltimore. Downriver traffic, moreover, was for the most part a one-way flow, for shipments upriver against the current were almost prohibitively expensive even for light and valuable merchandise. Similarly, textiles, hardware, hats, tea, and such other commodities of high value relative to their bulk as farmers could afford to import from across the Appalachians constituted, in the main, another one-way flow of goods (one of the chief exceptions being cattle driven on foot over the mountains to the East Coast). This difficult pattern of interregional trade depressed farm incomes in the West and encouraged self-sufficiency rather than commercial agriculture.

As the following readings make clear, Callender believed that "two events" changed this situation. The first was the introduction of the steamboat on the rivers of the West, and the second was the extension of cotton culture into the Southwest. The steamboat gave the first great impetus to Western growth. When it appeared on the Mississippi in 1817, it made possible a great volume of upriver traffic and greatly reduced shipping costs both up- and downstream. The reduction in upriver costs was, of course, far the greater of the two. By thus lowering the costs of imported merchandise the steamboat shifted the terms of trade—the relationship between prices received for farm products and prices paid for manufactured and other goods, which determines the farmer's purchasing power—sharply in favor of the farmer, encouraging settlement and the increased commercialization of agriculture. Table 4A in the statistical section reveals the great increase in both numbers and tonnages of steamboats operating on Western rivers between 1817 and 1860. It is scarcely to be wondered at that contemporary observers, contemplating the rapid economic rise of the West, should have rhapsodized in the manner of James H. Lanman's 1841 piece in *Hunt's Merchants' Magazine:* "Steam navigation colonized the West! It furnished a motive for settlement and production by the hands of eastern men, because it brought the western territory nearer to the east by nine-tenths of the distance."[1] James Hall, a sober and experienced observer, wrote in a quieter vein in 1835 or 1836: "The introduction of steamboats upon western waters . . . contributed more than any other single cause, perhaps more than all other causes which have grown out of human skill, combined, to advance the prosperity of the west."[2]

Callender's second important event, the growth and southwesterly movement of the cotton belt, forms one of the most remarkable features of the antebellum period. In 1790 cotton growing was largely confined to a few islands off the Carolina and Georgia coast and a few favored areas on the mainland within a few miles of the sea. Then, Whitney's invention of the gin permitted the cultivation of short-staple cotton to move into the back country of Georgia, where—with Augusta as center and chief market—it soon covered the upland parts of that state and South Carolina. For more than a quarter of a century this was the principal cotton-producing region of the nation. Indeed, as late as 1821 more than one-half of the entire crop was grown in these two states alone.

The first shift from its original center took the cotton belt north into North Carolina and Virginia and west over the mountains into Tennessee. Following the War of 1812, the decisive movement was to the Southwest, with the tide of cultivation flowing first into Alabama, Mississippi, and Louisiana, and eventually into Arkansas and Texas. By the mid-1820's South Carolina and Georgia had begun to lose their original dominant position; by the time of the Civil War they accounted for less than a quarter of the nation's cotton output. Mississippi and Alabama had become the leading states, with Louisiana not far behind (see Table 3D in the statistical section). New Orleans—the great central market for the cotton of the Western region—had received only 37,000 bales in 1816, but in 1822 the number was 161,000, in 1830, 428,000, and in 1840, 923,000 bales. Expressed in terms of changing proportions, the states and territories from Alabama and Tennessee westward

[1] James H. Lanman, "American Steam Navigation," *Hunt's Merchants' Magazine,* IV, No. 2 (Feb. 1941), p. 124.

[2] Quoted in Thomas S. Berry, *Western Prices Before 1861, A Study of the Cincinnati Market* (Cambridge: Harvard University Press, 1943), pp. 29–30. The characterization of Hall as "sober and experienced" is that of Berry.

increased their share of the nation's total output of cotton from one-sixteenth in 1811 to one-third in 1820, one-half before 1830, nearly two-thirds in 1840, and three-fourths in 1860.

Behind this shift of the center of cotton growing lay numerous forces, some of which pushed settlers on, others of which lured them. Among the pushing forces, surely one of the most impelling was the influence exerted by worn-out land. As in the case of colonial and post-colonial tobacco farming, continuous crops of cotton robbed the soil of necessary minerals, and yields fell. Under different circumstances—notably those of land-hungry older nations—this waste of land would have made no sense. But because of its abundance in the United States land was the relatively cheap factor of production; it was capital and labor that were scarce. For this reason it was cheaper to acquire new land than to devote scarce resources to improving the productivity of the old; so planter and farmer alike ignored the counsels of concerned observers, failed to rotate their crops, mined the soil for all it was worth, and moved on.

Yet, it is doubtful that pushing factors exerted as much influence as those that pulled settlers into the more fertile areas of the West. Prospects of profit—not only from agriculture but from the sale of improved lands to those who should come in the next wave of settlement—attracted thousands to the West and warmed the enthusiasm of land speculators, not least among whom were the farmers themselves. The call of the West was sounded in promoters' publications, in private letters, by word of mouth, and by newspaper reports of fabulous earnings, such as the one from an issue of *Niles Weekly Register* presented in the following readings. Still, economic motivations by no means explain everything—even everything economic—and one cannot overlook the elements of sheer restlessness and love of adventure that are found on all moving frontiers.

It was Callender's view that the plantation regime of the Southwest became the "first important market" for the farmers of the Northwest. Callender suggested that the relationship between the two agricultural communities was highly similar to that between colonial New England and the West Indies. In both cases communities of planters concentrated their resources on the production of profitable staples and depended on other communities of small farmers for their supplies of food. Very possibly it was David Christy's *Cotton Is King,* a book published before the Civil War and with which Callender was familiar, that suggested to him the idea of interdependence. As the excerpt from that book in the following readings shows, Christy thought in terms of a "tripartite alliance" uniting "the Western Farmer, the Southern Planter, and the English Manufacturer . . . in a common bond of interest. . . ."

Certain it is that until recently twentieth-century historians have followed Callender's emphasis on specialized and interdependent regions. In 1939, Louis B. Schmidt described that interdependence with the following phrases: "The rise of internal commerce after 1815 made possible a territorial division of labor between the three great sections of the Union—the West, the South, and the East. . . . Each section tended to devote itself more exclusively to the production of those commodities for which it was best able to provide. . . ." In 1961, Douglass C. North placed great emphasis on this idea in his important study, *The Economic Growth of the United States.* In this book North expressed the belief that the "southern demand for foodstuffs was the initial impetus to westward expansion." And in his 1966 study, *Growth and Welfare in the American Past,* North emphasized interregional trade as "the pivot on which America's economy swung during the period 1815 to 1860."

The great problem in verifying the strength of these interregional links has been the fragmentary nature of the surviving statistics on internal commerce. Besides calling on the testimony provided by such contemporary observers as James Silk Buckingham, Frederick Law Olmsted, David Christy, and others whose works are excerpted in the following readings, Callender built his case for interdependence between the Northwest and the Southwest on the increasing number of steamboats on Western rivers, the steady growth of the river towns handling produce for shipment, and the rising value of produce received at New Orleans. One difficulty of verification, however, is that contemporary testimony may be impressionistic or biased. Another is that none of Callender's indices points exclusively to a provisions trade between Northwestern farmers and Southwestern planters—all are broader than that. Receipts at New Orleans included cotton, tobacco, and lead destined for non-Southern markets, and the statistics pertaining to steamboats and river towns partly reflect that fact. Some of the produce arrived in New Orleans only to be transshipped to markets in the Caribbean or on the Atlantic coast—some of it, however, going to southern Atlantic ports. Another part of the New Orleans receipts was not transshipped at all but was retained by commission merchants (factors) in New Orleans and later shipped back upriver to Southern plantations.

Could previously overlooked records be found that would permit a determination of the relative amounts supplying Southern and non-Southern markets? If so, one could be more certain of the extent to which the South served as a market for Western produce (not altogether certain, of course, because of the possibility that West-to-South routes other than those ending in New Orleans brought provisions to the Cotton Kingdom).

In a major recent book, *American Railroads and the Transformation of the Ante-Bellum Economy,* Albert Fishlow throws new light on these questions. Fishlow provides newly developed statistics that reveal average receipts of Western produce at New Orleans (1823–60), retained receipts at New Orleans (1832–56), average annual Southern consumption of Western foodstuffs (1842–61), and the importance of the Southern market to the West (1839–60). Fishlow concludes that before the mid-1840's there was little consumption in the South of Western produce sent to New Orleans. While a substantial increase did occur in the 1840's and a more modest one in the 1850's, even at its high point in the latter decade the West-to-South trade was relatively quite small, amounting to only one-third of that between West and East. Before the increase during the 1840's, the small quantities destined for Southern consumption argue against an important exchange between West and South. Not only was the Southern market relatively unimportant to the West; Western produce was even less important to the South, since that region enjoyed substantial self-sufficiency in the production of foodstuffs. To illustrate Southern self-sufficiency Fishlow cites Richard Easterlin's finding that per capita production of corn, swine, and cattle in the South in 1840 was higher than the national average. William N. Parker has recently reached similar conclusions; after examining the original census schedules for 1850 and 1860, he finds that Southern plantations, except large ones devoted to sugar production, were probably generally self-sufficient in pork and corn at these dates.

As will be clear, the evidence introduced by various scholars is only partially comparable in time and place. For example, the data presented by Easterlin and Parker apply to the period 1840–60 and do not necessarily represent the situation of earlier years. Fishlow's findings, on the other hand, do constitute a formidable challenge to Callender's thesis. But, although those findings make it clear that interregional exchange between West and South was less important than has long been believed, the crucial question is whether or not the lessening of that supposed importance is so considerable as to require the abandonment of the thesis. Several reasons argue that it would be premature to do so.

Perhaps the most important of these reasons is that Fishlow's statistics on receipts at New Orleans of produce from the West are incomplete. The statistics are based on the annual reports of New Orleans commerce as reprinted in annual October issues of *Hunt's Merchants' Magazine*. These annual reports, however, are defective; as Thomas S. Berry, another student of the trade, has pointed out, "considerable quantities of goods, particularly those shipped by flatboat, were never counted by the Louisiana observers." [3] Since flatboat traffic increased rather than decreased following the advent of the steamboat on Western waters (1816), it undoubtedly carried an important part of the "shipments of flour, pork, other hog products, and whiskey," which, Berry notes, "increased at a tremendous rate" during the antebellum period. Presumably these unrecorded quantities of Western provisions would substantially add to the total "Other Commodities" given by Fishlow in his Table 1, included in the following readings.

Not all the unrecorded goods, of course, would have gone to Southern plantations. On the other hand, it cannot be assumed that the ratios between amounts received and amounts retained for Southern consumption that Fishlow presents for the years after 1832 also hold for the 1820's, because it was precisely during the dozen years before 1833 that the production of cotton in the Southwest began to overtake the original leadership of South Carolina and Georgia (see Table 3C in the statistical section). Indeed, by 1820, per capita production in Alabama and Mississippi exceeded that of any other cotton state; by 1830, that of Mississippi alone was triple the per capita output of South Carolina and double that of Georgia (see Table 3G in the statistical section). Furthermore, it is extremely important to note that Fishlow's ratios are for the South as a whole rather than for that part of the South where, it may reasonably be maintained, resources during these years were first concentrated on cotton, with a consequent high degree of dependence upon the Northwest for foodstuffs. It should be emphasized that Callender was speaking of the Southwest—not the South as a whole—and that he said the Southwest was the *first* important market for the farmers of the Northwest, not a market that would be permanently more important than any other. It is, then, precisely the dozen years before 1833 that are the ones in question.

If in fact the Southwest did import substantial quantities of provisions from the Northwest—and the preceding considerations suggest that it did—the "New South," as distinct from the older Southeastern states, did not during this period

[3] *Ibid.*, p. 4.

enjoy the substantial self-sufficiency that Fishlow, Easterlin, and Parker attribute to the South as a whole during the period 1840–60 on the basis of high regional per capita outputs. With respect to the later decades, certain other considerations reflect doubt on the thesis of substantial self-sufficiency in the Southwest. Douglass North has suggested one of them: that the richer yields of the more productive new lands of the Southwest invited a higher degree of concentration on cotton—and, in parts of Louisiana, on sugar—which made that area more dependent on outside supplies than was the case in the Old South, where self-sufficiency was more in evidence. Regional population statistics, when conjoined with regional production characteristics, strengthen the probability of the Southwest's dependence on outside sources for its food supply. The population of the rich food-producing states of the Old Northwest (Ohio, Indiana, Illinois, and Michigan) was almost exactly double that of the states of the Southwest (Alabama, Arkansas, Mississippi, and Louisiana) on every census date from 1820–60, inclusive. Surely the former region made a greater contribution than did the Southwest to the nation's output of foodstuffs. Indeed, given the relatively high degree of concentration on cotton in the Southwest, *that area alone* clearly could not have enjoyed a per capita production of corn and other foodstuffs that was higher than the national average.

With respect to livestock in particular, the question of self-sufficiency must be examined in relation not only to the Southwest but to the South as a whole. It is only by including the border states of Kentucky and Missouri in the South that one is able to conclude with Easterlin and Fishlow that Southern per capita production of livestock exceeded the national average. This inclusion is open to question. Douglass North, for one, believes the border states are more properly classified with the West. Thus, whether or not an important interregional trade existed between West and South turns on the simple question of how one classifies the border states. The question is all the more important because it involves a significant exchange that is not reflected in the statistics of New Orleans receipts. The trade in livestock was conducted overland, and it achieved considerable dimensions. According to Eugene Genovese, Kentucky and Missouri sent "great numbers of animals south throughout the antebellum period." Genovese continues . . .

> The two states sold almost $1,700,000 worth of animals to South Carolina alone in 1845, and work animals, hogs, cattle, and sheep worth more than that passed by the Cumberland Ford in 1838. In 1836 drovers of horses and hogs from Kentucky, Missouri, and neighboring states sold $2,000,000 worth of animals to South Carolina, and by 1839 Kentucky alone earned as much from its southern trade. This overland trade eventually gave way to railroad shipments, especially of bulk pork, but during 1849–1850 a total of 185,000 hogs went south from Kentucky and Tennessee; tobacco and cotton planters and farmers in North Carolina and elsewhere continued to buy large numbers of animals on the hoof.[4]

Even if Kentucky and Missouri are classified with the South, so that Southern per capita production of livestock is seen as being high in numbers, a further question must be raised about the quality of the livestock produced. Southern animals were poor, and while they existed in large numbers it was their

[4] *The Political Economy of Slavery* (New York: Random House, 1965), p. 107.

qualitative inferiority that explained the "paradox" of "an abundance of livestock and an inadequate supply of meat and work animals." [5]

The evident importance of the overland trade in livestock raises the question of whether additional flows of goods took place in channels other than those culminating in New Orleans. Fishlow's emphasis on the overwhelming importance of that port is strongly supported by Joseph Nimmo, Jr., whose valuable Report on Internal Commerce is excerpted in the following readings. Moreover, Fishlow himself raises and discounts the possibility that any significant trade between the West and the South bypassed New Orleans, either via various Western rivers or via reexports of Western produce from the coastal cities of the East to Southern ports. However, Robert W. Fogel has recently argued that the latter route was more important than Fishlow believes. With respect to river trade, there exists the possibility of an unrecorded direct flatboat traffic between the West and plantations located on tributaries that could not be negotiated by other craft. While the resolution of these uncertainties must be left to future research, there can be little ground for reasonable doubt that Fishlow has demonstrated, for the antebellum period as a whole, that the commercial interdependence between West and South was not as important to either region as tradition has held. It is less clear that Callender was wrong in his emphasis on the early years of the period and on the dependence of the Southwest rather than of the entire South.

In any case, the more general theme of regional specialization and interdependence, while somewhat narrowed, is not placed in jeopardy by the scholarly contributions just discussed. Exports of Western produce to the East, via the Mississippi to New Orleans and up the coast, continued throughout the antebellum period to increase in value. With the advent of canals and railroads the current began to flow with increasing directness. For some years, the principal result of the opening of the Erie Canal in 1825 and the Pennsylvania Main Line in 1835 was an increased volume of farm produce flowing East from western New York and Pennsylvania, respectively. Their influence was felt, however, in the agriculture and commerce of the whole Great Lakes area and the Ohio Valley after the completion of two canals across Ohio in 1833 and 1845 and the opening of the Illinois and Michigan Canal in 1848 (see Table 4E in the statistical section). The canals exerted a developmental impact upon the countryside, making possible a large new production of foodstuffs. By the mid-1840's the amount of tonnage shipped eastward via Lake Erie and the Erie Canal was slightly greater than that sent down the Mississippi River. By 1853, the former route accounted for 62.2 per cent and the latter for only 28.9 per cent of the total tonnage.

The growing volume of trade with the East and with the South increased the income of Western farmers and made it possible for them to purchase larger quantities of manufactured goods from the East. The value of merchandise shipped to the Western states on the Erie Canal amounted to less than $10 million in 1836, but in 1853 it rose to a peak of $94 million. The value of domestic Eastern manufactures sent to the South (financed by shipments of cotton to the East) is concealed in the unrecorded statistics of the coastal trade. Yet there is every reason, as we shall see in greater detail in Part IV, to believe that these shipments to the South were

[5] *Ibid.*, p. 106.

considerable. Both the West and the South thus provided widening markets for Eastern manufactures, and one effect of this expanding demand was to induce a higher level of investment in the East. At the same time, the expansion of production and transportation facilities in the East had the effect of raising the level of incomes there, permitting an increasing demand for Western commodities.

Thus, the opening of the West, regardless of the precise role played by cotton in that process, brought into being an economy made up of interdependent regions—East, West, and South. Because improved transportation and higher levels of income made it possible for each of the regions to depend to a great extent on the others for certain goods and services, each could specialize to an important extent on particular kinds of productive activities. This is not to say that the amount of diversified activity was insignificant. It is doubtful whether a single Southern plantation failed to devote some of its resources to the growing of corn, garden vegetables, hay, oats, or other foodstuffs needed for the sustenance of the owner's family, work force, and livestock. Many plantations also met part of their own needs for manufactured goods, especially cheap textiles for the slaves. It was particularly in the Southern states that the household system of manufacturing, especially of cotton goods, showed continued vitality even in the closing years of the antebellum period.

Although diversification continued to be important, the larger truth is that in each of the regions predominant types of industry tended to develop. In the South, the Southwest in particular concentrated on the production of cotton and a few other plantation staples and depended on the border and northwestern regions for an important part of its food supply and livestock. The Southeast, as well as the Southwest, looked to the East for the bulk of its manufactured goods and commercial and financial services. The East, devoting itself increasingly to manufacturing, commerce, and finance, supplied the products of its own and foreign industries—as well as a good deal of capital—to the West and South; it in turn depended upon those regions to an increasing degree for foods and raw materials. The West, including the border region, supplied the grains, meat, and animals required by the South and East.

A territorial division of labor thus tended to develop in the antebellum years, and, because specialization always involves interdependence or the need for exchange, a vast volume of internal commerce resulted. But the arteries of internal commerce were swelled by the pulsations of foreign commerce. It was the revenue from exported goods, of which cotton was more important than any other single commodity, that permitted the South to pay the East for its goods and services and the West for its food and livestock. The East and West thus received a large part of the income necessary for the payment of goods and services obtained from the other regions.

Territorial specialization rested upon an increasing degree of occupational specialization in agriculture, commerce and finance, and manufacturing. Diversity was still to be found, but the trend was towards specialization, and it was the productivity of specialized occupations, sectors, and regions that fostered economic growth. Less and less could one find the old-style "colonial merchant" importing and exporting, selling at both wholesale and retail, handling numerous commodities, and engaging also in banking, insurance, and the freight business. To an increasing degree men tended not only to specialize in just one of these occupations but also to develop even more refined categories of specialization, with commercial bankers and investment bankers, for example, becoming differentiated from those specializing in attracting and investing savings. There was occasionally even a central banker.

Thus, the advent of canals and then East-West railroads in the 1850's brought to the developing West stimuli that greatly reinforced those of the steamships and the movement of the cotton belt. Together these influences made possible an important degree of interdependence between the nation's principal regional markets, increased the efficiency of operation of the nation's economy, enormously enlarged the volume of internal commerce, and sped the pace of economic growth.

The following readings open with Guy Callender's analysis of the economic significance of the opening of the West. This selection is followed by Albert Fishlow's reexamination of West-South trade. Then comes Lewis C. Gray's detailed account of the movement of the cotton belt. Gray is the leading modern authority on Southern agriculture before 1860. Note his account of the topographical features of the states into which cotton planting moved, in addition to his discussion of railroad building in the Southwest as a stimulus to the expansion of cotton into large areas previously unsuited to commercial production. The next group of readings depicts some of the main forces behind the movement of the cotton belt. In the first of these another modern scholar, Avery O. Craven, analyzes the factors affecting soil fertility and exhaustion. While Craven's specific subject is the old tobacco regions of Virginia and Maryland, he explicitly relates his valuable description of the process of exploitation to the cotton lands of the lower South. The next selection, Frederick Law Olmsted's contemporary sketch of those barren areas, graphically shows the pertinence of Craven's discussion to the land of cotton. In the following reading, "An emigrant from Maryland" tells the planters of his home state and of Virginia about the lush profits to be won from the soil of Louisiana. The last selection in the group, extracted from the autobiography of Gideon Lincecum, gives an excellent example of the restless frontier spirit. Lincecum was born in Georgia in 1793; at various times in his career he was a schoolteacher, Indian trader, surveyor and school commissioner at Columbus, Mississippi, physician, Texas planter, and student of natural history.

The contribution of the steamboat forms the subject of the panegyric presented in the next selection, the 1841 article by James H. Lanman from which a passage has already been quoted. The discerning student will sift the corn for its kernels of fact and insight and look upon the piece as historical evidence of the importance of the steamboat in the eyes not only of the author but also of the audience for whom he was writing.

The remaining selections throw light on specialization in the South and its interdependence with other regions. In the first of these, David Christy, author of *Cotton Is King* (published in 1856), makes cotton the linchpin of the regional alliance. It is cotton, he insists, that links Western grain to foreign commerce. Note his attribution of slavery's "productiveness" to the ability of the South to concentrate its resources on the growing of cotton. In Part III we shall look more closely at agricultural practices in relation to productivity.

The next five brief selections, all taken from contemporary books published in the 30 years between 1826 and 1856, emphasize the high degree to which the South concentrated on cotton and depended on outside sources for much of its food, livestock, and other supplies. Then the following selection—excerpts from the records of expenditures made by the executors of the estate of Isaac Franklin—provides a specific example of this dependence. Franklin was a slave trader who became a Louisiana planter in 1835. At the time of his death in 1846 his vast West Feliciana plantations embraced 6,678 acres and 577 slaves and produced cotton, wood, and lumber. (The wood was sold to river craft and the lumber to nearby residents.) The dependence of this large establishment on outside food supplies is shown by the fact that while corn, hay, and oats were grown at home no less than $20,000 was spent on these items between 1846 and 1850. Records of other expenditures show that between 50 and 60 New Orleans merchants served Franklin and his executors, providing bagging, rope, and twine for cotton baling and also horses and mules, farm implements and tools, clothing and drugs, and such food supplies as pork, bacon, and corn. A score of firms helped supply the plantations with provisions, and nearly as many dry-goods merchants and clothiers also contributed to the maintenance of the estate. In addition, two hardware companies and three drug firms received large orders, and miscellaneous items were purchased from a dozen others. The great bulk of purchases was made from New Orleans merchants, but merchants in upriver towns—in Cincinnati, Louisville, Nashville, and St. Louis—also shared in the business. The case of Isaac Franklin clearly illustrates the general point that specialization generates the need for exchange, and the last selection in the group gives a clear idea of the growing volume of those exchanges. It consists of excerpts from the Report on Internal Commerce made in 1887 by Joseph Nimmo, Jr., Chief of the Division of Tonnage in the Treasury Department. The excerpts reveal the development of commerce on the Western rivers and the role of New Orleans as the major outlet for the produce of the region served by those rivers.

The final selection, a list of New York's commercial functions in 1846, is presented because of the advanced degree of occupational specialization that it reveals. The list was compiled by Robert G. Albion from *Doggett's New York Business Directory* for 1846 and 1847, Part II, "Classifications of Professions and Trade." Albion remarks that the groups in the list are not mutually exclusive: a general mercantile firm such as Grinell, Minturn & Co., for example, might appear in *Doggett's Directory* under several different headings. From the original list, which includes a very wide range of specialized functions, Albion omitted "the common functions not particularly distinctive of a seaport, such as retailers, lawyers, hotel keepers, etc." We shall see in later chapters something of the degree to which specialization of function touched other segments of economic life during the antebellum period.

# THE READINGS

## 1] The Opening of the West

### a] Guy Callender Stresses the Importance of West-South Trade

We will begin . . . with a brief sketch of [our economic] development during the first forty or fifty years of the nineteenth century. The most important event in our economic history during this period was the opening of the West. By the opening of the West I do not mean the early settlement of the region west of the mountains, which took place on a large scale during the thirty years after the Revolution. This in itself, as I shall attempt to show, had very little influence upon the economic life of the country. I refer rather to that improvement in the economic condition of the West which set in about the time of the second war with England, and which in a decade or two entirely changed the relation of that region to the rest of the country, lifting it for the first time into that important place in our economic life which it has until recently occupied. This event marks the shifting of the centre of interest in our economic activity from the ocean and foreign commerce to the interior and internal commerce. It was the ending of the colonial period in our economic development, and the beginning of what has been the chief object of our economic activity ever since; namely, the application of capital to the settlement of the interior and the development of its natural resources. In order to appreciate the significance of this change to the movement we are studying, it will be necessary to trace its history in considerable detail.

The settlement of new territory and the pushing of the frontier back into the interior are features of American life which began in colonial times. At the end of the Revolution the back country of Pennsylvania, Virginia, and the Carolinas, was full of people, and had its special frontier characteristics in industry and social life. Following the Revolution, these backwoodsmen and many emigrants from the tide-water region, who had been ruined by the war and the exhaustion of the soil, moved into the region west of the mountains. The census of 1790 showed 109,000 people in Kentucky and the region south of it, not to mention those who had settled in western Pennsylvania and Virginia, which must have amounted to as many more. According to the census the Western States and Territories contained 387,183 inhabitants in 1800; ten years later they contained 1,075,398; and in 1820, 2,207,476. To get the total Western population, it is necessary to add the

---

FROM Guy Stevens Callender, "The Early Transportation and Banking Enterprises of the States in Relation to the Growth of Corporations," *Quarterly Journal of Economics,* vol. XVII (1903), pp. 114–31.

number of inhabitants of western Pennsylvania and Virginia, which in 1820 amounted to 248,476 and 147,531 respectively, making a total for the whole West of 2,603,483. During the same period there was a great emigration to the wild lands of northern and western New York, as well as northern New England. In 1790 the census showed only 1,075 people in New York west of Seneca Lake; in 1800 there were still but 17,016; by 1810 this number had risen to 72,000; and in 1820 to 211,000. These figures show how large a movement of people from the older communities into the interior took place during the thirty years following the Revolution. There must have been between one and a half and two million people living west of the mountains at the outbreak of the War of 1812.

Great as was this movement of people into the West, its economic influence was very slight. The general character of the industry of the country remained what it had been since colonial times. The West at that time had few economic prizes to attract settlers. To the emigrant from the tide-water region it offered a refuge from the pressure of hard times, where he could easily gain a rich subsistence for a numerous family. To the backwoodsman it could add to this the wild, free life of adventure which was so attractive to men of this class. But to the investor or the man who wished to make a fortune it had as yet hardly anything at all to offer. Consequently, its settlement could have little economic influence upon the country as a whole. A little consideration of the conditions upon which the prosperity of a newly settled country depends, and a comparison of these conditions with those prevailing in the West at this time, will make this sufficiently clear.

Since Adam Smith's time, economists have generally accepted his explanation of the prosperity of newly settled countries. "The colonists carry out with them a knowledge of agriculture and of other useful arts, superior to what can grow up of its own accord in the course of centuries among savage and barbarous nations. . . . Every colonist gets more land than he can possibly cultivate. He has no rent, and scarcely any taxes to pay." . . . The application of this efficient labor to the abundant natural resources is supposed to result always in a large production of wealth. . . . "The colony of a civilized nation which takes possession, either of a waste country or one so thinly inhabited that the natives easily give place to the new settlers, advances more rapidly to wealth and greatness than any other human society." This explanation, though it appears to account for the prosperity of new countries, does not in reality do so; for it quite overlooks the fact that these conditions have not always resulted in rapid progress in wealth. The mere presence of a certain number of industrious people in a country abounding with fertile soil, forests, mines, and fisheries, by no means insures a rapid development of these resources and a consequent large production of wealth. The economic advantages possessed by a people so situated consist simply in the ability to produce food and raw materials with a small outlay of labor. Before they can utilize these advantages, certain favoring conditions must be present. They must be able to dispose of these commodities in exchange for the commodities which they cannot so easily produce,—in a word, they must have a market.

Theoretically, it is possible for the new country to secure this market by the development of manufactures at home, whereby a non-agricultural population is created; and it might conceivably be better for the community, both socially and economically, to secure its market in that way. But, practically, it is very difficult, if not impossible, for it to do this; and in any case the process of doing it would be so slow that the "advance to wealth and greatness" must be much less rapid than that of new countries is commonly supposed to be. Manufactures on a large scale cannot be carried on without a permanent wage-earning class; and in a community in contact with cheap, unoccupied land, where every one can easily become an independent proprietor, it is almost impossible to create such a class. The social attractions of land ownership outweigh those of high wages. Every one has heard of the difficulty which was encountered in this country during colonial times and the early part of the nineteenth century in securing laborers to work for hire. Franklin tells us that even the Scotch-Irish immigrants to Pennsylvania, who had been trained as artisans at home, would not continue more than a few years in that capacity; the early textile manufactures in New England had to depend chiefly upon female laborers, whose average period of service was less than five years; while the greatest difficulty was experienced by all the States in securing common laborers to construct the early canals. The creation of a wage-earning class in the North was in fact very slow and very difficult before the flood of immigrants came in, and the chief economic advantage of immigration to this country consisted not so much in the fact that the immigrants represented an actual addition to our laboring population as that they supplied material out of which we could easily create a wage-earning class at the time when we needed to organize labor in order to construct our railroads and develop manufactures. In the South, where even agriculture required the organization of labor in order to be conducted most efficiently, the difficulty or impossibility of inducing the whites to become wage-earners while they were in contact with cheap land is undoubtedly the chief reason why the cotton industry in this country was developed by slave instead of by free labor.

This difficulty of inducing men in a new country to give up the position of an independent proprietor and become a dependent wage-earner does not prevent the development of small manufactures, which are necessary for the immediate and pressing wants of the community, and require no great organization of workmen for their production. If the community for any reason is unable to secure these by trade, the manufacture of them will usually arise, as it did to some extent in the northern colonies in the eighteenth century. But the development of manufactures is not likely to go much beyond this, or, if it does, that development is sure to be very slow so long as the cheap land continues. Under such conditions there will be much rude comfort among the inhabitants and no lack of the necessities of life. But the community cannot advance rapidly in the production of wealth and the accumulation of capital; division of labor and development of skill do not take place; town life does not arise; and social and economic progress is slow. It may even happen that a community suffers a decline in both its economic efficiency and social life, if compelled to remain for several generations under such conditions. The Boers of South Africa and the Southern mountaineers are good examples of what may happen to a new community which remains for a long period of time in contact with cheap land and dependent upon the development of manufactures within itself for its economic prosperity.

It is evident from this that the condition necessary to enable the settlers of a new country to utilize their rich natural resources, and so to advance rapidly in wealth and social well-being, is a market for the commodities which its natural advantages enable it to produce cheaply. It must have commerce with the outside world. In the history of modern colonization it is impossible to find a new settlement which has made great progress in wealth where this condition of a market for its products has not been supplied. All the leading colonies have been concerned in the production of some two or three commodities for which there was already a demand in the markets of the world. It was so with the colonies of all the European countries in the sixteenth, seventeenth, and eighteenth centuries, which were concerned almost entirely with the production of precious metals, tropical and sub-tropical products, like sugar, tobacco, rice, cocoa, and dyestuffs, and a few products of the temperate zone, like furs, fish, and naval stores. These were the only commodities which Europe wished to buy of new countries at that time; and the colonies in many cases came into existence and in all cases grew in wealth because they could produce to supply this demand. The New England and Middle colonies are no exception to this rule; for, though they had few markets in Europe, the rise of the West India sugar industry, based on slave labor, supplied the market which created their prosperity. Of course, the founding of many of the colonies was due to other than economic motives; but the subsequent progress of these colonies in wealth was due to the rise of markets for their products. The same thing is true also of the great colonies and new countries of the nineteenth century, like Australia, South Africa, the Canadian North-west, California, and Argentina, whose economic progress has been primarily due to the rise of a market in old countries for wheat, meats, cotton, wool, and such commodities. There has always been a demand for gold and silver, and that accounts for the great part which their production has played in the settlement of new countries.

Let us see now what were the conditions existing in the West before 1812, and how far they correspond to those we have found to be necessary to secure the prosperity of a new community. Separated from the Eastern seaboard by complete lack of water communication, the Western people were unable to send any of their produce to the Eastern cities, except a few cattle, hogs, and horses, which could be driven to market over long distances, and a few commodities like furs, which could stand the expense of land carriage. They were compelled, therefore, to depend almost wholly upon such markets as could be found at the mouth of the Mississippi. With the exception of a small amount that went from northern Ohio and western New York, nearly all Western produce was sent down the rivers to New Orleans. Not only was this an expensive and dangerous voyage before the days of steamboats, but there was very little demand for the produce of the

West when it arrived at New Orleans. The population on the lower Mississippi was very small, and required little, if any, Western produce for its own consumption. The rest of the produce had to be sent around by sea to the Atlantic cities or exported to the West Indies, Mexico, or Europe. The total value of the produce received at New Orleans in 1807 was only $5,370,000, and by 1816 it had increased to only $8,773,000. 39 per cent. of this in the latter year came, however, from Louisiana and the lower Mississippi. The remainder represents the chief part of the exports of an agricultural community of nearly two million people, an average of only about $2.70 per head of population. The number and size of towns in the West at this time is another convincing proof of the slight development of trade which had taken place. The only town of any considerable size in the whole West was New Orleans, through which passed the bulk of the exports and a considerable part of the imports. This town had 24,562 inhabitants in 1810. Pittsburg, from which was distributed the larger part of the imports, and which contained the most important manufactories in the West, had only 4,768 inhabitants; Lexington, which Michaux tells us carried on nearly all the commerce of Kentucky and Tennessee, had only 4,326 inhabitants; and Cincinnati had only 2,540. The other commercial places like Louisville, Nashville, Natchez, and St. Louis, were little more than mere villages, with about one thousand inhabitants each. The significance of these figures will appear more striking if we compare them with similar ones for some new communities of later times. In 1891 the two colonies of Victoria and New South Wales, whose industry was almost entirely agricultural and pastoral, had an average export of $20 per inhabitant. Washington and Oregon, with a population of 663,198 in 1890, had commerce enough to build up four cities with an aggregate population of 145,150, besides several smaller towns of from 1,000 to 4,000 inhabitants. Kentucky and Tennessee had in 1810 almost exactly the same population,—namely, 668,-238; and the town which is said to have carried on the larger part of their commerce had but 4,326 inhabitants.

With regard to manufactories there were, as we should expect, a great number of small, local ones, producing articles of prime necessity. Almost every community had one or more grist and saw mills; and very many had forges, tanneries, and salt works, fulling and carding mills, and paper-mills. In Pittsburg, Lexington, and Cincinnati there were a number of industries that were not purely local in character. But the size of these towns, which were more largely commercial than manufacturing centres, shows how small were these industries; and travellers did not fail to note the obstacles which retarded their further growth. Michaux comments on the high price of labor, and says it "is occasioned by the inhabitants giving the preference to agriculture, there being but few who put their children to trade, because they require their assistance in their own employment."

A contemporaneous description of the West by one whose commercial connection gave him a thorough knowledge of it will suffice to confirm the views here presented. Congressman Porter, of western New York, made the following statement in a speech in Congress in 1810:—

> The great evil, and it is a serious one indeed, under which the inhabitants of the western country labor, arises from the want of a market. There is no place where the great staple articles for the use of civilized life can be produced in greater abundance or with greater ease, and yet as respects most of the luxuries and many of the conveniences of life the people are poor. They have no vent for their produce at home, and, being all agriculturists, they produce alike the same article with the same facility; and such is the present difficulty and expense of transporting their produce to an Atlantic port that little benefit is realized from that quarter. The single circumstance of want of a market is already beginning to produce the most disastrous effect, not only on the industry, but on the morals of the inhabitants. Such is the fertility of their land that one-half their time spent in labor is sufficient to produce every article which their farms are capable of yielding, in sufficient quantities for their own consumption, and there is nothing to incite them to produce more. They are, therefore, naturally led to spend the other part of their time in idleness and dissipation. Their increase in numbers far from encourage them to become manufacturers for themselves, but put to a greater distance the time when, quitting the freedom and independence of masters of the soil, they submit to the labor and confinement of manufacturers.

Such was the condition of the West before the War of 1812, and its economic relation to the rest of the country. Turn now to the changes which followed the war and their effect upon the West, and through it upon the country at large. As we have seen, the chief obstacle to the prosperity of this section was the lack of a market. Two events soon removed this obstacle, and started the whole country forward on its remarkable career of development. The first was the introduction of the steamboat; the second was the extension of cotton culture into the South-west. The steamboat was introduced on the Ohio at Pittsburg as early as 1811; but it was six years later before it had demonstrated its ability to stem the rapid current of Western rivers. With that event the Western country was suddenly supplied with a system of transportation which reached wide stretches of country, and brought them into easy communication with the seaboard. With the rise of the cotton industry in England and Whitney's famous invention in this country, cotton culture began its amazing growth. For more than twenty years it was confined almost entirely to the Eastern seaboard. A small amount was raised about New Orleans in Louisiana, near Natchez in Mississippi, and near Nashville in Tennessee; but in 1802 only 29,000 bales were exported from New Orleans, and this had increased to only 37,000 in 1816. About the latter date cotton planters began to turn their attention for the first time in considerable numbers to the South-west. The great body of fertile soil in this region suited to the cultivation of this staple, the numerous navigable rivers, coupled with the fact that cotton, having large value in small weight, could bear the expense of land transportation to the rivers from a long distance over poor roads, combined to make this extension of cotton culture into the South-west the source of the greatest profits in agriculture which the American people had ever enjoyed. A flood of emigrants from the older slave States now poured into this region. Alabama and Mississippi did not contain more than 75,000 people in 1816. Only four years later their population was 200,000, and it more than doubled during the next ten years. Louisiana, which contained about 76,000 people in 1810, had 143,000 in 1820, and 215,000 in 1830. Certain parts of Tennessee, Arkansas, and Florida, where cotton could be raised, were settled with equal rapidity. New Orleans was the great central market to which the cotton product of this region was sent; and it received, as we have seen, only 37,000 bales in 1816. That amount rose to 161,000 bales in 1822, 428,000 bales in 1830, and reached 923,000 in 1840. The cultivation of sugar in Louisiana was also increasing at this time, and was equally profitable.

The effect of this extension of cotton and sugar cultivation into the South-west upon the Southern States is well known. It opened up a very profitable field for the employment of the labor and capital of this section, and this economic advantage went chiefly to the revival and extension of the slave system. But its effect upon the Northern States, especially the newer States of the North-west, has hardly received the attention its importance deserves. In reality, it was that movement which gave to them their first important market, and thus supplied the one remaining requisite to their economic development. The use of slave labor on a large scale not only prevents the rise of manufactures, but it always causes a curious territorial division of labor in agriculture as well. Slave labor to be efficient, must be carefully supervised; and its maximum efficiency is therefore obtained only in those branches of agriculture which permit the close organization of labor. For this reason every slave community devotes itself for the most part to the production of a few staples, like cotton, sugar, tobacco, or rice, and finds it cheaper to purchase its food and other agricultural supplies, as well as its manufactured articles, from free labor communities. This gives rise to a trade in agricultural commodities between the slave communities and other agricultural communities. The important trade between the northern Continental colonies in the eighteenth century and the West Indies was a trade of this kind; and it was principally the development of the sugar colonies of the West Indies by slave labor, and the consequent dependence of these colonies on other communities for food and raw material, which provided New England and the Middle colonies with their most important market. In exactly the same way the introduction and spread of cotton and sugar culture into the southern part of the Mississippi Valley led to a division of labor between the planters of the South and the farmers of the North, and gave rise to an important trade in agricultural produce upon the Western rivers of the same character as that which went up and down the Atlantic coast during colonial times between the Northern colonies and the West Indies.

The development of this trade between the cotton planters and the farmers began with the first introduction of cotton culture into South Carolina and Georgia. Ramsey tells us that down to about 1793, when cotton began to be raised in South Carolina, that State produced both wheat and corn for export. By 1807, however, the greater profit to be earned in the production of cotton had attracted labor and capital to that industry, and the State was importing both wheat and corn. Olmsted said in 1856: "The slave labor of the State [South Carolina] is almost exclusively devoted to the culture of cotton and rice. Live stock, meat, corn, bread-stuffs, and forage, though the soil and climate of a large part are entirely favorable to that production, are very largely imported; and for nearly all sorts of skilfully manufactured goods the people are quite dependent on the Free States. Trade and skilled labor of all sorts is mainly in the hands of persons from the Free States or foreign countries.". . . Live stock was raised in great numbers in the back country of the Southern colonies in the eighteenth century, and was a considerable item of export; but, after the introduction of cotton culture, horses, mules, and swine were imported into these States from Kentucky and Tennessee. This trade had become very large by 1825, and played a considerable part in the discussions over the tariff and nullification in the years following. In the South-west the same tendency to concentrate attention upon the two great staple products, sugar and cotton, and to procure food and other supplies from the North, showed itself even more strongly than in the East. Flint says of Louisiana in 1825 that "corn, sweet potatoes, melons, and all northern fruit, with the exception of apples, flourish here; though the planters find the great staples, cotton and sugar, so much more profitable than other kinds of cultivation that many of them calculate to supply themselves with provisions almost entirely from the upper country." An English traveller in the South-west in the '50's had a similar comment to make: "Strange to say, it is more difficult to raise the requisite quantity of provisions for a southern plantation than to manufacture wagons, plows, houses, and articles of clothing. The bacon is almost entirely imported from the northern states, as well as a considerable quantity of Indian corn."

The extent of this commerce between the North-west and the South it is impossible to ascertain with accuracy, for there are no reliable statistics of it as a whole. The rapid growth in the number of steamboats on Western rivers, especially the number running between the Ohio and upper Mississippi and New Orleans, indicates a corresponding increase in the trade between these sections. Steamboats on the Western rivers increased from 20 in 1818 to 200 in 1829, 450 in 1842, and 1,200 in 1848, while their size and carrying capacity was also increasing. Besides this a large amount of flatboat tonnage existed, and a considerable part of the produce of the Ohio Valley was sent to market by this means. In 1845 the flatboat tonnage amounted to 620,000 tons, and the steamboat tonnage to 1,262,000 tons. The number of steamboat arrivals at New Orleans from the Ohio and upper Mississippi are not separated from the total arrivals before 1859, but in that year they were about 1,500 out of a total of 4,000. The value of the produce received at New Orleans increased from $8,700,000 in 1816 to $26,000,000 in 1830, $50,000,000 in 1841, and $185,000,000 in 1860. Between 1816 and 1820 about 61 per cent. of this tonnage was farm produce from the North-west. The proportion, though not the total amount, of farm produce declined until it reached 28 per cent. in 1860. The steady growth of the river towns which handled this trade also indicates its growth. Thus Cincinnati increased from 9,600 in 1820 to 115,000 in 1850, Louisville from 4,000 to 43,000, and St. Louis from 4,900 to 77,000. It was estimated in 1845 that during the twenty years previous planters had spent $900,000,000 in neighboring States for mules, horses, implements, and clothing. These are but rough indications of the extent of this trade; but they are sufficient to establish the fact that it was very large, and that it grew up almost entirely after 1815.

The influence of this extension of cotton culture upon the North was not confined to the agriculture of the North-west. It affected every other Northern interest as well. The prosperity which it brought to the whole Southern and Western population increased their ability to purchase such manufactures as they required, and thus provided Eastern manufacturers with a rapidly expanding market. This was the great influence which caused the steady growth of manufactures from 1816 to the Civil War, both under the protective policy of the earlier and the low tariff policy of the later years. Commercial interests also received great stimulus. The internal trade of the country sprang at once into commanding importance. A large and prosperous agricultural population in the South and West was devoting itself to the production of valuable crops of food and raw material, and exchanging them with the North-eastern States and Europe for manufactures. This trade opened new opportunities for the merchant, the banker, the ship-owner, the insurance company,–to the whole commercial class, in fact. The fact that all the capital which the South accumulated was put into cotton culture left this whole field open to the commercial capital of the North-east. An eager rivalry arose among the commercial cities of the seaboard to secure a share of this internal trade, and each appreciated that its future position would be determined chiefly by the success of its efforts in this direction.

The effect of all these changes upon the economic condition of the country at large was almost revolutionary. It opened the eyes of the people to the economic possibilities of their situation, and turned their attention for the first time to the exploitation of their natural resources. The West ceased to be a mere refuge of poverty and field for the adventure of pioneers. The enterprise and capital of the country turned away from the ocean and foreign commerce, and found here a new field for its operation. One of the most striking features of the new period was the increase of speculative activity everywhere in American industry. This was largely the result of the enormous increase in land values, to which the changes we have described gave rise. The choice cotton lands of the South-west and the coal lands of eastern Pennsylvania suddenly became worth fabulous sums. Along the canals and rivers, especially in western New York and central Ohio, farm produce more than doubled in value; and the value of the land rose correspondingly. From New York on the east to New Orleans on the west, new towns were springing up along the lines of trade, and old ones growing with a rapidity that was new in American experience. The population of New York increased from 123,000 to 203,000 in the ten years from 1820 to 1830; New Orleans, from 27,000 to 46,000; Cincinnati, from 9,000 to 24,000; and Louisville, from 4,000 to 12,000. Buffalo and Rochester were hardly in existence in 1816; in 1830 they had 18,000 inhabitants. The number of villages along the New York canals increased from 55 to 105 between 1817 and 1833. Of course, the growth of all these cities and towns caused a corresponding increase in the value of real estate. That of New York went up from $69,000,000 to $165,000,000 in ten years, and the increase in many others was still greater. It is easy to see how all these things would foster speculation. Josiah Quincy declared in 1826 "that the enormous increase in wealth without labor which has come to fortunate speculators since 1815 seems to make the invocation of chance legitimate business." This speculative tendency went on increasing until it culminated in the crisis of 1837–39,—the first of a series of such crises which have accompanied the development of the West.

## b] ALBERT FISHLOW REEXAMINES THE WEST-SOUTH TRADE

THUS FAR we have analyzed two of the channels of internal trade between America's three major pre-1860 regions. It remains only to consider the flow between the West and the South. The traditional view is that because the South was producing staple crops for export it was acquiring its foodstuffs from the West, whose comparative advantage conveniently lay along these lines. As Schmidt has summarized, and North recently reiterated: [1]

> The rise of internal commerce after 1815 made possible a territorial division of labor between the three great sections of the Union—the West, the South, and the East. . . . Each section tended to devote itself more exclusively to the production of those commodities for which it was best able to provide. . . . The South was thereby enabled to devote itself in particular to the production of a few plantation staples contributing a large and growing surplus for the foreign markets and depending on the West for a large part of its food supply. . . .

Such a model is simple, internally consistent, and not lacking the support of contemporary observation. Russell, one of many foreign visitors, noted the existence of specialization: "The bacon is almost entirely imported from the Northern States, as well as a considerable quantity of Indian Corn." Christy, a southern defender of slavery, emphasized the solidarity of western and southern commercial interests and commented in a like vein: "The West . . . had its attention now [after 1815] turned to the South, as

[1] Louis B. Schmidt, "Internal Commerce and the Development of a National Economy before 1860," *Journal of Political Economy,* XLVII (1939), 811. Cited by North, *Economic Growth,* p. 103.

FROM Albert Fishlow, *American Railroads and the Transformation of the Ante-Bellum Economy* (Cambridge: Harvard University Press, 1965), pp. 275–88. 

the most certain and convenient mart for the sale of its products—the planters affording to the farmers the markets they had in vain sought from the manufacturers." [2] The increasing flow of receipts at New Orleans often is used as evidence of the continuity of such exchange to a later period.

Such a position has come under recent attack.[3] Richard Easterlin's review of North's book points to the production statistics of the southern states as evidence of substantial self-sufficiency in foodstuffs.[4] The number of swine and bushels of corn produced per capita in the South from 1840 through 1860 were higher than the national average, for example. So too, the number of cattle, and the quantity of peas and beans produced. In this tally, the border states contribute more than proportionally, suggesting a flow of trade between different parts of the South, and not interregionally. The southern social structure, with large numbers of land owners with few or no slaves at all, also indirectly testifies to an economic structure with self-sufficiency and local production of foodstuffs for sale to nearby plantations.[5] Intrasouthern trade of some significance, apart from that with the border states, is a distinct possibility that has not yet been fully explored.

Although these data are obviously relevant to the question of southern dependence upon the West, their impact is dulled because they do not bear directly upon exchange between the two regions. It is necessary to focus upon such exchange if the matter is to be resolved. A good place to begin is with the receipts at New Orleans. Since the Ohio and Mississippi Rivers formed a continuous channel the largest volume of western produce for southern consumption passed to this market. So, too, however, did a large quantity of southern staples, which means that gross receipts at New Orleans are not a valid measure, absolute or relative, of the West-South trade. In Table 1, New Orleans receipts are separated into two components, one consisting of the southern staples, the other a residual comprising western products. These latter were largely foodstuffs, although lead was also important at the beginning of the period. From 1842 on these values are exact; for the earlier period they are estimates for the components, and exact for the totals. Included in Table 1, too, is a weighted index of physical receipts of western foodstuffs at New Orleans compiled by Thomas S. Berry.

These data yield two important conclusions. First, for the entire period, western products, and therefore western foodstuffs, make up less than half of New Orleans receipts. The very rapid rise in Berry's index between 1826–1830 and 1831–1835 does not contradict the simultaneously declining

[2] Both quotations in Callendar, *Economic History, 1765–1860,* pp. 292, 296.

[3] Although his is a far better study than Schmidt's brief summary, Isaac Lippincott's opposing views have not achieved wide circulation. See his "Internal Trade of the United States, 1700–1860," *Washington University Studies,* IV, pt. II, no. 1 (1916), 63–150. For the discussion of the trade between West and South, see pp. 130–132.

[4] *Journal of Economic History,* XXII (1962), 125. See also Donald L. Kemmerer, "The Pre-Civil War South's Leading Crop, Corn," *Agricultural History,* XXIII (1949), 236–39.

[5] For the number of slaveholders and slaves, see *Eighth Census, Agriculture,* p. 247. For a discussion of the different types of farmers in the context of a single plantation state see Herbert Weaver, *Mississippi Farmers, 1850–1860* (Nashville, 1945), especially chap. ii. Kenneth Stampp, *The Peculiar Institution* (New York: Alfred A. Knopf, 1956), pp. 51–53, also presents scattered evidence on self-sufficiency.

TABLE 1. AVERAGE ANNUAL RECEIPTS AT NEW ORLEANS, 1823–1860

| YEARS ENDING AUG. 1 | COTTON | TOBACCO | SUGAR | MOLASSES | OTHER COM-MODITIES | TOTAL [a] | INDEX OF RECEIPTS OF WESTERN FOODSTUFFS AT NEW ORLEANS (BASE—1810–62 AVERAGE) |
|---|---|---|---|---|---|---|---|
| | (millions of dollars) | | | | | | |
| 1823–1825 | 7.9 | 1.0 | 2.0 | — | 5.3 | 16.2 | 11 |
| 1826–1830 | 10.1 | 1.3 | — | — | 10.2 | 21.6 | 21 |
| 1831–1835 | 18.0 | 1.8 | — | — | 8.9 | 28.7 | 40 |
| 1836–1840 | 29.6 | 3.4 | — | — | 11.1 | 44.1 | 58 |
| 1841–1845 | 28.1 | 5.5 | 5.8 | 0.5 | 14.4 | 53.3 | 112 |
| 1846–1850 | 34.8 | 4.2 | 10.2 | 1.9 | 34.0 | 85.2 | 237 |
| 1851–1855 | 54.5 | 6.8 | 14.7 | 3.6 | 36.9 | 116.3 | 212 |
| 1856–1860 | 89.2 | 10.2 | 17.0 | 4.9 | 44.1 | 165.6 | 212 |

SOURCE: *1842–1849, except 1843:* Annual reports of New Orleans Commerce reprinted in the October issue of *Hunt's Merchants' Magazine* for the respective years.

*1850–1860* and Total *for 1823–1841:* U.S. Treasury Department, Bureau of Statistics, *Report on Internal Commerce for 1887* (Washington, 1888), pp. 191, 209.

*1823–1841, 1843:* Cotton: Receipts in bales at New Orleans, *Hunt's Merchants' Magazine,* XXI (1849), 557; average New Orleans price per pound given in Gray, *History of Agriculture,* II, 1027, multiplied by an assumed 500-pound bale. These values were reduced by 13 percent, the average overstatement produced by the method during the period covered by exact values and predicted ones in the 1840's. Values were further reduced for the earlier periods in proportion to the ratio of bale size in the given years and that prevailing in the 1840's. (Data on bale size from Gray, *History,* II, 705.)

Tobacco: Receipts at New Orleans, *Hunt's Merchants' Magazine,* XXI (1849), 557; average New Orleans price from Gray, II, 1038. Value of receipts inflated by 13 percent (average understatement in 1840's) to compensate for the exclusion of shipments by containers other than hogsheads and also for an understatement of price due to shipment of some higher valued tobaccos.

Sugar: Total values, 1843, Gray, II, 1033. Production, 1823, *Hunt's Merchants' Magazine,* XXI (1849) 557; 1824–1825, Gray, II, 1033. Prices, Gray, p. 1034. Receipts at New Orleans from 1826–40 exclude sugar entirely.

Molasses: In "Other commodities," 1823–1840; 1841, 1843 extrapolated from actual values of other years.

Index of western receipts at New Orleans: Berry, *Western Prices,* p. 581. An apparent typographical error in the entry for 1830 has been corrected although the same error is repeated in the text. With all components declining, the index goes up by 60 percent according to the printed version.

[a] May not add due to rounding.

value of receipts that is the basis for this observation. Not prices, but the declining trend of lead receipts is responsible for the divergence. With foodstuffs only a fraction of the 1826–1830 values and almost the complete 1831–1835 total, they could have gone up sharply, as Berry's index suggests, consistent with a small decline in value of all western products. To find a dominance of western products, therefore, it is necessary to go back before the depression of 1819 when the Southwest was not yet producing substantial quantities of cotton. In 1816–1818, Berry's index stands at 10 or at about its 1823–1825 level. Western prices were higher than in 1823–1825, and the total values of New Orleans receipts only $10 million a year.[6] Only

[6] *Report on the Internal Commerce of the United States for 1887,* pp. 191, 215; Berry, *Western Prices,* p. 580.

at that early date did the share of western products exceed 50 percent of the value of New Orleans receipts.

A second noteworthy result is the *absolute* decline in western shipments in the 1850's. The physical index brings this out nicely as do the value data once the rapid increase in the prices of agricultural products over the period is appreciated: bacon, pork, and lard, more than doubled in price between 1850 and 1857, flour was up by 25 percent, beef by 67 percent, and so on.[7] Since the South was expanding its cotton production rapidly exactly over this interval—output doubling—this is presumably when imports of western products should have shown a rapid increase! This disparity, and the seeming rapid growth in imports in the late 1840's, in part results from an inadequacy of these data that has not been fully recognized. Receipts of western produce at New Orleans were not entirely consumed but were also re-exported either to foreign or coastwise ports.

It is surprising that so little attention has been paid to this link in the argument. After all, the entire discussion of trade diversion in *De Bow's Review* revolved exactly upon the issue of whether it was cheaper to ship to the East via New Orleans or eastward by canal or railroad. Contemporaries clearly attributed the decline in receipts of western produce in the 1850's to the loss of transshipment, not to lesser southern consumption. A simple comparison in Table 2 of the total value of receipts of produce

TABLE 2. RETAINED RECEIPTS AT NEW ORLEANS (THOUSANDS OF DOLLARS)

| YEARS ENDING AUG. 1 | RECEIPTS FROM INTERIOR (1) | FOREIGN EXPORTS (2) | COASTWISE EXPORTS (3) | RESIDUAL (1)–(2)–(3) |
|---|---|---|---|---|
| 1832–1833 | 28,238 | 16,133 | 9,058 | 3,047 |
| 1836–1837 | 43,515 | 31,546 | 15,116 | – 3,147 |
| 1841–1842 | 45,716 | 27,427 | 19,444 | – 1,155 |
| 1845–1846 | 77,193 | 30,748 | 19,150 | 27,295 |
| 1850–1851 | 106,924 | 53,968 | 27,229 | 25,727 |
| 1855–1856 | 144,256 | 80,550 | 28,031 | 33,175 |

SOURCE: *Report on the Internal Commerce of the United States for 1887*, pp. 199, 215 285–286, 377.

at New Orleans with the volume of all exports, foreign and coastwise, emphasizes how little was retained, at least until the mid-1840's. Of the subsequent growth in the residual a good part consists of sugar and molasses either consumed directly in the South or exported up-river to Ohio Valley points. With annual value of sugar and molasses production at level of $20 million by the 1850's, and with coastwise exports of these not much more than half of output, the significance of this distortion is readily apparent.

[7] According to the valuations of western produce at New Orleans published along with the annual summaries of the trade of that city in the October number of *Hunt's Merchants' Magazine* for the respective years.

Fortunately, over the very interval in which there is some doubt concerning an increase in consumption of western foodstuffs, it is possible to be more precise. The records kept at New Orleans from 1842 on include re-exports of western produce to both foreign and coastwise ports; these compared with total receipts of such foodstuffs, give an exact notion of the quantity retained. Table 3 presents these data for the interval 1842–1861. From it we can see that the value of produce either retained at New Orleans or shipped coastwise to other southern ports approached one half of total receipts only toward the end of the period, finally reaching a fraction of almost three fourths in 1858–1861. In years of particularly large receipts, 1849 is a good example, the proportion consumed moves inversely, clearly indicating the re-export function of New Orleans. Only in the 1850's, moreover, do coastwise shipments to other southern ports begin to amount to a large fraction of total consumption. In 1842, the value of the produce retained at New Orleans is $1.9 million; that shipped to southern ports is $0.4 million. But in 1854 the corresponding values are $7.7 and $3.5 million.[8] This means that the small residual in New Orleans commerce before 1846 found in Table 2 may be taken as indicative of little *total* southern consumption, not only little consumption at New Orleans.

Such an aggregate result conceals substantial variation in the consumption of particular commodities. Despite some fluctuation, it seems on average about as much flour was sent on as was consumed, with possibly a slight upward trend. In the instance of provisions, on the other hand, an upward trend in consumption is obvious. So, too, do receipts of corn at New Orleans come more and more to represent southern needs. Yet both of these last commodities probably originated in Kentucky and Tennessee in large quantities and hence do not fully represent interregional trade. The consumption of lard and whiskey shows little variation over time—the former being almost wholly re-exported, the latter completely retained. The net result of these divergent patterns was to cushion consumption somewhat against the absolutely declining receipts of western produce at New Orleans in the 1850's. Nevertheless, the consumption data tell a tale similar to Berry's physical receipts index: substantial growth in the 1840's and much more modest advance in the 1850's. Consumption in 1850 dollars was $4.6 million in 1842–1845, $10.0 million in 1850–1853, and $12.3 million in 1858–1861. Even as its staple production proceeded apace the South was not becoming absolutely more reliant upon the West, and, relatively, less so.

These new consumption data permit us now to re-examine the West-South trade with respect to three basic characteristics: its absolute magnitude vis-à-vis other interregional trade, the relative importance of the exports to the West, and the relative importance of the imports to the South. First, we can conclude rather assuredly that the trade was relatively quite small. The $18 million consumption of foodstuffs in 1858–1861, although possibly augmented by imports of other western produce of equivalent size—as suggested by Table 36—is only a third of the exchange between West and East, and for that matter, a smaller proportion of the shipments from the

[8] Calculated from the data underlying Table 3.

TABLE 5. SOUTHERN CONSUMPTION OF WESTERN FOODSTUFFS ([illegible])

| | FLOUR (BARRELS) | PORK (BARRELS) | BACON (HOGS HEADS) | LARD (KEGS) | CORN (SACKS) | WHISKEY (BARRELS) | BEEF (BARRELS) | VALUE (THOUSANDS OF DOLLARS) |
|---|---|---|---|---|---|---|---|---|
| 1842–1845 [a] | | | | | | | | |
| Receipts [b] | 491,836 | 333,232 | 30,856 | 654,063 | 490,169 | 81,537 | 36,023 | 8,275 |
| Exports [c] | 245,542 | 244,115 | 8,012 | 575,974 | 189,573 | 7,274 | 19,835 | 4,823 |
| Consumption [d] | 246,294 | 89,117 | 22,844 | 78,089 | 300,596 | 74,263 | 16,188 | 3,452 |
| Cons./Rec. | 0.50 | 0.27 | 0.74 | 0.12 | 0.61 | 0.91 | 0.45 | 0.42 |
| 1846–1849 | | | | | | | | |
| Receipts [b] | 1,043,949 | 507,219 | 57,760 | 1,204,501 | 1,887,984 | 126,005 | 18,393 | 20,824 |
| Exports [c] | 726,399 | 308,492 | 25,303 | 1,064,975 | 1,446,457 | 15,948 | 49,417 | 13,830 |
| Consumption [d] | 317,550 | 198,727 | 32,457 | 139,526 | 441,527 | 110,057 | 28,976 | 6,994 |
| Cons./Rec. | 0.30 | 0.39 | 0.56 | 0.12 | 0.23 | 0.87 | 0.37 | 0.34 |
| 1850–1853 | | | | | | | | |
| Receipts [b] | 817,244 | 441,235 | 87,378 | 1,005,985 | 1,306,799 | 140,090 | 69,446 | 22,211 |
| Exports [c] | 304,836 | 234,578 | 30,232 | 910,169 | 496,277 | 8,970 | 49,624 | 10,803 |
| Consumption [d] | 512,408 | 206,657 | 57,146 | 95,816 | 810,522 | 131,120 | 19,822 | 11,408 |
| Cons./Rec. | 0.63 | 0.47 | 0.65 | 0.10 | 0.62 | 0.94 | 0.29 | 0.51 |
| 1854–1857 | | | | | | | | |
| Receipts [b] | 989,735 | 325,243 | 67,658 | 702,801 | 1,588,001 | 141,424 | 48,433 | 26,300 |
| Exports [c] | 529,863 | 139,447 | 16,127 | 724,726 | 820,267 | 7,179 | 28,340 | 13,053 |
| Consumption [d] | 459,872 | 185,796 | 51,531 | − 21,925 | 767,734 | 134,245 | 20,093 | 13,247 |
| Cons./Rec. | 0.46 | 0.57 | 0.76 | − 0.03 | 0.48 | 0.95 | 0.41 | 0.50 |
| 1858–1861 | | | | | | | | |
| Receipts [b] | 1,149,695 | 275,246 | 63,910 | 448,381 | 1,820,616 | 139,129 | 42,287 | 24,984 |
| Exports [c] | 425,542 | 39,543 | 4,907 | 405,351 | 410,004 | 4,425 | 15,051 | 6,873 |
| Consumption [d] | 724,153 | 235,703 | 59,003 | 43,030 | 1,410,612 | 134,704 | 27,236 | 18,111 |
| Cons./Rec. | 0.63 | 0.86 | 0.92 | 0.10 | 0.77 | 0.97 | 0.64 | 0.72 |

SOURCE: *Hunt's Merchants' Magazine*, VI (1842), 391–392; XI (1844), 419–421; XIII (1845), 370–372; XV (1846), 406–409; XVII (1847), 413–414; XIX (1848), 511–516; XXI (1849), 554–556; XXIII (1850), 536–537; XXV (1851), 602–605; XXVII (1852), 489–492; XXIX (1853), 624–629; XXXI (1854), 475–477; XXXIII (1855), 601–604; XXXV (1856), 474; *New Orleans Price Current*, Sept. 1, 1856; *Hunt's*, XXXVII (1857), 603–607; *New Orleans Price Current*, Sept. 1, 1858; Sept. 1, 1859; *DeBow's Review*, XXIX (1860), 521; *New Orleans Price Current*, Aug. 31, 1861.

[a] 1843 values were unavailable.

[b] Calculated in homogeneous physical units by dividing total value of receipts by price of specified physical unit.

[c] Foreign exports plus coastwise shipments to Boston, New York, Philadelphia, and Baltimore. Unspecified coastwise shipments were credited to southern ports, and hence consumption.

[d] Consumption equals receipts minus exports.

North to the South.[9] Before the 1850's, the small residual receipts at New Orleans contradict an appreciable exchange. It therefore does not appear that southern demands for foodstuffs were an important mechanism by which increasing exports of staples from the South transmitted a dynamic impulse to the West.

More direct evidence on this point, namely the proportion of selected western exports taken off by the South is available for the period after 1839. As Table 4 brings out, southern demands for every western product except whiskey were in a substantial minority by 1849. When weighted by relative values the meager extent of the southern market is yet more obvious. As early as 1839, at its peak, southern demands took off less than a fifth of western exports of foodstuffs. When receipts at New Orleans rallied owing to favorable river conditions or export demands, as they did both in 1849 and 1857, they were offset by increasing exports. That, after all, was the significance of New Orleans—as a gateway, not a terminal. Moreover, in the one important area in which southern demands held to a high level, provisions, the border states came to play a larger part. In 1853 Louisville contributed a fifth of the pork and bacon received at New Orleans, with additional amounts from the Cumberland and Tennessee rivers; in 1860 the share of Louisville alone increased to a third.[10]

If relatively unimportant to the West, the imports were minute compared with production of foodstuffs within the South itself. The 1842 corn consumption of 241,049 sacks (= 2 bushels each) may be compared with an 1839 crop in the South of 225,000,000 bushels; or the 1850 consumption of 763,014 sacks with 1849 production of almost 300,000,000 bushels; or 1860 consumption of 1,590,131 sacks against 1859 output of more than 340,000,000 bushels. Domestic production was augmented by imports to the extent of less than 1 percent in each of these years. Wheat imports represented a larger addition to productive capacity, to be sure, but still a modest one in absolute terms. Entering principally as flour (reckoned at 5 bushels to the barrel), imports of wheat amounted to 960,000 bushels in 1842, 2,600,000 in 1850, and 4,250,-000 in 1860. Output reached 25,000,000 bushels in 1839, 20,000,000 in 1849, and 38,000,000 in 1859. At best, due to the poor crop of 1849, imports supplemented production by 13 percent; but by 1860, due to a resurgence in southern wheat output during the simultaneous cotton boom, the ratio actually declined slightly to 11 percent. In meat products, the relative importance of external supplies is akin to the independence displayed in the case of corn. The 1850 census credited to the South more than $45,000,-000 in slaughtered animals, an estimate that must be raised beyond $100,-000,000 to compensate for understatement. The year 1850 saw imports of pork, bacon, and beef amounting to only $3,600,000. In 1860 the ratio of imports, similarly calculated, managed to climb only to the 5 percent mark.[11]

Only one possibility remains to refute these contentions. That would be a substantial flow of western produce directly to southern sites bypassing

[9] In "Antebellum Trade," eastern consumption of western products is estimated at $108 million. This is after an allowance for export of foodstuffs abroad; the gross flow is a larger $146 million.

[10] Kohlmeier, *Old Northwest*, pp. 118, 202.

[11] Census data for corn and wheat as reprinted in Gray, *History of Agriculture*, II, 1040. Delaware, Maryland, and Missouri are excluded in the totals given in the text. Value

New Orleans. It certainly does not seem to have occurred on the western rivers. The proportion of shipments from Cincinnati to downriver ports other than New Orleans is of no significance. In 1848–1850 less than 1 percent of the provisions shipped to New Orleans were destined to such other ports; of corn the ratio is 10 percent, but Cincinnati was not the leading forwarder; of flour, another growing export of St. Louis, the proportion is about 20 percent on average.[12] On the other side of the transaction, receipts at other southern cities do not appear to be substantial. Kohlmeier comments about shipments up the Cumberland and Tennessee rivers in the following vein: "they supplied a local market in western Kentucky and were comparatively limited in quantity." [13] The Vicksburg and Jackson Railroad is reported to have carried 297,119 pounds of meat from the river city to the interior in 1850.[14] This is equivalent to 371 hogsheads compared to receipts of 250,000 hogsheads at New Orleans in the same year. The Memphis and Charleston Railroad reported receipts from through freight eastward as $35,573.13. Converting to tons carried, this is only about 4,000 tons, an insignificant quantity.[15]

The underlying economics make shipment via New Orleans far more probable. With a predominantly downstream commerce, the trip upstream was necessary in any event and back haulage was presumably accommodated at low rates. The very marketing of the cotton in New Orleans also meant that factors could easily purchase the required foodstuffs there. In this instance, logic seems to have a counterpart in fact. The *Report on Internal Commerce for 1887* remarks: "There was no trade between the Western cities and the Southern plantations, very little even with the towns; it all paid tribute to New Orleans. . . . Of these shipments up-stream over 75 percent, strange to say, were articles which had previously been sent downstream." [16]

Finally, this was before efficient rail contact had been established between West and South. Gauge differences, lack of bridging, and actual physical breaks meant that southern railroads were "completely without rail connections with any other part of the nation." [17] Thus the range of alternative direct marketing routes from the West to the South was quite limited. While the Western and Atlantic Railroad could conceivably have received some shipments via a complicated routing on the Cumberland River, and then the Nashville and Chattanooga Railroad, the commerce was necessarily small because water shipments up the Cumberland were limited. In describing the increase in flour and grain brought to Charleston after 1852 by the

---

of slaughtered meat products from *Eighth Census, Agriculture,* pp. 187, 191. Wheat was converted to flour at 5 bushels to the barrel after an allowance of 12.5 percent of the crop for seed. The relationship between reported and actual values is derived from the national totals estimated by Gallman, "Commodity Output," p. 46.

12 Calculated from *Hunt's Merchants' Magazine,* XXIII (1850), 542.

13 Kohlmeier, *Old Northwest,* p. 202.

14 From a contemporary account quoted in John H. Moore, *Agriculture in Ante-Bellum Mississippi* (New York, 1958), p. 111.

15 *American Railroad Journal,* XXXIII (1860), 840–841. The receipts were converted to tons on the assumption of a 3- to 4-cent ton-mile charge and a length of road of 271 miles.

16 *Report on Internal Commerce for 1887,* p. 205.

17 Taylor and Neu, *Railroad Network,* p. 48.

TABLE 4. THE IMPORTANCE OF THE SOUTHERN MARKET TO THE WEST (PERCENT)

| COMMODITY | PROPORTION OF WESTERN EXPORTS SHIPPED VIA NEW ORLEANS | | | | | | PROPORTION OF RECEIPTS OF WESTERN PRODUCE AT NEW ORLEANS CONSUMED IN THE SOUTH | | | | | | PROPORTION OF WESTERN EXPORTS CONSUMED IN THE SOUTH | | | | | |
|---|---|---|---|---|---|---|---|---|---|---|---|---|---|---|---|---|---|---|
| | 1839 | 1844 | 1849 | 1853 | 1857 | 1860 | 1842 | 1844 | 1849 | 1853 | 1857 | 1860 | 1839 [a] | 1844 | 1849 | 1853 | 1857 | 1860 |
| Flour | 53 | 30 | 31 | 27 | 34 | 22 | 42 | 50 | 30 | 60 | 41 | 86 | 22 | 16 | 9 | 14 | 14 | 19 |
| Meat products | 51 | 66 | 50 | 38 | 28 | 24 | 41 | 31 | 34 | 62 | 69 | 95 | 21 | 19 | 17 | 24 | 19 | 23 |
| Corn | 98 | 90 | 39 | 37 | 32 | 19 | 46 | 70 | 21 | 44 | 65 | 91 | 45 | 63 | 8 | 16 | 21 | 17 |
| Whiskey | 96 | 95 | 67 | 53 | 48 | 40 | 80 | 95 | 89 | 90 | 93 | 98 | 77 | 90 | 60 | 48 | 45 | 39 |
| Total foodstuffs | 49 | 44 | 40 | 31 | 27 | 17 | 37 | 38 | 29 | 52 | 52 | 85 | 18 | 17 | 12 | 16 | 14 | 14 |

SOURCE: Proportion of western exports shipped via New Orleans: Kohlmeier, *Old Northwest*, pp. 33, 52–53, 83–85, 116–117, 146–148, 191–193, 248–249. Meat products include livestock (estimated for 1839–1853 as described in the technical appendix to "Antebellum Trade"). Some of the percentages deviate from Kohlmeier's text declarations due to divergence between those and absolute quantities separately given; the differences are small. Total foodstuffs include wheat, which is not shown separately. Current western prices have been used to weight the specific commodities.

Proportion of New Orleans receipts consumed in the South: Table 3. Meat products here are the weighted sum of bacon, pork, and beef. Total foodstuffs include lard and whiskey, but exclude wheat. This incomparability with panel 1 is not important.

Proportion of western exports consumed in the South: Panel 1 times panel 2.

[a] Exports for 1839 via New Orleans times 1842 retention ratio.

---

South Carolina Railroad, Derrick explains the result as a consequence of more efficient rail connections not to the West, but to northern Georgia, Alabama, and Tennessee.[18]

One further path bypassing New Orleans, namely coastal re-exports from northern cities, has recently been suggested as a challenge to these findings.[19] Although a possibility, it is not one that should be given undue weight. In the first instance, the growing shipments from New Orleans to other southern ports during the 1850's are indicative of increasing reliance upon a New Orleans route rather than the reverse. Secondly, there were actual exports to the North of corn and flour from Norfolk and Charleston during the decade, a situation which would lead to the belief that the return flow was limited and partially canceled, in any event.[20] Finally, the magnitude of the shipments required to alter the condition of substantial southern self-sufficiency would be quite large. In 1860, Baltimore, probably the prime source of supply to South Atlantic cities, exported 1,358,033 bushels of corn coastwise, 120,000 barrels of flour, and 562,339 bushels of wheat. Even if all went South—which we know from Boston receipts a goodly part did not—total imports of western corn would have supplemented output by less than 1½ percent, and reliance upon external supplies of wheat would not have exceeded 15 percent.[21] Some additional exports to the South beyond those received via New Orleans are certain, but it is doubtful whether they were large enough to matter.

## 2] The Expansion of the Cotton Belt: 1815–60

BEFORE the War of 1812 cotton production had developed mainly in regions already settled, and during the war there was probably little expansion of settlement in the South. The frontiers were endangered by

18 Samuel M. Derrick, *Centennial History of the South Carolina Railroad* (Columbia, S.C., 1930), pp. 211–212.

19 Fogel raised the point in his discussion of my "Antebellum Trade," in the *American Economic Review*, XIV (May 1964), 377–389. For a fuller reply see my "Postscript," in Ralph Andreano's forthcoming *New Perspectives on American Economic Development*.

20 See the Boston Board of Trade reports at the end of the 1850's for some receipts of corn and flour from southern ports. For exports from Charleston and Norfolk see *De Bow's Review*, XXIX (1860), 526, and *Hunt's Merchants' Magazine*, XLII (1860), 480.

21 For Baltimore exports see the *Eleventh Annual Report of the Baltimore Board of Trade for 1860* (Baltimore, 1861), pp. 21–56. From the Boston reports it appears that perhaps as much as half of the Baltimore flour and a quarter of the corn found their way to that city.

the Indians, and the market for Southern products severely restricted. The low prices from 1809 to 1814 inclusive probably served to discourage expansion. From 1815 to 1819, however, prices of cotton averaged nearly double the prices of the preceding period; it was easy to become rich in a few years, and "there were planters, who had thirty and forty thousand dollars a year, as the income of their crop." These conditions supplied the stimulus which initiated a period of unprecedented expansion. Cotton production rapidly expanded and became the vehicle for the introduction of Anglo-Saxon civilization into thousands of square miles. . . . The principal outlines of the Cotton Belt were formed in the twenty-five years from 1815 to 1840, with the exception of Texas. Even there the industry had made considerable headway, which appears graphically for the first time in 1849.

At the outbreak of the War of 1812 the principal centers of settlement in Alabama were in the neighborhood of Mobile; the post of St. Stephens, on the lower Tombigbee, established by Tories during the Revolution; and a group of settlements in Madison County in the Tennessee River valley, occupied by Georgia planters in 1809. The St. Stephens group were handicapped in marketing their products because of the Spanish occupancy of Mobile. Most of what is now Alabama, Mississippi, and Arkansas was still in possession of Indian tribes. The territory in southwest Mississippi ceded to Great Britain by the Choctaws was confirmed to the United States by the treaty of Fort Adams (1801). It comprised a small territory between the Mississippi and a line running for a short distance east of Vicksburg almost due south of the 31st parallel. In 1805 the Choctaws ceded a broad strip about fifty miles wide running eastward from the eastern boundary of the Fort Adams cession and nearly parallel with the line of 31 degrees north latitude. The successful Indian campaigns of Andrew Jackson opened up the fertile canebrake lands of the western half of central Alabama. In 1814 the territory between the Tombigbee and Coosa rivers and also the territory southeast of the Coosa were ceded by the Creeks. This acquisition was supplemented by the Chickasaw and Cherokee cessions in the Fall of 1816, which added a large strip in western Alabama between the Tombigbee and Tuscaloosa rivers, extending northward and broadening out to include the greater part of northern Alabama south of the Tennessee river. Cessions by the Choctaws in the same year added a large strip in southern Alabama, though not a region that proved well adapted to commercial production of cotton. In 1818 was effected the cession of the greater part of Arkansas south of the Arkansas river, including a portion of northern Louisiana. Most of the remainder of Arkansas had been acquired by treaty in 1808. In 1819 the Choctaws ceded a large block of territory, including much of the Yazoo Delta. The presence of Indian tribes for some years longer prevented progress of settlement in western Georgia, eastern Alabama, and much of eastern Mississippi.

## DEVELOPMENT OF ALABAMA AND WESTERN GEORGIA

The southern half of Alabama includes a number of physiographic regions of widely contrasting adaptability to cotton growing. Along the southern border of the State a strip of territory varying in width from twenty to sixty miles consisted largely of pine hills, open rolling pine woods, and pine flats. The same type of country was comprised in the southeastern portion of Mississippi and several parishes in southeastern Louisiana. Before 1830 the region maintained a considerable population and a few plantations; but after the opening of the rich lands in the central part of Alabama the planting population was largely drawn away. By 1840, as we have noted, the region was inhabited mainly by a population engaged largely in herding supplemented by farming for domestic consumption and here and there the production of small quantities of cotton. North of this sandy country is a broad belt of uplands running parallel with it, averaging in width about fifty miles and containing about 8,000 square miles. The original timber growth consisted of oak and hickory, interspersed with long-leaf pine, which was more abundant in the southern portion of the belt, decreasing gradually toward the north. The soil is less sandy and more fertile in the northern two thirds of the region, which was found well adapted to cotton. In the western portion of this belt is a hilly, calcareous region, belonging to the tertiary, comprising an area of about 1,200 square miles.

North of this region is the rich black prairie of central Alabama, which extends in a belt from east to west averaging about thirty miles in width. Near the Mississippi line the belt curves to the northwest and extends northward into northeastern Mississippi. A large proportion of the area consists of heavy, black clay, containing large quantities of disintegrated limestone, and when in a virgin condition contained abundant amounts of phosphorus, potash, and humus. Although the region as a whole was called a prairie, some of it was wooded. The early settlers found that cotton tended to suffer seriously from rust on the prairie itself, which, however, was extremely productive in corn and grass. Settlers were advised to select their farms so as to contain some woodland and some prairie. The tide of settlers began to enter this new region during the second and third decades, coming from eastern Georgia, the Carolinas, Virginia, and middle Tennessee. An examination of the tract books of certain counties of the calcareous belt indicates that prior to 1830 settlers had largely occupied the wooded bottom lands, not having yet learned how to deal with conditions in the prairie. However, between this time and 1837 the region was rapidly occupied, and by the latter year uncleared lands were selling at $35 an acre, the cost of clearing requiring an additional $15. The region as a whole comprised one of the most productive cotton areas in the South, and its rapid development is reflected in statistics of cotton production from southern Alabama which averaged annually about 11,000 bales from 1818 to 1820 inclusive, 46,000 from 1822 to 1824; 80,000 from 1827 to 1829; and 195,000 from 1834 to 1836.

In the extreme northern part of Alabama the new settlers came upon the fertile lands of the Tennessee River valley. In 1806 the Cherokees ceded a large part of this region, as far south as the Tennessee river, bounded by that river on the west and extending eastward to a line running from Chickasaw Old Fields to the most easterly source of Duck River, with the exception of a small reservation about Muscle Shoals. Although practically unsettled in 1810, Limestone and Madison counties contained by 1820 a free population of 27,352 and a slave population of 11,541. The following year it was estimated that the product of the "Big Bend of Tennessee River" would be not far short of 30,000 bales. In 1821 the product of north Alabama was estimated at 50,000 bales. This part of Alabama suffered a serious disadvantage in that its products could reach market only by being carried down the Tennessee river to the Ohio and thence to New Orleans, a distance of about fifteen hundred miles. Most of the imports were brought from the East to Pittsburgh by wagon, thence down the Ohio, and up the Cumberland and Tennessee. The region was separated from the plantation regions of central Alabama by the rugged lands of northern Alabama, occupied largely by small self-sufficing farmers with little commercial agriculture. There was not much commercial intercourse between the two plantation regions, for central Alabama shipped its products to Mobile by way of the numerous rivers tributary to the Gulf. Near the close of the ante bellum period the commercial isolation of northern Alabama was partly overcome by the construction of the Mobile and Ohio Railway.

Between 1820 and 1830 the cotton area of Georgia was greatly enlarged. In 1821 a large area between the Ocmulgee and the Flint rivers, ceded by the Creeks, was thrown open to settlement. Five years later a prolonged controversy between the Creeks, the State of Georgia, and the United States was brought to an end by the further cession of the territory between the Flint and the Chattahoochee rivers. By 1830 settlement in middle Georgia had extended to the western border of the State, and the area was rapidly peopled during the next decade.

### EXPANSION OF COTTON PRODUCTION ALONG THE LOWER MISSISSIPPI AND RED RIVERS

Before 1820 there appears to have been no unusually rapid development in the old plantation region of Louisiana. At that time the region produced some cotton, in addition to the main staple, sugar, but in the late twenties and early thirties turned almost completely to sugar production. In the early years of the century the old French plantation region between Baton Rouge and New Orleans was already the admiration of travellers. Although within a few years the region had been enriched by the huge profits from sugar production, there still remained much of the dignity and simplicity of the older régime. In 1818 a traveller wrote of this region:

> The plantations within these limits are superb beyond description. Some of them resemble villages. The dwelling houses of the planters are not inferior to any in the United States, either with respect to size, architecture, or the manner in which they are furnished. The gardens, and yards contiguous to them, are formed and decorated with much taste. The cotton, sugar, and ware houses are very large, and the buildings for the slaves are well finished. The latter buildings are, in some cases, forty or fifty in number, and each of them will accomodate ten or twelve persons. The plantations are very extensive, and on some of them there are hundreds of negroes. The planters here derive immense

> profits from the cultivation of their estates. The yearly income from them is from 20,000 to 30,000 dollars. . . .
>
> About seventy miles below Baton Rouge, the country is wonderfully fine. No description of mine can do justice to the appearance of its principal establishments. There are here the most superb dwelling houses. They are second to none in size, architecture, or decorations. The gardens attached to them are spacious, and elegantly ornamented with orange and fig trees. At a little distance from them are vast buildings, occupied for sugar mills and cotton presses, and for the storage of the immense productions of the plantations. Near these, are from fifty to one hundred neat buildings, for the negroes, beyond them are spacious and elegant oblong fields, constituting one hundred acres, and under the highest state of cultivation.

In 1810 the group of eight parishes which later comprised the most important sugar producing region contained 7,704 whites and 4,662 slaves. Ten years later the population had increased to 14,161 free people and 10,861 slaves. The rapid development of the western side of the lower Mississippi began in the decade 1820 to 1830, when the tide of planters from the Eastern States began to pour into the country. The initial antagonism between the earlier inhabitants and the newcomers was gradually mitigated by the advantages of rising land values. Woodbury estimated the product of Louisiana at only 2,000,000 pounds for 1811 and at 10,000,000 for 1821; but in 1826 it reached 38,000,000 and eight years later, 62,000,000.

While immigration from the Eastern Colonies had been slow to venture into the old and well established French civilization on the west side of the river, it was early attracted to the English settlements of the Natchez region. This ancient nucleus became the earliest section of extensive Anglo-Saxon expansion in the lower Mississippi. As late as 1772 there were but 78 families scattered through the territory surrounding Natchez, but by 1785 the population of the district had increased to 1,550 and by 1788 to 2,679, mainly composed of settlers from the Atlantic seaboard. This was a region of pioneer farmers who sold small quantities of tobacco and maintained a diversified and largely self-sufficing economy. When tobacco began to suffer severe competition from Kentucky and Tennessee, the region turned eagerly to cotton. By 1808 there was a well developed plantation system, devoted almost exclusively to cotton and dependent on Kentucky and Tennessee for flour, pork, beef, and horses. The wealthier planters had already built comfortable houses and were beginning to enjoy some of the elegancies of living, although some of the old pioneer conditions still continued. In the period 1800–1810 the free population of four counties of the region—Adams, Claiborne, Jefferson, and Wilkinson—increased from 2,403 to 10,542; and the slave population from 2,257 to 11,631. As late as 1827, however, on account of lack of an adequate levee system, there was little development on the eastern side of the river from a little below Natchez to Baton Rouge. The cotton crop of Mississippi, according to Woodbury, was 10,000,000 pounds by 1821. It increased threefold in the next five years, and more than eightfold by 1834.

Between 1810 and 1820 the so-called Attakapas and Opelousas country in southern Louisiana was beginning to attract the attention of eastern cotton planters. In the extensive prairies previously occupied by herds of cattle owned by easy-going Creole planter-herdsmen, the eastern immigrant found the establishment of a profitable cotton plantation unusually easy. There were "no forests to cut down, . . . no chopping, no grubbing." The planter had "nothing to do, but to build his house, inclose his field and commence ploughing." The high yields of the virgin lands combined with high prices of cotton in the years immediately following the War of 1812 enabled planters to earn $500 to $600 per hand in cotton production and up to $800 or more in sugar.

Similarly favorable conditions stimulated rapid development in the alluvial lands of Red River. By 1819 the planters near Alexandria, who had already made large fortunes raising cotton and sugar, were selling their lands for $40 to $50, and moving to the rich alluvial lands on the Ouachita or farther up Red River, which could be bought for $5 to $10. Near Natchitoches navigation was obstructed by a huge raft, originally from 128 to 160 miles in length. In 1833 the United States Government undertook its removal. In the first season the lower hundred miles, which was in a state of decay, was easily cleared as far as Shreveport, but the removal of the upper portion was not entirely completed until 1850. In 1839 the Indians were removed from the region immediately above the raft, but for some years settlers had been rapidly occupying the fertile lands of the upper Red river and its tributaries in Louisiana, southwestern Arkansas, and northeastern Texas. Before the Civil War this stream of settlers had extended as far west as Fannin County, Texas, whence cotton was hauled by wagon or shipped by boat to Shreveport. Before the annexation of Texas, southwestern Arkansas was the *ultima Thule* of southern agricultural expansion in the United States, and even in 1834 pioneer life there resembled in essential details the pioneer life of Kentucky and Tennessee before the close of the eighteenth century.

Whereas the lower prices of cotton for the crop years 1819 to 1832 inclusive, and especially 1826 to 1832, brought hardships and depression to the older cotton producing regions, it was still possible in the newer lands to produce cotton, though at somewhat lessened profits. Consequently in these periods immigration to the Southwest does not appear to have been materially retarded. Exports from New Orleans increased from 48,000 bales in 1819 and 156,000 in 1822 to 426,000 in 1830–31. Of the receipts for 1829–30, amounting to 362,969 bales, 179,094 were credited to Louisiana and Mississippi, 163,295 to northern Alabama and Tennessee, 3,512 to Arkansas, 193 to Missouri, and 7 to Illinois. The remainder consisted of transshipments.

When the Chickasaws surrendered title in 1818 to the region in Tennessee between the Tennessee and the Mississippi, another fertile area was made available for cotton. As early as 1816 some 1,500 bales were shipped to New Orleans from west Tennessee, but the beginnings of rapid development in this region did not occur until about a decade later. By 1840 receipts of cotton at Memphis were about 35,000 bales.

## SPECULATIVE MANIA OF THE THIRTIES

The decade 1830 to 1840 was a period of remarkable expansion. The removal of the tribes across the Mississippi between 1832 and 1834 opened to settlement large areas in northwestern Georgia and eastern Alabama held by the Creeks, the territories on the border of Alabama and Mississippi inhabited by the Choctaws, and the Chickasaw country in northern and northwestern Mississippi.

The opening of these new territories and a fuller realization of the opportunities in areas previously opened but not yet fully occupied paved the way for the craze for speculation which was stimulated by the easy credit and the period of high prices of cotton beginning with the crop year 1833–34. According to a traveller who visited Alabama just before the panic of 1837, the profit on cotton planting was commonly 35 per cent. One planter whom she met bought a plantation for $15,000, valued it two years later at $65,000, and in the second year expected to receive between $50,000 and $60,000 for his growing crop. A mania developed for buying land and slaves, fostered by the employment of State credit in the promotion of banks. During the years 1834 to 1837 inclusive $80,321,000 was invested in bank capital in Mississippi, Louisiana, Arkansas, Florida, and Alabama, over three fourths of the total in the first two States. Of the total, $32,321,000 consisted of State loans or private loans guaranteed by the States. The new banks loaned money lavishly on land, slaves, and cotton, at inflated values. In Alabama taxes were repealed in the belief that profits from the State bank would meet all State expenses.

Immigrants poured in from the older planting States: planters whose lands were exhausted, bankrupts with nothing to lose, and younger sons sent out from the parental roof with a dozen slaves to make a fortune in the new country. In many cases planters in the older States established plantations in the Southwest under the supervision of kinsmen or trusted overseers, without themselves removing thither. The psychology of this period of extravagant expansion has been so well portrayed by a contemporary that his description is worth quoting:

> A new theory, not found in the works on political economy, was broached. It was found out that the prejudice in favor of the metals (brass excluded) was an absurd superstition; and that, in reality, anything else, which the parties interested in giving it currency chose, might serve as a representative of value and medium of exchange of property; . . .
>
> . . . Money, or what passed for money, was the only cheap thing to be had. Every cross-road and every avocation presented an opening,—through which a fortune was seen by the adventurer in near perspective. Credit was a thing of course. To refuse it—if the thing was ever done—were an insult for which a bowie-knife were not a too summary or exemplary a means of redress. The State banks were issuing their bills by the sheet, like a patent steam printing-press *its* issues; and no other

> showing was asked of the applicant for the loan than an authentication of his great distress for money. . . .
>
> Under this stimulating process prices rose like smoke. Lots in obscure villages were held at city prices; lands, bought at the minimum cost of government, were sold at from thirty to forty dollars per acre, and considered dirt cheap at that.

The sudden collapse in 1837 not only ruined the mushroom banks but sent thousands of planters into bankruptcy, while many others fled precipitately to Texas to escape the execution of judgments on their slaves.

## RAPID EXPANSION OF COTTON PRODUCTION DURING THE DECADE 1830–1840

The speculative bubble called into cultivation so large an area of cotton land as to overwhelm the markets. Much of the land, it is true, was bought for mere speculation; but enough was put in cultivation to increase production enormously. From the three-year period centering on 1832–33 to the three-year period centering on 1841–42, New Orleans exports increased from 394,000 bales to 873,000; Mobile exports from 135,000 to 371,000. On the other hand, in the South Atlantic States as a whole the industry was nearly or quite stationary. South Carolina increased from 194,000 to 280,000, possibly by reason of larger shipments from Georgia to Charleston by the Hamburg-Charleston Railway; Georgia decreased from 269,000 to 225,000, in spite of the expansion in western Georgia; and North Carolina and Virginia decreased from 68,000 bales to 27,000 bales.

During the decade a number of newly occupied regions increased rapidly in population and production. The free population of seven counties in central Alabama increased from 22,613 in 1830 to 60,514 in 1840; and the slave population from 14,427 to 65,204. The population of three Mississippi counties—Noxubee, Lowndes, and Monroe—increased from 7,034 to 33,738. The settlement of southwestern Tennessee continued with great rapidity, and the same stream of population spread across the border into the fertile silt loam uplands of northern Mississippi, also tributary to Memphis. The receipts of cotton at Memphis increased from 35,000 bales in 1840 to 150,000 in 1850, and 361,000 in 1860. Cotton production was also rapidly expanded in the rich black prairie lands in northeastern Mississippi, tributary to Mobile by way of the Tombigbee river. The alluvial lands bordering the Yazoo and the Big Black, in the west central portion of the State, were settled with great rapidity, and there was also a substantial increase in the population of the older counties in the vicinity of Natchez. There was a steady increase of population in the alluvial lands of the Red river and the Mississippi in Louisiana, and scattered plantations had been established along the west bank of the Mississippi in Arkansas and in northern Louisiana. Another important extension of the plantation system during the same decade occurred in a wide area of southwestern Georgia, tributary to the Chattahoochee and Flint rivers. During the decade six counties in this region increased in population as a group from 5,678 to 42,269.

Although for the most part a region of good cotton soils, east central Mississippi did not become a well developed plantation region until after the building of the Mobile and Ohio Railroad. It was necessary to haul products long distances to the Tombigbee or south to the upper waters of the Pearl river. Small quantities of cotton were grown for market, and some grain was produced, but, like the counties of southeastern Mississippi, the region was largely devoted to stock-raising, being commonly known as the "cow-counties."

. . . . . . . . . . . . . . .

### ROUNDING OUT OF THE COTTON BELT AFTER 1840

Although by 1840 the main outlines of the "Cotton Kingdom" were filled in, except in Texas, the stream of slaveholders continued to pour into the newer regions not yet well settled. Development between 1840 and 1860 was especially rapid in central and northern Mississippi; along the Mississippi river, especially on the western bank; and along the streams flowing into the Mississippi from the west, including the Ouachita, Arkansas, White, and St. Francis river systems. In the thirties the bottom lands of the Arkansas were still in the log-cabin stage of development. Before 1860 these alluvial areas contained a well established plantation economy, although development was still far from complete. Considerable shipments of cotton occurred from the alluvial area of southeastern Missouri, but this region did not see an important development until many years after the Civil War.

Before 1840 a few scattering plantations and fragmentary levees had been established in the great alluvial area in Mississippi known as the Yazoo Delta, but the region was still largely unoccupied because subject to overflow. The great flood of 1842 showed the need for concerted action, and county supervisors began to organize levee districts. The flood of 1858 made it necessary to enlarge and consolidate these local systems, and a district was formed to include practically the whole of the Delta. The levees thus constructed withstood the great floods of 1861 and 1862, but the system was seriously disorganized and impaired by military occupation.

Nearly all the important plantation districts west of the Georgia-Alabama boundary enjoyed a substantial increase in population in the decades between the beginning of commercial cotton or sugar cultivation and 1860. In nearly all of these districts there was also a steady increase in percentage of slave population, representing not only an expansion of the plantation system and a displacement of the general farmers who had earlier settled in these regions but also probably an increase in the size of slaveholdings.

The expansion of the plantation system up to 1840 was in the Gulf plains —a region well provided with navigable streams, the use of which was considerably facilitated by the development of steam navigation, beginning on the Mississippi in 1816. The further rounding out of the Cotton Belt was greatly facilitated by the building of railroads. In 1831 a railroad five miles in length was built from New Orleans to Lake Pontchartrain, and in the same year a road from Richmond, Virginia, to Chesterfield—a distance of thirteen miles. In 1833 a railway was completed from Hamburg, South Carolina, via Augusta, to Charleston. By 1840 a considerable number of short local lines had been completed or were under construction, destined during the next two decades to be pieced together into continuous lines leading to strategic commercial centers. By the outbreak of the Civil War the South contained several important trunk lines, connecting many important agricultural regions more effectively with markets.

A significant aspect of railway building was the rivalry of the various ports for the trade of the hinterland. South Carolina and Georgia inaugurated ambitious programs of railway construction as a result of the rivalry of Charleston and Savannah for Western trade. In South Carolina lines were constructed connecting Columbia, Camden, Greenville, Spartanburg, and Abbeville with Charleston; and a branch line was built from Anderson Courthouse to Greenville—a connection which provided a continuous line from Charleston to Knoxville, Tennessee. A line from Columbia to Charlotte, North Carolina, tapped the fertile valleys of the Catawba and Yadkin rivers and furnished Charleston a connection with railways leading to northern cities.

The geographical position of Georgia was central and pivotal, and her railway system was closely connected with those of neighboring States. By 1860 a continuous line, made up of numerous shorter lines, connected Augusta, Georgia, with northern cities, by way of Richmond. The Central Railroad connecting Savannah and Macon, the Georgia Railroad from Augusta to Atlanta, the Western and Atlantic connecting Atlanta with Chattanooga, the Macon and Western, and the Southwestern, supplemented by a number of branch lines, tapped the most important cotton regions of the State, connected Savannah with the farming regions of Tennessee and eastern Alabama, and opened up hitherto undeveloped regions to the advance of commercial agriculture. Alabama was provided important connections with the Georgia railways and the Eastern seaboard by lines from Atlanta to West Point and from Montgomery to West Point. A second Eastern connection was furnished by the construction of the Alabama and Tennessee Railway from Selma, Alabama, to Rome, Georgia. A railroad from Mobile to Girard was planned to connect the Alabama port with the Georgia railways at Columbus.

There was also considerable development in the other cotton States or in areas with which they were economically interrelated. In Tennessee railroads were constructed uniting Nashville and Memphis with Chattanooga, Knoxville, and their eastern connections. The Mobile and Ohio was designed to connect the city of Mobile with northeastern Mississippi and the rich valley of the Tennessee river, the trade of which had hitherto traversed the river route to New Orleans, and ultimately to furnish a continuous route to St. Louis and Chicago by way of the Illinois Central. Connection was supplied with Louisville by the building of the Louisville and Nashville. In Mississippi a railroad was constructed connecting Vicksburg with Brandon, and finally with Selma, Alabama, thus furnishing direct connection between the Mississippi river and the eastern seaboard. In Arkansas a railroad was built connecting Little Rock with Memphis, and another connecting Fulton, on the Red river, with Gaines Landing, on the Mississippi.

The building of railroads stimulated the expansion of cotton into large areas hitherto not suitable for commercial production. Another result was the diversion of trade from New Orleans, especially that from east and middle Tennessee, which henceforth went to Mobile or to Charleston, Savannah, and Richmond. The trade from the upper Mississippi to New Orleans was cut off by construction of the trunk lines and development of the lake route. New Orleans commercial authorities consoled themselves with the belief that they could still count on much of the bulky produce of the Mississippi valley and that the rapid increase of production in the valley would compensate for diverted trade. A railway convention held at New Orleans in 1851 proposed nothing that could prove of great benefit to the city except the construction of railway connections with the upper Red river.

. . . . . . . . . . . . . . .

After the Texas Revolution [1836] planters with their slaves began to move to Texas in large numbers, settling on the alluvial lands of the Brazos, Trinity, Colorado, and Red rivers. By the late years of the fifth decade regular steamship connection with New Orleans was established, and extension of settlement on the Brazos and Trinity was facilitated by the development of steamboat navigation. From 1840 to 1860, and particularly from 1850 to 1860, the "Texas fever" developed almost into a delirium. Newspapers throughout the South were full of accounts of the wonderful fertility of Texas land, the salubrity of the climate, and the enormous fortunes made in planting cotton. Texas land companies were formed in various parts of the United States, and land speculation, facilitated by the loose land policy of the State, became the order of the day. Throughout the South thousands of planters caught the contagion, sold out their plantations, and moved to Texas. There was also a very substantial immigration of farmers. From 1850 to 1860 the total population increased from 212,592 to 604,215, and the slave population from 58,161 to 182,566; while cotton production increased from 58,072 to 431,463 bales. Before the Civil War, however, the plantation districts were still, for the most part, east of the fertile black prairie. This region, which became the most important cotton producing portion of the State after the Civil War, was occupied principally by herdsmen and small self-sufficing farmers. Its full development awaited the introduction of railroads. The principal plantation districts before 1860 were along the lower courses of the rivers flowing into the Gulf, on the Red river, and in the "oak and hickory" uplands west of the coastal plain.

. . . . . . . . . . . . . . .

# 3] Forces Behind the Movement of the Cotton Belt

## a] DEPLETION OF THE SOIL

THE DESTRUCTIVE character of agricultural methods in the old tobacco regions of Virginia and Maryland has been commented on by almost every writer who has dealt with that section. From an early day the visitor to that Old South was struck with "tumbledown" conditions and returned home to tell of abandoned fields, "worn out by tobacco culture," that spread out everywhere behind the great staple as it sought the "newly-cleared ground." More harsh in condemning the system were the intelligent planters who wrought the ruin, and who, with rising debts, stoically awaited the time when the whole order "would tumble about their ears." All unite in proclaiming the system bad, and the modern investigator finds abundant evidence to support the charges of carelessness, inefficiency, and even wanton destruction.

The fact of soil exploitation has long been known, but the causes for such rapid depletion and the wide-spread and long continued use of methods that permitted it, have not been satisfactorily explained. Some have believed that tobacco is an unusually exhausting crop, quickly reducing the soils upon which it grows; others have stated that the extensive nature of tobacco cultivation made scientific and progressive methods impossible; some few have left the blame with the cultivator, and inferred, at least, that it might be attributed to the easy-going, spendthrift, short-sighted qualities supposedly developed in those who dwell in warmer climes and of which the Southern planters had more than a normal share; while still others turn to that unfailing refuge of those who are puzzled by "things Southern," and charge it to the institution of negro slavery.

There may be truth in some of these explanations, but they fail to reach the fundamental forces that were at work to produce and extend the exhaustive system and send it on, almost unchanged, into the cotton fields of a later day. They fall into error when they assume that southern practices were unique and arose from peculiarly southern characteristics and institutions. They overlook the force of markets in shaping the economic activities of frontier regions and fail to consider certain general conditions that characterize all sections where agriculture predominates. When properly understood the agricultural practices of Virginia and Maryland appear as normal developments with only such variation as geography and markets imposed. They were but one phase of the exploitation of natural resources

---

FROM Avery O. Craven, *Soil Exhaustion as a Factor in the Agricultural History of Virginia and Maryland, 1606–1860,* University of Illinois Studies in the Social Sciences, vol. XIII, no. 1 (Urbana, Ill.: 1926), pp. 11–13, 18–22, and 162–64. Reprinted by permission of the publisher.

which has characterized the occupation of our continent. The story of ruin and recovery in this section forms but a normal chapter in general agricultural history.

There are two distinct problems in the depletion of any soil. The one has to do with those factors which work immediately upon the soil to lower its yielding capacity, while the other deals with those forces which determine the use of such agricultural practices as permit destruction. The one is a problem for the scientific specialist, the other may be of interest to the student of social affairs. Physico-chemical agents deplete soils, but the degree to which these agents operate is determined largely by the crops produced and the methods of cultivation employed—things which are seldom determined by the individual cultivator but are fixed by his markets and profits. Men produce what they can sell and, in the long run, use those methods which yield them the greatest returns. The two problems are entirely different in kind, yet they deal with forces that are so closely linked together as direct agents and conditioning factors that they cannot be entirely separated. The historian who would fairly place the blame for "soil exhaustion" in any region must first have some understanding of the direct agents which work the ruin and of those conditions which determine the intensity of their activity.

Soils serve plants in a four-fold way—as a mechanical support, giving room for the development and spread of roots; as a medium through which oxygen and water are admitted and retained for future use; by furnishing substances to the soil solution from which the plants secure a part of their food materials; and by harboring numerous micro-organisms which assist the plants in making a healthy growth. Other classifications might be offered but the essential facts are that the growth of plants is profoundly affected by the condition of the growing medium as to root room, water and air supply, temperature, supply of nutrients, the presence of favorable organisms and the absence of harmful factors.

It will be noted that a part of these services depends upon the chemical composition of the soil particles, but that the larger part has to do with their mechanical arrangement and other outside conditions. Soils are not "mere casual mixtures of particles, but these are mingled in what amounts to almost a loose state of combination," and intermingled with organic and living substances. The old idea that a soil's fertility is measured by the sum of the chemical properties of its various constituents has given way to a new dynamic conception which takes into consideration the "condition of soil in respect to compound particles and their colloidal properties; the mass and condition of organic matter in the soil; the micro-organic population . . . ; and lastly a number of conditions that are unfavorable to plants by reason of some toxic action on the plant itself or on some of the bacteria essential to the plant as mediators between the crude materials of soil and the substances that can actually be used by the plant in the manufacture of food."

. . . . . . . . . . . . . . .

The question of soil toxicity is one about which there has been, and still is, considerable dispute. The theory that plant roots excrete substances that are harmful to the growth of the same plants or to their near relatives, but not to other plants, was early set forth by DeCandolle. Often disputed, it has been revived by Whitney and Cameron and their associates in the United States Bureau of Soils and, in a modified form, has gained acceptance as one of the forces at work to require the rotation of crops for continued fertility. The present position on the subject, as stated by Russell, is that while most of the elements essential to plants may, under certain conditions, produce a toxic effect, "there is no evidence of the presence of soluble toxins in normally aerated soils sufficiently supplied with plant food and with calcium carbonate, but that toxins may occur in 'sour soils' badly aerated and lacking in calcium carbonate or in other exhausted soils. . . ." The conclusion seems to be, therefore, that where drainage is poor, plowing insufficient, or the addition of organic matter neglected, soils may become toxic under continued planting and deterioration result from this cause.

The relation of soil fungi, protozoa, bacteria and other microorganisms to soil fertility and exhaustion is a matter of growing recognition. Our knowledge of this complex life and its work, either favorable or harmful to plant growth, is as yet decidedly limited. Some of the numerous soil inhabitants in their search for food, decompose an excess of protein and leave it for the growing plant; others alter the physical condition of the soil favorably to the plant, while others decompose toxins which, if allowed to accumulate, would be decidedly harmful. But not all are friendly. Soil fungi, root rots, wilts, etc., are often injurious to such crops as corn, cotton, flax, and tobacco. Some seem to interfere with the work of favorable bacteria and thus do harm—soil protozoa in particular working in this way to lower the productivity of the soil. Much is yet to be learned along this line but enough is known to justify the inclusion of these factors among the important agents of depletion.

These are, in general, the factors which work directly in lowering the yielding power of soils under cultivation. Their effects vary with physical conditions and methods employed, yet they present a constant menace to the fertility of any soil under cultivation and especially those whose crops and methods are ill fitted to their needs. But every soil that is tended is threatened. The farmer who would escape must be ever alert and intelligent and the social order must enable him to take such a course as will give protection.

The newer understanding of fertility and exhaustion, placing greater emphasis upon the factors which are to a degree under the control of the cultivator, adds importance to the second problem in depletion, i.e., why men employ methods which permit of ruin. And here we face not only the individual but also social conditions of which the individual is often the victim. The crops produced and the methods employed, as has been said, are seldom matters of intelligent choosing on the part of the planter. Men may, because of ignorance or habit, ruin their soils, but more often economic or social conditions, entirely outside their control, lead or force them to a treatment of their lands that can end only in ruin. Some men may be less favorably placed than others in the matter of soils, topography, rainfall, etc., and thereby face a more serious and a more constant threat, yet in most cases where practices are uniformly bad, the forces which produce them are of a social nature and appear often enough and universally enough to permit of some general classification.

Frontier communities are, by their very nature, notorious exhausters of their soils. The wants and standards of living of such communities have been developed in older economic regions and they make demands upon the newer sections that cannot be met from normal returns. The first efforts must be spent in producing the things with which to satisfy the primal wants and until exchange can be developed with older economic regions the material standards of life will be set by the natural resources of their immediate surroundings. An early period of simplicity and even lack of comforts may develop a new standard of living, but there will be also a decided effort to create a surplus and find a staple of some kind for that exchange which will widen the field of supply and lift the standard of living set by the available materials. Such exchange, when developed, can seldom be on equal terms and the surplus produced must come from an extravagant spending of the natural resources of the newer community. Seeming abundance of raw materials encourages waste; the lack of capital forbids the economies of production, and the heavier burdens of carriage and marketing fall upon the producer of the raw materials in exchange. The greater the trade, therefore, and the wider the new life which rises upon this exchange, the greater the demands upon the resources of the region until partial exhaustion limits the class who may enjoy the new imports or time brings the home production of things desired.

All the natural resources of frontiers suffer from such pressure, and the soils are no exception. Less spectacular than furs, precious metals, or timber, they, nevertheless, are more universal and are called upon more often to bear the burden of frontier production than any other single agent. The frontier farmer, where a long continued isolation does not force a shiftless self-sufficing life, always struggles to create an agricultural surplus and find a way to market with it. Where he is fortunate enough to find some staple, the demand for which is constant, and the value of which is great enough to pay the burdens of transportation, a single-crop type of agriculture developes and long persists. The one crop with highest value in outside exchange, drives all other major crops from the fields and becomes the object of first endeavor. Early advantages give it a magnified value and habit fixes it as the dominant product of the region long after its first advantages have ceased.

Furthermore, the abundance of land, combined with a scarcity of capital and labor—a condition which characterizes all frontiers—throws the burden of intensified production upon the soil as the cheapest factor. Only the most fertile soils will be used and only those methods employed which give greatest immediate returns regardless of future consequences. The problem is one of rapid spending, not of conservation. The speed with which the privations of the frontier may be passed, depends upon the rapidity with which the riches of the soil may be exploited. The section is most fortunate whose fertility may be most easily spent, and its progress toward a complex life will be most rapid.

This process of exploitation has gone on from one end of our land to the other, and from the earliest times down to the days of the "last American frontier." What sugar production was to the West Indies, tobacco to Virginia and Maryland, cotton to the Lower South, corn to the Mississippi Valley, wheat and flax have been to the Northwest of our own day. And the social order has invariably reached the highest degree of complexity in the shortest period of time where the soils have been spent with the freest hand. If Virginia society early became like that of old England, it was because the people found the means of exploiting their soils; if Massachusetts failed to approximate that standard, too much emphasis should not be placed on Puritan origins. "The American planters and farmers," declared a British traveler through New England in 1775, "are the greatest slovens in Christendom," and then added significantly, "their eyes are fixed upon the present gain, and they are blind to futurity." Seventy-five years later the Wisconsin farmer, who grew wheat crop after wheat crop on his weakening lands, confessed himself a "sloven farmer" but pleaded the necessities of exchange conditions as his excuse. And it is well to remember that the exhausted and abandoned lands behind the advancing frontier were but a counterpart to the mineral waste and charred stumps in the train of the exploiter of mineral wealth or of virgin forest. Frontiers, like those who come to sudden wealth, are inclined to be spendthrifts.

. . . . . . . . . . . . . . .

From this survey of one phase of the agricultural development in Virginia and Maryland a few general conclusions may be drawn. In the first place, the part played by soil depletion in this section must be recognized as constant and important in shaping not only the course of agricultural development but of the larger social-economic order as well. Throughout the colonial period and afterward, agriculture was based upon a single crop produced by exploitive methods which caused yields to decline and lands to reach a condition in which the planters declared them "exhausted." Abandonment took place on a wide scale and the planters always accepted expansion as a matter of course. An agricultural life was developed which was based upon the exploitation of the soil's natural fertility. To the evil of a single crop was added insufficient plowing and shallow cultivation, which, on loose soils and rolling lands and under heavy and concentrated rainfall, invited destructive erosion; a constant replanting of the same crop in the same soils rapidly depleted the available plant food materials and encouraged soil toxicity and the development of harmful soil organisms; and the failure to add organic matter or artificial fertilizers prevented recovery or even the checking of the work of destruction. Expansion was the only escape, and expansion from the small to the large unit and from the older to the newer regions became a normal part of life in the section;

and when expansion became difficult, lowering standards of living, hardening of social lines, and conflict between the various agents in the social, economic and political life, developed.

. . . . . . . . . . . . . . .

The destructive practices of the Old South were, in fact, in the beginning merely the normal product of frontier conditions. The dependence upon a single crop produced by whatever methods gave largest immediate returns regardless of the waste entailed; the thrusting of the burdens of abnormal production upon land because it was more plentiful than either capital or labor; the placing of an exaggerated value upon the crop which first furnished the surplus by which exchange with the outside world was established—all these were typical frontier practices which have characterized all frontiers.

And practices begun by the frontier were continued under the influence of markets and government, and the pressure which they added made the continuance of early practices almost compulsory. Their burdens were adjusted to exploitive production and as long as these burdens remained, new methods could not be introduced. The force of government lessened with the Revolution, but the influence of markets continued to a degree that can be appreciated only when the part which more favorable conditions played in the work of recovery is understood. Here, as in most places, markets and profits determined to a large extent the agricultural practices in vogue.

Such an understanding of causes makes the agricultural practices of the Old South but normal developments under the social and physical conditions which surrounded them. It robs the story of any features that belong to the South alone as a section and rising out of its peculiar institutions and characteristics. The story of soil depletion in this region becomes but a normal chapter in the story of the farmer and his lands wherever he may be in time and in place.

## b] Consequences of Soil Depletion in the Lower South

. . . . . . . . . . . . . . .

The following is a graphic sketch by a native Georgian of the present appearance of what was once the most productive cotton land of the State:—

> The classic hut occupied a lovely spot, overshadowed by majestic hickories, towering poplars, and strong-armed oaks. The little plain on

FROM Frederick Law Olmsted, *The Cotton Kingdom*, vol. II (New York: 1861), pp. 296–99, and 303.

which it stood was terminated, at the distance of about fifty feet from the door, by the brow of a hill, which descended rather abruptly to a noble spring, that gushed joyously forth from among the roots of a stately beech, at its foot. The stream from this fountain scarcely burst into view, before it hid itself in the dark shade of a field of cane, which overspread the dale through which it flowed, and marked its windings, until it turned from sight, among vine-covered hills, at a distance far beyond that to which the eye could have traced it, without the help of its evergreen belt. A remark of the captain's, as we viewed this lovely country, will give the reader my apology for the minuteness of the foregoing description: "These lands," said he, "will never wear out. Where they lie level, they will be just as good, fifty years hence, as they are now." Forty-two years afterwards, I visited the spot on which he stood when he made the remark. The sun poured his whole strength upon the bald hill which once supported the sequestered school-house; many a deep-washed gully met at a sickly bog, where had gushed the limpid fountain; a dying willow rose from the soil which had nourished the venerable beech; flocks wandered among the dwarf pines, and cropped a scanty meal from the vale where the rich cane had bowed and rustled to every breeze, and all around was barren, dreary, and cheerless.

I will quote from graver authority: Fenner's Southern Medical Reports:—

The native soil of Middle Georgia is a rich argillaceous loam, resting on a firm clay foundation. In some of the richer counties, nearly all the lands have been cut down, and appropriated to tillage; a large maximum of which have been worn out, leaving a desolate picture for the traveller to behold. Decaying tenements, red, old hills, stripped of their native growth and virgin soil, and washed into deep gullies, with here and there patches of Bermuda grass and stunted pine shrubs, struggling for subsistence on what was once one of the richest soils in America.

Let us go on to Alabama, which was admitted as a State of the Union only so long ago as 1818.

In an address before the Chunnenuggee Horticultural Society, by Hon. C. C. Clay, Jr., reported by the author in De Bow's "Review," December, 1855, I find the following passage. I need add not a word to it to show how the political experiment of the Carolinas, and Georgia, is being repeated to the same cursed result in young Alabama. The author, it is fair to say, is devoted to the sustentation of Slavery, and would not, for the world, be suspected of favouring any scheme for arresting this havoc of wealth, further than by chemical science:—

I can show you, with sorrow, in the older portions of Alabama, and in my native county of Madison, the sad memorials of the artless and exhausting culture of cotton. Our small planters, after taking the cream off their lands, unable to restore them by rest, manures, or otherwise, are going further west and south, in search of other virgin lands, which they may and will despoil and impoverish in like manner. *Our wealthier planters, with greater means and no more skill, are buying out their poorer neighbors, extending their plantations, and adding to their slave force. The wealthy few, who are able to live on smaller profits, and to give their blasted fields some rest, are thus pushing off the many, who are merely independent.*

Of the twenty millions of dollars annually realized from the sales of the cotton crop of Alabama, nearly all not expended in supporting the producers is reinvested in land and negroes. Thus the white population has decreased, and the slave increased, almost *pari passu* in several counties of our State. In 1825, Madison county cast about 3,000 votes; now she cannot cast exceeding 2,300. *In traversing that county one will discover numerous farmhouses, once the abode of industrious and intelligent freemen, now occupied by slaves, or tenantless, deserted, and dilapidated; he will observe fields, once fertile, now unfenced, abandoned, and covered with those evil harbingers—foxtail and broom-sedge; he will see the moss growing on the mouldering walls of once thrifty villages; and will find "one only master grasps the whole domain" that once furnished happy homes for a dozen white families. Indeed, a country in its infancy, where, fifty years ago, scarce a forest tree had been felled by the axe of the pioneer, is already exhibiting the painful signs of senility and decay, apparent in Virginia and the Carolinas; the freshness of its agricultural glory is gone; the vigour of its youth is extinct, and the spirit of desolation seems brooding over it.*

What inducement has capital in railroads or shops or books or tools to move into districts like this, or which are to become like this? Why, rather, I shall be asked, does it not withdraw more completely? Why do not all, who are able, remove from a region so desolate? Why was not its impoverishment more complete, more simultaneous? How is it that any slaveholders yet remain? The "venerable Edmund Ruffin," president of the Virginia State Agricultural Society, shall answer:

The causes are not all in action at once, and in equal progress. The labours of exhausting culture, also, are necessarily suspended as each of the cultivators' fields is successively worn out. And when tillage so ceases, and any space is thus left at rest, nature immediately goes to work to recruit and replace as much as possible of the wasted fertility, until another destroyer, after many years, shall return, again to waste, and in much shorter time than before, the smaller stock of fertility so renewed. Thus the whole territory, so scourged, is not destroyed at one operation. But though these changes and partial recoveries are continually, to some extent counteracting the labours for destruction, still the latter work is in general progress. It may require (as it did in my native region) more than two hundred years, from the first settlement, to reach the lowest degradation. But that final result is not the less certainly to be produced by the continued action of the causes.

As to the extent to which the process is carried, Mr. Gregg says:

> I think it would be within bounds to assume that the planting capital withdrawn within that period [the last twenty-five years] would, judiciously applied, have drained every acre of swamp land in South Carolina, besides resuscitating the old, worn-out land, and doubling the crops—thus more than quadrupling the productive power of the agriculture of the State.

. . . . . . . . . . . . . . .

The following picture of the condition of Virginia, the great breeding ground of slaves, is drawn by the last governor of that State, Henry A. Wise. It was addressed to a Virginia audience, who testified to its truthfulness.

. . . . . . . . . . . . . . .

> You have had no commerce, no mining, no manufactures.
>
> You have relied alone on the single power of agriculture—and such agriculture! Your sedge-patches outshine the sun. Your inattention to your only source of wealth has scared the very bosom of mother earth. Instead of having to feed cattle on a thousand hills, you have had to chase the stump-tailed steer through the sedge-patches to procure a tough beefsteak.
>
> The present condition of things has existed too long in Virginia. The landlord has skinned the tenant, and the tenant has skinned the land, until all have grown poor together. I have heard a story—I will not locate it here or there—about the condition of the prosperity of our agriculture. I was told by a gentleman in Washington, not long ago, that he was travelling in a county not a hundred miles from this place, and overtook one of our citizens on horseback, with, perhaps, a bag of hay for a saddle, without stirrups, and the leading line for a bridle, and he said: "Stranger, whose house is that?" "It is mine," was the reply. They came to another. "Whose house is that?" "Mine, too, stranger." To a third: "And whose house is that?" "That's mine, too, stranger; but don't suppose that I'm so darned poor as to own all the land about here."

. . . . . . . . . . . . . . .

## c] An Emigrant from Maryland on the Lushness of Louisiana

VIEWS OF LOUISIANA.
TO THE PLANTERS OF MARYLAND AND VIRGINIA.
FROM THE NATIONAL INTELLIGENCER.

[Copied at the particular request of the author.]

ATTAKAPAS, (LOU.) Aug. 6.

I have received several letters during the last year from gentlemen in your states, requesting me to give them some information relative to Louisiana, and particularly of the counties of Attakapas and Opelousas. It appears that this beautiful and interesting section of the United States is but little known. As there are many of you, who have determined to leave your native state and to 'seek your fortunes in a distant land,' I do not think that I can render you a greater service, than by directing you to Attakapas or Opelousas, in Louisiana, and by shewing you the decided advantages which these two counties have over any other part of the United States. In doing it, I will not rely upon *assertions,* but prove it by *facts;* and for this purpose I ask you to read and to reflect upon the statements and observations which I am about to make. I address this publication to you, because the emigrants from your states are generally the owners of negroes; and of all kinds of property the negroes are the most valuable in Louisiana. My observations will be confined solely to Attakapas and Opelousas.

*Soil and Products.*—The lands are generally *prairie,* and a very small portion of woodland for cultivation. The *prairies* are mostly level, but sometimes waving. Nothing can surpass the soft beauty of these prairies. In places for many miles, they are as level as if they had passed under the roller, and as even as if they had been cut by the shears; then again they undulate, resembling the gentle but lofty rolling of the sea, after a storm has subsided. Such is the appearance of that part of the Attakapas situated upon the bayou Fortue, and the river Vermillion, which has been called by a French traveller in his history "*le Paradise du Monde.*" These prairies resemble natural meadows, covered with eternal verdure; they are interspersed here and there with clumps of trees and groves of timber. The banks of the bayous and rivers which flow in every direction, are covered with woods, filled with the sweetest songsters of the groves. It is in these prairies, some of which are 150 miles in length, the large flocks of horses and horned cattle range. The soil is very rich and produces beyond any that has yet been tried, some fields having been in cultivation for forty years in succession, without any diminution of their strength; this is owning not only to the soil but to the levelness of the country, which precludes all washing.

---

FROM An Emigrant from Maryland, "Views of Louisiana," *Niles Weekly Register,* vol. XIII (Sept. 13, 1817), pp. 38–41.

The earth is very soft and easily worked. There are no stones or pebbles in the country. The soil of Attakapas is black or of a dark brown, that of the Opelousas is of a lighter color and not as durable as that of Attakapas. It is in these prairies that the planter establishes himself, and nature has done here what it takes art and hard labor years to accomplish elsewhere. The fields are already cleared for cultivation, there are no forests to cut down before the crop can be made, no chopping, no grubbing. The planter has nothing to do, but to build his house, inclose his field and commence ploughing. Once that the crop is sown, with moderate industry, the excellent quality of the land will furnish abundant crops of sugar, rice, indigo, cotton, corn, potatoes, oats, &c. all of which are made in Attakapas in great abundance. The staples of Opelousas are cotton, corn, and oats. Sugar succeeds also very well in Opelousas, but the lands of Attakapas yield much more sugar than those of Opelousas, and are far superior to those upon the banks of the Mississippi, and immediately in the neighborhood of New-Orleans. On the Mississippi an hogshead of sugar per acre is considered as a common crop, but in Attakapas a hogshead and a half and two hogshead to an acre are the common crops. Our sugar lands can be purchased at present for one third of the price they are selling for on the Mississippi; and the water carriage to market at New-Orleans, is at the door of the planter. I will annex a list of the crops made by some of our planters, which will convey a more correct idea of the advantages of this country, than any written description can give.

*Joseph Theall*—1816.

| | |
|---|---|
| 18 bales cotton as per acct. sales | $1585 17 |
| 100 barrels corn sold | 125 00 |
| | 1710 17 |

3 hands only—$570 per hand, besides provisions in abundance for the next year.

*Nicholas Lorsselle*—1816.

| | | |
|---|---|---|
| 40 bales of cotton<br>1 barrel of indigo | acct. of sales | 4150 |
| | | 4150 |

7 hands only—$593 per hand, besides provisions in abundance for the next year.

*Peter Roberts*—1816.

| | |
|---|---|
| 5484 lbs. of cotton 28 cts. | 1525 |
| 20,000 lbs. sugar $13 | 2600 |
| 200 barrels corn sold $1 25 | 250 |
| | 4375 |

7 hands only—620 dollars per hand, besides provisions, &c.

*Joseph Berwick*—1816.

| | |
|---|---|
| 10 hhds. of sugar 130 dollars | 1300 |
| 2 hands only—650 dollars per hand, besides provisions, &c. | |

*Michael Gordy*—1816.

| | |
|---|---|
| 25 hhds. of sugar 130 dollars | 3250 |
| 4 hands only—812 dollars per hand, besides provisions, &c. | |

*James Saunders*—1816.

| | |
|---|---|
| 13 bales of cotton 28 cts. | 1260 |
| 3 hands—420 dollars per hand, besides provisions, &c. | |

*George Singleton*—1816.

| | |
|---|---|
| 24 bales of cotton | 2520 |
| 4 hands—630 dollars per hand, besides provisions, &c. | |

*Samuel Rice*—1816.

| | |
|---|---|
| 18 hhds. sugar, each 110 dollars | $ 1980 |
| 700 gallons molasses, at 33⅓ cents | 267 |
| | 2247 |
| 3 hands only—$749 per hand, besides provisions, &c. | |

*John Theall*—1816.

| | |
|---|---|
| 12 hhds. sugar, 110 dollars | 1320 00 |
| 400 galls. molasses, at 33⅓ cents | 133 33 |
| | 1453 33 |
| 3 hands only—$484 44 per hand, besides provisions, &c. | |
| His sugar mill and kettles cost him only 120 dollars. | |

*Jackson and Caffery*—1816.

| | |
|---|---|
| 54 acres of cane, 72 hhds. sugar, 1100 lbs. each | 9360 |
| 10 bales coton, 26 cents | 965 |
| 3000 galls. molasses, 33⅓ cents | 1000 |
| 1000 barrels corn, sold at $1 25 | 1250 |
| | 12,575 |
| 27 hands—$465 per hand, besides provisions, &c. | |

*Jett and James Thomas*—1816.

| | |
|---|---|
| 84 hhds. sugar sold for | 14,000 |
| 3000 galls. molasses, sold for | 1,000 |
| | 15,000 |

36 hands—$417 per hand, besides provisions, &c.

*Peter Regnier*—1816.

| | |
|---|---|
| 105,000 lbs. cotton, at 28 cents | 2940 |

8 hands—$367 per hand, besides provisions, &c.

*John M. Watson*—1816.

| | |
|---|---|
| 70 hhds. sugar, 1100 lbs. each, at 130 dollars | 9100 |
| 13 bales cotton, 28 cents | 1250 |
| 3000 galls. molasses, at 33⅓ cents | 1000 |
| 700 barrels corn, sold at $1 25 | 875 |
| | 12,225 |

35 hands—$350 per hand, besides provisions, &c.

I could name the products of many other plantations, but I think these will suffice to shew the great advantage this country has over the other parts of the United States; and after knowing these things, can you prefer any other part of the union! or will you prefer the rocky lands of the west or north, to the beautiful picturesque meadows of Louisiana, whose prolific soil more than amply repays the laborer for his toils; where nature smiles upon every thing, and where industry and enterprize never fail to ensure wealth and comfort in a very few years? I leave these things to your reflections.

This is one of the finest countries in the world for vegetables; they grow during the whole year; and our gardens are as green in the winter as in the spring. I have seen the rose in full bloom, in all our gardens, in the month of January.

We have the best fruit trees. The orange, the fig, the pomegranate, the peach, plumbs of every description, pears, &c. flourish in the greatest perfection, as well as all the vine fruits, such as the grape, melons, &c.

There are many inhabitants here who raised horned cattle, and the stocks of some are almost innumerable. Many of our citizens brand from 500 to 1000 calves every year, and some of them 2000 and 3000 calves. Amongst the largest stock owners are William Wikoff, of Opelousas, Joseph Sorrel, Jean Mouton and his sons, the family of Guidorys, of Attakapas, and Chretiens (freres) of Opelousas. The stocks of these gentlemen are so numerous, that they can form no idea themselves of their number. It is a beautiful sight to see these large herds of cattle feeding and ranging in the large prairies. In the time of gathering these cattle, I have seen at least 12,000 in one gang, where the owners had assembled them for the purpose of facilitating the branding, as the law requires every man to have a particular brand, which is recorded. The breeds of these cattle are very fine; they keep fat in the prairies and cost the owners nothing, except men to guard them: the largest of these stocks not requiring more than six horsemen in the time of gathering, and the half that number at other times.

*Rivers.*—The Teche and Vermillion, in Attakapas, and the Mermentau, in Opelousas, are the only rivers which flow through these countries. The Vermillion and Teche take their rise in Opelousas, and flow entirely through Attakapas from north to south, when they empty themselves into the sea. These two rivers are connected by the Bayou Fusilier. Both the Teche and Vermillion are navigable for large boats and vessels, drawing not more than eight feet, at all times, for one hundred miles from their mouth—the Teche particularly so. It is generally slow and sluggish in its course, but at times very rapid from freshes. It is never liable to overflowings, like the Mississippi, is generally very deep, and as high up as the town of St. Martinsville, 100 miles from its mouth, is ten feet deep at all times. Besides these rivers, there are many smaller ones, called bayous here, such as Ne pique Plaquemine Brule, Boeuf, Cortablau, &c. in Opelousas and Caron Crow, Tortue, Salle, Cypre mort, Petitance, &c. in Attakapas; added to these, are two large and beautiful lakes in Attakapas, from which the finest fish are caught. These and the water courses communicating with the Mississippi by the Bayous Plaquemine and La Fourche, are the only rivers, Bayous, &c. worth mentioning, and form at all times a safe and good conveyance to market.

*Towns.*—The most important town in these two counties is that of St. Martinsville, which has been lately incorporated. It contains about 40 dwelling houses, besides out-houses; it has one Roman Catholic church and residence for a priest, one court house and a public jail, one academy, a small market house, for meat only, three taverns, three blacksmiths' shops, two hatters' shops, three tailors' shops, one saddler's shop, two boot and shoemakers' shops, one joiner's shop, one silversmith's shop, two bakers' shops, one timer's shop and ten stores. It is the seat of justice for the county of Attakapas.—In this town there reside four attornies at law and three physicians. Its inhabitants are industrious and enterprizing, and amongst them several very respectable families. The inhabitants are generally decent in their deportment and friendly amongst themselves. They are chiefly French and Americans, and some Irish and Scotch. It is beautifully situated upon the bank of the Teche, which is about fifty yards wide opposite to it, and about fifteen feet deep. It is destined one day to become a very respectable inland town, being in the centre of a rich and populous country.

Nova Iberia is the port of entry for the district of Teche, and is beautifully situated upon the Teche, in Attakapas, about ten miles from St. Martinsville.

Franklin, in the parish of St. Mary, in Attakapas, has been lately laid off, and will become a place of much business, as it not far from the mouth of the Teche, and upon the right bank of that river.—It is in the centre of that part of Attakapas where the largest sugar establishments are made. At present its buildings are not numerous, consisting of a public jail, a school house, two taverns, two stores, two saddler's shops and three or four dwelling houses.

The only town in Opelousas, is called 'Opelousas church.' It is handsomely situated upon the east side of a point of woods jutting into the prairie.—It began to flourish before the war, but during its existence, it went to decay. Since peace has been established, it looks up again, and their can be no doubt but in a few years it will rapidly increase.—Its buildings are a Roman catholic church, an academy, a court house and public jail. There are four taverns, five stores, one saddler's shop, one tanner's shop, one tailor's shop, two boot and shoemakers' shops, one silversmith's shop, and about twenty-five dwelling houses, besides out-houses. It is built six miles from any navigable stream, which is one of the causes why the growth of the town has been impeded.

There is another town about being laid off, ten miles from Opelousas church, at the place where Mr. Charles Smith, a rich and respectable planter of Opelousas, is erecting an elegant large Roman catholic church and an academy, which he intends as a present to the public. It is by acts like these, that an essential and lasting service is rendered to the public, and such men deserve the thanks of their country, and are an example worthy of imitation.

*Climate.*—An idea has gone forth that this country is sickly—it is the reverse. I have resided in Virginia and Maryland, in which last state I was *born,* and I prefer this climate to any that I have experienced. I believe the Attakapas and Opelousas countries are as healthy as any part of the United States, and much more so than either Virginia or Maryland, or any of the southern Atlantic states. After a residence of several years here, both myself and my family, white and black, have enjoyed better health than we ever did in Maryland. We have not as many fevers here as in the other parts of the union. That fatal species of the dysentery which rages with such violence in your states is unknown here. Those violent putrid and malignant fevers which too often make their appearance amongst you, have never yet reached our happy climate. Those epidemics which prevail almost annually with you, never exist here. The only fever which this climate, or rather Opelousas and Attakapas, are subject to, is the common bilious fever of the country, which is slow in its approach, and easily cured if taken in time; fatal only when neglected. This constitutes the only fever of the country. To be sure, upon the Mississippi, at New-Orleans, and in those parts of Louisiana which are covered with woods, more violent and dangerous fevers exist, and and [sic] there are causes for some complaints; but this is a very different country—our wide, open and extensive prairies, the continual current of air which sweeps over them and the sea breezes continually blowing during the sickly and warm months, prevent those dangerous consequences, as to disease, which follow those establishments made in the midst of the woods, and removed from the influence of the sea. Attakapas and Opelousas are washed by the sea upon their southern boundaries. The pure air of the ocean passes over their entire surface, without meeting any swamps of wood or putrefaction in its course. It reaches them as unadulterated as when it first left old Neptune's domain, and gives a softness, elasticity and freshness to the atmosphere, which is truly agreeable and pleasant to the feelings. During the three last years the thermometer of Farenheit has seldom been higher than 86° in the summer, and only five times as high as 93°. As far as I can ascertain from my observations during the last three years, the average mean heat of Attakapas and Opelousas, has been about 78° in the months of July, August and September. That close, suffocating heat so often felt to the northward, and so injurious to health, is seldom experienced here. The nights during the summer, are very pleasant, always fanned by the sea breezes, and generally cool enough to cover with a sheet, and often with a counterpane. The dews here are far from being unhealthy, so great is the influence of the salt particles wafted in the sea air. It is impossible for me in this address, to enter into a train of reasoning to prove to you the salubrity of our climate; all I can do is to state the facts such as they are—and so I have done.

If any of you determine to emigrate, I will ask you, after the exhibits I have given you of the produce of our soil, and the description of our climate and country, to what more advantageous section of the union can you go, than to the two counties I have described? Is not this the country for the slave holder? Do not the climate, the soil and productions of this country furnish allurements to the application of your negroes on our lands? In your states a planter, with ten negroes, with difficulty supports a family genteelly; here, well managed, they would be a fortune to him. With you the seasons are so irregular, your crops often fail; here the crops are certain, and want of the necessaries of life, never for a moment causes the heart to ache—abundance spreads the table of the poor man, and contentment smiles on every countenance. Perhaps you will scarcely believe me, but I declare to you I have not seen one beggar in Atakapas or Opelousas nor do I know an object of charity from want. Oh! that at this moment as much could be said for the whole world!

I shall make no further remarks at present; and, should any person who reads this publication, wish to obtain further information relative to this country, the editor who publishes this will furnish them with my name and address, and I will most cheerfully give them every information in my power.

AN EMIGRANT FROM MARYLAND.

## d] THE RESTLESS FRONTIER SPIRIT

ABOUT THIS time, [1802] Tyre Kelly, James and John Hickman, of Tennessee, three brothers-in-law, wrote my father frequent letters urging him to sell out and go to that rich country. He, being naturally of a restless disposition, was very willing to try the experiment. He soon found a purchaser for his rich, money-making home. Three years of successful

FROM Ulrich B. Phillips, ed., *Plantation and Frontier,* pp. 185–96, John R. Commons, ed., *A Documentary History of American Industrial Society,* vol. II (New York: Russell & Russell, 1958). Reprinted by permission of the publisher.

farming had tired him out. He sold out everything he could not carry with him, bought a good road wagon and four fine horses, and set out for Tennessee. The amount of freight he had to transport was a big chest, four beds, four white and four negro children, and his mother, who was at that time 88 years of age. She was a little indisposed when we started, and her sickness became so serious that the violence of her paroxysms frightened my father so much that he went to the house of a Mr. Morris, who was nearest our camp, and got him to agree to let her have shelter with him while her sickness lasted. Her sickness continued three weeks, and my father, concluding that the fates were opposed to his removal to Tennessee, became discouraged, rented Mr. Morris's place and moved the family into Morris's house. Morris was an old man, had no children with him, and he and his old wife went to live with one of his sons. My father worked hard that year, made a large crop of cotton, which he sold for $5.00 a hundred in the seed. He had kept his wagon and fine horses and with the money he got for his cotton and corn crop, he was better prepared to meet the expenses of the long journey than he had been the year before.

So he fixed up again. . . . We rolled on, four days, until we came in view of a little, dilapidated village on the bank of the Savannah river; just below the mouth of Broad river. There was other company ahead of us, and we could not get our wagon into the flat till near sundown. Just as the wagon was turning to go down into the ferry boat, a quite handsome young lady came up and, without asking any questions, threw a small budget into the wagon, and crossed over with us. After getting over into South Carolina, we had only time to get out of the timber when it was night. Here we camped. While they were collecting wood to make a fire, the before mentioned young lady came into camp with a heavier log of wood on her shoulder, my father said, than a man could carry. In a few days this young lady who proved to be Miss Melinda Nevils was married to my cousin, Asa Lincecum, who had joined us a few days previous to our setting out from Georgia.

We remained at that camp three days, during two of which my father had been away with an old drunken Irishman, who had come there the day after we pitched camp. Mother was uneasy and said she did not understand it; that it was too bad to lose three days of pretty fair weather in such a long journey. But father came back the evening of the third day and astonished us all by informing us that he had rented an excellent farm on Calhoun's creek, Abbeville district, S.C.

We went there the next day and found the house a very good one and the land excellent. There was another good house on the farm, and Asa agreed to make a crop with my father, as there was plenty of open land on the place. He and his wife had nothing but their health and strength to begin life with, not even a blanket. But they had courage, and they went bravely to work, clearing the land and fixing up their house. Mother lent them a bedstead and some blankets. Asa made a fine crop of cotton and corn and Melinda spun and made cloth sufficient for clothing and household use. In the course of a year they had accumulated a wagon load of property.

My father paid Asa for his share of the large crop they made, and it enabled them to supply all their immediate necessities.

My father sold his cotton for a good price and made a visit to his sister, living in Clark county, Ga. He was gone two or three weeks, and when he returned, he told my mother that he had purchased a tract of land with a good house on it, one mile from Athens, Ga. We were soon on the road again, returning to Georgia. In the course of a week we reached our new home. Father exerted every power at his new place. He planted and raised a large crop of cotton; and as soon as it began to open, every one that could pick five pounds a day was forced into the cotton field. . . . We succeeded in gathering the cotton by Christmas, and father took it to the gin and got the receipts for 4,643 pounds, for which he received five cents a pound.

He again became restless, and selling his place, put his wagon in good repair, set out on a third attempt to get to Tennessee. This time his cargo, besides the beds, trunks, etc., consisted of grandmother, four white and four black children. He had also two white children and one negro child walking. The weather was fine, and we made good progress. I was delighted that we were on the road. Being in my twelfth year, I was an expert with a bow and arrow, and could run far ahead, shooting and killing many birds in the course of a day.

Father hired a straggling old fellow to drive for this trip, and we rolled on bravely until we came to the Saluda river. There was there a store and a blacksmith shop, and we stopped until the smith nailed a pair of shoes on the out-riding horse. Father and his teamster became somewhat intoxicated and got two bottles of whiskey to carry with them. The river was wide and swift, but shallow. We forded it, and in the course of two hours were all safely landed on the border of South Carolina again. After going about five miles my father and the driver became more deeply intoxicated. The latter fell off the wagon and frightened the horses. They ran away and tore up the wagon, hurting all who were in it. My grandmother was very seriously wounded. It became necessary for us to remain in this place three weeks before my grandmother was able to travel again. At the end of this time my father told us that he had decided to purchase a place from a man by the name of Hamilton, who lived on a hill nearby. My father gave him some money and his wagon and two horses for the place. This was in Pendleton district, S.C.

We had on this place a large orchard. There were in it fifty peach trees, said to be forty-four years old. They made a very fine crop of peaches, which my father gathered and carried to a still, where he had them made into brandy. This, with all his corn and fodder that he could spare, he sold to travelers for ready money at a good price. It was an easy place to make a living, and my father seemed to be quieting down to a settled state of mind. All of the family were satisfied and willing to remain there. Unfortunately my uncle, Tyre Kelly, who had been living in Tennessee, stopped with us on his way to Georgia. He and his eight motherless children remained with us a month. After they left, my father became restless again, and sold his place at the first opportunity.

We were soon on the road again. The next time we stopped it was at a place a mile from where we lived the previous year.

The lands beyond the Oconee river had been obtained by the United States from the Muskogee Indians. No one had moved into this new purchase, and as father intended to settle there as soon as the Indians had completed the twelve months' hunting which had been by a stipulation in the treaty with the United States reserved to them, he took an overseer's place instead of purchasing land.

There came a man by the name of Young Gill, with his family, and made up a school, which was to be kept in a little old log cabin, a mile and a half from our home. Father entered my sister, brother and me as day scholars at the rate of $7.00 each per annum. We three started the next day and did not miss a day until father moved to the new purchase five months later. I was fourteen years old, and it was the first schoolhouse I had ever seen. I began in the alphabet. There were some very small boys, seven years old, who could read.

Whenever Mr. Gill would storm out, "Mind your book," the scholars would strike up a loud, blatant confusion of tongues, which surpassed anything I had ever heard before. There I sat in a sea of burning shame, while the clatter and glib clap of tongues rattled on. I soon accustomed myself to this method of studying aloud and felt myself very much at home. . . .

When the Indians had finished their year of hunting and retired from the new purchase my father took me with him to explore the country. We crossed the Oconee river and traversed the lands of the new purchase ten or twelve days. He preferred the country on Little river, selected a place and we returned home to make ready for the removal as soon as possible. The newly acquired land belonged to the State, and the Legislature enacted that it should be surveyed into lots of 202½ acres each, and have it drawn for by her citizens in general lottery. Men having families were entitled to two tickets; single men and women of age, and sets of orphaned children, one ticket each. My father had been moving and shackling about so much that he was not entitled to a chance in the lottery,—and the place he had selected on Little river had been drawn by a man who would not part with it. This discovery was not made until we had moved on to it. Father then found a place belonging to Thomas McLellon, with a double cabin on it. For this place he gave all the money he had, with "Mammy Pat" and two of her children. It was situated in the wild woods, on a beautiful clear running creek, in one mile of where Eatonton now stands.

Great numbers of people flocked into the country, and the next year after we came there the county seat was laid off and named Eatonton. I was one of the chain carriers to survey the streets and lots though I was but fourteen years old. We had cleared and planted ten acres of ground the year before, and this year we cleared fifteen acres more. About this time my father and I had a misunderstanding and I decided to leave home. I hired to a man by the name of William Wilkins, a merchant at Eatonton. I worked for him two years remaining in his home during this time. At the end of the first year I had a serious difficulty with a man by the name of Clark, who had insulted me several times. He was discharged by Mr. Wilkins, who put me in entire charge of his business. After my second year with Mr. Wilkins I was employed by Mr. Thompson, a more prosperous merchant, who paid me a salary of $500.00 a year.

In the meantime I had studied medicine during odd moments. The War of 1812 was approaching. I left the store and confined myself entirely to the study of medicine until the declaration of war. I then enlisted in a company of volunteers, but as the people of Putnam county had elected me tax collector, I could enlist for only five months. I had to begin collecting in January, and it was in the month of August when I went into the army. I served until the first of January; then went home, collected the taxes, paid the money into the treasury and married. I served another period of three months after I was married, and in the spring of 1815 went home and gave my father a faithful year's work.

The next year I joined forces and farmed with Judge Strong. He had three hands and sixty acres of open land. I had forty acres of open land and two hands. He was to furnish all the provisions, smithing, etc. I was to superintend the farm and we were to make an equal division of the proceeds of the crop. I planted sixty acres in cotton and forty in corn. I cultivated the ground carefully and both crops were very good. That year cotton was worth 31½ cents a pound, but I became restless and did not feel like staying in that country until the crop could be gathered. The Alabama, Black Warrior, Tombecbee, and Chatahoochie countries had all been acquired by conquest, and I was determined to seek a home in the wilderness. My father had made up his mind to go to the new country with his large family and he had been insinuating to me the propriety of breaking up to go with him. There was another little thing that increased my restlessness. My wife's relations were all wealthy and my wife said they had been mean enough to cast little slurs at her and her poverty. She also persuaded me to sell out and go with my father to the new country. All these influences confirmed me in the resolution to get ready and bid adieu to my native State.

Father and I sold out our possessions and were soon on the road to the new country. We had proceeded about forty-five miles when we came to the Ocmulgee river, which at that time was a dividing line between the Georgians and the Creek Indians. A man by the name of Ferguson came to our camp and getting a little "tight" with my father, in a kind of frolic, sold my father his land and cattle. All along the river the people owned herds of cattle which they kept in the range on the Indian side of it. There was plenty of deer over there, too; and being satisfied that my father would not remain more than a year, I concluded to stop also and do what I had never done in my life; idle away the time until he got tired of his bargain and made ready to move again.

I could continue my medical reading, fish in the river, and hunt the deer beyond it; and in this way have a pleasant time. I had made two or three very successful hunting excursions, had been fishing at my baited hole, and caught some fine fat red horse, and was highly pleased at the prospects for a pleasant year's amusement. . . .

My father loved a border life, and the place he had purchased on the Ocmulgee, as the people had already commenced settling on the opposite side of the river, was no longer looked upon as a border country. He sold his place and was soon equipped and geared up for the road, and so was I. I had been reared to a belief and faith in the pleasure of frequent change of country, and I looked upon the long journey, through the wilderness, with much pleasure.

Our company consisted of my father and mother and eight children, with six negroes; Joseph Bryan, my brother-in-law, and his wife and two negroes; my wife and me and two small sons and two negroes. We had good horses and wagons and guns and big dogs. We set out on the 10th of March, 1818. I felt as if I was on a big camp hunt.

The journey, the way we traveled, was about 500 miles, all wilderness; full of deer and turkeys, and the streams were full of fish. We were six weeks on the road; and altogether it was, as I thought and felt, the most delightful time I had ever spent in my life. My brother Garland and I "flanked it" as the wagons rolled along and killed deer, turkeys, wild pigeons; and at nights, with pine torches, we fished and killed a great many with my bow and arrows, whenever we camped on my water course. Little creeks were full of fish at that season.

At length we reached Tuscaloosa, Ala. It was at that time a small log cabin village; but people from Tennessee were arriving daily, and in the course of that year it grew to be a considerable town.

I concluded to stop there, and my father and his family and Bryan and his family continued their journey to a small improvement eight miles below Tuscaloosa, on the river, where they settled, and, cutting down a canebrake, made corn; and killed bear, venison, and fish enough to supply the family.

I fished and had as much as we needed of that kind of food, but there were no bear nor deer in reach of the town, and I had to buy provisions at enormous rates. Flour, $25 a barrel; corn, $2½ a bushel; sugar, 50 cents a pound; coffee, 62½ cents a pound; salt, $8. a bushel; bacon, 37½ cents a pound. There was no beef to be had.

I built a little clapboard house on the river side of the town, which had not yet been surveyed. The land hunters from Georgia found us and continued their friendly calls on us until what money I had left from the long journey was eaten up. This was a circumstance for which I had made no provisions. I felt no uneasiness on that account; for I was as strong as two common men and could do anything from cutting and splitting fence rails to fine cabinet work. And in mercantile action was familiar with all the duties from the lumber house to the counting room. I could mix drugs and practice medicine as far as it was known in the interior of the country in those days. I felt no alarm at the fact that my money was gone. . . .

[In the fall of 1818, he set out to remove his family to the Tombigby River.]

Our wagons being the first that had ever traversed that unhacked forest, we of course, had to make a sufficient road for them to pass. It fell to my lot to go in advance and blaze the way, and by taking advantage of the open spaces amongst the trees, I saved a great deal of time. The woods having been burnt every year by the Indian hunters, there were but few logs remaining, and we got along very nicely. Except when we came to the water courses, we had but little difficulty. There are three little rivers and several creeks that crossed our path. We were forced to dig down the banks of these streams before crossing them.

In the afternoon of the twelfth day we landed on the banks of the Tombecbee river, three miles by land above where Columbus, Miss., now stands. . . .

Soon all the families had houses, and all the hands went to work, cutting down and clearing the maiden forest to make fields to plant corn in. I cut down six acres of cane brake that jammed itself almost down to the place where I built my house. I burnt off the cane on the 5th of May, and planted it with a sharp stick on the 6th. Twice while it was growing I cut and beat down the young cane that sprouted up from the old cane stumps. That was all the work the crop got. The bear and racoons ate and destroyed a good deal of it, and yet I gathered 150 Bushels of good corn. . . .

In 1819, the government marked or surveyed a road from Nashville, Tenn., to Natchez, Miss. It crossed the Tombecbee river where Columbus, Miss., now stands; ten miles by water and three by land below where I had settled. I went down there to see what kind of a place it was. I found it a beautifully elevated situation, being about the head of navigation. I thought it was an eligible town site, and that it would be a town as soon as the country should settle up. I was so fully impressed with the belief that a big town would some day loom up on that beautiful bluff that I went home, sawed a thousand boards; put them on a raft and floated them down the river with the intention of building a snug little house on a nice place I had selected, hoping to be able to realize a profit from it, as soon as people should move into the country.

## 4] Steamboats on the Western Rivers

. . . . . . . . . . . . . . . . . . . . . . .

WE NOW arrive to the consideration of the present condition of steam navigation in the United States. What is this condition? Taking our stand upon the New York dock, and looking abroad upon those ships which border it, like flying monsters of oak that have folded their canvass wings and now lie chained to the wharves, as racehorses to the manger when their race is run, we perceive scattered among the thicket of masts numerous strange craft, without spars or sails, that appear like piratical new-comers, more fanciful in color and more fragile in form than the black and solid vessels that surround them.

. . . . . . . . . . . . . . . . . . . . . . .

We change the scene, and transport ourselves to one of the blue peaks of the Highlands, and from that eminence look down upon the silver Hudson,

---

FROM James H. Lanman, "American Steam Navigation," *Hunt's Merchants' Magazine*, vol. IV (February, 1841), pp. 120–21, and 123–24.

as it winds its way through valley and mountain, as far as the eye can reach, like an enchanted stream. What are those vehicles that are constantly passing before us with a cloud of smoke by day and a pillar of fire by night issuing from their smoke-pipes, as they glide along their dazzling tracks with the speed of the sunbeam? They are floating hotels, the swiftest in the world, with the banner of the republic waving at their masthead—steamboats, the carrier-pigeons of commerce, on their way from the commercial mart of the nation to the political capital of the state. We advance further, to the borders of those inland seas that water the forests of the northwest, and looking out at midnight, our attention is arrested by numerous fiery bodies which seem as meteors. As they approach, we perceive that they are not like the baleful comet . . . but smoke and sparks streaming from the chimneys of numerous steamers passing and repassing to and from the west, advancing with emigrants and their merchandise, who are about to turn up the rich mould of the prairies, or returning from the west with loads of wheat and flour, the product of that soil, for the markets of New York. Or let us ascend the fruitful Mississippi, and take a long view of its brimming flood, and we perceive its sky blackened here and there by clouds of ascending smoke. They issue from the hundreds of splendid though unsafe high-pressure boats of that river, rushing down from St. Louis or Cincinnati to New Orleans, with machinery, emigrants, and agricultural products, with barrels of sugar, casks of tobacco, or bales of cotton, produced by the plantations upon its shores, and which are to be consumed in this country, or to be shipped abroad to return in harvests of gold. Look at the price current of New Orleans, and mark those long columns that denote the receipts of produce from the interior. Their sentences commence with the words "per steamer." What is the cause of all this? *Steam!* It has made safe tracks across the ocean, from Liverpool to Boston, from New York to Liverpool and London. It has ploughed its furrows around the coast, from the great commercial mart of the country to Charleston, Cuba, and New Orleans, and has established regular packets upon that track. It has produced rapid and elegant navigation around the republic and through it. The little steamboat that rides upon the village stream like a sea-gull, has connected that stream with the lakes; the large steamships are about to connect the lakes with the ocean. Wherever there is a sufficient depth of water to float its fabrics, there its banners wave. Its vessels crowd the docks of New York and Baltimore, Buffalo and Detroit, Pittsburg and Cincinnati, Louisville, St. Louis, and New Orleans, as well as our other principal ports, both at the east and the west.

. . . . . . . . . . . . . . . . . . . . . . . . . .

What, then, is the influence which steam navigation has produced, and is producing upon the country? The position, it is thought, may be safely maintained, that it has effected a more powerful, physical, and moral revolution, upon this republic, than any agency that has been devised, or could be devised, within the present knowledge of man. In order to ascertain this fact, it will be only necessary to look back at the condition of the country before this agent was introduced, and when the vessels worked by sails were the only vehicles of commerce. What would now have been the extent of colonization in this broad empire had we been shut out from its benefits? We have already seen that, previous to the year 1811, the great navigable waters of the interior were destitute of safe and rapid means of intercommunication. The few feeble colonies that had penetrated the forests of the Muskingum, the Ohio, and the Detroit, were in effect cut off from the rest of the world; and even at a later period, the eloquent geographer of the western valley, Mr. Timothy Flint, could creep up the Mississippi in his boat only by grasping the reeds that bordered its banks. What motive was held out for the cultivation of lands, however fertile, when the producer was deprived of a market? What other agent upon the face of the earth, but steam, could stem the current of that flood, and provide convenient access to the plantations scattered along its winding shores? What motive would have been presented for ages for the colonization of the wilderness around the lakes, were the western waters traversed only by the canoe or pirogue of the Indian and fur-trader, or the straggling shallop, cast about by storms, which occasionally made a solitary voyage to the western ports? Where now would have been Buffalo and Cleveland, Cincinnati, Louisville, and St. Louis, had not steam navigation made them entrepots of trade and commerce? How many emigrants would have left their peaceful hearthstones at the east, and have ventured into an unbroken wilderness, removed from the uncertain and inconvenient means of navigation, by months of travel from the firesides they had left? How many golden wheat-fields in that region would have waved with yellow harvests, were the western husbandman deprived of eastern intercourse and an eastern market? Steam navigation colonized the west! It furnished a motive for settlement and production by the hands of eastern men, because it brought the western territory nearer to the east by nine tenths of the distance. It opened new channels of intercommunication, and new markets for its products. A journey from the western borders of New York to Detroit, requires but a little more than two days. Steam palaces float by scores upon almost every point of the western waters. The western farmer can receive his friend, and ship his wheat and cotton and sugar and corn, by steamers, almost within stones-throw of his granary. Steam is crowding our eastern cities with western flour and western merchants, and lading the western steamboats with eastern emigrants and eastern merchandise. It has advanced the career of national colonization and national production, at least a century!

. . . . . . . . . . . . . . .

# 5] Specialization and Interdependence

## a] COTTON: "LINCH-PIN OF THE REGIONAL ALLIANCE"

THE INSTITUTION of slavery, at this moment, gives indications of a vitality that was never anticipated by its friends or foes. Its enemies often supposed it about ready to expire, from the wounds they had inflicted, when in truth it had taken two steps in advance, while they had taken twice the number in an opposite direction. In each successive conflict, its assailants have been weakened, while its dominion has been extended.

This has arisen from causes too generally overlooked. Slavery is not an isolated system, but is so mingled with the business of the world, that it derives facilities from the most innocent transactions. Capital and labor, in Europe and America, are largely employed in the manufacture of cotton. These goods, to a great extent, may be seen freighting every vessel, from Christian nations, that traverses the seas of the globe; and filling the warehouses and shelves of the merchants over two-thirds of the world. By the industry, skill, and enterprise employed in the manufacture of cotton, mankind are better clothed; their comfort better promoted; general industry more highly stimulated; commerce more widely extended; and civilization more rapidly advanced than in any preceding age.

To the superficial observer, all the agencies, based upon the sale and manufacture of cotton, seem to be legitimately engaged in promoting human happiness; and he, doubtless, feels like invoking Heaven's choicest blessings upon them. When he sees the stockholders in the cotton corporations receiving their dividends, the operatives their wages, the merchants their profits, and civilized people everywhere clothed comfortably in cottons, he can not refrain from exclaiming: "The lines have fallen unto them in pleasant places; yea, they have a goodly heritage!"

But turn a moment to the source, whence the raw cotton, the basis of these operations, is obtained, and observe the aspect of things in that direction. When the statistics on the subject are examined, it appears that nearly all the cotton consumed in the Christian world is the product of the slave labor of the United States. It is this monopoly that has given slavery its commercial value; and, while this monopoly is retained, the institution will continue to extend itself wherever it can find room to spread.

. . . . . . . . . . . . . . .

The cotton planting States, toward the close of the contest, found themselves rapidly accumulating strength, and approximating the accomplish-

---

FROM David Christy, *Cotton Is King,* reprinted in E. N. Elliott, ed., *Cotton is King, and Pro-Slavery Arguments* (Augusta, Ga.: Pritchard, Abbott & Loomis, 1860), pp. 55–56, 92, 94–95, and 124–27.

ment of the grand object at which they aimed—the monopoly of the cotton markets of the world. This success was due, not so much to any triumph over the North—to any prostration of our manufacturing interests—as to the general policy of other nations. All rivalry to the American planters from those of the West Indies, was removed by emancipation; as, under freedom, the cultivation of cotton was nearly abandoned. Mehemet Ali had become imbecile, and the idolent Egyptians neglected its culture. The South Americans, after achieving their independence, were more readily enlisted in military forays, than in the art of agriculture, and they produced little cotton for export. The emancipation of their slaves, instead of increasing the agricultural products of the Republics, only supplied, in ample abundance, the elements of promoting political revolutions, and keeping their soil drenched with human blood. Such are the uses to which degraded men may be applied by the ambitious demagogue. Brazil and India both supplied to Europe considerably less in 1838 than they had done in 1820; and the latter country made no material increase afterward, except when her chief customer, China, was at war, or prices were above the average rates in Europe. While the cultivation of cotton was thus stationary or retrograding, everywhere outside of the United States, England and the Continent were rapidly increasing their consumption of the article, which they nearly doubled from 1835 to 1845; so that the demand for the raw material called loudly for its increased production. Our planters gathered a rich harvest of profits by these events.

. . . . . . . . . . . . . . .

The West, which had long looked to the East for a market, had its attention now turned to the South, as the most certain and convenient mart for the sale of its products—the planters affording to the farmers the markets they had in vain sought from the manufacturers. In the meantime, steamboat navigation was acquiring perfection on the Western rivers—the great natural outlets for Western products—and became a means of communication between the Northwest and the Southwest, as well as with the trade and commerce of the Atlantic cities. This gave an impulse to industry and enterprise, west of the Alleghanies, unparalleled in the history of the country. While, then, the bounds of slave labor were extending from Virginia, the Carolinas, and Georgia, Westward, over Tennessee, Alabama, Mississippi, and Arkansas, the area of free labor was enlarging, with equal rapidity, in the Northwest, throughout Ohio, Indiana, Illinois, and Michigan. Thus, within these provision and cotton regions, were the forests cleared away, or the prairies broken up, simultaneously by those old antagonistic forces, opponents no longer, but harmonized by the fusion of their interests—the connecting link between them being the steamboat. Thus, also, was a *tripartite alliance* formed, by which the Western Farmer, the Southern Planter, and the English Manufacturer, became united in a common bond of interest: the whole giving their support to the doctrine of Free Trade.

This active commerce between the West and South, however, soon caused a rivalry in the East, that pushed forward improvements, by States or Corporations, to gain a share in the Western trade. These improvements, as completed, gave to the West a choice of markets, so that its Farmers could elect whether to feed the slave who grows the cotton, or the operatives who are engaged in its manufacture. But this rivalry did more. The competition for Western Products enhanced their price, and stimulated their more extended cultivation. This required an enlargement of the markets; and the extension of slavery became essential to Western prosperity.

We have not reached the end of the alliance between the Western Farmer and Southern Planter. The emigration which has been filling Iowa and Minnesota, and is now rolling like a flood into Kansas and Nebraska, is but a repetition of what has occurred in the other Western States and Territories. Agricultural pursuits are highly remunerative, and tens of thousands of men of moderate means, or of no means, are cheered along to where none forbids them land to till. For the last few years, public improvements have called for vastly more than the usual share of labor, and augmented the consumption of provisions. The foreign demand added to this, has increased their price beyond what the planter can afford to pay. For many years free labor and slave labor maintained an even race in their Western progress. Of late the freemen have begun to lag behind, while slavery has advanced by several degrees of longitude. Free labor must be made to keep pace with it. There is an urgent necessity for this. The demand for cotton is increasing in a ratio greater than can be supplied by the American planters, unless by a corresponding increased production. This increasing demand must be met, or its cultivation will be facilitated elsewhere, and the monopoly of the planter in the European markets be interrupted. This can only be effected by concentrating the greatest possible number of slaves upon the cotton plantations. Hence they must be supplied with provisions.

. . . . . . . . . . . . . . . . . . . .

Commerce supplied us, in 1853, with foreign articles, for consumption, to the value of $250,420,187, and accepted, in exchange, of our provisions, to the value of but $33,809,126; while the products of our slave labor, manufactured and unmanufactured, paid to the amount of $133,648,603, on the balance of this foreign debt. This, then, is the measure of the ability of the Farmers and Planters, respectively, to meet the payment of the necessaries and comforts of life, supplied to the country by its foreign commerce. The farmer pays, or seems only to pay, $33,800,000, while the planter has a broad credit, on the account, of $133,600,000.

. . . . . . . . . . . . . . . . . . . .

But is this seeming productiveness of slavery real, or is it only imaginary? Has the system such capacities, over the other industrial interests of the nation, in the creation of wealth, as these figures indicate? Or, are these results due to its intermediate position between the agriculture of the country and its foreign commerce? These are questions worthy of consideration. Were the planters left to grow their own provisions, they would, as already intimated, be unable to produce any cotton for export. That their present ability to export so extensively, is in consequence of the aid they receive from the North, is proved by facts such as these:

In 1820, the cotton-gin had been a quarter of a century in operation, and the culture of cotton was then nearly as well understood as at present. The North, though furnishing the South with some live stock, had scarcely begun to supply it with provisions, and the planters had to grow the food, and manufacture much of the clothing for their slaves. In that year the cotton crop equaled 109 lbs. to each slave in the Union, of which 83 lbs. per slave were exported. In 1830 the exports of the article had risen to 143 lbs., in 1840 to 295 lbs., and in 1853 to 337 lbs. per slave. The total cotton crop of 1853 equaled 485 lbs. per slave—making both the production and export of that staple, in 1853, more than four times as large, in proportion to the slave population, as they were in 1820.[1] Had the planters, in 1853, been able to produce no more cotton, per slave, than in 1820, they would have grown but 359,308,472 lbs., instead of the actual crop of 1,600,000,000 lbs.; and would not only have failed to supply any for export, but have fallen short of the home demand, by nearly 130,000,000 lbs., and been *minus* the total crop of that year, by 1,240,690,000 lbs.

In this estimate, some allowance, perhaps, should be made, for the greater fertility of the new lands, more recently brought under cultivation; but the difference, on this account, can not be equal to the difference in the crops of the several periods, as the lands, in the older States, in 1820, were yet comparatively fresh and productive.

Again, the dependence of the South upon the North, for its provisions, may be inferred from such additional facts as these: The "Abstract of the Census," for 1850, shows, that the production of wheat, in Florida, Alabama, Mississippi, Louisiana, Arkansas, and Texas, averaged, the year preceding, very little more than a peck, (it was 27/100 of a bushel,) to each person within their limits. These States must purchase flour largely, but to what amount we can not determine. The shipments of provisions from Cincinnati to New Orleans and other down river ports, show that large supplies leave that city for the South; but what proportion of them is taken for consumption by the planters, must be left, at present, to conjecture. These shipments, as to a few of the prominent articles, for the four years ending August 31, 1854, averaged annually the following amounts:

| | |
|---|---|
| Wheat flour . . . . . . . . . | 385,204 bbls. |
| Pork and bacon . . . . . . . . | 43,689,000 lbs. |
| Whisky . . . . . . . . . . . | 8,115,360 gals. |

Cincinnati also exports eastward, by canal, river and railroad, large amounts of these productions. The towns and cities westward send more of their products to the South, as their distance increases the cost of transportation to the East. But, in the absence of full statistics, it is not necessary to make additional statements.

1 The progressive increase is indicated by the following figures:

| | 1820 | 1830 | 1840 | 1853 |
|---|---|---|---|---|
| Total slaves in United States . . . . | 1,538,098 | 2,009,043 | 2,487,356 | 3,296,408 |
| Cotton exported (lbs.) . . . . . . . | 127,800,000 | 298,459,102 | 743,941,061 | 1,111,570,370 |
| Average export to each slave (lbs.) . | 83 | 143 | 295 | 337 |

From this view of the subject, it appears that slavery is not a self-sustaining system, independently remunerative; but that it attains its importance to the nation and to the world, by standing as an agency, intermediate, between the grain-growing States and our foreign commerce. As the distillers of the West transformed the surplus grain into whisky, that it might bear transport, so slavery takes the products of the North, and metamorphoses them into cotton, that they may bear export.

. . . . . . . . . . . . . . . . . . .

## b] THE DEPENDENT SOUTH

### [1] Excerpts from Five Contemporary Writers

#### I

TOBACCO and indigo could be as extensively cultivated as cotton, but neither of the former offers as alluring prospects to the planter as the latter. Tobacco and indigo have each been staples of Carolina, but have long been abandoned, and their places supplied by rice and cotton. In all parts of the state cotton is the general staple. . . .

For domestic use, maize, wheat, rye, barley, tobacco, potatoes, (the sweet and Irish,) indigo, hemp, flax, madder, and a variety of smaller articles are raised. Indian corn, wheat, barley, tobacco, hemp, flax, and indigo, were formerly exported from this state, but they have all given place to cotton and rice. The upper parts of this state yield the finest of wheat, large heavy grains, producing the whitest and sweetest flour. Indian corn flourishes in great luxuriance; the lowlands on the rivers yielding in good seasons from 50 to 75 bushels to the acre. This fact tends to show the superior value of the cotton plant when it supersedes an article which can be raised to such advantage as corn. The planter only cultivates enough of this grain to answer his domestic purposes; in some years he has actually to purchase it in Charleston, where it is imported from the northern states in large quantities. . . .

There is not a finer grazing country in the world than South Carolina; and were attention paid to the raising of cattle, sheep, goats, hogs, horses, mules, &c., this state might supply itself as well as all the West India islands, &c. with these useful animals; but every other object gives place to cotton. Immense numbers of cattle, hogs, horses and mules are driven from the western country annually into this state, and sold to advantage.

. . . . . . . . . . . . . . . . . . .

---

FROM Guy S. Callender, ed., *Selections from the Economic History of the United States, 1765–1860* (Boston: Ginn & Co., 1909), pp. 290–94. The five writers, in the order presented above, are: 1) Mills, *Statistics of South Carolina* (1826); 2) Stuart, *Three Years in North America* (1828); 3) Buckingham, *Slave States of America* (1841); 4) Russell, *North America: Its Agriculture and Climate* (1856); and 5) Olmsted, *Seaboard Slave States* (1856).

## II

THE BUSINESS of the merchants here is very extensive. They buy up the produce of the land, consisting of wheat, maize, and other grain, of cattle, salted pork, butter, cheese, and other articles, which they carry to New-Orleans, and there they purchase sugar, coffee, tea, foreign wine, woollen cloths, and all those articles which the Illinois planters require for their own use. The merchant, of whose store Mr. Stephens was taking charge, had some time ago sent down to New-Orleans 200,000 weight of salted pork.

. . . . . . . . . . . . . . . .

One of our stopping-places for wood, not far above the confluence of the Mississippi and Ohio, was at Mr. Brox's farm, on the west side of the river. He has 700 acres of fine land, about 100 head of cattle, and an innumerable quantity of pigs. He says he has no difficulty in selling all the produce of his farm; he disposes of his stock to the New-Orleans' butchers, who go all over this country to make their purchases;—and there are merchants who have great depôts of grain, salted pork, and other agricultural produce, which they scour the country to collect, and afterward carry to New-Orleans. The prices are variable—and Mr. Brox thinks, as every farmer or planter does, are too low; but there is no want of a ready market in any part of the western states hitherto settled. Navigable rivers, generally fit for steamboats, are within reach.

. . . . . . . . . . . . . . . .

## III

. . . . . . . . . . . . . . . .

ON OUR way we met a small caravan, as it might be termed, of fine horses, and beautiful mules, conducted by two drovers, one of whom rode in advance, the other in the rear; and the cattle were driven like sheep, without halter, bridle, or other fastening, between the two. These were all proceeding, to the number of about a hundred, from Kentucky and Ohio to South Carolina and Georgia for sale; and some idea may be formed of the extent of this traffic, when it is mentioned that not less than 10,000 horses and mules, from these middle and Western States come down every year for sale to the purchasers in the Atlantic States, and the cities of the coast, as many as 500 at a time frequently passing through Greenville [South Carolina] in a single day. The horses were quite as fine as ordinary horses seen at fairs and markets in England; but the mules were by far the most beautiful I had ever seen, surpassing even the finest of those in Spain and Portugal.

. . . . . . . . . . . . . . . .

## IV

. . . . . . . . . . . . . . . .

STRANGE to say, it is more difficult to raise the requisite quantity of provisions for a Southern plantation, than to manufacture waggons, ploughs, harness, and articles of clothing. The bacon is almost entirely imported from the Northern States, as well as a considerable quantity of Indian corn. This is reckoned bad management by intelligent planters; and in one case I found it forming the subject of lamentation by a slave-dealer, who maintained that planters could not possibly thrive while they bought their bacon and corn at such high prices, and sold their cotton so low. When provisions are cheap, a great impulse is given to the extension of the culture of cotton, more especially on the inferior class of soils, which are not equally well adapted for Indian corn. It is said that planters who cultivate little else than cotton, which has hitherto fluctuated much in value, and who make it a practice to buy the greater part of their provisions, seldom do well.

On this plantation [in Louisiana] as much Indian corn was raised as was needed; but little bacon, which is imported from Ohio. The average sum annually expended on this article was upwards of £800. Large plantations are not suited to the rearing of hogs; for it is found to be almost impossible to prevent the negroes stealing and roasting young pigs. This is one of the disadvantages in raising certain kinds of produce incidental to a system of slavery. The number of cattle which can be raised on the large cotton plantations, do little more than replace the draught oxen that are required. The sheep only supply the wool needed for clothing; and the mules used for ploughing are bred in the Northern States. The bad qualities of the soil and climate for producing the finer grasses, and the great expense of cattle food cultivated by slave labour, render the raising of stock for exportation, under present circumstances, in a great measure undesirable.

. . . . . . . . . . . . . . . .

Rearing mules for the southern markets is carried on to a great extent in Kentucky and Tennessee. The gentleman who occupied the farm above described usually grazed forty of these animals during the summer. In winter it costs 16s. 8d. (four dollars) a month for keeping a mule, which is allowed as much Indian corn or oats as it can consume. An ox on grass is kept for one dollar a month. Though often the cold is so intense that the Ohio is frozen over in winter, the cattle are not stabled; the wood pastures affording good shelter from the high winds. They are fed upon hay and Indian corn: the latter being given to them as it is cut from the fields. One would be very apt to suppose that great loss would arise from the imperfect manner in which cattle would masticate the unground grain of Indian corn; but a lot of pigs are usually wintered with the cattle, and act in the character of a save-all. Some of the pasture-fields, too, are often allowed to grow after the middle of July, and thus afford good winter grazing. . . .

Clover and Timothy succeed well in Kentucky, and the latter is in great repute for hay. When the land is allowed to remain in pasture, the blue-stem grass occupies the ground and puts all the others out. Large quantities of hay are made in the western parts of the State, pressed into bales, and sent down the Mississippi to New Orleans; for this is a scarce and high-priced article in all the States south of Tennessee.

. . . . . . . . . . . . . . . .

## V

THE PRINCIPAL other freight of the train was one hundred and twenty bales of northern hay. It belonged, as the conductor told me to a planter who lived some twenty miles beyond here, and who had bought it in Wilmington at a dollar and a half a hundred weight, to feed to his mules. Including the steam-boat and railroad freight, and all the labor of getting it to his stables, its entire cost to him would not be much less than two dollars a hundred. This would be at least four times as much as it would have cost to raise and make it in the interior of New York or New England. Now, there are not only several forage crops which can be raised in South Carolina, that cannot be grown on account of the severity of the winter in the free-States, but, on a farm near Fayetteville, a few days before, I had seen a crop of natural grass growing in half-cultivated land, dead upon the ground; which, I think, would have made, if it had been cut and well treated in the summer, three tons of hay to the acre. The owner of the land said that there was no better hay than it would have made, but he hadn't had time to attend to it. He had as much as his hands could do of other work at the period of the year when it should have been made.

Probably the case was similar with the planter who had bought this northern hay at a price four times that which it would have cost a northern farmer to make it. He had preferred to employ his slaves at other business.

The inference must be either that there was most improbably-foolish, bad management, or that the slaves were more profitably employed in cultivating cotton, than they could have been in cultivating maize, or other forage crops.

I put the case, some days afterwards, to an English merchant, who had had good opportunities, and made it a part of his business, to study such matters.

"I have no doubt," said he, "that, if hay cannot be obtained here, other valuable forage can; with less labor than anywhere at the North; and all the Southern agricultural journals sustain this opinion, and declare it to be purely bad management that neglects these crops, and devotes labor to cotton, so exclusively. Probably, it is so—at the present cost of forage. Nevertheless, the fact is also true, as the planters assert, that they cannot afford to apply their labor to anything else but cotton. And yet, they complain that the price of cotton is so low, that there is no profit in growing it; which is evidently false. You see that they prefer buying hay, to raising it, at, to say the least, three times what it costs your Northern farmers to raise it. . . ."

. . . . . . . . . . . . . . .

## [2] Evidence from a Planter's Accounts

Estate of Isaac Franklin,

| | | | Dr. |
|---|---|---|---|
| | To Peters and Millard,[1] | | |
| 1846. | | | |
| April 21. | 6 lbs tobacco at 80c, 1 bbl sugar 258 lb | | 22 86 |
| | 1 box bl[ac]k tea 8 lb at 8c, 1 bbl crushed sugar 217 lb at 13½c | | 37 29 |
| | 2 boxes candles 67½ lb at 29c | | 19 58 |
| | ½ lb 4b 47 15 almonds at 18c | | 8 96 |
| | 1 box raisins 18b, 6 jars prunes 14b | | 12 75 |
| | 1 box preserves $12, 1 doz guava $2 | | 14 00 |
| | 12 boxes sardines 90c, 2 bxs claret 8c | | 26 80 |
| | Drayage | | 25 |
| | | | $184 12 |
| | Received by J. S. Clack. | | |
| July 1. | 2 galls brandy 2 50, demijohn 6b | | 6 75 |
| 7. | 1 box sp[erm] candles 34½ lb, at 30c | 10 35 | |
| | 84 lb loaf sugar, bbl 4b, 13½c drayage 2b | 12 09 | 22 44 |
| | | | $212 31 |

. . . . . . . . . . . . .

Messrs. Hill, McLean & Co. will please pay the above account and charge the same to account of Estate of Isaac Franklin.

March 4th, 1848. John Armfield.

[1] Samuel J. Peters and Charles Millard, grocers, corner Bienville and Old Levee streets, New Orleans. Peters was prominent in New Orleans politics and served as president of the New Orleans City Bank. *New Orleans Annual and Commercial Register for 1846,* pp. 421, 465; appendix, 58; New Orleans *Price-Current,* January 8, 1848.

Invoice pork shipped by Dick and Hill, per steamer "Paul Jones," consigned to M. Gilbert, "Bellevue," and for account and risk Isaac Franklin, deceased.

Bought of John Ferguson,[2]

| | | |
|---|---|---|
| 20 bbls. mess pork, at 9⅛c. | 182 50 | |
| Drayage, | 2 00 | 184 50 |
| 2½ Commission, | | 4 61 |
| Debit Isaac Franklin, deceased, | | $189 11 |

Dick and Hill, per James Brandt.

New Orleans, 26th June, '46.

Executors of Isaac Franklin. [July 14, 1846.]

Bought of William Owen.

10,000 lbs. of bacon, to wit:

| | |
|---|---|
| 250 sides, and 133 shoulders, at 4½c. | $450 00 |
| 14 hogsheads, at 50c. | 7 00 |
| Drayage, | 1 75 |
| | $458 75 |

Invoice bacon, &c., shipped by Dick and Hill, per Cora, consigned to James Watson, Esq., for account and risk of estate Isaac Franklin.

Bought of J. and R. Geddes,[3]

| | |
|---|---|
| 10 casks bacon sides, 7194, at 5½ | 395 67 |
| 2 shoulders, 1657, at 3½ | 58 00 |
| Drayage, | 1 50—455 17 |

Bought of McAlpin and Tagert,[4]

| | | |
|---|---|---|
| 10 lbs. black tea, at $1, | 10 00 | |
| Drayage, | 25 | 10 25 |
| 2½c. commission, | | 11 63 |
| Debit estate Isaac Franklin, | | $477 05 |

Dick and Hill, per C. J. Estlin.

New Orleans, 14th July, '46.

[2] Probably John Ferguson, Jr., sometime of the firm of Ferguson & O'Dowd, commission merchants, 84 Tchoupitoulas Street, New Orleans. *Cohen's New Orleans and Lafayette Directory . . . for 1849,* p. 64.

[3] Produce merchants, 102 Tchoupitoulas Street, New Orleans. *New Orleans Annual and Commercial Register for 1846,* p. 272. In 1849 the two were listed as "agents for N. O. and Mobile Daily U.S. mail line" with offices at 12 Bank Place. *Cohen's New Orleans and Lafayette Directory . . . for 1849,* p. 73.

[4] Robert M. McAlpin (McAlphin) and Joseph Tagert, grocers, corner Common and New Levee streets, New Orleans. *New Orleans Annual and Commercial Register for 1846,* pp. 402, 543.

Nashville, September 26, 1846.

Executors of Isaac Franklin,

Bought of John W. Martin,[5]

For the Bellevue Plantation:

| | |
|---|---|
| 1680 lbs. bacon, at 4½ cents per lb., | $76 60 |
| 365 lbs. shoulders, 4 | 14 60 |
| 2 hogsheads, 1 00 | 2 00 |
| 1 cask, to pack shoulders, | 75 |
| | $92 95 |

Received payment of O. B. Hayes, executor,
September 28, 1846. Jno. W. Martin. By J. C. Harris

$922 74 Nashville, Nov. 7, 1846. No. –

At sight, pay to the order of Geo. McGregor,[6] Esq., agent, nine hundred and twenty-two dollars and seventy-four cents, value received, and charge the same to account of supplies for the Bellevue plantation,

O. B. Hayes, Executor of Isaac Franklin, deceased.

To Messrs. Dick & Hill, New Orleans.
*Paid,* 19th *Nov.* 1846. George McGregor, Agent.

New Orleans, January 7, 1847.

Executors of Isaac Franklin,

Bought of Dudley and Nelson.[7]

| | |
|---|---|
| 1 hhd. fine sugar, 1205–120–1085, at 7¼, | $78 68 |
| 5 bags Rio coffee, 820, at 8, | 65 60 |
| 1 demj. fine brandy, demj., 6b., 2 gal. 450, | 5 75 |
| Drayage, | 50 |
| Executors Isaac Franklin. | $154 51 |
| Bellevue, | 213 91 |
| Pr. Concordia | $368 42 |

[*Received payment from Messrs. Nalle and Cox.*
*Dudley and Nelson, Pr. Chas. E. Barklay.*

5 Although this item is dated at Nashville, it may have been ordered through John Martin of Martin, Pleasants & Co., commission merchants, 92 Common Street, New Orleans. *Ibid.,* 396.

6 Located at 87 Common Street, New Orleans. *Cohen's New Orleans and Lafayette Directory . . . for 1849,* p. 116.

7 W. H. Dudley and J. P. Nelson, wholesale and retail grocers, 6 Old Levee Street, New Orleans. *New Orleans Annual and Commercial Register for 1846,* pp. 222, 441.

New Orleans, January 8, 1847.

Executors Isaac Franklin Estate,

Bought of Dudley and Nelson.

| | |
|---|---|
| 20 barrels molasses, 816 gal., at 26c., | 212 16 |
| Drayage, | 1 75 |
| Bellevue, per Magnolia. | $213 91 |

Received payment from Messrs. Nalle and Cox.

Dudley and Nelson, per Charles E. Barklay.

Estate of Isaac Franklin,

Bought of Dudley & Nelson,

| 1847. | | | | | | |
|---|---|---|---|---|---|---|
| Jan'ry. | 25 | 5 | gallons Cog[nac] brandy, | 2 50 | | |
| | | | dem. $1 | | 13 50 | |
| | | | Drayage to s'bt. Concordia | | 25 | 13 75 |
| Feb'ry. | 26 | 4 | boxes sardines | | 4 00 | |
| | | 1 | HF powder | | 6 00 | |
| | | 1 | bag buck shot | | 1 75 | |
| | | 3 | small do | 1 50 | 4 50 | |
| | | 1 | catty tea | | 2 75 | |
| | | 30 | loaf sugar, | 16c | 4 80 | |
| | | 2 | kegs mustard | 6b | 1 50 | |
| | | 2 | jars pickles | 4b | 1 00 | |
| | | 1 | box soap, 48 | 6¾ | 3 24 | |
| | | | Per st'bt. Sam Dale, drayage | | 25 | 29 79 |
| May | 6 | 1 | tierce rice 671–67–604 | | 31 71 | |
| | | | nett | 5¼ | | |
| | | | Drayage to st'bt. Sam Dale | | 25 | 31 96 |
| November | 2 | 5 | black tea | $1 | 5 00 | |
| | | 24 | best loaf sugar | 16c | 8 84 | 8 84 |
| | | | Per Magnolia, | | | |
| December | 21 | 15 | bags co[arse] salt | 85 | 12 75 | |
| | | 5 | fine do | 1 25 | 6 25 | |
| | | | Drayage | 75 | 75 | 19 75 |

| | | | | | | |
|---|---|---|---|---|---|---|
| Jan'ry. | 11 | 1 | box sperm candles, 33¼ | 36 | | 11 97 |
| | 17 | 5 | bags Rio coffee, 818, | 7½ | 61 35 | |
| | | 1 | hhd. sugar, 1170–117–1053, | 5¼ | 55 28 | |
| | | 25 | bbls molasses, 1103 | 19½ | 215 08 | |
| | | | Drayage, | | 2 50 | $334 21 |
| | | | | | | $450 27 |

. . . . . . . . . . . . .

Messrs. Nalle & Coxe will please pay Dudley & Nelson or order, the amount of the within account and charge, to the estate of Isaac Franklin.

New Orleans, February 17, 1848. John Armfield,

Dudley & Nelson.

Received of James Watson, for estate of Isaac Franklin, one hundred and thirty dollars and eight cents for 2168 lbs. bulk pork at 66[6c].

Feb. 20th, 1847. Wm. A. Pearcey.

Received of James Watson, one hundred and forty-two dollars [and] fifty-one cents, on acc't of pork sold to the estate of Isaac Franklin, dec'd. $142 51

[March ? 1847] McCoy and Stocking.

Angola, March, 5th, 1847.

$260 Messrs. Dick and Hill: Gentlemen, you will please pay McCoy and Stocking, two hundred and sixty dollars; it being for pork bought for the estate of Isaac Franklin.

James Watson.
G. Coates
McCoy and Stocking.

*Paid*, 19 *March*, '47.

1847, March 10. Franklin Woodyard.

Received of James Watson eighteen dollars and twenty-five cents, for 1440 lbs. hay at 90c per cwt., and 62 lbs. of bacon hams at 8½c per lb.

H. W. Hughes.

Angola, March 12th, 1847.

$2300 Messrs. Dick and Hill. Gentlemen, you will pay at sight to Richard Plummer, the sum of twenty-three hundred dollars, it being for corn and pork bought for the use of the plantation, and charge the same to the estate of Isaac Franklin.

Very respct. yours, James Watson.

Attest: Jas. S. Clack, Agent.
*Paid, 15 March, '47.* Richard Plummer.

. . . . . . . . . . . . .

## c] The Fruits of Interdependence

### [1] The Growth of Commerce on the Western Rivers

. . . . . . . . . . . . . . .

THE RECEIPTS of New Orleans during the first year of successful steam navigation, 1816, amounted in value to $8,062,540. . . .

This is independent of the produce raised in Louisiana, such as cotton, corn, indigo, molasses, rice, sugar, tafia or rum, and lumber. These were brought to the market in the planters' crafts, and often taken from the plantation direct in foreign-bound vessels, a ship loading directly with sugar and molasses, which thus never went through New Orleans. But little account was taken of this system in the commercial reports of the time, although sea-going vessels ascended the river as far as Natchez for cargoes. They were, of course, of small size, of but little more tonnage and draught than the steam-boats themselves.

The value of receipts shows to what extent the produce of the West passed through New Orleans. Cotton, which in later days rose to be 60 and even 75 per cent. in value of all the receipts, was then barely 12 per cent. At least 80 per cent. of the articles came from the West, that is, from the Ohio and the Upper Mississippi, above the Ohio. They represented the surplus products of the Mississippi Valley, for but little found any other exit to market. Much of the produce shipped from the West to New Orleans was lost en route. A rough estimate places the loss from disasters, snags, etc., at 20 per cent. Many boats, moreover, stopped along the river on their way down to sell supplies to the planters. Thus, at Natchez, flour, grain, and pork were purchased from the Kentucky boats.

From these losses and sales the shipments down the river in 1816, including the products of Louisiana, may be estimated at $13,875,000.

The river traffic required 6 steam-boats, 594 barges, and 1287 flat-boats, of an actual tonnage of 87,670.

. . . . . . . . . . . . . . .

FROM U.S. Congress, House, *Report on the Internal Commerce of the United States.* House Executive Document No. 6, part 2. 50th Congress, 1st Session, 1888. (Washington: Government Printing Office, 1888), pp. 191, 199, 205, and 214–15. Reprinted in Guy S. Callender, *Selections from the Economic History of the United States, 1765–1860* (Boston: Ginn & Co., 1909), pp. 313–21.

During all this period [1816–'40], and despite all these difficulties, the number of arrivals at New Orleans and the amount of river business on the Lower Mississippi continued to steadily increase. The growth of the river traffic is well shown in this table.

In regard to the steam-boats, it should be remembered that the steady increase in arrivals each year does not fully express the increase in tonnage, because the boats were not only growing more numerous, but were increasing in size each year, and thus while they doubled in number between 1825, and 1833 they more than trebled in their carrying capacity.

In regard to the flat-boats and other craft, there is no sufficiently definite information for most of this period. It should be said, however, that while the steam-boats supplanted the flat-boats in many lines of trade, they did not entirely drive them off the river for fifteen or twenty years afterwards. During all this period when the Western cities were building steam-boats the flat-boats also were increasing in numbers. They were found serviceable in carrying hay, coal, etc., and in reaching the interior streams. The Mississippi counted some hundreds of tributaries. On some of these the settlements were sparse, and the surplus products afforded at best one or two cargoes a year, and these were sent much more conveniently and cheaply in flat-boats than in steamers. The steamers had passed the flats between 1820 and 1830 in the business transacted and the freight hauled, and from this time they increased the lead steadily. The number of flats, however, arriving at New Orleans kept but little if any behind the steamers, and as late as 1840 nearly a fifth of the freight handled in the Lower Mississippi went by flat-boat, keel, or barge. The early flat-boats had depended altogether on the current of the river to carry them down. The system of towing was tried in 1829, and a small steamer, which would be called a tug to-day, was successfully used in towing keel-boats up and down stream. The idea did not seem, however, to meet with much favor, the flat-boat men having a superstition that their conjunction with a steamer was not favorable to them, and it was reserved for a later generation to definitely try in the barge the system of towing freight up and down stream. . . .

As the first two decades of the century showed the settlement of the Ohio basin, and a rapid increase in population and production, so the next two resulted in the settlement of the Lower Mississippi region from Louisiana to the mouth of the Ohio. The removal of the Indian tribes to the Indian Territory, the building of levees, and the immense increase in the demand for cotton, hastened the development of West Tennessee, Mississippi, Arkansas, and Northern Louisiana. The Western products received at New Orleans, although they did not fall off, constituted a smaller percentage of the city's total trade, while cotton and sugar became each year more important items commercially. In other words, the Western trade, while not growing less, did not increase as fast as that section advanced in population and production, nor as fast as the cotton trade.

It was during this period that the South first began to insist on the sovereignty of King Cotton, and New Orleans claimed, like Mahomet, to be its prophet. The rapid development of the cotton manufacturing industries in Europe incited the planters to devote more and more acres to it, and it became highly profitable to cultivate cotton even on credit. New Orleans was overflowing with money in those flush times, and lent it readily, and the credit system of the South was firmly established, to last even to this day. The system became universal among the planters, particularly those engaged in raising cotton and sugar, and New Orleans became not only the lender of money at a high rate of interest, but the depot of western supplies, which it advanced in large quantities to the planters throughout the vast region then tributary to it. The whole agricultural country along the Lower Mississippi and its bayous and streams became, in a manner, the commercial slaves of the New Orleans factors, and were not allowed to sell to any one else or buy from them. The western produce shipped down the river never stopped at the plantation, but was sent direct to New Orleans, and thence transshipped up the river over the same route it had just gone. When the big collapse of 1837 came the banks of New Orleans, with a circulation of $7,000,000, purported to have a capital of $34,000,000, a great majority of them being wrecked in the storm. Within a few years, however, New Orleans recovered from the shock and strengthened its hold on the planters.

While the Mississippi Valley was listening at the Memphis convention to the story of its glories to come, and river men were calculating on the immense traffic that was assured the future, New Orleans was confident of the future. Few of its people anticipated any danger of its future, and it was predicted not only in American papers but in the British Quarterly Review that it must ultimately become, on account of the Mississippi, the most important commercial city in America, if not in the world.

That eminent statistical and economical authority, De Bow's Review, declared that "no city of the world has ever advanced as a mart of commerce with such gigantic and rapid strides as New Orleans."

It was no idle boast. Between 1830 and 1840 no city of the United States kept pace with it. When the census was taken it was fourth in population, exceeded only by New York, Philadelphia, and Baltimore, and third in point of commerce of the ports of the world, exceeded only by London, Liverpool, and New York, being, indeed, but a short distance behind the latter city, and ahead of it in the export of domestic products. Unfortunately, its imports were out of all proportion with its exports. It shipped coffee, hardware, and other heavy articles like this up the river, but it left the West dependent on New York and the other Atlantic cities for nearly all the finer class of manufactured goods they needed.

Later on, when the West began to go into manufacturing itself, and Cincinnati and Pittsburgh became important manufacturing centers, New Orleans imported their goods and reshipped them to the plantations. Of these shipments up-stream over 75 per cent., strange to say, were articles which had previously been sent downstream. Cincinnati sent its lard, candles, pork, etc., to New Orleans to be carried up by the coast packets to Bayou Sara and Baton Rouge. From these latter towns were shipped so many hogsheads of sugar and barrels of molasses to New Orleans to be thence sent by the Cincinnati boats to the Ohio metropolis. There was no trade between the Western cities and the Southern plantations, very little even with the towns; it all paid tribute to New Orleans.

The upper Mississippi had from 1850 become the center of immigration and production, and New Orleans, which had formerly depended on the Ohio River country almost wholly for its supplies, now largely got them from Saint Louis. About 1850 the traffic with Saint Louis exceeded that with Cincinnati. In 1859, 32 steamboats of 48,726 tons were required for the Saint Louis and 36 of 26,932 tons for the Cincinnati trade. . . .

The extent of the commercial area covered by the river traffic of New Orleans in 1860 will show what was lost in the four years of war that followed, and never fully regained. New Orleans then absolutely controlled the entire river trade, commerce, and crops of the State of Louisiana. In Texas, through the Red River, it secured the crops of the northern half of the State; through the Arkansas and the Red it secured the products of the greater portion of the Indian Territory. It controlled the trade of the southern two-thirds of Arkansas, all the Ouachita and Arkansas valleys, all the river front, and a portion of the White River trade running up into Missouri. It controlled Mississippi with the exception of the eastern portion of the State, through which ran the Mobile and Ohio railroad and the tributaries of the Alabama. All the produce of western Tennessee and half that of middle Tennessee went to New Orleans; and in Kentucky a large proportion of the business went to the Crescent City. The bulk of the produce of the Ohio valley had been diverted to the lakes and Atlantic seaboard, but probably one-fifth of it found its way to New Orleans direct or by way of the Cincinnati and Louisville packets.

In the upper Mississippi probably a third of the surplus, or exported crops, similarly reached market by way of New Orleans, either direct or via Saint Louis.

The territory immediately tributary to New Orleans included all Louisiana, half of the settled portion of Texas, half of the Indian Territory, three-fourths of Arkansas, three-fourths of Mississippi, a third of Tennessee, and considerable portions of Kentucky and Alabama, probably 300,000 square miles, while indirectly tributary to it, through Saint Louis, Cincinnati, and Louisville, was a region twice as great.

Yet it was admitted at the time that New Orleans and the river route were losing some trade, and it was felt that the railroads were diverting traffic away from it. They had tapped the river at various points. The tributaries running into the Upper Tennessee, had formerly sent down their produce by flat-boats to New Orleans, the boats reaching the city in fleets of thirty and forty. Railroads had diverted much of this traffic to Charleston, Savannah, and the Atlantic cities. The trade of northern Alabama had formerly come via the Tennessee to New Orleans. It was almost gone and the receipts from North Alabama were actually less in 1860 than in 1845, although the crops had grown manifold larger. The lead trade of the upper Mississippi had been diverted from the river by the railroads. At Cincinnati a large portion of the flour and grain that had been formerly sent down the river traveled either up it to Pittsburgh or went direct by rail to New York, or by canal to Cleveland, Buffalo, and thence by the Hudson. In the twenty years between 1840 and 1860, during which the competition of river and rail had been inaugurated, the production of the Mississippi

Valley had increased far more rapidly than the receipts at New Orleans. The river traffic had increased in the aggregate, but lost relatively.

The Mississippi carried a much larger tonnage, but a far smaller percentage of the total traffic of the valley. The loss was most marked in Western products. Forty years before, these had constituted 58 per cent of the total receipts at New Orleans. In 1859–'60 they had fallen to 23 per cent. although in that period the West had made the greatest increase in population and production. What was lost here, however, was more than made good in the cotton and sugar crops, and the river trade of New Orleans therefore showed no decline but a steady, active, and positive advance.

During all this period "the levee" of New Orleans, as the river landing of that city was called, was the wonder of every visitor. It was beyond doubt the most active commercial center of the world. Here, side by side, lay the steam-boats and flat-boats of the river, the steamers, ships, and numerous ocean vessels. Here the entire business of New Orleans and of the greater portion of the valley was transacted. The levee was the landing, warehouse, commercial exchange of half a continent, and the freight handled there exceeded that to be seen on any single dock-yard of London or Liverpool. . . .

The flat-boat trade slowly went out during this period [1840–'60]. It had been a cheap but very unsafe way of getting produce to market. It is estimated that not more than three-fourths to four-fifths of the flat-boats when started down river to New Orleans ever reached that port, the others being snagged or lost. A squall on the river would sink a dozen at a time. At the same time the flat-boat offered great advantages to the farmers living along the smaller streams penetrating into the center of Indiana and Ohio. Indeed, there was no other way of their getting their produce to market, as the low water, snags, etc., rendered it impossible for the steam-boats to penetrate there. A flat-boat was accordingly built after the crop was gathered, loaded down with produce, and the spring tide waited for to float it out. . . .

The steady decline of this trade can be here studied. The only State which shows an increase is Pennsylvania, due to the coal trade. Indiana, particularly the Wabash country, sent a considerable amount of produce, largely hay, to New Orleans by flat-boats; and so did the upper tributaries of the Tennessee River, whence the tobacco was shipped on flat-boats. On the other hand, the flat-boat traffic of the upper Mississippi had given way to the steam-boats, and neither Missouri nor Iowa sent a single flat to New Orleans. Some remarkable fluctuations will be noticed in the arrivals from year to year, attributable to the condition of the river. When the water was high, as in 1851–'52, the flat-boats got out without any difficulty. On the other hand, in the previous season, which was a low one, the flat-boat tonnage was reduced much below the average. After 1856 the flat-boat played so unimportant a part in the river traffic that it ceased to be enumerated among the arrivals.

. . . . . . . . . . . . . . .

## [2] Commercial Specialization in the Port of New York (1846)

*Merchants*

| | |
|---|---|
| General | 31 |
| "Importing and Commission" | 51 |
| "Shipping and Commission" | 138 |
| "Shipping and Importing" | 8 |

*Importers*

| | |
|---|---|
| Artificial flowers | 5 |
| Baskets, willow | 5 |
| Bolting cloths | 3 |
| Bristles | 9 |
| Bronzes | 2 |
| Burr blocks | 2 |
| Buttons | 6 |
| China, glass & earthenware | 53 |
| Cloths, cassimeres & vestings | 36 |
| Coffee | 69 |
| Drugs | 37 |
| Dry Goods | 89 |
| Dundee goods (burlaps, duck, etc.) | 5 |
| Essential oils | 4 |
| Fancy goods | 59 |
| "General" | 17 |
| Goat skins | 4 |
| Guns & pistols | 10 |
| Hairdressers' articles | 4 |
| Hardware & Cutlery | 86 |
| Hatters' trimmings | 1 |
| Hemp | 8 |
| Hides | 17 |
| Homeopathic medicines | 1 |
| Hosiery & gloves | 16 |
| Indigo | 28 |
| Laces & embroideries | 24 |
| Linen | 2 |
| Looking glass plates | 6 |

*Importers (cont'd)*

| | |
|---|---|
| Marble | 5 |
| Morocco | 1 |
| Musical instruments | 5 |
| Needles & fish hooks | 6 |
| Oil paintings | 1 |
| Olive oil | 9 |
| Perfumery | 2 |
| Plate glass | 2 |
| Precious stones | 3 |
| Rice | 30 |
| Russia goods | 9 |
| Sail duck | 4 |
| "Segars" | 44 |
| Sewing silks | 15 |
| Silks & fancy dry goods | 42 |
| Slates | 2 |
| Stationery | 4 |
| Steel | 1 |
| Steel pens | 1 |
| Straw goods | 8 |
| Sugar | 45 |
| Suspenders | 1 |
| Tea | 17 |
| Toys | 7 |
| Twine | 2 |
| Watches | 40 |
| Watchmakers' tools | 2 |
| Wines & liquors | 89 |
| Woollens | 6 |
| Worsted goods | 6 |

*Commission Merchants*

| | |
|---|---|
| Dry goods | 91 |
| General | 317 |
| Hardware & cutlery, domestic | 8 |
| Produce (flour, etc.) | 86 |

FROM Robert G. Albion, *The Rise of New York Port* (New York: Charles Scribner's Sons, 1939), pp. 421–22. Reprinted by permission of Charles Scribner's Sons.

| *Auctioneers* | 66 |
|---|---|

| *Jobbers* | |
|---|---|
| Boots & shoes | 42 |
| China, glass & earthenware | 93 |
| Clothiers | 24 |
| Cloths, cassimeres & vestings | 14 |
| Druggists | 46 |
| Dry goods | 224 |
| " " (also importers) | 23 |
| Fancy goods | 30 |
| Fruit, foreign | 24 |
| Grocers | 221 |
| Hardware & cutlery | 35 |
| Hats, caps & furs | 42 |
| Hosiery & gloves | 8 |
| Laces & embroideries | 6 |
| Ready made linen & stocks | 3 |
| Silks & fancy dry goods | 40 |
| Tea | 1 |
| Wines & liquors | 22 |

| *"Merchants" or "Dealers"* (Not differentiated in respect to above functions) | |
|---|---|
| Carpet dealers | 33 |
| Coal dealers | 95 |
| Cotton merchants | 3 |
| Flaxseed dealer | 1 |
| Flour dealers | 39 |
| Fur dealers & furriers | 55 |
| Grindstones & plaster | 55 |
| Hide & leather dealers | 33 |
| Leather only | 18 |
| Iron merchants | 38 |
| Lumber dealers | 60 |
| Mahogany yards | 22 |
| Military goods | 10 |
| Molasses merchant | 1 |
| Oil merchants | 42 |
| Pot & pearl ash & saleratus dealers | 5 |
| Produce dealers | 6 |
| Rice dealer | 1 |
| Salt dealers | 4 |
| Stave yards | 4 |
| Stone yards | 32 |

| *Brokers* | |
|---|---|
| Bill | 5 |
| Bullion | 1 |
| Commission | 5 |
| Cotton | 13 |
| Custom House | 9 |
| Drug | 22 |
| Dry goods | 4 |
| Dye woods | 1 |
| Exchange | 114 |
| General | 9 |
| Hide & skin | 1 |
| Insurance | 4 |
| Merchandise | 18 |
| Metal | 3 |
| Money | 2 |
| Note | 3 |
| Oil | 2 |
| Produce | 17 |
| Rice | 2 |
| Ship | 8 |
| Tea | 3 |
| Tobacco | 2 |
| Wine | 4 |
| Wood | 1 |
| Wool | 3 |

| *Agents* | |
|---|---|
| Collecting | 3 |
| General | 4 |
| Miscellaneous | 17 |
| Passenger | 2 |

| *Other Functions* | |
|---|---|
| Accountants | 12 |
| Bankers, private | 17 |
| Barometer & thermometer makers | 3 |
| "Boarding houses—sailor" | 70 |
| Boat builders | 19 |
| Booksellers, foreign | 3 |
| Chain cables | 2 |
| Chocolate & cocoa mfrs. | 6 |
| Chronometer makers | 5 |
| Coffee roasters | 7 |
| " " & spice factors | 24 |

| *Other Functions (cont'd)* | |
|---|---|
| Commercial agency | 1 |
| Consulates | 45 |
| Cordage mfrs. | 5 |
| Cordage, rope & twine dealers | 4 |
| Cotton, damaged, dealers | 2 |
| " menders | 2 |
| " presses | 4 |
| Distillers | 25 |
| Dock builders | 2 |
| Docks (dry, & marine railways) | 4 |
| Expresses | 13 |
| Forwarding & transportation merchants | 27 |
| Gaugers | 8 |
| Harbor masters | 4 |
| Hide currier | 1 |
| Inspectors (flour, tobacco, etc.) | 21 |
| Insurance companies, marine | 19 |
| Leather dressers | 24 |
| Lighter offices | 3 |
| Map & chart publishers | 8 |
| Marine surveyor | 1 |
| Mathematical & nautical instrument makers | 16 |
| Mercantile agencies | 2 |
| Packet offices | 14 |
| Passage offices | 3 |
| Port wardens | 5 |
| Rectifiers of spirits | 14 |
| "Refinishers, pressers & packers of dry goods" | 5 |
| Riggers & stevedores | 18 |
| Sailmakers | 35 |
| Ship builders | 9 |
| Ship chandlers | 57 |
| Ship joiners | 28 |
| Ship smiths | 22 |
| Ship wrights | 13 |
| Shipping offices | 9 |
| Spar makers | 6 |
| Steam engine builders | 8 |
| Sugar refiners | 9 |
| Weighers | 43 |

# PART III
# Production

# INTRODUCTION

When we look away to Dixieland we are apt to see only vast plantations on which hundreds of Negro slaves toiled "from day clean to first dark" to produce the South's cotton crop. To be sure, the large plantation was an essential part of the picture, but the part must not be mistaken for the whole. In 1860 there were in the South 1,516,000 free families, of whom only 385,000 were owners of slaves; nearly three-fourths of all free Southern families owned no slaves at all! The "typical" Southerner, as Kenneth Stampp points out, was not only a small farmer but a non-slaveholder. A large majority of the slave-owning families, moreover, owned only a few slaves. As the following table reveals, in 1850, 89 per cent of the owners held less than 20 slaves, 71 per cent less than 10, and almost 50 per cent less than 5. If we accept the usual definition of a planter as a man who owned at least 20 slaves, these proportions make it clear not only that the "typical" slaveholder was not a planter, but also that the "typical" planter worked only a moderate-sized gang of from 20 to 50 slaves. The "planter aristocracy" was made up of some 10,000 families living off the labor of gangs of more than 50 slaves. Yet it was on the large agricultural units that most of the slaves were to be found. Ownership was so highly concentrated that only one-fourth of the slaves belonged to masters holding less than 10, considerably more than half lived on plantations holding more than 20, and approximately a quarter belonged to masters owning more than 50.

PERCENTAGE DISTRIBUTION OF SLAVEHOLDING FAMILIES ACCORDING TO NUMBER OF SLAVES HELD, 1790 AND 1850[1]

| NUMBER OF SLAVES | PERCENTAGE OF FAMILIES | |
|---|---|---|
| | *1790* | *1850* |
| 1 | 24.5 | 17.4 |
| 2 and under 5 | 30.5 | 29.5 |
| 5 and under 10 | 22.0 | 24.4 |
| 10 and under 20 | 14.3 | 17.4 |
| 20 and under 50 | 6.4 | 9.1 |
| 50 and under 100 | 1.0 | 1.7 |
| 100 and under 200 | 0.2 | 0.4 |
| 200 and under 300 | [a] | 0.1 |
| 300 and over | [a] | [a] |
| Unknown | 1.0 | |

1 Ross M. Robertson, *History of the American Economy* (New York: Harcourt, Brace & World, 1964), p. 119.
[a] Less than one-tenth of 1 per cent.

As is suggested by the fact that a large majority of the owners held only a few slaves, cotton was the crop of the "little" man as well as the big. Indeed, its cultivation required no slave labor at all, and it was accordingly grown on small farms without slaves—or with only a few—and on middling- to large-sized farms as well as on plantations. Unlike rice and sugar cane, which required large investments of capital for processing machinery, cotton required little. A small farmer could cultivate it with the assistance of his wife and children, and he had little trouble getting it ginned and prepared for market. As a rule, the value of cotton in relation to its bulk was sufficiently high to bear the costs of transport over considerable distances without jeopardizing the hope of profit. Cotton stood abuse much better than many other farm commodities; it was nonperishable and hence suffered relatively little from rough handling, exposure, long delays, and poor warehousing while in transit to market. Smaller agricultural units were thus enabled to make substantial contributions to each year's crop. Nevertheless, in all probability the bulk of the crop came from the plantations, where most of the slaves were concentrated.

Total output, Table 3B makes plain, increased remarkably each decade before the Civil War, in large part because of the increasing size of the Cotton Kingdom itself. The volume of output naturally rose as more resources were attracted into production. The contribution made by each of the states to this result, in terms of both total and per capita output, is shown in Tables 3C and 3G, respectively. Probably the per capita output of the slave labor force, as well as that of the population of each state as a whole, also rose. David Christy calculated in the 1850's that average cotton exports per slave rose from 83 pounds in 1820 to 143 in 1830, 295 in 1840, and 337 in 1850 (see selection 5a in Part II). Christy was willing to give some credit for this increase in productivity to the superior fertility of Western soils, but his main explanation was essentially that the South pursued its comparative advantage in the production of cotton and other staples and looked elsewhere for the goods others could produce more cheaply. It specialized, and the natural result was greater efficiency in production.

However, when one descends from the safe heights of generalized deduction and begins to ask questions about practices followed at different times and under varying conditions—price, size of plantation, and methods of management—enormous complexities appear. On small agricultural units—the great majority of the units in the South—the masters usually gave close personal supervision to the unspecialized labor of a few slaves. Many were obliged to work in the fields alongside their hands, although those in command of as few as half a dozen slaves sought a more elevated social status by refraining from such labors. Nevertheless, small slave forces lacked skilled craftsmen, and their masters found it necessary to repair tools, do carpentry work, and perform other specialized tasks. At picking time in the fall the master usually supplemented his small force with his own labor.

Substantial farmers and small planters who owned from 10 to 30 slaves normally lived on their own land and devoted full time to the management of their enterprise. They did not as a rule employ overseers, although they might have the aid of a slave foreman or driver, whose essential function was to urge on the slave gangs by word or whip. Agricultural units of this size usually benefitted from some labor specialization. Besides the field hands and driver, a few slaves might exercise manual skills or perform domestic work. Even so, the unit was too small for full-time carpenters or cooks, so that the latter often had to work in the fields as well.

Maximum specialization was possible for those planters who owned 30 or more slaves. Only rarely did such owners fail to use overseers, whose functions are well described in the following readings by a planter's written instructions to his overseer. Overseers were generally retained on a year-to-year basis under a written contract that could be terminated at will by either party, and as a rule each overseer made use of one or more drivers in working the slave gang. The "gang system" was one of two basic methods of labor management. Under the other—the less frequently used "task system"—each hand was given a specific daily assignment and could quit work when the task was completed. The planter who hired a full-time overseer was able to devote his own attention to problems of marketing, finance, and general plantation administration. He also enjoyed sufficient leisure to be able to absent himself from his plantation more or less at his own discretion. But absentee ownership was not characteristic on plantations of any size.

Plantations containing 30 or more slaves enjoyed a considerable degree of labor specialization. Household servants and field hands were clearly distinguished from each other, and the latter were divided between plow gangs and hoe gangs. On the larger plantations slaves were able to devote their full time to such occupations as ditching, tending livestock, driving wagons, and taking care of vegetable gardens. In 1854 one Virginia planter had 8 plowmen, 10 hoe hands, 2 wagoners, 4 oxcart drivers, a carriage driver, a hostler, a stable boy, a shepherd, a cowherd, a swineherd, 2 carpenters, 5 masons, 2 smiths, a miller, 2 shoemakers, 5 spinners, a weaver, a butler, 2 waitresses, 4 maids, a nurse, a laundress, a seamstress, a dairy maid, a gardener, and 2 cooks attached to the field service. The owner of a very large establishment employed a general manager or steward to help him run the estate. If several plantations were involved he might run one himself, but as a rule he hired an overseer for each of them.

That numerous plantations were managed with a high degree of efficiency is clear from the record. Just as certainly, others were not. Note in the following readings the detailed and informed charges made by R. Abbey, himself a Mississippi planter. The essence of Abbey's indictment is that his fellow planters are unenterprising, and are uninterested in anything new or in ways of cutting costs. Also note the complaints by Liverpool merchants and cotton brokers about the careless packing of cotton, which echoes one of Abbey's points. Some views of the well-known editor Freeman Hunt are also presented; making the same general observation as Christy, but drawing a different lesson from it, he says that from 1800 to 1860 it had taken progressively fewer slaves per bale to produce the cotton crop. Hunt's explanation differs from that of Christy, though. In part, he says, slaves have been "drafted from other pursuits to the cotton plantations." This meant, of course, that the output of cotton of the slave population as a whole rather than the productivity of the cotton-working proportion of that population had risen. But Hunt also claims that the "most advanced planters" have realized increased output per acre "by improved methods of culture," and he concludes that "there can be no doubt that the introduction of the same enlightened views among the Southern planters will issue in a large increase in our cotton crops." Surely the testimony of these varied witnesses leads to the conclusion that, however great the efficiencies achieved by the planters, there was indeed room for improvement.

That improved techniques were sometimes adopted is clear enough. For example, improvements in baling methods between 1820 and 1860 made possible an increase in the average weight of bales from 250 to 400 pounds. Other improvements appear to have increased the number of acres each hand could cultivate. According to *The American Farmer,* in 1820 the usual crop in middle Georgia for each full hand was 6 acres of cotton and 8 of corn. Ulrich B. Phillips reports that in the following decades mules were advantageously substituted for horses and oxen, implements of tillage were improved, and greater expertness was achieved by harvesters, with the result that the number of acres per hand rose to 10 of cotton and 10 of corn. Obviously, however, the number of acres a hand could cultivate also depended on the nature of the terrain. If the land were flat prairie or river bottom, as many as 10 acres per hand might be planted; if it were hilly or rolling, the limit might range from 3 to 8. In his valuable report on cotton, included in the following readings, Secretary of the Treasury Levi Woodbury arrives at an average of 8 acres. "Some say five to seven, and others ten," the Secretary explains. He places at 5 to 8 the number of acres of corn the hand could also assist in raising. The Woodbury Report is dated 1836; this illustrates the point that the variable of time as well as those of place and differing conditions must be taken into account in any full-scale investigation of planter efficiency. Given our present knowledge, the significance of particular influences in rising productivity—whether of labor or land—are difficult to assess; it is uncertain how generally they made themselves felt, and how strong was the pull of opposing tendencies. It is difficult, therefore, to generalize.

Whatever the degree of efficiency attained by the planters in producing their cotton—a complex problem that still awaits careful study of differing periods, areas, and conditions—their general disposition to produce as much of it as possible seems clear. Small crops, Professor McCay of the University of Georgia argues in the following readings, are an "injury to the planter." Not only do they bring in less money to the planter, but by stimulating prices they encourage the production of cotton in India and elsewhere "and thus endanger the monopoly which we now possess in the European market." They also bring on other specified woes. On the other hand, "over-production and ruinously low prices are a still greater injury." Nevertheless, McCay's counsel is clear: "The proper course for the planter, and the one he is sure to pursue, is to make as much cotton as he can, while the price is fair and remunerative. As soon as it falls below this, he should apply both his capital and labor to other pursuits." Note particularly that the course McCay recommends is the one the planter "is sure to pursue" anyway. Note too that the planter is advised to diversify only after the price of cotton becomes unremunerative. Only then should he "undertake new schemes, not yet tried and proved, which promise fair profits to capital"; only then should he encourage "every new enterprise calculated to diversify our labor, develop our resources, and divert capital and labor from our great staple."

Are not these words clear expressions of the cotton conservatism of the planting South against which the selection by R. Abbey is tilting its lance of enterprise? The call is clear: the planter must make as much cotton as he can while the price is fair and remunerative. Whether or not he is so advised, he will do this anyway. Perhaps this conservative commitment to cotton reflected, in part at least, the fact that the crop brought the planter a generally good livelihood. Perhaps it also reflected in part the planter's supreme confidence in Europe's insatiable demand for the South's "great staple." But there is an alternative explanation of the tendency to maximize production, and this explanation is so deep-set in the literature of the subject that it amounts to an historical tradition.

According to the tradition, it was not the planter but the factor or commission merchant who was responsible for the constantly growing crops, for the pouring of resources into the production of cotton to the neglect of a more diversified agriculture, for the failure of cities to grow and of manufactures and shipbuilding to develop—in a word, for the economic bondage of an underdeveloped region. The villain in the piece is the so-called penalty commission clause of the factorage contract, which required the planter to pay a penalty on the shortage if production fell below a certain quota. Planters are said to have signed such contracts to get credit. Factors are said to have frequently refused to advance credit unless given the exclusive right to sell the planter's crop. Their fundamental purpose in extending credit was to gain control of the sale of crops in order to earn commissions on the sales, and their purpose in inserting the penalty commission clause was to make sure that the sales would be large.

It is certain that factors sometimes demanded and received written contractual guarantees of the right to market the crop of a planter to whom they had advanced money. However, the careful research of the most recent student of this question, Harold D. Woodman, establishes beyond reasonable doubt that written contracts were the exception rather than the rule. The obligation on the part of the planter to consign his cotton to a factor from whom he had received an advance was at most "moral" rather than legal. No doubt some planters felt bound by the obligation and acted accordingly. But many others did not, and it is therefore difficult to believe that the value structure of the community was decisively arrayed against such conduct. There can be no doubt that factors making advances hoped that planters would thereby be induced to give them their business. This hope is plain in the correspondence of William Bostwick, selections from which are presented in Part IV. It is certain that the hope was sometimes not realized. In fact, planters who had received advances often consigned their cotton to two or more factors simultaneously and changed factors even in mid-season, an impossible act if they had been tightly or legally bound to a particular factor.

Thus, in all probability it was not an institutional imperative—the factorage contract—that was responsible for the planter's tendency to maximize production and concentrate investment in lands and slaves. The ownership of land and slaves not only afforded him an economic livelihood but also served as a prime source of prestige and status in Southern society. Is it possible that the most fundamental elements in production policy —what to produce and in what quantities—were questions that were sometimes not answered in the light of business judgment? In attempting to answer this question we must not overlook—as the selection by Professor McCay does not do—the difficulty faced by thousands of scattered units of production in adopting policies conducive to their common interests. That has almost always been a basic element of the "farm problem" in the United States, after the Civil War as well as before it.

In the first of the following readings a contemporary, writing in *Harper's Monthly Magazine,* describes the process of "making cotton" from the readying of the field for the seed to the baling of the harvested crop. The next selection consists of excerpts from the diary of a Mississippi planter depicting the routine of the cotton year. The two following readings relate to plantation management. In the first, we see the written instructions of a Mississippi planter to his overseer, and in the second we see the techniques of another planter from that state for managing his slaves. The four following selections, falling under the head of "Efficiency and Enterprise," are the selections from Abbey, McCay, and Hunt, together with the complaint from Liverpool over poor packing. The next selection, an estimate of the capital and labor employed in the growing of cotton, is the product of that indefatigable Secretary of the Treasury, Levi Woodbury. Note particularly the kinds of considerations that the Secretary takes into account in arriving at his estimate and the three different modes of computation he shows to be possible.

The final selection provides a revealing glimpse into the personal side of plantation life. The author, Susan Dabney Smedes, here memorializes her father, Thomas Smith Gregory Dabney. Born in 1788 at Bellevue, his father's country seat in Virginia, Dabney had two children, Benjamin and Samuel, by his first wife, Mary A. Tyler. She died in 1823, and Dabney married Sophia Hill in 1826. Nine years later (in September, 1835), he left Virginia with his wife and children for Mississippi, where he had "succeeded in purchasing four thousand acres from half a dozen small farmers." They arrived in early December of that year, and the Dabneys proceeded to raise corn as well as cotton. Note Mrs. Smedes' fond recollections of her father's techniques for increasing the efficiency of his slaves. Note, too, the pathos of such remarks as "After the mules and horses were fed in the evening the negroes carried home all they cared to have," which—like the measures for increasing efficiency—were clearly looked upon by Mrs. Smedes as tributes to an astute and kindly man. Few memoirs are more painful than those that—like this one—show how far short of fullness was the cup of kindness tendered under the slave system.

# THE READINGS

## 1] The Cultivation of Cotton

### a] "Making Cotton"

. . . . . . . . . . . . . . . .

THE PREPARATIONS for planting cotton begin in January; at this time the fields are covered with the dry and standing stalks of the "last year's crop." The first care of the planter is to "clean up" for plowing. To do this, the "hands" commence by breaking down the cotton stalks with a heavy club, or pulling them up by the roots. These stalks are then gathered into piles, and at nightfall set on fire. This labor, together with "housing the corn," repairing fences and farming implements, consume the time up to the middle of March or the beginning of April, when the plow for the "next crop" begins its work. First, the "water furrows" are run from five to six feet apart, and made by a heavy plow, drawn either by a team of oxen or mules. This labor, as it will be perceived, makes the surface of the ground in ridges, in the centre of which is next run a light plow, making what is termed "the drill," or depository of the seed: a girl follows the light plow, carrying in her apron the cotton seed, which she profusely scatters in the newly-made drill; behind this sower follows "the harrow," and by these various labors the planting is temporarily completed.

From two to three bushels of cotton seed are necessary to plant an acre of ground; the quantity used, however, is but of little consequence, unless the seed is imported, for the annual amount collected at the gin-house is enormous, and the surplus, after planting, is either left to rot, to be eaten by the cattle, or scattered upon the fields for manure.

If the weather be favorable, the young plant is discovered making its way through in six or ten days, and "the scraping" of the crop, as it is termed, now begins. A light plow is again called into requisition, which is run along the drill, throwing the *earth away from the plant;* then come the laborers with their hoes, who dexterously cut away the superabundant shoots and the intruding weeds, and leave a single cotton-plant in little hills generally two feet apart.

Of all the labors of the field, the dexterity displayed by the negroes in "scraping cotton" is most calculated to call forth the admiration of the novice spectator. The hoe is a rude instrument, however well made and handled; the young cotton-plant is as delicate as vegetation can be, and springs up in lines of solid masses, composed of hundreds of plants. The field-hand, however, will single one delicate shoot from the surrounding

---

FROM T. B. Thorpe, "Cotton and its Cultivation," *Harper's New Monthly Magazine,* vol. VIII, no. XLV (February, 1854), pp. 452–57 and 459.

multitude, and with his rude hoe he will trim away the remainder with all the boldness of touch of a master, leaving the incipient stalk unharmed and alone in its glory; and at nightfall you can look along the extending rows, and find the plants correct in line, and of the required distance of separation from each other.

The planter, who can look over his field in early spring, and find his cotton "cleanly scraped" and his "stand" good, is fortunate; still, the vicissitudes attending the cultivation of the crop have only commenced. Many rows, from the operations of the "cut-worm," and from multitudinous causes unknown, have to be replanted, and an unusually late frost may destroy all his labors, and compel him to commence again. But, if no untoward accident occurs, in two weeks after the "scraping," another hoeing takes place, at which time the plow throws the furrow *on to the roots* of the now strengthening plant, and the increasing heat of the sun also justifying the sinking of the roots deeper in the earth. The pleasant month of May is now drawing to a close, and vegetation of all kinds is struggling for precedence in the fields. Grasses and weeds of every variety, with vines and wild flowers, luxuriate in the newly-turned sod, and seem to be determined to choke out of existence the useful and still delicately-grown cotton.

It is a season of unusual industry on the cotton plantations, and woe to the planter who is outstripped in his labors, and finds himself "overtaken by the grass." The plow tears up the surplus vegetation, and the hoe tops it off in its luxuriance. The race is a hard one, but industry conquers; and when the third working over of the crop takes place, the cotton plant, so much cherished and favored, begins to overtop its rivals in the fields—begins to cast a *chilling shade of superiority* over its now intimidated groundlings, and commences to reign supreme.

Through the month of July, the crop is wrought over for the last time; the plant, heretofore of slow growth, now makes rapid advances toward perfection. The plow and hoe are still in requisition. The "water furrows" between the cotton rows are deepened, leaving the cotton growing as it were upon a slight ridge; this accomplished, the crop is prepared for the "rainy season," should it ensue, and so far advanced that it is, under any circumstances, beyond the control of art. Nature must now have its sway.

On some plantations there is no "overseer;" the owner manages his place with the help of a skillful and truthworthy negro, termed the "driver." These drivers are very ambitious, and are, like their masters, exceedingly sensitive if a stranger, or other disinterested person, gives an unfavorable opinion of the general appearance of the crop under their management. If much grass is seen in the cotton field, it is supposed to be an unfavorable testimony of the industry or skill of the driver. Upon a certain occasion, a gentleman riding along a cotton field remarked to the negro manager, "You have a good deal of grass in your crop." The negro felt mortified, and, anxious to break the force of the insinuation, coolly replied, "It is poor ground, master, that won't bring grass." The finest intellect could not, under the circumstances, have said a better thing.

The "cotton bloom," under the matured sun of July, begins to make its appearance. The announcement of the "first blossom" of the neighborhood is a matter of general interest; it is the unfailing sign of the approach of the busy season of fall; it is the evidence that soon the labor of man will, under a kind Providence, receive its reward.

It should perhaps here be remarked, that the color of cotton in its perfection is precisely that of the blossom—a beautiful light, but warm cream color. In buying cotton cloth, the "bleached" and "unbleached" are perceptibly different qualities to the most casual observer; but the dark hues and harsh look of the "unbleached domestic" comes from the handling of the artisan and the soot of machinery. If cotton, pure as it looks in the field, could be wrought into fabrics, they would have a brilliancy and beauty never yet accorded to any other material in its natural or artificial state. There can not be a doubt but that, in the robes of the ancient royal Mexicans and Peruvians, this brilliant and natural gloss of cotton was preserved, and hence the surpassing value it possessed in the eyes of cavaliers accustomed to the fabrics of the splendid court of Ferdinand and Isabella.

The cotton blossom is exceedingly delicate in its organization. It is, if in perfection, as we have stated, of a beautiful cream color. It unfolds in the night, remains in its glory through the morn—at meridian it has begun to decay. The day following its birth it has changed to a deep red, and, ere the sun goes down, its petals have fallen to the earth, leaving inclosed in the capacious calyx a scarcely perceptible germ. This germ, in its incipient and early stages, is called "a form;" in its more perfected state, "a boll."

The cotton plant, like the orange, has often on one stalk every possible growth; and often, on the same limb, may sometimes be seen the first opened blossom, and the bolls, from their first development as "forms," through every size, until they have burst open, and scattered their rich contents to the ripening winds.

The appearance of a well-cultivated cotton field, if it has escaped the ravages of insects and the destruction of the elements, is of singular beauty. Although it may be a mile in extent, still it is as carefully wrought as is the mould of the limited garden of the coldest climate. The cotton leaf is of a delicate green, large and luxuriant; the stalk indicates rapid growth, yet it has a healthy and firm look. Viewed from a distance, the perfecting plant has a warm and glowing expression. The size of the cotton-plant depends upon the accident of climate and soil. The cotton of Tennessee bears very little resemblance to the luxuriant growth of Alabama and Georgia; but even in those favored states the cotton-plant is not every where the same, for in the rich bottom lands it grows to a commanding size, while in the more barren regions it is an humble shrub. In the rich alluvium of the Mississippi the cotton will tower beyond the reach of the tallest "picker," and a single plant will contain hundreds of perfect "bolls;" in the neighboring "piney-woods" it lifts its humble head scarcely above the knee, and is proportionably meagre in its produce of fruit.

The growing cotton is particularly liable to accidents, and suffers immensely in "wet seasons" from the "rust" and "rot." The first named affects the leaves, giving them a brown and deadened tinge, and frequently causes them to crumble away. The "rot" attacks the "boll." It commences by a black spot on the rind, which increasing, seems to produce fermentation and decay. Worms find their way to the roots; the caterpillar eats into the "boll" and destroys the staple. It would be almost impossible to enumerate all the evils the cotton-plant is heir to, all of which, however, sink into nothingness compared with the scourge of the "army-worm."

The moth that indicates the advent of the army-worm has a Quaker-like simplicity in its light, chocolate-colored body and wings, and, from its harmless appearance, would never be taken for the destroyer of vast fields of luxuriant and useful vegetation.

The little, and, at first, scarcely to be perceived caterpillars that follow the appearance of these moths, can absolutely be seen to grow and swell beneath your eyes as they crawl from leaf to leaf. Day by day you can see the vegetation of vast fields becoming thinner and thinner, while the worm, constantly increasing in size, assumes at last an unctuous appearance most disgusting to behold. Arrived at maturity, a few hours only are necessary for these modern locusts to eat up all living vegetation that comes in their way. Leaving the localities of their birth, they will move from place to place, spreading a desolation as consuming as fire in their path.

All efforts to arrest their progress or annihilate them prove unavailing. They seem to spring out of the ground, and fall from the clouds; and the more they are tormented and destroyed, the more perceptible, seemingly, is their power. We once witnessed the invasion of the army-worm, as it attempted to pass from a desolated cotton-field to one untouched. Between these fields was a wide ditch, which had been deepened, to prove a barrier to the onward march of the worm. Down the perpendicular sides of the trench the caterpillars rolled in untold millions, until its bottom, for nearly a mile in extent, was a foot or two deep in living mass of animal life. To an immense piece of unhewn timber was attached a yoke of oxen, and as this heavy log was drawn through the ditch, it seemed absolutely to float on a crushed mass of vegetable corruption. The following day, under the heat of a tropical sun, the stench arising from this acidulated decay was perceptible the country round, giving a strange and incomprehensible notion of the power and abundance of this destroyer of the cotton crop.

The season of cotton picking commences in the latter part of July, and continues without intermission to the Christmas holidays. The work is not heavy, but becomes tedious from its sameness. The field hands are each supplied with a basket and bag. The basket is left at the head of the "cotton-rows;" the bag is suspended from the "picker's" neck by a strap, and is used to hold the cotton as it is taken from the boll. When the bag is filled it is emptied into the basket, and this routine is continued through the day. Each hand picks from two hundred and fifty to three hundred pounds of "seed cotton" each day, though some negroes of extraordinary ability go beyond this amount.

If the weather be very fine, the cotton is carried from the field direct to the packing-house; but generally it is first spread out on scaffolds, where it is left to dry, and picked clean of any "trash" that may be perceived mixed up with the cotton. Among the most characteristic scenes of plantation life is the returning of the hands at nightfall from the field, with their well-filled baskets of cotton upon their heads. Falling unconsciously "into line," the stoutest leading the way, they move along in the dim twilight of a winter day with the quietness of spirits rather than human beings.

The "packing-room" is the loft of the gin-house, and is over the gin-stand. By this arrangement the cotton is conveniently shoved down a causeway into the "gin-hopper." We have spoken of the importance of Whitney's great invention, and we must now say that much of the comparative value of the staple of cotton depends upon the excellence of the cotton-gin. Some separate the staple from the seed far better than others, while all are dependent more or less for their excellence upon the judicious manner they are used. With constant attention, a gin-stand, impelled by four mules, will work out four bales of four hundred and fifty pounds each a day; but this is more than the average amount. Upon large plantations the steam-engine is brought into requisition, which, carrying any number of gins required, will turn out the necessary number of bales per day.

The *baling* of the cotton ends the labor of its production on the plantation. The power which is used to accomplish this end is generally a single but powerful screw. The ginned cotton is thrown from the packing-room down into a reservoir or press, which, being filled, is tramped down by the negroes engaged in the business. When a sufficient quantity has been forced by "foot labor" into the press, the upper door is shut down, and the screw is applied, worked by horse. By this process the staple becomes almost as solid a mass as stone. By previous arrangement, strong Kentucky bagging has been so placed as to cover the upper and lower side of the pressed cotton. Ropes are now passed round the whole and secured by a knot; a long needle and a piece of twine closes up the openings in the bagging; the screw is then run up, the cotton swells with tremendous power inside of its ribs of ropes—the baling is completed, and the cotton is ready for shipment to any part of the world.

Nothing would be more difficult than to give a correct idea of the profits arising from the cultivation of cotton. Statistics afford no certain data. The growing crop is liable to so many accidents, that the amount to be raised the current year can never be calculated with any exactness, and the demand for cotton seems to vary with every ship arrival to this country from Europe. The difficulty of obtaining the number of bales of cotton that will be raised any given year is illustrated in a remarkable manner by the fact that certain commercial men in New York advertised for estimates of the "coming crop," and the result may be given as follows: The written opinions of two hundred and nine parties, scattered over the United States, were sent in and recorded, and between the lowest and highest estimate there was found to be *a range of one million four hundred thousand bales!*

A "great yield" is one thousand pounds of "seed cotton" to the acre, which makes two thirds of a bale of ginned cotton of four hundred and fifty pounds. Cases could be given where twice this quantity has been produced, but these examples would not be fair illustrations of the general production. The average of a bale of ginned cotton to every cultivated acre is set down by the most experienced planters as a very liberal reward for their labor. Ten acres of cotton and five acres of corn are considered the work of each "field hand;" yet five or six bales of cotton, of four hundred and fifty pounds to the hand, would greatly exceed the average production, for it will be found, on examination, that an average of two acres are cultivated in order to produce one bale.

. . . . . . . . . . . . . . . .

The "cotton-picking season" is generally brought to a close by the middle of December. The crop ready for shipment, the negroes are permitted to relax from their labors, and are in fine spirits, because "the work of the year is finished." . . .

## b] THE ROUTINE OF THE COTTON YEAR

SATURDAY, 28th March, 1829. Ploughs commenced in new ground by Mackeys & finished on the South side of the Bayou at night. Hoe hands finished rolling logs & burning brush, at an hour by sun, David putting new beam in a plough broke the other day.—

Sunday, 29th. Left home after breakfast rode to Jeff Montgomeries,—Digned at Mr. Kings—Commenced to rain at 2 o'clock. Showery the balance of the evening. Came home in a shower—

Monday, 30th. Rain all day. 3 men drawing the Well, some platting Shucks, & some Shelling Corn—Women Spinning—Altered Coult (Fiddler) to day—

Tuesday, 31st. Rained hard all night last night too weet to plough, all hands pulling stalks, till dinner then made sheep' pasture fence—Altered & marked 17 Calves & 26 Lambs to day—

Wednesday, 1st April, 1829. Six Ploughs in Poplar tree cut of No. 2—Commenced planting cotton in Groces field after breakfast. Covering with a harrow and a roler—Women and children cleaning up before the Ploughs in No. 2 Abraham & Moses hall [haul] rails in sheep pasture fence—David making another roler—Jack & Jerry finishing last Quarter—P. K. Montgomery staid with me to night on his way to Natchez—

Thursday, 2nd. Six Ploughs in long cut by the old road—Finished planting Groces field at an hour by Sun, & commenced in Sheep Pasture—Women cleaning up before Ploughs in No. 2. Moses & Abram still halling for fence across sheep pasture—Jack & David making new invented Cleaver for opening lists for sowing cotton.

Friday, 3rd. Six Ploughs still in cut by the old road—Cleaver opening, & harrow covering Cotton seed in Sheep pasture—Women put up fence on the line by Mackeys down to the large hollow—Moses & Abraham finished halling for pasture fence—& halled two loads to horse lot at Barn.

Saturday, 4th. Finished planting Sheep pasture in Cotton at 10 o'clock

---

FROM Extracts from the Diary (1829–30) of Leven Covington, Mississippi Planter, in Ulrich B. Phillips, ed., *Plantation and Frontier*, pp. 231–44, John R. Commons, ed., *A Documentary History of American Industrial Society*, vol. I (New York: Russell & Russell, 1958). Reprinted by permission of the publisher.

A.M.—Stephen & Ben then commenced opening for corn in circle cut of No. 3—Women planting after them, planted all the soked Corn & then finished putting up, & stakeing Horse pen—Ploughs still in cut by the old Road. Stopped at 4 P.M. by rain, and commenced Shelling corn—Dr. Walton sent for medicine for Sick Horse.

Sunday, 5th. To Salem meeting—Digned at Mackeys, and got home at sunset—

Monday, 6th. 7 Ploughs in long cut by old road till 10 o'clock—then commenced small cut by the Ditch in same field & nearly finished it at night—Women & three men finished fence on the line by Mackeys and mended the water gap—team halling rails as they ware put up on the fence—

Tuesday, 7th. 7 Ploughs finished cut by the ditch & long cut by the old Road (except a small part of each too wet to Plough) at 11 A.M. and commenced on the bottom cut of No. 2—Women, & three men cleaning up before the ploughs,—Team halling rails to finish fence arround Deadn's.

Wednesday, 8th. Wind very high from the South & quite clowdy; rain commenced at breakfast, a very hard shower & considerable wind from the West at half past 9 A.M. Stopped raining at 11 and cleared off beautifully at 12. Plough boys rolled logs in Potato patch and cotton ground of No. 1 and 2 & commenced in slip of new ground in No. 3—Women finished Sheep pasture fence—William came up from Natchez for a horse for cousin Dick.

Thursday, 9th. The ground too wet to plough in No. 2. All hands pulling stalks in upper cut on the old road of No. 1 till breakfast, then started 3 Ploughs in same cut and 3 in No. 3 to finish small piece left by the pond. Finished that & then commenced ridging for Potatoes—Started Cleaver to open, and a harrow covering Cotton in the upper cuts of No. 2—Two women sowing seed the balance pulling stalks, & making fence across wry patch—

Friday, 10th. Commenced planting corn in No. 3. Six Ploughs opening before the hoes—Stephen, Ben & Moses, opening & harrowing Cotton in long cut of No. 2—Mare Fanny Foulded.

Saturday, 11th. Finished all of No. 3 that was dry enough replanted the middle, & small cut next the road of No. 4, & planted circle cut in the same—Ploughs finished opening that & the piece in Sheep Pasture at dinner & commenced listing for cotton again, in bottom cut of No. 2—I met board of Road Commissioners in Natchez & got home at dark Cousin Dick returned from N. Orleans—Messrs. Farnsworth & Rucker here.

Sunday, 12. Mr. F. and myself attended Preaching at Christs Church—I digned at Col. Woods—& staid all night at Jas. Woods—

Monday, 13th. Came home from Mr. Woods, home to breakfast—Ploughs in bottom cut of No. 2 till breakfast, then commenced in the deadning by Mackeys, North side of branch—Hoe hands planted corn in Sheep Pasture the second time (destroyed by the hogs) & then commenced to burn brush and hill the new potato patch—Commenced to rain at half past 2 & rained moderately till night, not hard enough to stop work—Sent Jim to Natchez for cotton seed—

. . . . . . . . . . . . . . .

Friday, 1st. May, 1829. Ploughs in branch cut of No. 2–Hoes finished old field part of No. 4 & commenced in circle cut by the Brick Kiln Left Mr. Shields' at 10 o'clock digned at Jeff Montgomeries attended Writing School & got home at night–

. . . . . . . . . . . . . . . .

Friday, 8th. Ploughs in bottom cut of No. 2–Hoes scrapeing cotton in Sheep pasture commenced after breakfast, finished scrapeing, & replanting Groces field at breakfast–Still planting middle cut of No. 1–Jack & David halled timber for fence across Coles creek–Sprinkled of rain at 4 P.M. Cleared off by eight.

. . . . . . . . . . . . . . . .

Monday, 11th. Ploughs finished No. 2 & commenced at 12 o'clock in cut below the Gin of No. 1–Hoes finished circle part of long cut of No. 2 & commenced in Poplar tree cut–Planting of left side of road to Gin–Spent the day in the board of Road Commissioners, got to Washington at dark & staid all night.

Tuesday, 12th. Ploughs still in cut below the Gin–Hoes finished all the first planting in No. 2 at 5 P.M.–(Gulf Seed) & commenced replanting corn in No. 3–Two ploughs commenced throwing off in new field at Mackeys (Warren Seed) finished planting on the left of the road & commenced on the right after dinner, dropping seed given me by Mr. Hall–Came home to breakfast from Washington–Dr. Walton started for the purchase via Warren County.

Wednesday, 13th. Ploughs in Appletree cut of No. 1. Hoes finished replanting No. 3 & commenced Scrapeing New ground by Mackeys at 10 o'clock. Two ploughs throwing off before the hoes–Planting in branch cut of No. 2.

Thursday, 14th. Ploughs in appletree cut of No. 1. Hoes in new ground till 12 o'clock then stopped by the rain–Planted Potatoes by the Barn, in the evening–Started after dinner to Shields Wedding–

Friday, 15th. Ploughs finished Appletree cut at dinner & commenced in the Tasker field–Hoes in new ground till stopped by rain at 3 P.M.–All hands shelling Corn–Staid at P. Harrison's all night on my way from the wedding–Phillips finished pecking Mill-Creek rose over my fence without injuring it–

Saturday 16th. Ploughs finished small piece by the Fodder house in No. 1 at dinner, & returned to Tasker field–Hoe hands making fence between the upper field & Sheep pasture, Chopping briers, & setting up corn in Sheep pasture–Six men makeing upper fence across the creek–Ground till dinner–Rain commenced at 12 o'clock. Came home to breakfast from Harrisons–Planting in bottom No. 1.

Sunday, 17th. Rucker digned with me & started to Natchez after dinner –I rode to Mr. Halls saw his crop & returned at sunset in a shower of rain–

Monday, 18th. Ploughs in field across the Spring branch. Hoe hands fencing along the creek at the same place till dinner then moved the rails along the old road, & commenced scraping in long cut of No. 2 (Sum Seed two rows above willow stump) about two hours by sun—Rain at 3 P.M. not enough to stop work—Finished planting bottom cut of No. 2 at 5 P.M. & commenced in new part of No. 1.

Tuesday, 19th. Ploughs still in upper field across spring branch—Hoes still scraping long cut of No. 2 till Dinner, then scraped part of upper cut by old Road of No. 1, considerable showers of rain at dinner—D. Chambers arrived at night.—

Wednesday, 20th. Ploughs finished upper field at dinner, started two in the orchard to plough for Pease & four in No. 4—Hoes in New ground by Mackeys—Showery all the fore part of the day—On settlement with Chambers deducted from rent proceeds of Cotton $419.08 & half of Bagging & Cordage—Rode to Washington with Chambers after dinner—Edm'd & Clem arrived in the evening—Planting in Appletree cut of No. 1.—

. . . . . . . . . . . . . . . .

Thursday, 28th. Stopped the Plough in No. 3 & started the hoes in the same at dinner—Two Ploughs breaking middles in Popular tree cut of No. 2 after dinner & two listing old Rice patch, two still moulding in Groces field—finished scraping potatoes at dinner—stopped by a shower of rain at 4 P.M.—Thrashed pease, Shelled corn & ground the balance of the day—

Friday, 29th. Finished moulding Gulf Seed cotton in No. 2, at breakfast & started to moulding in the deadning. Two still in Groces field—Hoes finished circle cut and part of upper cut of No. 3 at breakfast, & commenced at 2 O'Clock & continued till 5—Thrashed Pease, laid up pasture fence below the Gin, & moved cotton Seed out of the Gin—

Saturday, 30th. All hands transplanting corn in No. 4 till breakfast, then started 4 Ploughs throwing off from corn in old Sheep pasture, finished that & broke up middles in cotton part of same—Hoes finished transplanting and commenced after the ploughs to scrape corn at 12 o'clock, finished and scraped small piece of cotton the second time & stopped an hour by sun—Considerable thunder & a sprinkle of Rain at half past 3 P.M.—

Sunday, 31st. To Union Chapple to hear Dr. Cooper preach and an Indian give his experience—Digned at Jeff Montgomeries to see Caleb King in the evening & home at night—

. . . . . . . . . . . . . . . .

Thursday, 25th. [February, 1830] Caleb, Rucker & Alden took breakfast on their way from the wedding, & wated till eleven o'clock for the creek to fall—Men at the press till 3 P.M. then chopping in clearing—Women piling brush.

Friday 26. Four Men malling rails for Hog pasture, balance cleaning up in Deadning by Mackeys—Women puling stalks in long cut of No. 2 till Dinner, then in the mackey field till night—Started ploughs again in upper part of field No. 1 ground still quite wet—

Saturday, 27th. Men & women making fence from the mouth of Branch to the line of division on the creek. Doctor Walton digned & staid all night with us—Cass and I rode out after dinner, & met mother, and Mr. W. Winston, at Mr. Mecuens—Two ploughs still following upper part of No. 1.

Sunday, 28th. Ben & Dr. Walton left after breakfast Ben for Mr. Tuckers, Dr. W. to see a patient at Hoggatts Quarter. Mother & Mr. Winston started home after Dinner. Cass & I rode a part of the way & called at Mr. McCuens on our return—Cassandra had considerable fever when we got home—Took medicine & was quite sick all night—

March 1st, Monday. Started two more ploughs in field No. 1. Four men malling. Nick and the women fencing at the bottom of No. 1 till dinner, then chopping briers, and sprouts, at the bottom of the same field. Team halling coal till dinner, then halling rails in hog pasture. Thunder and lightning and excessive hard rain commenced at 9 P.M.

Tuesday, 2nd March. All hands pulling stalks in long cut of No. 2 till breakfast;—then started the ploughs in upper cut of No. 1, 4 men malling—Women cleaning up in the same field—Team halling rails arround hog pasture—Clowdy & Cool all day.

Thursday, 4th. Heavy rain all day. Commenced at 4 A.M. Wind S.E. Shelled, & ground allowance for next week. Assorted, & nubbed Corn for planting—Cleaned up corn crib—Clem & Jo in the shop making Ploughs—

Friday, 5th. All hands puling Stalks till 3 P.M. finished field No. 2, then roling logs & cleaning up in bottom part of No. 1. Weather clowdy, & misty about 1 o'clock—Ground very wet with yesterday & last night's rain—

Saturday, 6th. Men belting trees in new ground, in field No. 2 Women cutting briers in the same—All stopped at 4 P.M.—Cass & I started for Sandy Creek at 10 A.M. As soon as we left home Mr. & Mrs. Walton came.

Sunday, 7th. From Gen'l Winstons after breakfast, digned at Mt. Wellcome & home in the evening—Jo Winston with us.

Monday, 8th. Five Ploughs in No. 1, finished upper, and commenced in bottom cut after dinner—Four men malling—Women making a ditch on the N side of same field—Team halling rails for pasture—weather clear, & fine—. . .

## 2] Plantation Management

### a] A PLANTER INSTRUCTS HIS OVERSEER

RULES AND directions for my Thorn Island Plantation by which my overseers are to govern themselves in the management of it.—ALEXANDER TELFAIR.

(The directions in this book are to be strictly attended to.)

1 The allowance for every grown Negro however old and good for

FROM Ulrich B. Phillips, ed., *Plantation and Frontier*, pp. 126–29, John R. Commons, ed., *A Documentary History of American Industrial Society*, vol. II (New York: Russell & Russell, 1958). Reprinted by permission of the publisher.

nothing, and every young one that works in the field, is a peck of corn each week, and a pint of salt, and a piece of meat, not exceeding fourteen pounds, per month.

2 No Negro to have more than Fifty lashes inflicted for any offence, no matter how great the crime.

3 The sucking children, and all other small ones who do not work in the field, draw a half allowance of corn and salt.

4 You will give tickets to any of the negroes who apply for them, to go any where about the neighborhood, but do not allow them to go off it without, nor suffer any strange negroes to come on it without a pass.

5 The negroes to be tasked when the work allows it. I require a reasonable days work, well done—the task to be regulated by the state of the ground and the strength of the negro.

6 The cotton to be weighed every night and the weights set down in the Cotton Book. The product of each field to be set down separately—as also the produce of the different corn fields.

7 You will keep a regular journal of the business of the plantation, setting down the names of the sick; the beginning, progress, and finishing of work; the state of the weather; Births, Deaths, and every thing of importance that takes place on the Plantation.

8 You are responsible for the conduct of all persons who visit you. All others found on the premises who have no business, you will take means to run off.

9 Feed every thing plentifully, but waste nothing.

10 The shade trees in the present clearings are not to be touched; and in taking in new ground, leave a thriving young oak or Hickory Tree to every Five Acres.

11 When picking out cotton, do not allow the hands to pull the Boles off the Stalk.

12 All visiting between this place and the one in Georgia is forbidden, except with Tickets from the respective overseers, and that but very seldom. There are none who have husbands or wives over there, and no connexions of the kind are to be allowed to be formed.

13 No night-meeting and preaching to be allowed on the place, except on Saturday night & Sunday morn.

14 Elsey is allowed to act as midwife, to black and white in the neighborhood, who send for her. One of her daughters to stay with the children and take charge of her business until she returns. She draws a peck of corn a week to feed my poultry with.

15 All the Land which is not planted, you will break up in the month of September. Plough it deep so as to turn in all the grass and weeds which it may be covered with.

16 If there is any fighting on the Plantation, whip all engaged in it—for no matter what the cause may have been, all are in the wrong.

17 Elsey is the Doctoress of the Plantation. In case of extraordinary illness, when she thinks she can do no more for the sick, you will employ a Physician.

18 My Cotton is packed in Four & a half yard Bags, weighing each 300 pounds, and the rise of it.

19 Neither the Cotton nor Corn stalks to be burnt, but threshed and chopped down in every field on the plantation, and suffered to lie until ploughed in in the course of working the land.

20 Billy to do the Blacksmith work.

20 [sic] The trash and stuff about the settlement to be gathered in heaps, in broken, wet days to rot; in a word make manure of every thing you can.

21 A Turnip Patch to be planted every year for the use of the Plantation.

22 The Negroes measures for Shoes to be sent down with the name written on each, by my Raft hands, or any other certain conveyance, to me, early in October. All draw shoes, except the children, and those that nurse them.

23 Write me the last day of every month to Savannah, unless otherwise directed. When writing have the Journal before you, and set down in the Letter every thing that has been done, or occurred on the Plantation during the month.

24 Pease to be planted in all the Corn, and plenty sowed for seed.

25 When Picking Cotton in the Hammock and Hickory Ridge, weigh the Tasks in the field, and hawl the Cotton home in the Wagon.

26 The first picking of Cotton to be depended on for seed. Seed sufficient to plant two Crops to be saved, and what is left, not to be thrown out of the Gin House, until you clean it out before beginning to pick out the new Crop.

27 A Beef to be killed for the negroes in July, August and September. The hides to be tanned at home if you understand it, or put out to be tanned on shares.

28 A Lot to be planted in Rye in September, and seed saved every year. The Cow pens to be moved every month to tread the ground for this purpose.

29 When a Beef is killed, the Fifth quarter except the hide to be given to Elsey for the children.

30 Give the negroes nails when building or repairing their houses when you think they need them.

31 My Negroes are not allowed to plant Cotton for themselves. Every thing else they may plant, and you will give them tickets to sell what they make.

32 I have no Driver. You are to task the negroes yourself, and each negro is responsible to you for his own work, and nobodys else.

33 The Cotton Bags to be marked A. T. and numbered.

34 I leave my Plantation Shot Gun with you.

35 The Corn and Cotton stalks to be cut, and threshed down on the land which lies out to rest, the same as if it was to be planted.

## b] A Planter's Techniques for Managing his Slaves

. . . . . . . . . . . . . . . . . . .

. . . Some very sensible and practical writer in the March No. of "The Review," under the *"Agricultural Department,"* has given us an article upon the *management of negroes,* which entitles him to the gratitude of the planting community, not only for the sound and useful information it contains, but because it has opened up this subject, to be thought of, written about, and improved upon, until the comforts of our black population shall be greatly increased, and their services become more profitable to their owners. Surely there is no subject which demands of the planter more careful consideration than the proper treatment of his slaves, by whose labor he lives, and for whose conduct and happiness he is responsible in the eyes of God. We very often find planters comparing notes and making suggestions as to the most profitable modes of tilling the soil, erecting gates, fences, farm-houses, machinery, and, indeed, everything else conducive to their comfort and prosperity; but how seldom do we find men comparing notes as to their mode of feeding, clothing, nursing, working, and taking care of those human beings intrusted to our charge, whose best condition is slavery, when they are treated with humanity, and their labor properly directed! I have been a reader of agricultural papers for more than twenty years, and while I have been surfeited, and not unfrequently disgusted, with those chimney-corner theories (that have no practical result, emanating from men who are fonder of using the pen than the plough-handle) upon the subject of raising crops, and preparing them for market, I have seldom met with an article laying down general rules for the management of negroes, by which their condition could be ameliorated, and the master be profited at the same time. One *good article* upon this subject would be worth more to the master than a hundred theories about "rotations" and "scientific culture;" and infinitely more to the slave than whole volumes dictated by a spurious philanthropy looking to his emancipation. For it is a fact, established beyond all controversy, that when the negro is treated with humanity, and subjected to constant employment without the labor of thought, and the cares incident to the necessity of providing for his own support, he is by far happier than he would be if emancipated, and left to think, and act, and provide for himself. And from the vast amount of experience in the management of slaves, can we not deduce some general, practicable rules for their government, that would add to the happiness of both master and servant? I know of no other mode of arriving at this great desideratum, than for planters to give to the public their rules for feeding, clothing, housing, and working their slaves, and of taking care of them when sick, together with their

---

FROM "A Mississippi Planter," in J. D. B. DeBow, ed., *Industrial Resources of the Southern and Western States* (3 vols., Washington, D.C. and New Orleans: J. D. B. DeBow, 1852), vol. II, pp. 330–33.

plantation discipline. In this way, we shall be continually learning something new upon this vitally interesting question, filled, as it is, with great responsibilities; and while our slaves will be made happier, our profits from their labor will be greater, and our consciences be made easier.

I would gladly avail myself of the privilege of contributing my mite to the accomplishment of this end, by giving my own system of management, not because there is any thing novel in it—that it is better, or differs essentially from that of most of my neighbors—but because it may meet the eye of some man of enlarged experience, who will necessarily detect its faults, and who may be induced to suggest the proper corrections, and for which I should feel profoundly grateful. To begin, then, I send you my plantation rules, that are printed in the plantation book, which constitute a part of the contract made in the employment of the overseer, and which are observed, so far as my constant and vigilant superintendence can enforce them. My first care has been to select a proper place for my "Quarter," well protected by the shade of forest trees, sufficiently thinned out to admit a free circulation of air, so situated as to be free from the impurities of stagnant water, and to erect comfortable houses for my negroes. Planters do not always reflect that there is more sickness, and consequently greater loss of life, from the decaying logs of negro houses, open floors, leaky roofs, and crowded rooms, than all other causes combined; and if humanity will not point out the proper remedy, let self-interest for once act as a virtue, and prompt him to save the health and lives of his negroes, by at once providing comfortable quarters for them. There being upwards of 150 negroes on the plantation, I provide for them 24 houses made of hewn post oak, covered with cypress, 16 by 18, with close plank floors and good chimneys, and elevated two feet from the ground. The ground *under* and around the houses is swept every month, and the houses, both inside and out, whitewashed twice a year. The houses are situated in a double row from north to south, about 200 feet apart, the doors facing inwards, and the houses being in a line, about 50 feet apart. At one end of the street stands the overseer's house, workshops, tool house, and wagon sheds; at the other, the grist and saw-mill, with good cisterns at each end, providing an ample supply of pure water. My experience has satisfied me, that spring, well, and lake water are all unhealthy in this climate, and that large under-ground cisterns, keeping the water pure and cool, are greatly to be preferred. They are easily and cheaply constructed, very convenient, and save both doctors' bills and loss of life. The negroes are never permitted to sleep before the fire, either lying down or sitting up, if it can be avoided, as they are always prone to sleep with their heads to the fire, are liable to be burnt and to contract disease: but beds with ample clothing are provided for them, and in them they are *made to sleep*. As to their habits of amalgamation and intercourse, I know of no means whereby to regulate them, or to restrain them; I attempted it for many years by preaching virtue and decency, encouraging marriages, and by punishing, with some severity, departures from marital obligations; but it was all in vain. I allow for each hand that works out, four pounds of clear meat and one peck of meal per week. Their dinners are cooked for them, and carried to the field, always with vegetables, according to the season.

There are two houses set apart at mid-day for resting, eating, and sleeping, if they desire it, and they retire to one of the weather sheds or the grove to pass this time, not being permitted to remain in the hot sun while at rest. They cook their own suppers and breakfasts, each family being provided with an oven, skillet, and sifter, and each one having a coffee-pot, (and generally some coffee to put in it,) with knives and forks, plates, spoons, cups, &c., of their own providing. The wood is regularly furnished them; for I hold it to be absolutely mean for a man to require a negro to work until daylight closes in, and then force him to get wood, sometimes half a mile off, before he can get a fire, either to warm himself or cook his supper. Every negro has his hen-house, where he raises poultry, which he is not permitted to sell, and he cooks and eats his chickens and eggs for his evening and morning meals to suit himself; besides, every family has a garden, paled in, where they raise such vegetables and fruits as they take a fancy to. A large house is provided as a nursery for the children, where all are taken at daylight, and placed under the charge of a careful and experienced woman, whose sole occupation is to attend to them, and see that they are properly fed and attended to, and above all things to keep them as dry and as cleanly as possible, under the circumstances. The suckling women come in to nurse their children four times during the day; and it is the duty of the nurse to see that they do not perform this duty until they have become properly cool, after walking from the field. In consequence of these regulations, I have never lost a child from being burnt to death, or, indeed, by accidents of any description; and although I have had more than thirty born within the last five years, yet I have not lost a single one from teething, or the ordinary summer complaints so prevalent amongst the children in this climate.

I give to my negroes four full suits of clothes with two pair of shoes, every year, and to my women and girls a calico dress and two handkerchiefs extra. I do not permit them to have "truck patches" other than their gardens, or to raise any thing whatever for market; but in lieu thereof, I give to each head of a family and to every single negro, on Christmas day, five dollars, and send them to the county town, under the charge of the overseer or driver, to spend their money. In this way, I save my mules from being killed up in summer, and my oxen in winter, by working and hauling off their crops; and more than all, the negroes are prevented from acquiring habits of trading in farm produce, which invariably leads to stealing, followed by whipping, trouble to the master, and discontent on the part of the slave. I permit no spirits to be brought on the plantation, or used by any negro, if I can prevent it; and a violation of this rule, if found out, is always followed by a whipping, and a forfeiture of the five dollars next Christmas.

I have a large and comfortable hospital provided for my negroes when they are sick; to this is attached a nurse's room; and when a negro complains of being too unwell to work, he is at once sent to the hospital, and put under the charge of a very experienced and careful negro woman, who administers the medicine and attends to his diet, and where they remain until they are able to work again. This woman is provided with sugar, coffee, molasses, rice, flour, and tea, and does not permit a patient to taste of meat or vegetables until he is restored to health. Many negroes relapse after the disease is broken, and die, in consequence of remaining in their houses and stuffing themselves with coarse food after their appetites return, and both humanity and economy dictate that this should be prevented. From the system I have pursued, I have not lost a hand since the summer of 1845, (except one that was killed by accident,) nor has my physician's bill averaged fifty dollars a year, notwithstanding I live near the edge of the swamp of Big Black River, where it is thought to be very unhealthy.

I cultivate about ten acres of cotton and six of corn to the hand, not forgetting the little wheat patch that your correspondent speaks of, which costs but little trouble, and proves a great comfort to the negroes; and have as few sour looks and as little whipping as almost any other place of the same size.

I must not omit to mention that I have a good fiddler, and keep him well supplied with catgut, and I make it his duty to play for the negores every Saturday night until twelve o'clock. They are exceedingly punctual in their attendance at the ball, while Charley's fiddle is always accompanied with Ihurod on the triangle, and Sam to "pat."

I also employ a good preacher, who regularly preaches to them on the Sabbath day, and it is made the duty of every one to come up clean and decent to the place of worship. As Father Garritt regularly calls on Brother Abram (the foreman of the prayer-meeting,) to close the exercises, he gives out and sings his hymn with much unction, and always cocks his eye at Charley, the fiddler, as much as to say, "Old fellow, you had your time last night; now it is mine."

I would gladly learn every negro on the place to read the Bible, but for a fanaticism which, while it professes friendship to the negro, is keeping a cloud over his mental vision, and almost crushing out his hopes of salvation.

These are some of the leading outlines of my management, so far as my negroes are concerned. That they are imperfect, and could be greatly improved, I readily admit; and it is only with the hope that I shall be able to improve them by the experience of others, that I have given them to the public.

Should you come to the conclusion that these rules would be of any service when made known to others, you will please give them a place in the "Review."

A MISSISSIPPI PLANTER

## RULES AND REGULATIONS FOR THE GOVERNMENT OF A SOUTHERN PLANTATION

1. There shall be a place for every thing, and every thing shall be kept in its place.

2. On the first days of January and July, there shall be an account taken of the number and condition of all the negroes, stock, and farming utensils of every description on the premises, and the same shall be entered in the plantation book.

3. It shall be the duty of the overseer to call upon the stock-minder once every day, to know if the cattle, sheep, and hogs have been seen and counted, and to find out if any are dead, missing, or lost.

4. It shall be the duty of the overseer, at least once in every week, to see and count the stock himself, and to inspect the fences, gates, and water-gaps on the plantation, and see that they are in good order.

5. The wagons, carts, and all other implements, are to be kept under the sheds, and in the houses where they belong, except when in use.

6. Each negro man will be permitted to keep his own axe, and shall have it forthcoming when required by the overseer. No other tool shall be taken or used by any negro without the permission of the overseer.

7. Humanity on the part of the overseer, and unqualified obedience on the part of the negro, are, under all circumstances, indispensable.

8. Whipping, when necessary, shall be in moderation, and never done in a passion; and the driver shall in no instance inflict punishment, except in the presence of the overseer, and when, from sickness, he is unable to do it himself.

9. The overseer shall see that the negroes are properly clothed and well fed. He shall lay off a garden of at least six acres, and cultivate it as part of his crop, and give the negroes as many vegetables as may be necessary.

10. It shall be the duty of the overseer to select a sufficient number of the women, each week, to wash for all. The clothes shall be well washed, ironed, and mended, and distributed to the negroes on Sunday morning; when every negro is expected to wash himself, comb his head, and put on clean clothes. No washing or other labor will be tolerated on the Sabbath.

11. The negroes shall not be worked in the rain, or kept out after night, except in weighing or putting away cotton.

12. It shall be the duty of the driver, at such hours of the night as the overseer may designate, to blow his horn, and go around and see that every negro is at his proper place, and to report to the overseer any that may be absent; and it shall be the duty of the overseer, at some hour between that time and daybreak, to patrol the quarters himself, and see that every negro is where he should be.

13. The negro children are to be taken, every morning, by their mothers, and carried to the houses of the nurses; and every cabin shall be kept locked during the day.

14. Sick negroes are to receive particular attention. When they are first reported sick, they are to be examined by the overseer, and prescribed for, and put under the care of the nurse, and not put to work until the disease is broken and the patient beyond the power of a relapse.

15. When the overseer shall consider it necessary to send for a physician, he shall enter in the plantation book the number of visits, and to what negro they are made.

16. When the negro shall die, an hour shall be set apart by the overseer for his burial; and at that hour all business shall cease, and every negro on the plantation, who is able to do so, shall attend the burial.

17. The overseer shall keep a plantation book, in which he shall register the birth and name of each negro that is born; the name of each negro that died, and specify the disease that killed him. He shall also keep in it the weights of the daily picking of each hand; the mark, number, and weight of each bale of cotton, and the time of sending the same to market; and all

other such occurrences, relating to the crop, the weather, and all other matters pertaining to the plantation, that he may deem advisable.

18. The overseer shall pitch the crops, and work them according to his own judgment, with the distinct understanding that a failure to make a bountiful supply of corn and meat for the use of the plantation, will be considered as notice that his services will not be required for the succeeding year.

19. The negroes, teams, and tools are to be considered under the overseer's exclusive management, and are not to be interfered with by the employer, only so far as to see that the foregoing rules are strictly observed.

20. The overseer shall, under no circumstances, create an account against his employer, except in the employment of a physician, or in the purchase of medicines; but whenever any thing is wanted about the plantation, he shall apply to his employer for it.

21. Whenever the overseer, or his employer, shall become dissatisfied, they shall, in a frank and friendly manner, express the same, and, if either party desires it, he shall have the right to settle and separate.

. . . . . . . . . . . . . . . .

## 3] Efficiency and Enterprise

### a] A SLAVEOWNER URGES ECONOMY AND ENTERPRISE

. . . . . . . . . . . . . . . .

WHETHER we regard the cultivation of cotton then, as it exists at present, or in its prospective appearances, it is the most important branch of agriculture in the world; and yet we may venture to believe that it is prosecuted with less economy and enterprise than any other considerable branch of business in our country. There is a slovenlesness about it, almost universally seen, that is really unaccountable, since it is admitted that cotton planters are among the most intelligent and well informed of our citizens. Why it is that agriculture is so far behind the enterprise of the age we live in, cannot be told—nor are we able to tell why cotton growing is so far in the rear of the very slow march of the other branches of agriculture around us. But that it is so, is but too apparent. If it was not in *too* bad taste, I would just allude here, by way of parenthesis, to my negro man John. He is the best fellow to work in the world, but never knows or cares *what* he is doing, or *how* he is doing it; to *do enough of it,* is his sole aim. It is hoped the refined and intelligent planter will pardon this unseemly piece of pleasantry.

The cultivation of cotton, as a branch of productive industry, ought to take the lead in agriculture. But instead of this, it lags lazily behind every

FROM R. Abbey ("of Mississippi"), "Cotton and the Cotton Planters," *DeBow's Review*, vol. III (January, 1847), pp. 2–6 and 8–19.

thing else. The fact, that unlike other articles it cannot be raised in different climates or lattitudes, shows the similarity that would be observed, were the best plans generally adopted. It is a fact, too, that there is a much greater diversity in the profits arising from cotton plantations than from other agricultural investments; for while some yield large profits others do not pay expenses. And it is also true that the cotton we sell at the lowest range of prices, costs us nearly as much as that which sells at twice the money. Another reason why cotton growing ought to take the lead in agriculture, is, that with us, it is more of an exclusive business than the product of any one article is with the farmer of the West or North. And moreover, it is supposed, that without disparagement to any, it may be assumed that cotton growers, as a class, are more intelligent and better informed than the mass of farmers generally. We do not say they are more intelligent *farmers,* or better informed *in their business*—that is the very thing complained of.

As a proximate cause to these disadvantages under which the country labors, one or two things may be hinted at. There is among the cotton planters no dissemination or concentration of professional knowledge or practice. No means are in use—no money is expended to conduct an interchange of opinions. The views, theories and experience of one man, be they ever so sound and valuable, are of no public utility what ever, and consequently, in many instances, of but limited benefit to himself. Every farmer lives in an agricultural world of his own. He is monarch of all he surveys, but holds no communion with the rest of the world. His fence is his Chinese walls, and his grandfather's ghost is his emperor. The *man* goes abroad often enough, but the *farmer* never. It is thought by many that at this time it would be greatly to the advantage of the planter if the amount of the crop could be known. Well, most certainly the number of bales could as well be counted on the first of November as July. At the middle of March next every planter ought to know precisely the number of acres of cotton, corn &c., to be planted the next year, with a thousand other items of profitable information. Look at commerce, with his thousand cohorts his million of couriers and his army of printers! a merchant scarcely thinks until every other merchant catches the sound and profits by it. Every mercantile operation is influenced, more or less, by every other similar one, all over the country. Merchants act advisedly—farmers in the dark. How many agricultural newspapers are there in the country? Two or three seven-by-nines, starving for patronage! When and where do agriculturalists assemble for consultation. Who legislates for agriculture? Who pleads her cause or sustains her interests? Are we not content with the notion that agriculture, like a town in the country I once heard of, is *finished?*

Again it might be stated, that farmers are opposed to innovation. There is almost an organised opposition to change or reform in any particular. A slight modification in a plough or a hoe, once in a great while, might possibly be tolerated; but any kind of change in plan or arrangement—any doing of a thing different this year from what it was last, or from what "every body always done it," is *"theorising,"* the highest crime known to the laws forbiding innovation.

Considering then, the many positive and negative disadvantages under which the cotton grower labours, is it not strange that a spirit of enterprise and economy is not cherished and prosecuted more than it is? Allow then Mr. Editor, to be pointed out, some of what are conceived to be the most glaring and easily remedied errors under which our business labours, and which may probably result in part from some of the above named disadvantages.

In relation to THE GROUND WE PLANT there is much room for reformation. *To wear out land,* or to make it *grow poorer* by cultivation, is unquestionably bad farming. We know that agricultural chemistry is too young to enable us to apply science properly in this respect; yet we all know that the propogation of particular plants requires the use of particular properties in the soil; and as these properties become exhausted unless they be restored the land becomes poor. Now, obviously, the proper course is to restore to the land as much as practicable of *the same thing* we take away. That portion of the product we send to market we cannot restore *in kind,* but surely we can and ought to restore all the rest. The best vegetable manure certainly is that which the land produced, especially if the same crop is to be raised the next year. But instead of that we see many persons refuse even to let the land have the cotton stalks back again, but actually *burn them up!* The seed too, are in many instances as unjustly withheld, or if restored at all, it is after the rains of a winter or two have destroyed the most of its fructifying quality. That which we necessarily remove from the soil, and cannot therefore restore in kind, we can easily restore in some other way. In fact if we afford the opportunity Nature will do it herself. Land has a resusitating and invigorating tendency, or in other words Nature is constantly endeavoring to bring back impoverished land to its original state of richness. This supply of that of which the land has been robbed, is derived chiefly from the atmosphere; and if the land be placed in favorable circumstances it will soon obtain a sufficient supply. To this end land should be suffered, as farmers say, to *rest* a year or two. But it is not enough in order to rest land that you merely cease to cultivate it; because its rest may be greatly disturbed. It cannot repose much with its bosom exposed to a summer's sun. Nor will its slumber be healthful or invigorating with the same crop of weeds or grass growing on it which heretofore, from year to year, have been *cultivated,* or suffered to grow in the process of cultivation. The way is to give the land a coating of something, the growth of which requires chiefly other properties of the soil than those already exhausted, and with such verdure as it can support easiest, it will acquire, upon its surface, that degree of humidity necessary to a favourable supply of atmospheric food. Chemistry, were we sufficiently acquainted with it, would immediately point out the proper article for this purpose in every particular instance. But in our lack of knowledge here, we must depend upon experiment. After cotton we usually sow rye, or after corn, oats.

But the great difficulty in all this is that most planters plant all their open land every year. We lack twenty-five per cent. of having enough land open, and plant twenty-five per cent. too much of the land we have open. What is called over-cropping is a very common fault with the cotton planters, and results in great disadvantages; a less quantity of land cultivated better, will produce a greater amount of cotton. And moreover, the same number of bales of cotton, on a less number of acres of land; requires less labour in picking. And the picking of cotton being more than one-third of the whole labour requisite to produce it, this is a very important consideration. It is a very uncommon thing to see a cotton crop cultivated well, throughout the season. Nine-tenths of the cotton crops suffer for the plough and hoe during three-fourths of the growing season. How much room for reform is here!

One of the greatest disadvantages under which the cotton planting labours, is in regard to THE SEED WE PLANT. The popular notion is that seed runs out very rapidly, or in a few years, and that a fresh supply of *"Gulf seed"* is necessary to take a new start from. Again, we hear that changing seed among different plantations, or to and from different kinds of soil, is of great advantage; and again that seed two or more years old is far preferable, for that then the poorest seed will not germinate. To expose these egregious whims and set forth what is deemed the correct reasoning upon the subject, it is not necessary for us to speak of any particular variety of cotton grown in this country, but to state principles equally applicable to all.

. . . . . . . . . . . . . . .

*What is degeneration, or "running out" in cotton seed?* And what is the cause of it? These are the only questions that need to be answered, and certainly, it seems to me, they are very simple. *It is the production and continued reproduction from the smaller and less perfectly grown seeds.* And how is it to be prevented? *Use the large and full matured seed exclusively, to produce from.*

There is on every stalk and in every boll of cotton some seed which are large, full grown, and of vigorous stamina, whilst others are smaller in size, imperfectly matured, and consequently weaker in stamina.—These differences in the same boll are perhaps very slight, but in different bolls on the same stalk, very perceptible, and in different stalks in the same field still more so.

Suppose, then, you take from a single stalk of Cotton one half of its bolls which are the largest and best, and from these bolls you select the best seed. On the other hand, you select from the poorest bolls the poorest seed. These two parcels of seed are the product of single seed, and are now planted in separate fields. From the cotton growing from the large seed you continue to select and plant from year to year the best seed, and from that growing from the poor seed, you pursue the contrary course, and produce from the poorest seed from year to year. After three or four years how will these two fields of Cotton compare? The one will unquestionably be perfectly "run out," and the other will have *run* considerably in a contrary direction. This I undertake to suppose is very common sense, and accords fully with the experience of every man every day. And yet with this full knowledge of all the facts and theory before us, there seems to be comparatively few who bring their minds fully up to the very great and apparent propriety of excluding these lesser seed occasionally as they make their appearance in any considerable quantity. The trouble and expense of excluding imperfect seed is far less than is generally supposed. It depends, however, upon circumstances. If you have a large proportion, half or two thirds, as is generally the case, of poor seed, it is considerable trouble to pick out the good seed. But if there is but little depreciation and but a few green, black or small seed in the mass, mostly of large white seed, it is but little labor to select them out and throw them away.

. . . . . . . . . . . . . . . . . . . .

It is quite probable, also, that a scientific examination, thoroughly made, into all the botanical principles of the plant, and with the chemical principles of its production with us might illustrate facts not so near the surface of observation as those I have stated, and which would show other lateral causes of depreciation. For instance, cotton, as is the case with every other species of plant, requires not only a particular climate and atmosphere, but particular proportions in the soil, and peculiar modes of cultivation at all the different stages in its growth; and there requires in all these a perfect system of adaptation and correspondence, in order to the most perfect product. Now, our rough system—rather the total abuse of all system—of cultivation, consults none of these things, and, therefore, we lose all the means we might otherwise have of preserving all the valuable properties of the plant.

. . . . . . . . . . . . . . . . . . .

Experiment has abundantly shown that different kinds of soil except you go far North or South, does not very materially change the character either of the cotton or the seed. The best and most careful planters have the best seed, and usually the best cotton. And whether they live a mile, or ten or a hundred miles from Rodney in Mississippi, is not very material.

The idea that cotton seed is benefitted by itinerating among different plantations from year to year, is unphilosophical, and has nothing to support it but a whim that started some where, and has been kept in use for want of a better. The *fact* of such benefits by change, from one place to another, is not doubted, but the *reasons* therefor are to be found in the principles stated above.

. . . . . . . . . . . . . . . . . . .

Another impediment of great magnitude and of extensive disadvantage is in regard to THE PREPARATION OF COTTON FOR MARKET. This consists chiefly in *picking, guining* and *baleing*.

The great improvements that have been made in Cotton Factories in cleaning Cotton, and preparing it for the spindle, ought to indicate to us that one of two modes, widely different from each other, ought to be pursued in picking. The lower qualities of cotton are not enhanced much in value by keeping the cotton very clean of *trash* or leaf. The manufacturers can clean it sufficiently for coarse fabricks much cheaper than we can. And on the other hand, pretty good or fine cotton, if somewhat trashy, is lessened in value materially thereby. We should then, when we *go in*—as we say in the country—for fine cotton, take pains in picking, keep it clean, suffer it to remain in the field the shortest possible time after opening, and handle and gin it with great care. But in any portion of the crop when this should become unproffitable, we ought to go to the other side entirely, or nearly so, and *go in* for the greatest quantity. The state of the market, present and prospective, and the condition of the manufactories seem to point out this course.

Far too little attention is usually paid to GINNING COTTON. For many years past the rage has been for fast ginning, and the value of a cotton gin was measured by the number of bales per day, that could be ginned upon it. In this way the value of a crop, in thousands of instances, has been reduced three, five, or eight dollars a bale rather than expend a dollar more upon the ginning. Fast ginning injures cotton more than all other defects and disadvantages in this part of the preparation of cotton for market. And yet I have seen opinions the reverse of this stated, if I mistake not, in the Review. Nothing can be more unreasonable, and nothing is more at variance with the experience of every observing planter. Next to fast ginning is the great error of using *cheap gins.* It is a very easy thing to save fifty or a hundred dollars in the price of a gin stand, and then as a consequence very probable, loose five or ten dollars a day while you use it. A cotton gin requires the most perfect mechanical precision in all its parts. Small objects are as fatal to making cotton as large ones. Nothing is more familiar to a cotton merchant than this, that two samples of cotton are separate twenty or thirty per cent. value by the mode of ginning alone. And yet to make a planter believe this, who is alone interested in the great and important truth, you have to thunder in his ears loud enough to wake the dead; and then oftentimes the first cheap gin manufacturer can soon dissipate all his anxiety on the subject, by offering him fifty dollars to injure his five successive crops five hundred dellars [sic] each.

It was stated in the September number of the Review that *Carver, Washburn & Co.* of Massachusetts were making gins designed expressly for Mastodon cotton, and some of them would be tried in Mississippi and Louisiana this fall. The writer has now the satisfaction of saying that these experiments have resulted as advantageously as was anticipated. They are highly approved of in every instance, so far as is known, and are believed to be the best gins now in use: certainly much the best the writer has seen.

The next process is to pack the cotton into BALES for shipment. The circular which the writer received from the Editor last summer contained some inquiries on this subject, and it was then briefly attended to.

*The present mode of packing cotton, on the plantations, results in a direct and immediate loss to the planters, of a sum fully equal to the whole amount of expenses, direct and indirect, of repressing the bales at the sea ports.* So great a truth as that, if it be true, deserves to be repeated with an emphasis. The position cannot be successfully controverted. And although it has frequently been stated by several of our most intelligent planters, it is not known that any man has ever undertaken publicly to call its truth in question. It is unhesitatingly asserted that the same expense and labor now generally used in packing cotton, will, with a little modification in the process, together with the substitution of good presses for poor ones when it is necessary, put the cotton in better shipping order than it generally comes from the Presses in New Orleans or the other ports. And moreover by the putting of bales in shipping order at the gin, several other important advantages will accrue to the planter. These may appear very bold and hazardous declarations. They would not be made, most assuredly, but for the consciousness of the great ease with which they are capable of being maintained.

But how is this truth to be proved? It seems to be rather a question of fact and veracity, than of argumentation. The simple fact is, that it is less labour to pack bales with a good press, 22 inches square, 4 feet 6 inches long, weighing 400 pounds, and bind them with iron hoops, (when they are in the best shipping order the cotton is capable of being put in,) than it is to put them up in the usual mode, when they not only regain all the expenses of repressing but other additional expenses of freight, &c. &c. It is difficult to prove this on paper, but any man to have been on this plantation yesterday, would have been compelled to know that all here stated is strictly true. The only remaining question then is, whether there are any collateral, indirect or incidental disadvantages arising from putting bales in *shipment size* and banding them with iron, to hold them firmly there at the gin? This will be looked at presently; but first, assuming that there are none, how does the case stand? The first object that strikes the eye is the payment to the citizens of the seaports, by cotton planters whose cotton is shipped thence, one million of dollars annually, for which the latter receive *no benefit*. Is this a matter unworthy of thorough investigation? Should it call forth the *attention* of planters or should it not? Are we the guardians of our own interests or are we not? What is enterprise, and what is it for? and what are the disabilities of industry without it? Are we to learn nothing? Does the *law* against innovation absolutely and unconditionally require that we shall *always* carry the stone in one end of the bag and the meal in the other? Are we wedded indissolubly to the crude blunders of early processes, or may we walk out like a grown up man, with his eyes open, profiting by past experience, and look and see where is the best place to put his foot next? Cannot the strides of valuable improvement that commerce and mechanism is making every day around us, stimulate us a little? Has emulation left us quite?

It is assumed that 25 to 30 pounds to the cubic foot is as small as cotton should be pressed. Greater pressure than that would probably injure the cotton, and that being quite as small as it usually comes from the presses—New Orleans, say. 4½ feet long, 22 to 24 inches square, for bales weighing, 400 to 450 pounds. The cotton must not only be put into this size, but the bales must be so banded that they will not enlarge. Bales of this kind, well put up, may be considered of *shipment size,* or in as good *shipping order* as the cotton is capable of being put in.

Now, the question is, can every planter put his cotton in this condition with the same labour and expense now bestowed upon it? The affirmative is so simple a truth that it not only cannot be successfully opposed, but no man can examine carefully into it and doubt for a moment. Then why do we not all do it? Why do we employ thousands of men, agents, clerks, labourers, draymen, warehouses, machines, makers, &c., &c., to do for us that which we can do for ourselves without the expense of a desire? Why do we do this? The answer is plain—because our fathers did so—Because we did so last year. No other answer than this can be given. And thus it is that we, year after year subject ourselves to these exceedingly onerous disabilities.

Some explanation of the *process* by which cotton is thus packed may not be amiss, as there are many who have not thought much on the subject. There is a great error abroad as to the amount of power necessary to put bales into shipment size, and it is not unfrequently the case that bales are put mainly or quite into the proper size, but the elasticity of the hemp ropes put upon them suffers the bale to expand one third or more, when the presses at the ports have little else to do than press it back again where it was originally, and the ropes being perfectly distended, and being retied, hold it there.

A *good* Newell press, especially the large size screw, which of late is going into general use, or any press of about that power, is sufficient to press cotton into the size indicated. The difficulty is not in pressing the cotton small enough, but in keeping the bales firmly, at that size. The only way in which this has been known to have been done, is the use of IRON HOOPS. The best and easiest mode, of using the hoops is not be presumed to be taught or explained here but it is confidently believed—nay, it is certainly known, that bales may be packed with the use of them with greater facility than is usual with ropes, so far as some little experience in both, with the writer has led him to observe. And if his experience may be attended here, it is advised first to *get ready*. This item of instruction, in this form, I obtained from my overseer, when describing the process to a neighbor, and it is considered too valuable to be left out of these observations. First, get ready, and you will have very little difficulty afterwards.

A very important thing to be attended to in the process of getting ready, is first to obtain the proper kind of iron. The iron should be *sufficiently strong*, but not *unnecessarily heavy*. The size most approved is about three quarters or seven eights of an inch in width, and about number eighteen, of the wire guage. This will weigh about a pound, or perhaps a little over, to the band, which is the weight of rope that is tolerably small; so that the weight of iron and rope are about equal. Then if the iron be *very soft*, it will have sufficient strength.

The next thing is to cover the iron, so as to give it a handsome black, glossy, or jappan appearance. The chief advantage in this is, that it gives the bend a handsome appearance. It also prevents the possibility of the slightest *rust*. It is confidently believed that the raw hoopison could not, under any circumstances, afford rust in quantity sufficient to do the least injury to the cotton or bailing, although this has been stated in New Orleans by those whose interest it was to discourage the use of iron in this particular. But be this as it may, the process now about to be decided will, as observed, perfectly prevent the slightest rust, and at an expense next to nothing. For this purpose *coal tar* is used, which is bought in New Orleans at five dollars a barrel. Not over a gallon or two will be required to cover iron enough for a hundred bales. It is applied in the following manner. Take a hundred or two of hoops and place them in a pile spread a little, and elevated six or eight inches from the ground upon blocks. Underneath is put a light fire of shavings or other light material, so that the hoops are heated, equally all along the pile, to a degree of warmth so that they can barely be handled in the following manner. The operator, having a small tub of tar along side, wraps his hands with pieces of blanket, or something of the kind, several thicknesses, tying them about his wrists, so as to form a kind of mitten. These he saturates in the tar, and taking up one piece of iron at a time draws it from end to end through his hands, and drops it in another pile. He thus proceeds, removing the pieces quickly, from the pile over the fire to the other, taking care to let the piece pass its whole length through his hands, and seeing, meanwhile, that an equal fire is kept up under the heating or hot pile, and that they are kept so hot as to require him to handle them pretty fast to prevent burning his hands. As the iron cools the tar becomes perfectly hard, black and glossy in appearance. To cover, in this way, hoops enough for a hundred bales, requires the labor of a negro but a few hours.

The rivets are purchased already made, and if the holes are not already punched in the hoops (which ought to be the case) you require a good punch, such as blacksmiths use, and a punching block, you also want a riveting hammer; the puncture in the riveting tool of course being the size of the rivet, as also the punch. These four tools can be made by any good blacksmith. In punching the iron, care is to be taken, that when the ends come together, the two smooth sides of the hole will come together, and the two feather sides outward; you then bend the two middle corners of the hoop, forming the two squares upon the back side of the bale, so that the hoop is to be introduced to the bale from the back side of the bale, putting both ends through, above and below at the same time. The rivets are also put in its place in one of the holes, when the hoops are ready for use, and are placed in a pile on the back side of the bale. All this is done before you commence baling. You then want a bar of iron four inches wide, and half an inch thick, and probably seven or eight feet long. When the doors are thrown open and the follower down, this wide bar of iron is placed lengthwise along the middle of the front side of the bale, where the ties come, it falls into latches prepared for it, and hugs closely to the bale; and you are now ready to put on your hoops. The hoops are all first slipped in from the back side. The man on the front side with his tools at hand, bends the one end up and the other down, and they of course meet on the bar of iron. The head of the rivet is inward next the iron bar, and the other end of the hoop is slipped on the outer end of the rivet and with the riveting tool is driven up to its place firmly, when nothing remains to be done but to batter down the end of the rivet. The man handling the riveting hammer will soon find that small quick blows will rivet faster than to strike heavy and slow. It will be found useful for the man on the back side of the bale to use a small mallet at the corners, above and below, upon the hoop to make it hug closely round the bale, while the one on the front side is fastening it. The most of the time required in putting on the hoops is in hammering down the rivets, but a man to hammer smartly will soon head the seven rivets. When all is previously made ready; the process requires about two-thirds or three-fourths the time it takes to put on ropes.

To prepare the bagging, no bale cloth is made, you only cut off two strait pieces of proper length, the bottom the same as the top, which are all sufficient. The bales are square neat and uniform, and they make a steamboat laugh to look at them. When well marked and numbered and carefully weighed, and placed in a dry shed on the bank of the river, off the ground, clean and dry, they are *in shipping order*—the best order for transportation they can be put in.

The fluctuations in the prices of rope and iron vary the comparative value somewhat, but considering the saving in bagging the hoopiron covering will be found sometimes probably to have the advantage in price in the first instance. The iron is worth about five or five and a half cents a pound. So far, the comparative cost of using rope and iron is about equal, but after this there are several decided advantages on the side of the latter.

If the practice was uniform, or if a considerable portion of cotton was put up in this way, the cost of freight would be materially lessened. These bales can be handled with so much greater ease, that boats can be loaded and unloaded in much less time.

The cost of insurance would be materially lessened. It is always perfectly protected against loss by fire. The bands cannot come loose so as to let the bale expand, and it would be, therefore, impossible to burn a pile of cotton, whether on a boat or in a ware house.

Cotton packed up in this mode would go to market in much better order than it does now. On this point reference need only be made to the horridly, ragged and wasteful manner in which cotton for sale is now usually introduced to the purchaser. When a cotton buyer now examines a sample of cotton, he knows that the cotton he buys is not in the condition of the sample. Why? Because the bagging is torn, the ends out, several pounds of cotton is materially injured by being exposed to mud, and much of it has become trashy and worthless. In the other case he knows that every pound he purchases is *like* the sample he has in his hand. And the price he is willing to give is of course, in both cases, regulated accordingly. No man at all acquainted with this subject can fail to know, that if our cotton went to market *in good order,* great advantage would accrue to the planter in prices.

Another important advantage of putting cotton in iron hoops, and in shipment size bales, is the fact that it is always ready for shipment. It not unfrequently happens now, that much delay is experienced in New Orleans, and at the other ports in consequence of the cotton not being in a condition to transport. Parcels frequently are known to remain in port for weeks at a time—not for the want of freight—not because the cotton is not there to ship, but because it is not in shipping condition. The purchaser is thus placed under circumstances often highly disadvantageous; which on the other hand, if the bales were put in shipment size at the gin, it is always ready for the vessel the moment it is purchased. This would often facilitate sales considerably, and prices too, somewhat, for it is always a matter of great importance in a seller of any thing, to place the purchaser in the most favorable position—to clear all obstructions and difficulties out of his way, as far as possible, and to make the vended article as immediately available to him as practicable. We know that nothing more certainly or immediately affects the price of cotton in New Orleans, than the question of *"freights."* Well, how suppose you, a freight could be contracted for, to best advantage? By saying to the master of the vessel, "Sir, the cotton is ready for you, now, you can commence loading in an hour," or on the other hand: the presses will be ready to commence it in a few weeks, and you can probably in a month or so commence taking it?

This difficulty is always felt, though to a less extent, than at the sea ports, in the market, at the river towns in the interior, at seasons when the smaller rivers are not navigable. In such cases the rise and fall of water, in the fall and winter seasons, affects the price of cotton directly and even more than that sometimes. The sea freight of cotton in hoops would also be lessened, by being thus packed. The apparent reason ableness of the thing as well as conversations with several sea captains, have abundantly demonstrated this position; and further, *cotton never could be burnt at sea.* It is no more labour to load two vessels with cotton in hoops, than one with the same number of bales in ropes, as they usually come from the steam presses.

The advantage of having cotton put in shipment size at the gin would be felt to a still greater extent in cases where cotton is to be only re-shipped at the sea ports, for sale in another market. In such cases there need be often but a single drayage, no warehousing, no piling in press rooms, no waiting to have it got ready to ship. The operation is performed at once, and the cotton is at sea or in market over the Atlantic, rather than receiving the winter rains of the South, being eat partially by cattle, pilfered by vagabonds on the wharves or streets, or suffering loss and damage in any of the various ways in which such things are known very extensively to occur.

The recommendation that cotton be always put in shipment size by the planter himself, at his own gin press, is not so wild a stride of innovation as might be supposed by those who have not *thought* much on the subject. A few years ago it was impracticable, but now it is quite easy. Cotton was sent to the sea ports, to be repressed there and steam presses erected there for the purpose, because the plantation presses could not do it, and the practice is continued because it was commenced, not because the same reason still exists. But within the last fifteen years, great improvements in plantation presses have been introduced, and still greater improvements are being made. It is not presumed that every plantation is now furnished with a suitable press for their purpose, but it is confidently asserted that every plantation can easily so supply itself. The present condition of machinery of this kind is such that the power of two horses is sufficient for the purpose indicated. The writer does not pretend to be acquainted with the most approved kind of plantation presses now in use, but he does know enough to justify the above remark. He is now using a press of a kind not approved by himself; it is a single wood screw, but with it there is no difficulty in pressing *mastodon* cotton to the size indicated with two mules, and it is to be observed that the mastodon in consequence of the *body* and firmness of its staple, is harder to press than the common Mexican. The largest size

Newell screw cannot fail of exerting sufficient power. And the *Bullocks Patent Press,* if it is capable of receiving a box of sufficient length, will no doubt be found far preferable. With it one mule will give sufficient power. If the expense of erecting such presses is thought an objection to this introduction, it may be stated that the wood press above alluded to, cost one hundred dollars, besides getting out and hawling the timber. The large size iron screw will cost perhaps fifty dollars more than the old fashioned Newell press that every body has, and the Bullocks Patent will cost a hundred and twenty-five to a hundred and fifty dollars.

These evils, thus hastily sketched and hurriedly run over, deserve a loud and long complaint. They speak in tones of thunder to the pockets of cotton growers and ought not to pass by unheeded. In the state of Georgia the oldest and until recently the largest cotton Growing state, it is astonishing to learn that at the present time *one half* of the cotton is put up for market, not in bales at all, but bundled up in something like old meal bags. The other half of the crop of Georgia is put up in the most clumsy, awkward and miserable looking bales, very seldom in passable shipping order, these are called *"square"* the other "round" bales. Both kinds are indescribably shapeless, but the packing in the *"round"* bundles is so excessively miserable that the regular mercantile deduction from the market price of such cotton is *half a million of dollars annually!* This deduction is over and above the next deduction consequent upon the *"square"* bales not being in shipping order. Is there here no room for reform?

The Georgia and South Carolina and Florida planter, who thus ties his cotton up in bags, loses money enough *every year* to put up a press at a cost of a thousand dollars, and the Alabama, Louisiana and Mississippi planter will also save money enough *annually* to pay for a press, by putting his cotton in shipment size. Large planters will save five or ten times the cost of such presses.

The present condition of our business, calls for *immediate* reform. The ravages of the cotton worm the present season, admonishes the planter to look around him. To cultivate a certain number of acres of land, in cotton, or to put a given number of bales into the hands of a commission merchant are not the only questions to be inquired into, nor yet are they the most important. To realize the largest amount of nett money from a given amount of means invested, looking carefully and economically into all parts of the operation, is the part of wisdom and enterprise.

. . . . . . . . . . . . . . .

## b] A College Professor Urges a Production Policy

. . . From year to year, almost without exception, the reports of a short crop are circulated everywhere on this side of the Atlantic; and on the other side, with the same regularity, are heard the tales of ruinous prices of goods, and of bankrupt brokers and manufacturers. These rumors are not, however, peculiar to the dealers in cotton. They are common to all the pursuits of business where the supply and demand are irregular and uncertain. The bulls and bears in Wall street are engaged in the same efforts as the cotton sellers of New-Orleans and the buyers of Manchester. The trade in flour, tobacco, and coffee, as well as wines, spices, and fruits, is subject to the same false reports. They are found everywhere; they are unavoidable, and they cannot be prevented.

These reports sometimes imply fraud and falsehood—but often this is not the case. In a country like ours, where cotton is cultivated in every variety of soil and climate, the drought which is so disastrous to one is often a blessing to another. The frost, the worm, the rust, and the floods, are seldom universal. Partial showers may relieve the general absence of rain. The wet bottoms do not require the same seasons as the thirsty uplands. The early crops do not demand the same supply of rain and sunshine as the late plantings. While thus from numerous localities the rumors of ruin and destruction may be true, they may not be general or universal. Those who meet with calamities make the loudest noise, for it affects them deeply. Those who do not suffer say but little, for they obtain only their wishes or expectations, and there is nothing in this to call particular attention to their condition. The losses affect not only the planter, but the factor, the merchant, and others, and thus many join in the cry of disasters. The good fortune of others has no one to herald it, because few have any particular interest in the result.

But though these false reports may always be expected, and do not of themselves imply fraud and deception, they do nothing but harm to all concerned. Sometimes they appear to help the planter, but this is fully balanced at another time by a loss equal to his former gain. As the profit and loss are thus sure at last to be fairly balanced, the unnecessary fluctuations in price caused by these false reports are a serious and important injury to both parties. It would be a great advantage to all, if greater steadiness could be given to prices. When the planter makes his purchases and expenditures, expecting to receive fifteen cents for his cotton, and sells at last for nine, the loss and inconvenience are greater than the gain and gratification that attend an advance from nine to fifteen. So it is with the manufacturer. If he contracts to deliver his cloth or his yarn, when cotton is low, a rise in the raw material forces him to ruinous sacrifices, perhaps to pay extraordi-

---

FROM C. F. McCay, "Cotton Trade of the South," in J. D. B. DeBow, ed., *The Industrial Resources of the Southern and Western States* (New Orleans: J. D. B. DeBow, 1852), vol. I, pp. 139–41.

nary interest to the money lender, or close his business in bankruptcy. Goods will not rise immediately with an advance in cotton. They fall sooner with a decline than they rise with an advance. The loss is thus more than the gain. As greater regularity and uniformity would be promoted by correct and accurate knowledge of the crops and markets, the truth, the whole truth, and nothing but the truth, would be of advantage to all.

It is a common opinion among the planters and factors of the South, that a short crop not only brings a higher price, but actually produces a larger amount of money than a large or an average crop. It would be strange if this were true. Fine seasons, instead of being the kind gifts of a bountiful Providence, would then be an injury and a curse. The destructive drought and early frosts would be a positive advantage to the agriculturist. The planter would be acting wisely for his own interests if he should destroy a large portion of what he had produced. These seem like strange propositions, and at first sight, are very improbable. Let us examine them by the history of prices for twenty-five years past.

The receipts for our cotton are constantly changing; they rise and fall like a wave of the sea. At times they go up for several years, and then decline suddenly. At other times the rise is rapid, and the fall gradual. In twenty-five years the value of our cotton exports, according to the official reports of the Secretary of the Treasury, has six times reached the highest point, and five times the lowest. Of these six years of large receipts, three of them were large crops, two an average, and one small. Of the five years of small receipts, four of them were small crops, and one an average. In these eleven years, the rule therefore was true but once.

Perhaps, however, the rule deserves a fuller examination. We have supposed above that the crop and its proceeds were large when they exceeded the amounts of the year before and the year after, and small when they were less than both. It would be fairer, perhaps, to take the average of every five years, both of the crop and of the money it was sold for, and to call that an average crop which was near—say within 5 per cent. of this average. Thus, for the year 1847 the number of bales delivered at the seaports was 1,779,000; the average of 1845, '46, '47, '48, and '49 was 2,270,000 bales, so that the receipts were less than the average of 471,000 bales, or 21 per cent. below. This would, therefore, be regarded as a very short crop, because more than 5 per cent. from the average. So with the amounts for which the cotton was sold. In 1848 the value of our cotton exports was $62,000,000. For 1846, '47, '48, '49, and '50, the average of the values was $57,300,000. The real receipts were, therefore, large, being $4,700,000, or 8 per cent. above the average of the five years of which 1848 was the middle one.

If, now, we compare the rule with the facts of the last twenty-five years, the crops were large, according to this definition, in 1827, '30, '31, '40, '43, '45, '48, and '49, and short in 1828, '32, '37, '41, '42, '47, and '50. Of these fifteen years no short crop brought a large value, and only one large one—that of 1831—brought a small value. If we had taken the exports in pounds instead of the crops in bales, there would not have been a single year that the rule would have been found true; so that the only case where the rule appears to hold, in the twenty-five years, occurred when a large crop brought a small price, because a great deal of it was retained at home and unsold. In table I., at the end of this article,[1] may be seen all the crops, values, and exports for the twenty-five years, with the average for each, and every one may examine the facts for himself. In 1827 the exports were 5 per cent. above the average, and the money received for them 32 per cent. above. In 1828 the exports were 15 per cent. below, and the value 17 per cent. below. In 1829 the crop was an average one, and so was the cash received for it. In 1830 both were large, and in 1831 both were small. For the six years, from 1832 to 1837, the exports were about an average, but the values were sometimes large and sometimes small. In 1838 and 1839 the amount exported was first large and then small, and both years brought average values. In 1840 it was large, and the money was large. In 1841 and 1842 we had two very short crops succeeding each other, yet the sales of the second year were 12 per cent. lower than the average. In 1843 the exports were large, and the proceeds were within the average limit. From 1844 to 1851 we have had three large crops—1845, '48, and '49—and each of them brought average values. In the same time we had three short crops—1846, '47, and '50; the first brought a small return—the other two were about the average. And thus, for every year in the whole twenty-five, the rule entirely fails, and cannot therefore be regarded as true.

No doubt it sometimes happens that a small crop brings more money than a large one. Thus, in 1847, 1,779,000 bales brought more money than 2,395,000 bales in 1845. But neither year brought large returns—both were an average. The large crop of 1848 brought more money than either; and the very large one of 1849, although it succeeded a large crop, brought still more. The small exports of 1850 were sold for a large amount, but the money received will not exceed the average sales of 1849, 1850, and 1851.

If it be, then, true that short crops are an injury to the planter on account of the diminished amount of money he receives for them, there are other reasons which render the calamity still greater. They stimulate prices to such a high limit that they encourage the production of cotton in India and other places, and thus endanger the monopoly which we now possess in the European market. They discourage the use of cotton in the place of hemp, flax, wool, and silk, and thus put down still further the price of the raw material when favorable seasons have enlarged the supplies. They raise the price of many articles that planters are compelled to buy, and thus lessen the net amount of his income. They increase the price of all kinds of property, so that the gains of the planter with high prices, when invested in anything but money, seldom obtain a larger amount than with low or inordinate prices. They disturb the regular operation of business, tempt the producer to increase his expenditures, to contract debts, to purchase land and negroes on credit, and when the decline comes, as it is sure to do, he is forced to pay for property purchased at high prices, with the sales of his crop at low prices. They lead to the neglect of other products, so that hay is carried from Massachusetts, flour from New-York, corn from Balti-

[1] Here omitted—S.B.

more, bacon from Cincinnati, not only to the seaports of the South, but far into the interior; and when cotton falls, the planter cannot begin at once to supply all his own wants, because he is out of stock from which to raise his hogs, horses, or mules, and some time must elapse before he can obtain them.

These, and many other evils that might be mentioned, show that the interest of the producer is not diverse and opposite to that of the consumer—that the blast and mildew, the drought and the flood, the caterpillar and the boll-worm, which reduce the supply and raise the price to the manufacturer, are also an injury to the planter—that favorable seasons—a proper succession of rain and sunshine, are twice-told blessings, both to him that buys, and to him that sells.

While thus short crops are sources of serious evils to the planter, over-production and ruinously low prices are a still greater injury. How can these be prevented? Not by the combination of half a million of planters scattered over a wide extent of country; not by state conventions and paper resolutions; not by monster schemes of monopoly and governmental interference; not by banks or corporations, or factors or brokers forestalling the markets of New-Orleans, New-York, and Liverpool; not by false rumors—by retaining the crop of the country till the season is far advanced—by publishing in the newspapers every disaster from frost or flood, and withholding the reports of abundance and plenty. These plans are all either useless or injurious. Free trade, unshackled industry, is the motto of the South, not only in commerce and manufactures, but in agriculture. Capital is best employed when let alone. The keen-sightedness of self-interest will discern the proper remedy for over-production, and no one need be concerned lest trade should not regulate itself better than he would do it, if he had full power to manage and control it. God is wiser than man, and the laws he has imposed require no aid from us to adjust and adapt them to the circumstances around us. The proper course for the planter, and the one he is sure to pursue, is to make as much cotton as he can, while the price is fair and remunerative. As soon as it falls below this, he should apply both his capital and labor to other pursuits. By the home manufacture of cotton, wool, paper, iron, and machinery; by producing at the South his flour, corn, bacon, mules, and horses; by the increased planting of the sugar-cane and tobacco; by the introduction of new agricultural products; by devoting his capital to the construction of railways and plank-roads; by building ships and steamers to carry on our own trade with the north and with Europe; by importing directly from abroad our foreign supplies, and by sending our cotton directly to European ports, without the transhipment at New-York; by these, and many other means, his capital and labor can be diversified and rendered profitable, when the price of cotton will no longer bring fair returns. It is the duty of the intelligent and public-spirited men of the South not to attempt to reverse the laws of trade by forcing up the prices to some arbitrary level at which the planter can afford to produce cotton, but to seek out new modes of profitable investment; to undertake new schemes, not yet tried and proved, which promise fair profits to capital; to encourage by words and actions, by legislative enactments, by public and private commendation, every new enterprise calculated to diversify our labor, develop our resources, and divert capital and labor from our great staple.

. . . . . . . . . . . . . . .

## c] LIVERPOOL URGES BETTER PACKING

### REGULATIONS FOR COTTON PACKING

THE FOLLOWING statement, on behalf of the Liverpool American Chamber of Commerce and the Cotton Brokers' Association, respecting the evils arising from the false packing of cotton, is entitled to a place in this department of the *Merchants' Magazine:—*

LIVERPOOL, October 23.

*To the Chamber of Commerce of New Orleans, Mobile, Charleston, and Savannah, and to all concerned in the cotton trade of the United States:—*

The magnitude and importance of the commerce of Great Britain with the United States in the article of cotton, is sufficiently known, and to those who are acquainted with the details of the trade it is a matter of satisfaction that the machinery by which the distribution of so enormous a quantity of material is effected has, up to this time, worked so smoothly owing to the honorable character of all concerned, from the planter to the manufacturer.

But, in order to sustain the character of the trade, and to retain the mutual confidence which has hitherto existed, it is essential that every sample of cotton offered in the market should fairly represent the quality of the bulk from which it is taken, as every deviation from this rule tends to create a distrust.

Of late, however, so many instances of careless packing have occurred, causing a discrepancy between the sample and the bulk, that serious loss has been sustained both by the manufacturer and the merchant, and it has become a duty to call the attention, not only of the American planters and factors, whose reputation is thereby injured, but also of the trade generally, to the present growing increase in the proportion of irregular and false packed bales, and to invite their serious consideration of the evils which must inevitably follow the continuance of the practice, and to solicit their assistance in checking it.

In most cases, the irregular packing is only discovered when the bale has reached its ultimate destination and is opened by the manufacturer, and the trouble, cost, and inconvenience of repacking, and the difficulties which attend a prosecution of his claim, frequently induced him to bear the loss in silence. Similar reasons have prevailed with the merchants to suffer the

---

FROM [Freeman Hunt] "Regulations for Cotton Packing," *Hunt's Merchants' Magazine*, vol. XXXVI (March, 1857), pp. 351–52.

loss resulting from such cotton returned by the manufacturer, rather than resort to the tedious and often useless process of seeking redress against the planter abroad.

It is on this account that so few instances have occurred in which the real offender has borne the consequences of neglect, and presuming on this forbearance, the evil complained of has, from carelessness or otherwise, increased to such an extent that in a large proportion of shipments arriving in Liverpool, instances of false or irregular packing are discovered, and occasionally whole parcels, consisting of 20, 50, and even 100 bales, are found mixed in the bale, and sometimes plated—in other words, the outer bale from which the sample is taken is more or less superior in quality to the interior of the bale.

It is hoped that all parties will see the urgent necessity of promptly co-operating to stop and remove this serious and increasing evil, which will otherwise disorganize the trade, and destroy that mutual trust and confidence, without which such an extensive and important branch of commerce cannot be carried on.

THOMAS SELLAR, President American Chamber of Commerce.
THOMAS HAIGH, President Cotton Brokers' Association.

## d] AN EDITOR PINS HIS HOPES ON EFFICIENCY

THE NEW YORK *Shipping List* remarks:—Not a little anxiety has been excited among the cotton manufacturers of England by the prevalence of an opinion that the demand for cotton is increasing much more rapidly than is the slave population of the United States. It is supposed that each slave can produce a fixed quantity and no more, and that, as the increase of the number of slaves is limited by certain fixed natural laws, the limit of the production of cotton is defined by the ratio in which that part of the population is augmented. This method of estimating the prospective crops of the United States is commonly resorted to by writers and practical men in Europe, with all confidence that its results are as certain as the demonstrations of Euclid. It is singular that it should never have occurred to these parties that it might be well to test their calculation by the facts of experience. Nothing could be easier, and one would suppose nothing more accordant with common sense. To have done so, however, would have scarcely accorded with the purpose which writers on this subject across the Atlantic generally have in view, viz.: to depreciate the capacity of North America as a cotton producing country.

A simple comparison of any two decades in the history of our cotton crops would have shown the entire fallacy of their estimates. They would have ascertained that what they assume as a fixed fact, viz.: an unfluctuating proportion between the number of the slave population and amount of cotton produced, is in truth a mere fiction, and that consequently the ground

FROM [Freeman Hunt] "Cotton Production," *The Merchants' Magazine and Commercial Review,* vol. 44 (January, 1861), pp. 101–02.

work of their calculations is fallacious. It has not yet been ascertained what is the largest amount of cotton that can be produced by slave labor in this country; for the crops have been constantly increasing in a larger proportion than has the slave population. In proportion as the value of cotton has advanced, the slave population has been drafted from other pursuits to the cotton plantations; and hence it will be found that the production of other staples in the South has progressed much less rapidly than has the growth of cotton.

In 1800, when the cotton crop was only 35,000 bales, the number of slaves in the country was 857,095, showing an average of twenty-four slaves to the bale. Twenty years later the number of slaves had nearly doubled, while the production of cotton had increased nearly fifteen fold, so that then there were three slaves to each bale of cotton. During the ten succeeding years the cotton crop increased in the ratio of seventy-five per cent, and the number of slaves thirty-three per cent, which brought down the number of slaves to each cotton bale to 2¼. From 1830, up to the present time, the proportion has continued to decline steadily, until now the production of cotton is as 1⅛ bale to each of the slave population.

The following table shows this progress during each decade since 1800:—

| | Crop, bales. | Slave population. | Slaves per bale. |
|---|---|---|---|
| 1800 | 35,000 | 857,095 | 23 |
| 1820 | 509,158 | 1,524,580 | 3 |
| 1830 | 870,415 | 2,005,471 | 2¼ |
| 1840 | 2,177,532 | 5,486,226 | 1⅛ |
| 1850 | 2,796,796 | 3,204,051 | 1⅛ |
| 1860 | 4,500,000 | 4,000,000 | 9–10 |

It is strikingly apparent from this comparison that the number of the slave population is a most imperfect criterion by which to judge of the probable future production of this staple. Experience teaches us to expect a larger ratio of increase in the cotton crop than in the number of slaves; but how much larger the ratio will prove in the former case than in the latter, it is impossible to estimate. This must depend to a certain extent on the numbers that can yet be drawn from other kinds of labor by reason of the greater profitableness of cotton culture. But not by any means on this alone, nor perhaps on this chiefly. The most advanced planters have shown that very much may be done towards increasing the produce per acre by improved methods of culture. The history of agriculture during the last ten years shows that, by skillful management, land may be made to produce nearly double what it has yielded under old systems of culture; and there can be no doubt that the introduction of the same enlightened views among the Southern planters will issue in a large increase in our cotton crops, and the more so as the fertility of the virgin soil has to such a large extent become exhausted as to cause a need for artificial aids.

# 4] An Estimate (1836) of Capital and Labor Employed in the Growing of Cotton

. . . . . . . . . . . . . . .

THE CAPITAL employed in growing cotton, with the income it yields, is a question of much interest and importance. But very little can be found concerning it in books, and the information obtained on it from different correspondents in the United States is defective, and is founded on quite different data in different States and by different persons.

The elements of any computation must be, the average cost per acre of cotton lands, wild or cleared, and if the former, the expense of clearing them: the amount of labor necessary per acre to produce a given quantity of raw cotton; the cost of labor, whether in the form of wages or otherwise; the expense of tools, horses, &c. with salaries of overseers, taxes paid, &c. &c.

One mode of making the computation is as follows: The average cost of cotton lands when wild, in the old States, did not probably exceed often half a dollar per acre, including fees for patents, &c. In the new States it has generally ranged from $1 25 to $20 00 per acre, depending on its quality, location, and the price of cotton. The actual settlers, in purchasing of capitalists, have generally been compelled to give an advance from 50 to 100 per cent.; sometimes much more.

The expense of clearing wild land averages from ten to fifteen dollars per acre. Land in a condition to be cultivated, will, on an average, in the United States, yield from 250 lbs. to 300 lbs. of clean cotton. In the old States, 125 lbs. clean, or 500 lbs. in the seed is an ordinary crop. Cox, in 1810, estimated it at 138 lbs. and others at 120 lbs.

It is believed, that one field hand or laborer, with the aid hereafter named, can cultivate, on an average, eight acres. Some say five to seven, and others ten. He will at the same time assist in raising five to eight acres of corn.

It is usual to employ in this business slave labor, and the next element in the calculation must be the capital invested in slaves for this purpose, and the annual cost of their maintenance.

The price of field hands has nearly or quite doubled in ten years; and they now often cost eight hundred or one thousand dollars, when formerly four and five hundred dollars were the usual rate each.

The maintenance of them is another item very differently computed. Sometimes it is done by the purchase of more land and cultivating it, put-

FROM U.S. Congress, House, Treasury Department Report [by Levi Woodbury] *Cotton, Cultivation, Manufacture and Foreign Trade of,* House Document no. 146. 24th Congress, 1st Session, pp. 18–22. [Authorities cited in the text have been deleted.]

ting stock on it of cows, sheep, &c. so as, with the aid of other slaves, kept partly for that purpose and partly for the culture of cotton, to raise corn, pork, &c. to feed, and other materials to clothe the whole. In such case the additional land put in cultivation, the additional slaves bought, and the stock on the plantation, &c. must be considered as so much more capital.

The additional slaves in such case, being more youthful, or more aged ones, or infirm females, may be fairly computed at an equal number with the field hands, but costing only about half the price. The additional land should be for cultivation, about twenty acres for each field hand. The capital in oxen, horses, sheep, tools for husbandry, &c. about thirty dollars to each slave on the plantation.

To these must be added the capital which may be deemed temporary, and not as a permanent investment, and hence is to be all yearly returned, such as expense for extra clothing not made on the plantation, for medicine, overseers, tools for labor, taxes, freight, &c. which may be forty-five dollars to each slave.

Differing from these last data, in some respects, in substance, and wholly unlike in form, is another mode of computing all the capital invested except that in the mere cotton lands. Instead of estimating the price of slaves, &c. it may be considered that slave labor could be hired, with food, clothing, medicine, &c. at a cost for each field hand from one hundred to one hundred and twenty dollars per year. That from thirty to forty dollars each would defray the annual expense of overseers, tools, horses for each, and that the additional and equal number of slaves, not prime field hands, could be hired and supported for less than half the annual cost of the others.

On these data the cotton crop, as estimated for 1835, at 480 million pounds, would grow on 1,600,000 acres at 300 lbs. per acre, or 1,920,000 at 250 lbs. each. Considering that some lands wear out quick and are changed, probably the whole quantity cultivated for cotton in the United States, at this time, should be estimated at two millions or more of acres.

From the above elements the whole capital invested in growing the cotton crop in the United States can be readily computed. On one hypothesis, converting the whole capital into that which is permanent, and partly invested in lands, slaves, and tools, as fixed capital, and partly invested in bank or other stocks, or in loans so as to yield an income, and not a capital sufficient to defray those kinds of expenses which are usually deemed temporary, and are yearly remunerated, or require what is called a circulating or floating capital, and the whole will amount to more than 900 millions of dollars. On another hypothesis, considering the capital, as it generally is, divided into fixed and circulating; the capital as fixed, which is invested in lands, slaves, stocks of horses, tools, &c. and only about thirty millions of dollars for other expenses, as circulating or temporary, and to be itself, and not its income or interest, used and repaid yearly, and the whole capital of both kinds will not quite equal 800 million dollars.

This last amount accords nearly with a still different mode of testing the quantity of capital, by supposing that the whole crop of 480 million pounds, at ten cents per pound, being 48 million dollars, would yield six per cent. on all the money invested in any way in raising the crop. If the capital used was all permanently invested, it would, on this hypothesis, amount to near 800 million dollars; but as from 25 to 30 million dollars is temporarily invested, and must itself be repaid yearly, the whole may, in the usual mode of treating of capital employed in such business, be considered rather under than over 800 million dollars.

That amount, however, has been assumed as about correct, in the table, and is near enough for the estimate and comparisons at different periods in this country, and at the same period between this and other countries. In others, as in India, Brazil, and Egypt, the cost of labor is less, and perhaps the value of land, though the latter is doubtful; and the crop per acre, and the amount of labor performed by each hand, is believed to be less, independent of the failure there to use much the improved cotton gin.

Here, at 250 pounds per acre as an average crop, and eight acres an average cultivation by one hand, the product would be 2,000 pounds per hand, or at ten cents per pound, would be the average of two hundred dollars per field hand. All the planter obtains over ten cents per pound would yield him a large rate of interest above 6 per cent. to pay for the greater risk and uncertainty of capital invested in this species of property. The whole crop of 1834 was probably worth 75 million dollars at the actual market prices, though at 10 cents per pound only 48 millions.

It is difficult to institute any just comparison between the profits of capital invested here in the growing of cotton, and in the manufacture of it; as in the latter so much more in proportion is invested in temporary or circulating capital to pay for wages and stock, and the whole of which is to be annually repaid. Neither have I leisure for the details.

Indeed it might have comported better with the technical language of political economy to have divided the whole expenditures in raising cotton into three heads, viz: labor, capital and land; to yield in return, wages for the labor, profit or interest on the capital, and rent for the land. It will be easy, for those who prefer it, to throw the calculation into that form; but the results then, would not be such as accord best with the views proposed . . . which are, to present to the community here, in plain terms, and in a form as intelligible as possible to people at large, the amount of capital actually employed at different periods in growing the cotton crop in the United States; whether invested in the original purchase of lands, the clearing, or the culture of them; in the purchase of slaves, or in procuring an income for the payment, or in the actual payment of wages of free labor to raise the crop; for buying seed, tools, food, raiment, horses, &c. and for payment of taxes, overseers, or any other expense, incidental or direct, connected with the production of the crop.

Two brief statements of a very general character are subjoined, in illustration of some of the above remarks.

| | |
|---|---|
| 1st. The capital invested in cotton lands under cultivation, at two million acres, and worth cleared, on an average, $20 per acre, is | $ 40,000,000 |
| The capital in field hands, and in other lands, stock, labor, &c. to feed and clothe them, at $100 per year, on 340,000 in number, would require the interest or income of a capital, at six per cent. of | 544,000,000 |
| The maintenance of 340,000 more assistants, &c. at $30 each per year, would require the income of a capital at six per cent. of | 167,000,000 |
| The capital to supply enough interest or income to pay for tools, horses for ploughing cotton, taxes, medicines, overseers, &c. at $30, for the first 340,000, would be | 167,000,000 |
| Making in all a permanent capital, if so used, equal to | $918,000,000 |
| 2d. The capital in cotton lands, as stated above | $ 40,000,000 |
| Capital in the purchase of 340,000 field hands, at $800 each, on an average | 272,000,000 |
| Capital in the other 340,000 to aid, and to raise food, clothing, &c. at half price | 136,000,000 |
| Capital in horses, cattle, sheep, utensils, &c. for plantation, about $30 to each person, to aid in making food and clothing, &c. | 20,400,000 |
| Capital in other lands to support stock, raise corn, &c. at 20 acres to each of the 680,000, worth $20 per acre cleared | 272,000,000 |
| Capital, temporary, or floating, to buy clothing not made on plantation, pay taxes, overseers, freight, tools cotton, &c. $45 to each | 30,600,000 |
| | $771,000,000 |

Making, in all, about $740,000,000 of capital permanently invested or fixed, and about $30,000,000 temporarily or circulating.

The crop in Demarara, per acre, is said to be 400 pounds clean. Edinburgh Encyclopedia, article "Cotton," 1815. But, in another place, the crop in Guiana is computed, on an average, at only 200 pounds, and costs 14 cents or (7*d.*) per pound to raise it.

The capital, per acre, invested there in land, buildings, slaves, &c. is computed for 1814, at about $730, which is nearly double the amount computed above for the United States. (See same book.) He states also the cost of cotton land in Louisiana at about $12½ per acre, slaves at $430 each, and assigns 30 for a plantation of 600 acres and over; horses and sheep for same, costing about $2,250, or $75 for each slave. Those 30 slaves will raise 1,000 pounds of cotton each; (and, it is presumed, maintain themselves from the land not in cotton, and stock on it.) The annual expenses of overseers, physician, tools, clothing and taxes, with freight of cotton to market, are computed at about $1,350, or $45 each per year; which, deducted from the price of the cotton, valued at 21 cents per pound, or about $6,450, leaves about $5,100 as a return on the original investment of about $22,500, (or at the rate of nearly 25 per cent.) viz:

| | |
|---|---|
| 600 acres at $12½ per acre | $ 7,500 |
| 30 slaves, at $430 each | 12,900 |
| Horses, sheep, &c. | 2,250 |
| | $22,650 |

The number of persons is computed on similar data and principles to those suggested in the first mode of estimating the capital. Some allowances are made in certain cases, but for comparison there has been preserved similar proportions in all the years for which the computation is carried out in the table.

Thus two millions of acres, at one field hand to every six acres, would require about 340,000 laborers: but many compute that the number in the United States is over 550,000, who are chiefly, though not entirely, engaged in field labor. Suppose the whole number to be double the field hands, as above computed, or 680,000, who are engaged in field labor, picking and otherwise assisting in the cultivation of cotton and corn, and the estimate of laborers is complete at about 680,000. But allowing that a number more should be added, who are connected with the cultivators, as infirm women, very young children, and too aged persons, &c. unable to labor in the field besides overseers, owners and their respective families, dependent on the cotton crop, and it is presumed that then, a million of persons would be considered as now engaged in the United States, directly and indirectly, in the growing of cotton: but the actual laborers are only about two-thirds of that number.

The numbers are, for comparative views, in all other countries stated on the same principle, though they are doubtless more, in most nations, to raise the same quantity of cotton for reasons too obvious for recital, and especially where the saw gin and horse power are less used.

. . . . . . . . . . . . . . .

## 5] Life on a Mississippi Plantation

. . . . . . . . . . . . . . .

IN SELECTING his plantation, Thomas showed his usual sound judgment in practical matters. It comprised four thousand acres in a compact body, not all bought at one time, but as he saw opportunity to secure the prop-

---

FROM Susan Dabney Smedes, *Memorials of a Southern Planter* (Baltimore: Cushing & Bailey, 1887), pp. 63–65, 67–71, and 73–74.

erty of small farmers whose land adjoined his. In this way he shaped his place to suit himself; and it was characteristic of his exact methods that after making his final purchase the section lines fell so as to form an almost exact square, with Tallahala Creek crossing it diagonally from northeast to southwest. The lowland bordering the creek, called "The Bottom," was inexhaustibly fertile, and ensured heavy crops in the dryest season. From the creek-bottom the land gradually rises and runs back in a series of hills and plateaus. Those not already cleared for cultivation were covered with a magnificent growth of timber,—oaks of many species, yellow pine, hickory, elm, sweet- and black-gum, besides countless other trees and shrubs of less value. Walnut-trees of magnificent size, magnolia, beech, and laurel grew on the banks of the creek.

Crops raised on the hills flourished best in wet weather; so with the admirable diversity of soil on the plantation there was never a failure of a whole crop in the most unfavorable season.

The land was well watered throughout by Tallahala Creek, with its tributary branches, Indian Jumper and Snake Creek, and a number of smaller bayous. In the hills springs bubbled out, giving rise to spring "branches," which did not go dry in the most prolonged drought. There was always pasturage for cattle along these water-courses, and in the bitterest cold of winter they found abundant green food in the canebrakes of the creek. In this mild climate many wild flowers adorn the fields and woods till late in the fall. Tiny blue innocents dot the grass as early as January. Later come wild violets, roses, the wild lily, rhododendron, clematis, woodbine, snapdragon, and a host of flowering trees, shrubs, and vines. Among these we find the red-bud, maple, dogwood, crab-apple, hawthorn, and wild peach; but supreme in beauty and in fragrance we have the yellow jasmine. It is the crown and glory of Southern woods, throwing its drapery of golden bells over trees and shrubs for whole acres.

It was Thomas's plan in the management of this large estate to bring under cultivation a certain portion of new land every year. His rule was to clear one hundred acres each season. The cotton-plant delights in a virgin soil, and he counted on making a bale and a half of cotton to the acre on all new ground. This was, of course, above the average. In the hill country a planter thinks himself rewarded for his labor by an average yield of half a bale to the acre. Thomas one year made six hundred bales on six hundred acres, but that was an exceptional season. The fact that this place would be as productive now as ever with the same cultivation goes to show how well the land lies, and how wise Thomas was in the choice of his plantation.

In entering on this pioneer life many difficulties had to be met that were a new experience to people coming from lower Virginia. One of the first was the unavoidable delay in getting supplies of meat for the servants. For two weeks after their arrival they had none. Sophia's sister Emmeline, Mrs. Lewis Smith, was so conscientious that she refused during this period to touch a morsel of meat, although the supply on hand was ample to last the white families till more could be procured.

The roof of the house in which Thomas had to put his wife and children was so leaky, that he had sometimes at night when it rained to sit up in bed and hold an umbrella over her and the baby.

There were then no railroads, and the cotton crop had to be hauled in wagons forty miles, to Grand Gulf. The roads were so bad that to trust the teams to negro-drivers alone was not to be thought of, and the master went with every wagon.

Not more than a quarter of a mile from Thomas's home, in those early days in Mississippi, lived a man named Jack Cotton. He was one of a band of highwaymen who infested the road from Vicksburg to Memphis. Their practice was to waylay planters and rob them on their return from selling their cotton. Jack Cotton's house was a half-way station and a rendezvous for the band. Jack was civil to the new neighbors, and they were ignorant of his reputation as a desperado till he ran away to Texas to escape the law.

. . . . . . . . . . . . . . .

Thomas was misunderstood and misjudged by the people in Mississippi by whom he found himself surrounded. The plainer classes in Virginia, like those in England, from whom they were descended, recognized the difference between themselves and the higher classes, and did not aspire to social equality. But in Mississippi the tone was different. They resented anything like superiority in breeding.

Thomas Dabney was considered cold and haughty. It took them long years to find out that he was a true friend to the poor. As years passed on they learned to look on him as one to be relied on, not only for substantial help but for sympathy. Under the look of stern dignity the heart was tender and compassionate as a woman's.

It was the custom among the small farmers in his neighborhood to call on each other to assist when one of them built his house, usually a log structure. Accordingly, one day an invitation came to the new-comer to help a neighbor to "raise" his house. At the appointed time he went over with twenty of his men, and he did not leave till the last log was in place and the last board nailed on the room, handing over the simple cabin quite completed to the owner. This action, which seemed so natural to him, was a serious offence to the recipient, and, to his regret, he was sent for to no more "house-raisings." On another occasion, a small farmer living a few miles from him got "in the grass," as the country people express it when the grass has gotten ahead of the young cotton-plants and there is danger of their being choked by it. Again Thomas went over with twenty men, and in a few hours the field was brought to perfect order. The man said that if Colonel Dabney had taken hold of a plough and worked by his side he would have been glad to have his help, but to see him sitting up on his horse with his gloves on directing his negroes how to work was not to his taste. He heard a long time after these occurrences that he could have soothed their wounded pride if he had asked them to come over to help him to raise his cabins. But he could not bring himself to call on two or three poor white men to work among his servants when he had no need of help.

Another neighbor he found more grateful. This man was very sick during the season when his field should have been ploughed. His wife and only servant were quite taken up with nursing him. One day they heard the voices of workers in their field, and, on looking out, recognized Colonel Dabney and his servants. He had heard of the trouble, and had ordered his men to go to this place with their mules and ploughs, and to put everything in order for the crop, not failing to take their dinners along. The man got well, and he and his wife and children were life-long friends to the family at Burleigh.

A young doctor moving to the neighborhood said in his hearing that he found it difficult to buy corn. Thomas made no comment, but the next morning the doctor saw a six-mule wagon at his gate. The driver, whom he recognized as a Burleigh negro, asked where the corn should be stowed away. He showed him his corn-crib, and a day or two after, meeting Thomas, asked what he owed for the corn. "Oh, nothing," was the answer; "I do not charge a neighbor for a wagon-load of corn." This incident is hardly worth mentioning were it not that little things make up a man's life and show the spirit.

His plantation was considered a model one, and was visited by planters anxious to learn his methods. He was asked how he made his negroes do good work. His answer was that a laboring man could do more work and better work in five and a half days than in six. He used to give the half of Saturdays to his negroes, unless there was a great press of work; but a system of rewards was more efficacious than any other method. He distributed prizes of money among his cotton-pickers every week during the season, which lasted four or five months. One dollar was the first prize, a Mexican coin valued at eighty-seven and a half cents the second, seventy-five cents the third, and so on, down to the smallest prize, a small Mexican coin called picayune, which was valued at six and a half cents. The decimal nomenclature was not in use there. The coins were spoken of as "bits." Eighty-seven and a half cents were seven bits, fifty cents four bits, twenty-five cents two bits. The master gave money to all who worked well for the prizes, whether they won them or not. When one person picked six hundred pounds in a day, a five-dollar gold-piece was the reward. On most other plantations four hundred pounds or three hundred and fifty or three hundred was considered a good day's work, but on the Burleigh place many picked five hundred pounds. All had to be picked free of trash. No one could do this who had not been trained in childhood. To get five hundred pounds a picker had to use both hands at once. Those who went into the cotton-fields after they were grown only knew how to pull out cotton by holding on to the stalk with one hand and picking it out with the other. Two hundred pounds a day would be a liberal estimate of what the most industrious could do in this manner. A very tall and lithe young woman, one of mammy's "brer Billy's" children, was the best cotton-picker at Burleigh. She picked two rows at a time, going down the middle with both arms extended and grasping the cotton-bolls with each hand. Some of the younger generation learned to imitate this. At Christmas Nelly's share of the prize-money was something over seventeen dollars. Her pride in going up to the master's desk to receive it, in the presence of the assembled negroes, as the acknowledged leader of the cotton-pickers, was a matter of as great interest to the white family as to her own race.

The negroes were helped in every way to gather the cotton, not being interrupted or broken down by any other work. Some of the men were detailed to carry the cotton-hampers to the wagons that the pickers might lift no weights. Water-carriers, with buckets of fresh water, went up and down the rows handing water to the pickers. They would get so interested and excited over the work that they had to be made to leave the fields at night, some of the very ambitious ones wishing to sleep at the end of their rows, that they might be up and at work in the morning earlier than their rivals. The cotton was weighed three times a day, and the number of pounds picked by each servant set down opposite to his or her name on a slate. Quite a remarkable feat of memory was exhibited by one of the negro men one day in connection with this. His duty was to help the overseer to weigh the cotton. One day the slate was caught in a rain and the figures were obliterated. This man came that night to the master's desk and gave from memory every record on the slate, the morning, mid-day, and evening weights of each picker. The negroes stood near enough to hear if he had made a mistake in any man's figures. It was the more remarkable as he could not have expected to be called on to do this. In addition to the cotton crop, corn was raised in such abundance that it was not an unusual thing to sell a surplus of a thousand or two bushels or more. A maxim with the master was that no animal grew fat on bought corn. In putting in his corn crop he made full allowance for a bad season, hence there was never a scarcity. A lock on a corn-crib was not known. After the mules and horses were fed in the evening the negroes carried home all that they cared to have. They raised chickens by the hundred. One of the chicken-raisers, old Uncle Isaac, estimated that he raised five hundred, unless the season was bad. Uncle Isaac's boast was that he was a child of the same year as the master, and that the master's mother had given to him in her own arms some of the baby Thomas's milk, as there was more of it than he wanted. He would draw himself up as he added, "I called marster brother till I was a right big boy, an' I called his mother ma till I was old enough to know better an' to stop it myself. She never tole me to stop."

The negroes sold all the chickens they did not eat. They were taken to Raymond or Cooper's Well in a four-mule wagon, provided by the master. As he paid the market price, and as there was some risk of their getting less than he gave, there was not often a desire to send them off if he would take them. And he had need to buy all he used after the death of our faithful Granny Harriet. Different servants were given the care of the poultry, and all failed so signally that Aunt Kitty, who was renowned for success in her own poultry-yard, was placed in charge. She was given all the conveniences and facilities she asked for,—chicken-houses, coops, and separate enclosures for young chickens. The result of all this outlay was not a chicken the first year, and only one the second. The history of that one deserves to be recorded. It was hatched out in the hedge and raised by its mother hen without the aid of our accomplished hen hussy.

The thrifty negroes made so much on their chickens, peanuts, popcorn, molasses-cakes, baskets, mats, brooms, taking in sewing, and in other little ways, that they were able to buy luxuries. Some of the women bought silk dresses; many had their Sunday dresses made by white mantua-makers. Of course they had the clothes of the master and mistress in addition; and in later years, as the house grew full of young masters and young mistresses, theirs were added. As the family knew that the servants liked nothing so well as the well-made clothes that they laid aside, they wore their clothes but little. They justly considered that those who had labored for them had rights to them while still fresh. Under these circumstances it did not seem wasteful for a daughter of the house to distribute, at the end of a season, as many as a dozen or more dresses that had been made up but a few months before. It was quite funny to see among the gallants three or four swallow-tail coats of the master's come in at the gate for the grand promenade on Sunday evenings, escorting the colored belles in all their bravery of hoop-skirts, and ruffles, and ribbons, and flowers.

. . . . . . . . . . . . . . .

For some years the master accompanied every wagon loaded with cotton that went to market from his plantation. He slept on these journeys under the wagons, and sometimes on awakening in the morning he found that his great-coat, in which he was wrapped, was frozen hard to the ground. His negro drivers were more heavily clad than himself, each one being provided with a thick woollen great-coat that reached to his heels, home-knit woollen socks and gloves, and an enormous comforter for the neck. No illness resulted from the exposure. In the morning a hot meal, cooked by one of the negroes—and all the race are admirable cooks—was shared by the master and his men.

Until over seventy years old, he was singularly indifferent to cold or heat, or to discomforts of any sort. But he felt compassion for his negroes. He knew that the warm African blood in their veins was not fitted to endure what he could stand. He never regarded the weather for himself, but was very careful about sending them out in bad weather, and never did it unless it seemed a necessity. On such occasions he wore an anxious look, and said that he could not go to bed until his servants had gotten home safely. They were always sure of finding a hot fire and a warm drink ready for them on their return.

Every other year he distributed blankets on the plantation, giving one apiece to each individual. Many of the families were large, and as the fathers would move off under a load of twelve or fourteen blankets, some, whose quivers were less full, would be heard to exclaim over the good fortune of the lucky ones. There were usually a dozen or so left over in these distributions, and they were thrown in for good measure to those who had the large families. "Poor things, they have so many children," seemed to my dear mother a sufficient explanation for special favors that she often bestowed on those who had no other claim. Some of the negro men with the big families of children had a funny little affectation of feigning not to know either the names or the number of their boys and girls. "I disremember, missis, dyar's so many on 'em," with a little pleased laugh, was considered a sufficient answer to inquiries on the subject on every-day occasions. But not so on the days when blankets were to be given out. Then their memories were fresh. Then the babies that had not been in their cradles more than a few days, mayhap hours, were remembered and mentioned in due turn, with no danger of being forgotten or overlooked because there were "so many on 'em."

In addition to the blankets, comforts were quilted in the house by the seamstresses for every woman who had a young baby. The every-day clothes of all the negroes were cut out and made in the house; two complete woollen suits for winter and two cotton ones for summer. For Sundays, a bright calico dress was given to each woman. The thrifty ones, and, with scarcely an exception, these negroes were thrifty, had more than they needed, and the clothes were in their chests a year before they were put on. The woollen socks and stockings for both men and women were knit in the cabins by old women, and in the "great house" by young girls. These last were set a task by the mistress, with the privilege of holiday the rest of the day when it was done. This had the desired effect of making them quick and industrious, and so interested that they would be at their work betimes in the morning. The clever ones sometimes get through with the allotted task before breakfast.

On rainy days all the plantation women were brought into the house. Then Mammy Maria, who was in her way a field-marshal on such occasions, gave out the work and taught them to sew. By word and action she stimulated and urged them on, until there was not on the Burleigh plantation a woman who could not make and mend neatly her own and her husband's and children's clothes.

. . . . . . . . . . . . . . .

# PART IV

# Financing and Marketing the Cotton Crop

# INTRODUCTION

¶ INSIGHT into the ways in which the antebellum South marketed its cotton crop can be gained by examining the colonial tobacco trade, which is discussed in an earlier volume in this series, *The Colonial Merchant*.[1] The key figure in both trades was the factor, or commission merchant, whose essential functions were to market the crop and supply merchandise on credit. At the beginning of the era, when volume was small and the tidewater plantations were easily accessible to ocean-going ships, the factor with whom the planter dealt resided in England—in London or one of the outports for colonial tobacco, in Liverpool for post-colonial cotton. The case of the late seventeenth-century Virginia tobacco planter and storekeeper Colonel William Fitzhugh nicely illustrates these beginnings. By dealing directly with a number of factors in London and other English ports, Fitzhugh ordered manufactured goods in great variety; when the English vessels had come upriver to his plantation landing and had unloaded their cargoes, he saw to it that his tobacco was loaded on board for the return trip. He then retailed the imported merchandise from his two local stores or from small boats sent upriver to other planters in the area.

Even in the early nineteenth century, Tidewater cotton planters sometimes still dealt directly with English houses in the same manner. But they did so with increasing rarity, and in the tobacco trade the practice of direct dealing had begun to die in the early eighteenth century. In both cases the reason was the same: as population grew, settlers moved inland, and as the cultivation of staples increased, a growing number of middlemen was required in order to move the crops to their final markets. In the case of colonial tobacco, English houses sent a younger partner or other representative to reside in the American coastal ports; Scottish houses, finding the English dominant on the seaboard, sent factors into the interior to establish chains of stores at convenient points to supply merchandise on credit and purchase tobacco. Since the cotton trade was a post-Revolutionary development it was dominated by American merchants from the beginning, but the need for additional middlemen again made itself felt as soon as cotton pushed into the backcountry. To move cotton out and merchandise in required a chain of supply, and the links that made up the chain were forged from a series of forwarding and receiving agents spread from England and the northern United States (especially the port of New York) to the frontier.

In the early years of the nineteenth century, foreign goods necessarily bulked large among purchases made by planters, but native wares appear to have become more important with the rise of manufacturing in the Middle Atlantic and

[1] *The Colonial Merchant,* Stuart Bruchey, ed. (New York: Harcourt, Brace & World, 1966).

New England states. Whether domestic or foreign, the goods were likely to be sent south by New York merchants, for the same merchant houses that had begun as importers often continued in business as marketers of domestic manufactures. In a sense, they may be said to have plugged into the New York–Liverpool distribution network created earlier by the demands of the English Industrial Revolution. Unfortunately, our relative ignorance of the composition of coastal cargoes makes it difficult to say when and to what extent native manufactures began to predominate over foreign ones. It is almost certainly true that domestic manufactures were more important than is commonly realized. The Andrews Report to the United States Senate (1853) observes that "the increase of importations is mainly for the use and consumption of those portions of the country that do not produce cotton." The report concludes, "A statement fairly exhibiting the movement of merchandise *coastwise* would show a domestic importation into the southern cities having a much nearer ratio than the foreign importations to their export trade." Andrews' point is considerably strengthened by Robert Russell, who, writing in 1861, made the observation that "A mere fraction of our foreign imports finds its way to the Southern States. These States do not consume foreign but *domestic* merchandize. They import from the North ten dollars in domestics for every one imported, directly or indirectly from Europe."

Whether domestic or foreign in origin the goods were sent from the North to coastal merchants in the leading cotton ports of the South—New Orleans, Mobile, Savannah, and Charleston. Sometimes the goods were ordered in advance; at other times Northerners took the initiative by sending goods to be sold by coastal factors on commission. The orders, as we shall see, by no means originated with coastal factors alone. Frequently, they came by mail from merchants residing in the interior. Even so, the coastal factor first received the goods and then forwarded them to the inland factors via wagon, steamboat, or railroad. The inland factors, who resided in the leading interior towns—which by 1860 included Fayetteville, Columbia, Augusta, Milledgeville, Macon, Atlanta, Montgomery, Nashville, Memphis, and Shreveport—supplied the needs of planters, farmers, and keepers of general stores in the smaller towns and villages. Surprisingly, the latter appear sometimes to have been in direct correspondence with New York merchants—although, once again, they depended upon inland factors who in turn depended upon coastal factors to transmit ordered goods. Finally, at the approaches of the frontier, where the volume of business was too small for even a village store, wandering peddlers formed still another link in the chain of middlemen.

The South's cotton crop passed through the same channels of supply. Throughout the antebellum period Liverpool was the great market for most of the cotton, but some also went to Havre and elsewhere in Europe. With the rise of the New England textile industry, an increasing amount went to Boston. The largest amount of overseas shipments went directly to Europe from the southern ports, but from the early 1820's till the mid-1850's large quantities were sent to New York for transshipment.

The planter or farmer started the cotton crop on its way by carting the bales by wagon to the warehouse of the inland factor, who resided—let us say—in the important market town of Augusta, Georgia. If the planter lived upriver from Augusta he floated his bales down the Savannah on flatboats. According to the compiler of a "gazateer" for the state of Georgia, published in 1837, the 30 or 40 flatboats owned in Macon could "carry at a time from 400 to 700 bags of cotton and return with 70 and 80 tons." Sometimes the factor sold the cotton in the Augusta market, occasionally before it had even been unloaded. Often, however, cotton was stored in the factor's warehouse to wait for available shipping to the coast or for a more favorable market. It was not at all uncommon for the planter to give precise instructions concerning the disposition of his cotton—including "limits" beneath which he did not wish it sold. The typical arrangement, however, was one in which the factor decided when and where to sell and at what price. Being on the spot, he could closely follow changing trends in his own market, while the coastal factors and the Northern merchants kept him informed of prices in Savannah, other southern ports, and Liverpool.

It was the factor's business to watch the markets and move in the right direction at the right time. He was a specialist in cotton—as were the rice, sugar, and tobacco factors in their lines, for the volume of trade permitted this high degree of specialization. The amount he earned in commissions (almost always 2.5 per cent of the gross proceeds of cotton sales) depended substantially on how good his judgment was. If it were poor the planter could, and often did, change to a factor in whom he had confidence. No one can read the correspondence of a cotton factor—such as William Bostwick of Augusta, for example—without becoming deeply aware of the competition among factors for the business of planters. Visits to the country, circular letters, a constant stream of price and other market information, plus the hope—sometimes not realized—that goods and money advanced on credit would induce the planter to consign the cotton crop to him rather than to a business rival, attest to the reality of competition. And competition sharpened the factor's need to make wise market decisions.

A sale in the Augusta market saved the cost of transport and insurance for transshipment to the coast. On the other hand, buyers were more numerous in the larger coastal markets and prices often more attractive. Frequently, therefore, the factor in Augusta hired professional wagoners, freighted space on a steamboat (after 1816), or sent the cotton by railroad (after the early 1830's) to the care of one or more coastal factors with whom he had established relations—and sometimes a partnership—in Savannah or Charleston. If the cotton was for the account of a New York merchant, the coastal factor might be instructed to ship to that port. If it went to a coastal buyer among the resident agents of English merchants or manufacturers—or of Baltimore, New York, and other northern houses—it might then be shipped north or direct to Liverpool.

Even these routes, and numerous alternatives, did not exhaust the possible modes of selling cotton. In the early days of the cotton trade—before the volume of business made possible the institutional arrangements just described—inland factors personally accompanied the cotton to the coast, travelling from Nashville to New Orleans, perhaps, and sold it there in exchange for store goods that they laboriously hauled upstream (before steamboats appeared on the Western rivers in 1817). Or else they took a coasting vessel to New York where they bought their stock and returned home by wagon. Some planters consigned their cotton to coastal instead of inland factors, and some travelled to coastal cities and bought merchandise for themselves.

Inland factors frequently made summer trips to New York to select merchandise for their stores; the case of William Bostwick in the readings illustrates the practice.

What the inland factor was to the larger planter, the country storekeeper was to the smaller planter and farmer. Factors and storekeepers performed highly similar functions: both groups sold equipment, food, dry goods, and other supplies on book credit and received cash and cotton in payment. One major difference between the two was of scale: country stores were located in the villages and smaller towns, and their volume of business with individual customers was comparatively quite small. Their total business, however, was sufficiently large to make them of interest to factors. Storekeeper John Read, for example, shipped over $25,000 worth of cotton from his general store at Huntsville, Alabama, in 1835. As we shall see, William Bostwick dealt with country stores as well as planters.

A second major difference between factors and storekeepers derived from the first: because of their small volume of business storekeepers could specialize to a lesser degree. They dealt in numerous commodities and sold dry goods, hardware, and other merchandise not only for cash and cotton but for a large variety of farm products, often taken in barter exchange. These farm products—horses, mules, hogs, pork, bacon, and corn among others—were frequently disposed of to the planters, who were thus able to concentrate their resources more completely upon cotton. Thus, general stores, which existed even in the rich black-belt areas dominated by planters, served as intermediaries between the inland factors and the planters and farmers. Once again, it is frequently difficult to draw a fine line of distinction between the marketing functions of inland factors and storekeepers. "In the largest sense," as Harold D. Woodman observes in an excellent recent study, "the country store served as an adjunct to the factorage system, extending that system deep into the interior, into areas often far from the rivers and railroads." [2] And it extended the system in the more settled areas as well.

Credit made the factorage system possible, sustained the inward and outward flows of goods, and enabled planters to specialize in cotton, farmers in foodstuffs, and factors in the handling of particular staples. It originated abroad as well as at home. In colonial days, English credit had been of great importance to plantation agriculture and trade, and the well by no means dried up after the Revolution. Incomplete evidence suggests that credit lessened in importance, however, probably in part because of increasing success in capital accumulation by American merchants and the development of institutions—especially commercial banks—that increased the mobility of domestic capital. That individual American merchants enjoyed English credit is certain. Outstandingly successful American merchants—Robert Oliver and Robert Gilmor of Baltimore, for example—were beneficiaries of unusual credit arrangements. Each had been granted uncovered credits (credits not based upon collateral) with the great London merchant banking house of Baring Brothers. It is known in Oliver's case, however, that this credit did not serve as a "trading capital" but rather as a fund upon which, when exchange rates were high, he could draw bills and sell them at a profit. That is to say, the English credit

[2] Harold D. Woodman, "King Cotton and His Retainers" (unpublished Ph.D. dissertation, Department of History, University of Chicago, 1964), p. 92.

granted was short-term, even in Oliver's case. It is probable that American importers in general rarely, if ever, obtained long-term credit. The bills of exchange that English exporters drew on American importers and sent along with their goods were usually payable 60 or 90 days after sight. In contrast, we shall see the testimony of William Bostwick that the usual credit extended by New York merchants to factors in the Southern back country ran from 6 to 9 months. It was in large part because inland factors received long-term credit from New York merchants that they themselves were able to sell goods and make cash advances to planters and farmers on long credits.

While the length of long-term credit varied from case to case and from period to period, the fundamental consideration was that planters needed foodstuffs and supplies long before the sale of their cotton could afford them the means of repayment. Sometimes they received advances against a crop even before the seed was in the ground. While the length of credit might be short, it often ran from 10 months to a year and even longer. Large sums, as a rule, do not appear to have been involved. While scholars have not sufficiently studied the available account books of inland factors to make any generalization secure against the possibility of error, present indications are that the sums involved ran in the hundreds—and often less—rather than in the thousands. As a rule the factor seems merely to have charged the account of the planter for cash advances and supplies, but sometimes—possibly when the amount was somewhat larger than usual, the credit standing of the planter a bit unsteady, or the likelihood present that the factor might need his funds before the debt matured—he obtained an IOU from the planter. He could then endorse the note and discount it at a bank in case of need.[3]

In any assessment of the credit institutions available to the South, banks of three kinds must be taken into account: the so-called plantation or property banks, state banks, and ordinary commercial banks. Property banks made loans and issued bank notes on the basis of capital secured by mortgages on real estate, while state banks did so on the basis of the state's credit. In the words of Guy Callender, the early twentieth-century economic historian, "The business of all of them consisted in providing the capital for producing and marketing the cotton and sugar of this region." The charters of many of the state banks explicitly permitted the making of long-term loans to the agricultural community, sometimes stipulating that one-half of the bank's capital be used in this way. And, like the property banks, they sometimes made such loans on the security of land, slaves, and other possessions.

The commercial banks played a very important indirect role in financing cotton transactions. They seldom offered loans directly to planters or farmers, but, as we have seen, they did discount the notes of planters that had been endorsed by a factor. In short, behind the factor's credit to the planter was Southern bank credit as well as New York mercantile credit. In one way or another the banks were involved in almost every transaction arising from the marketing of the cotton crop. If a fac-

[3] To discount is to sell for cash, with a sum deducted from the face value of the note. Since the note matures *at a future date,* the deduction (discount) represents the bank's charge for present cash. The amount of the charge is determined by the interest rate and the length of time the note has to run before it matures.—S.B.

tor made advances on the crop in the form of a draft, the planter could discount it at a bank. Inland factors discounted their drafts on coastal factors, and the latter their drafts on Northern or English merchants after they consigned cotton for sale. Finally, if a coastal factor received a sterling bill from the agent of some Liverpool dealer to whom he had sold cotton, the bill could be discounted at a local bank. Normally, the bank sent the bill to New York for sale, because that city was the importing center of the country and hence the largest market for sterling and other foreign bills.[4]

The special role of New York in the cotton trade deserves more than passing notice. We have already noted the likelihood that manufactured goods, whether domestic or foreign, were apt to be sent to Southern coastal cities by way of New York merchants, and that substantial quantities of cotton were sent from Southern ports to New York for transshipment. We may now add that the cotton sent direct from the South to Europe was likely to be shipped in a vessel owned by a New Yorker and insured by a New York firm. Indeed, since numerous New York mercantile houses had partners from that city in residence in the Southern coastal ports, all the arrangements for the shipment were often made by New Yorkers. Frequently, then, it was New Yorkers—and also to some extent New Englanders and men from other northern cities—who earned part of the profits, and who also collected the freight charges, insurance premiums, commissions, and handling charges arising from the cotton trade.

[4] Importers wanted the bills in order to obtain a means of paying their foreign suppliers. Thus, cotton (or other) exports generated a *supply* of bills, and imports a *demand* for them.—S.B.

To explain the prominent role played by New Yorkers, and even more broadly by Northerners—in what one would naturally expect to have been a trade dominated by Southerners—is no easy task. Prior to the recent studies of Robert G. Albion, historians tended to point to such factors as New York's excellent harbor and geographic position. By accident, so to speak, New York lay closer than any other principal port to the heart of the mill and factory belt that developed in the Middle Atlantic and New England states. Among the reasons for her emergence as a principal port, main emphasis was placed upon her daring construction of the Erie Canal (1817–25). When completed, with its system of branches and other extensions, the canal permitted the city to tap the resources of the Great Lakes and the vast Ohio Territory. With lumber, grain, and meat products flowing in from the West after the mid-1830's and textiles, hardware, machinery, leather, and other goods moving in the opposite direction, New York increasingly became an entrepôt where jobbers and wholesalers could join specialized importers and exporters in assembling cargoes of many types for many destinations. By 1860, two-thirds of the nation's imports and one-third of its exports moved through the port of New York. Not least in contribution to the prominence of the port as an import center was the passage of legislation (1817) establishing sales by auction under a system that discouraged the withdrawal of goods when bids ran low and that attracted buyers to the city in search of bargains. Finally, profits from flourishing internal and foreign commerce generated the banking capital that in turn made possible further increases in the volume of trade.

All of these considerations indeed deserve emphasis, although on reflection it will be clear that an assessment of the importance of each of them and of the total causal complex to which they belong requires comparison with the conditions under which all other ports have risen to prominence. Two other factors, however, receive special emphasis in Albion's work: the establishment of packet line service by groups of private vessels for transatlantic (1818) and coastal (1822) trade. Sailing on regular schedules at specified times, packet service on the ocean was dependable and did much to cause the channels of European trade to flow to New York rather than to Boston or Philadelphia. The coastal packets, in turn, provided the cargoes of cotton and other Southern products that helped make profitable the eastbound trips of the ocean packets. Together, ocean and coastal packets made possible the "cotton triangle" which, Albion emphasizes, was established before the Erie Canal was completed in 1825. Interestingly enough, the same entrepreneurs who started the "regular traders" (ships which, unlike tramps, shuttled between fixed ports) and then the packet lines were also the pioneers in developing the cotton triangle. Quakers connected by birth or marriage, they included such well-known mercantile names of the time as those of Jeremiah Thompson and Benjamin Marshall. They had originally come to New York as agents of Lancashire manufacturers in order to obtain raw materials and market finished goods.

New York lay at one of the corners of the cotton triangle, a Southern cotton port at another, and Liverpool (or Havre) at the third. Most vessels sailed around the three sides, carrying cotton from Charleston, for example, direct to Liverpool, returning to New York with general freight or immigrants, and then sailing south on the coastal leg with freight or in ballast. A considerable part of the cotton and other Southern products, however, traversed only two sides of the triangle, eliminating the normal direct run between the Southern port and Europe. The cotton and other Southern products, that is to say, were shipped some 200 miles out of their way to New York before being transshipped to Liverpool. An even larger part of the European goods reaching the South also travelled only two sides of the triangle, being shipped from Europe to New York and from New York to the South, with direct shipment from Europe to the South once again eliminated. In sum, Southern cotton usually went direct to Europe from the South, but manufactured goods did not come direct to the South from Europe.

In Albion's view, the New Yorkers were guilty of a kind of entrepreneurial impudence, and he found "no logical need" for what he called their interference with the commerce of the cotton ports. Still more recently, Eugene D. Genovese has argued that the arrangement made good economic sense. There was insufficient demand in the South for manufactured goods, he maintains, and if the ships carrying cotton had sailed from Southern ports direct to Europe and back they would have had to return in ballast. Yet Genovese acknowledges that "the South depended upon Europe as well as the North for manufactured goods." The question, then, still seems pertinent as to why it was Northern rather than Southern entrepreneurship that supplied those needed goods. Is Albion right in his suggestion that "The uncommercial attitude of the southerners, who found it more congenial to have the Negroes raise cotton than to engage in countinghouse routine and risks, gave New York port its opportunity"?

Certainly the colonial planters of the Lower South were merchants as well as planters, and certainly those of the Upper South (Virginia and Maryland) were storekeepers as well as planters. As we have seen, cotton planters near the coast sometimes handled their own cotton shipments and purchases of needed supplies. Surely, throughout the South one may find examples of intense entrepreneurial concern with costs and profits. On the other hand, one repeatedly encounters the charge, from the writings of Thomas Jefferson to those of the New Orleans editor J. D. B. DeBow, that large numbers of Southerners were somewhat less concerned in their daily lives than were Northerners with ways of reducing costs and improving incomes. The pages of *DeBow's Review* are filled with editorials and articles urging agricultural diversification, direct shipments, technological improvement, manufacturing in the South, and other ameliorative devices. A number of commercial conventions and planters' conventions met to consider similar possibilities. Yet little came of these efforts.

How is this most satisfactorily explained? As we know, staple agriculture—in the case of both colonial tobacco and post-colonial cotton—moved steadily into the interior, multiplying the number of middlemen intervening between planter and market. Was the commercial-mindedness of the planter reduced by his typical delegation of market decisions to his factor? Apparently planters did not as a rule keep systematic records of income and expenditures, so that their factors served them as bookkeepers as well as moneylenders, suppliers, and market specialists. Is this too an indication of something less than a keen interest in the details of business? Did the fact that agriculturalists bought and sold only occasionally, in contrast with the daily business dealings of merchants and storekeepers, sharpen the contrast between the agricultural South and the commercial, urban, and industrializing North? Was the fundamental fact the existence of a value system reflecting the preference of a persistently agricultural region for things as they were? If so, when did the elements of this system evolve and in response to what influences? Does one find the same values among other agricultural peoples? Among other slaveowning groups?

It has long been believed that the economic growth of the South lagged well behind that of the rest of the nation, but recent estimates of trends in per capita income suggest that it was growing in the South at only a slightly lesser rate than the national average. Other recent studies establish the strong probability that slavery was indeed a profitable form of investment. Is the explanation for the South's failure to industrialize simply that profits earned from cotton and slave sales were equally attractive as those that might have been earned in manufacturing? Did the agrarian value system of the planters merely adapt itself to this underlying economic reality? Or can one maintain that had the Southern value system been geared to business goals agricultural profits would probably have been even higher than they were?

The following readings open with letters that illustrate the part played in the cotton trade by merchants residing in states north of the cotton belt. The previous discussion has properly emphasized the credit and other contributions made by the merchants of New York. But the activities of individuals in other cities sometimes rivaled—if they did not exceed—in importance those of the New Yorkers. An instance of this is provided by Alexander Brown & Sons of Baltimore. Founded in 1800, the firm moved successively from concentration on imports of Irish linens to the cotton trade, to dealings in foreign exchange based on that trade, and to investment banking, a business in which it continues to engage as the oldest such firm on the American continent. Some indication of its early scale of operations is provided by a remark that appears in a popular sketch of the Browns' history: "Between 1824 and 1834 it was not unusual for the firm to deal in as many as twenty thousand bales of cotton,"[5] presumably in the course of a single year. A recent scholarly study of the period rates the volume of the Browns' dealings in foreign exchange as second only to that of the Second Bank of the United States (1816–36).[6] The resources of the Bank, which was capitalized at $35 million and had some 25 branches located in various parts of the country, of course gave it immense advantages over any private competitor.

The Browns entered the cotton trade to an increasing extent after establishing a branch house, William Brown & Company (later W & J Brown & Co.) in Liverpool in 1810. How new the trade was to them in that year is clearly suggested in the following readings by their letter to the Liverpool branch of December 15, 1810. Note the use of the older English term "cotton wool" to refer to cotton, and note even more particularly a passage which shows the apparently accidental origins of what was to develop into a standard technique. Messrs. Keller & Forman, they complain, have followed up their consignment of cotton to the Liverpool branch by calling on the Browns to endorse the bills of exchange drawn against that shipment. It was precisely by this method that the Baltimore firm was to emerge as one of the nation's largest operators in the cotton trade and foreign exchange business.

The developed technique, clearly delineated in the letter of Alexander Brown & Sons of April 22, 1819, to Adger & Black of Charleston, was this: utilizing the services of coastal factors resident in the principal cotton ports—and also to some extent those of inland factors, for example in Augusta, Georgia—the Browns offered in normal times to advance apparently the full value of cotton shipments consigned to the Liverpool branch. The advance was made in the form of bills drawn by the exporter on the Liverpool house and endorsed by the Brown agent. But that was not all: apparently beginning in 1819, the Browns instructed their agents also to purchase the bills which their agents had just endorsed. Thus, by a single operation, the Browns: (a) built up their short-term assets in Liverpool in the form of sales proceeds of cotton consigned there; (b) earned commissions on those sales; (c) purchased, and later sold at a profit in Northern import centers the bills drawn against those assets. It was, of course, the continual building up of their Liverpool balances by means of cotton that they were provided with the quantities of exchange that made them so formidable a factor in the bill market.

These services did not exhaust the Browns' connections with the cotton trade. Besides acting as commission merchants and bill dealers, they also bought and sold cotton on their own account, shipped merchandise to coastal ports for sale, supplied shipping in which exporters might find cargo space to Liverpool, and, on at least one occasion, offered expert advice on ship construction techniques in Baltimore to a Southerner in the market for a vessel. These and other aspects of the Browns' business are re-

[5] Frank R. Kent, *The Story of Alexander Brown & Sons* (Baltimore, 1925), p. 102.

[6] Walter B. Smith, *Economic Aspects of the Second Bank of the United States* (Cambridge: Harvard University Press, 1953), p. 46.

vealed in the group of letters included in the readings.[7]

From the more northerly coast we move in the next group of readings to the inland South. Selected from a "gazateer" of Georgia published in 1837 by A. Sherwood these excerpts depict important facets of the commercial geography of Augusta (including the Savannah River), Augusta's cotton trade, storage and commission rates in Augusta, and stages available from that inland town. These selections serve as an introduction for excerpts from one of the richest known sources of information concerning the activities of the inland factor, the business records of William Bostwick and his various partnerships in Augusta in the 1820's, 1830's, and 1840's. These records include copies of outgoing correspondence (Letterbooks) and an unusually full set of such bookkeeping records as Ledgers, Journals, Daybooks, Notes and Bills Payable, Invoice Books, Memorandum Books, and the like. Originally of New Haven, Connecticut, Bostwick was typical of a large group of New Englanders and New Yorkers who settled in Southern coastal and inland cities to seek their fortunes as commission merchants in the cotton trade. Apparently beginning in 1826 as a partner in the firm of Edward Campfield & Company, Bostwick subsequently became an associate of Burton & Bostwick (1826–29) and Bostwick & Baird (1829–32). From 1832 on (till 1856?) he did business as an individual proprietor.

Like commission merchants of other times and places, Bostwick dealt in cotton on his own account as well as on that of others. In one instance—apparently the only one—he had a cargo of cotton shipped to Liverpool for sale on his own account. Valued at $8,000, the shipment, made in May, 1838, netted him a loss of $909. Closures from the Cotton account to the Profit & Loss account reveal that he did better when he sold his cotton in domestic markets. But his main earnings appear to have come in the form of commissions charged on cotton sales for the account of planters and country storekeepers and from profits on merchandise sold them, interest on credit advances, and charges for such services as storing cotton, receiving and forwarding merchandise, and accepting drafts.

Bostwick's records reveal his intimate connections with New York merchants, a number of whom supplied him with the almost incredibly large number of articles that he in turn sold to planters and storekeepers. He appears to have made frequent annual trips to New York, apparently in late summer and fall, to buy goods in person. Sometimes he purchased at auction, but mainly from mercantile firms, often paying cash but apparently more often receiving credit ranging from 4 to 10 months. After returning to Augusta he proceeded from time to time during the year to order additional goods via letters to New York and other cities. Besides buying heavily from New York such items as sugar, tea, nails, bales of cotton cloth, shirting, buttons, and other hard and soft goods too numerous to mention, he also bought whiskey from Baltimore and Philadelphia, barrels of mackerel from Boston, cheese from New Haven, cotton cloth

[7] The history of this important mercantile banking firm is yet to be written. Note the intimate references in the Browns' letters to the business depressions that we now know as the Panics of 1819 and 1837. While a number of studies have been made of these and other "panics," the cause of scholarship would be much advanced by a detailed account of business fluctuations in various industries and regions, based on the surviving letters and accounts of businessmen. In other words, studies of economic growth and decline need to "disaggregate" if one is to deal effectively with the causes of these phenomena.—S.B.

from "Richmond Factory," molasses, coffee, bales of bagging and numerous other items from Charleston, rice from Savannah, and rum, candles, raisins, flour, cotton bags, and much else from fellow merchants in Augusta. An idea of the scale of his operations is provided by the fact that the invoices of his purchases from June 16, 1830, to April 1, 1833—a period of less than 3 years—amounted in total to $170,348.59.

The following selections from the Bostwick Papers throw light on the nature of the relations between the inland factor and the New York merchant, coastal factor, planter, and storekeeper. The first group of letters, (a), reveals various aspects of the relationship with New York merchants. The first two letters in this group, to James Edmonson—evidently a young man about to set up in business as an inland factor—are especially valuable documents in that they disclose what Bostwick characterizes as the usual credit terms given by New York merchants to back country factors. Also included in the group are several letters to Leeman Reed of New York that bespeak Bostwick's early difficulties in paying a modest balance owed in that city. These difficulties were compounded by the destruction of Bostwick's warehouse and counting room by lightning in August, 1826, a misfortune in which all his "Books and papers were burnt." According to A. Sherwood, whose 1837 "gazateer" of Georgia has already been mentioned, such incidents were not at all uncommon.

Also in this group are letters describing Bostwick's cotton shipments to Thaddeus Phelps of New York. Phelps appears to have become his main New York consignee, for in 1841 we find Bostwick writing:

> In my case, every bale of cotton that I have shipped to your market in the last *ten years* has been consigned to you. Every order I have executed has been by you. Every draft I have drawn, in short every transaction in your city during that period upon which I have paid a commission has been with yourself.[8]

The occasion for the remarks was his dissatisfaction with Phelps' increase in the interest rate on his account, for just as the planters were indebted to him so was he to New York wholesale grocers, textile jobbers, and other merchants. But as we have seen, he made purchases in other cities too, and the first letters end with an order for "Segars" to a supplier in Westfield, Massachusetts. Note the numerous middlemen whose services would be required for the cigars to reach Bostwick in Augusta.

Group (b) of the Bostwick selections touches on some of the services performed by coastal factors for inland factors and also some of the problems involved in their relationships. Group (c) presents numerous aspects of the inland factor's relations with planters, showing how he sent them price information, advances, and the like. Group (d) reproduces the accounts of three planters. Items on the left-hand side (debits) are charges for merchandise and cash advances and for interest, while items on the right-hand side (credits) reveal the way in which the planter paid off his debt. Note that 10 months after receiving book credit for sundry articles Isham Raney paid in cash; Lewis J. Duepree's account shows that 18 months after the granting of book credit the obligation was converted into an IOU—more formal evidence of indebtedness (Notes Receivable); Dr. Edward Hughes repaid a substantial part of his 5-months old obligation with "Produce," a word

[8] Quoted in Robert Greenhalgh Albion, *The Rise of New York Port* (New York: Charles Scribner's Sons, 1939), p. 113.

that means cotton in the Bostwick records. Following this, however, came a cash advance of $167.11 that was still not paid back nearly 6 years later. The final group of the Bostwick selections concerns country storekeepers.

In the alphabetical indices of his two surviving Ledgers will be found the credit ratings that Bostwick assigned his customers, with "M" standing for merchant and "P" or "Pl" for planter. Thus Thomas H. White was designated "M good" and John C. Wood "P good". But for Matthew Young (M) the firm noted "no more cr unless for Small amt." and for Hiram Young (P) the notation was simply "no more Credit." Interest rates on advances to planters were high by today's standards, frequently 8 per cent and more. Yet it must be remembered that these rates included an element of insurance on risks that might turn out to be poor ones. It would be interesting to learn whether the professional credit rating services soon to be made available by the predecessors of Dun & Bradstreet resulted in a demonstrable lessening of the insurance element in interest rates.

The final reading in Part IV is an excellent example of direct relations between village storekeeper and coastal factor. Like Jonathan Trumbull, the last governor of colonial Connecticut, Andrew Jackson was a storekeeper—for perhaps a dozen years—in early life. At the time of the letters presented, 1803–04, Jackson and his partner John Hutchings had stores in the Tennessee villages of Hunter's Hill, Gallatin, and Lebanon. Jackson & Hutchings did business by purchasing general assortments of groceries, nails, salt, and other supplies on 12 months' credit from New Orleans factors and then bartering the goods for cotton at their stores. They then shipped the cotton to New Orleans for sale. In 1804 their factors were Boggs & Davidson, a Philadelphia firm that appears to have done business by having one partner (Boggs) reside in Philadelphia and the other in New Orleans. The exchange of letters between these factors and Jackson & Hutchings reveals the kinds of differences that might arise in the course of business. Note the storekeepers' questioning of the justice of a number of commissions charged by the factors, the differences concerning advances, and the misunderstanding over the disposition of a cotton consignment. Differences of one kind or another are always to be found among men in business relationships, as they are also to be found among men in other kinds of relationships. The years 1803–04 were early ones for the cotton trade. It is a good question whether in later years the institutionalizing of the above-described arrangements for getting the South's great staple to market brought a higher degree of mutual understanding.

THE READINGS

# 1] The Role of Northern Capital in the Financing of Cotton Exports from Southern Ports: Selections from the Letters of Alex. Brown & Sons of Baltimore

## To Messrs William Brown & Co

BALTIMORE 15 Decemr. 1810

. . .Messrs Keller & Forman made you a Shipment of Some cotton wool by the [ship] Dumfries, and they have this date called on us to endorse their drafts on you against that shipment £ 850 which we have done, they ought to have informed us they would require this before the Ship sailed, that we might have advised you we were to make advances, to prevent your accepting and [sic; any?] but Such as we endorsed. however with them we do not Suppose there is any risk of this kind, we presume this is the only Bill that will be drawn by them until they receive the Sales. We expect prices will improve of that article, we expect you held up the Sallys and George Dyers Cotton until you received the Presidents Proclamation [.] that would Certainly give it a Start, there is Some Shipments of Cotton making to France, if that trade can be carried on with Safety, it will very much lessen the quantity going to england, Speculating on this event prices have been advancing in this country, notwithstanding their declining with you, New Orleans Cotton is 19 to 20 Cents here. it was 18 Cents in New Orleans last quotations, and 16 cents for upland at Savannah, it will be Surprising under these Circumstances if it does not advance very much with you . . .

ALEXR BROWN & SONS

## To Messrs Adger & Black (Charleston)

BALTIMORE 22 April 1819

GENTLEMEN

Your esteemed favours of 21 & 30 Ulto & 7 Inst are received, the last some days since, but we delayed writing until we could hand you invoice of a further quantity of oznaburgs shipped [per?] General Macomb to sail in 3 or 4 Days, We believe they are just the same as the last you sold and you will be pleased to make the best disposition of them you can— We would

---

FROM Papers of Alexander Brown, Manuscript Division, Library of Congress, Washington, D.C.

like you to close the sales of the [faded] Sheetings on the best terms you can, The proceeds of the General Macombs Cargo and of the Oznaburgs [1] as the payments come round, we wish invested in Sterling bills giving a decided preference to such as you have endorse[d] for the advance on shipments to W & J Brown & Co, that is you purchase from the shippers their Sterling bills on W & J B & Co at the current rate for such advance as you may have agreed on[,] making payment with our funds as far as in your hands and drawing on us for the balance, or we will remit you—In the month of May if southern funds are at a discount here we will probably make some remittances for that purpose—When you have occasion to write us you will please quote the rate of Exchange[.] You will observe we wish particularly to give the preference to bills on W & J B & Co against shipments to themselves, where you endorse the bills, if none such are to be had about the times the funds will be coming round, be very particular in other bills[,] taking none but such as you know to be undoubtedly good.

We believe the Genl Macomb is sold, otherwise she would no doubt return to you, but we think it probable if the owners here see a prospect of doing good they will soon have another and you may rely on it no opportunity will be lost of being serviceable to you,

We have seen a letter from Charleston dated 16 Inst stating Uplands of good quality could be bought at 16 cts, this decline we have confidently looked for for the last 5 mos. which makes us not regret, that nothing has been done earlier in the way of advances, the losses to early shippers will be heavy and its very unpleasant to be obliged to ask even part of an advance to be refunded[.] At low prices the risks of overdrawing are not so great[.]

Yours
AB & Co

Ex[change] 4/6 Stg to the dollar, Good bills scarce

## To Mr James Carruthers (Savannah)

BALTIMORE 22 April 1819

DR SIR

. . . We observe the great decline in the price of uplands[.] this was fully expected 5 months ago, the state of the many concerned in this place is such as precludes the possibility of raising funds without selling exchange . . . . the difficulty of raising money there [in Liverpool] in case of need may be so great that we would rather they [W & J Brown & Co of Liverpool] should forego their Coms, [Commission] business for a time than even run the chance of being slaves of money [i.e., of having to borrow at a high interest rate], this has been their steady course ever since their establishment, and from which no consideration of gain can ever induce them to deviate, we cannot therefore consent to their being drawn on untill the property is actually shipped and insurance ordered, nor are we yet so sanguine of great profits even at the price you mentioned, the decline on the other side will be in exact proportion to the accumulating stock of the article and the

[1] Osnaburgs were a species of coarse linen, originally made in Osnaburg, Germany.—S.B.

smallest check to the spinning business there added to the commercial distress now existing would produce a state of things heretofore unknown in that Country—

A B & Co

## To Messrs McLanahan & Bogart (New Orleans)

BALTIMORE 9 April 1819

GENTLEMEN

Having to forward a letter of Mr Bernards received this evening, we take the opportunity of acknowledging receipt of yours of 6 Ulto, by which we are glad to see nothing had been done for us & as our latest accounts from Liverpool quote

| | | | | |
|---|---|---|---|---|
| New uplands | 15 | @ | 15½ | |
| Orleans | 17 | , | 17½ | [sic] |
| Uplands | 14[?] | | | |

we think it not improbable they may go something lower[.] we wrote you by Mr McLanahan stating our preference to haveing our funds in your hands used in making *moderate advances* to that of shipping on our account—. . .

A B & Co

## To Mr John Cumming (Augusta)

BALTIMORE 6 April 1819

DEAR SIR

. . . We annex J C & Cos account current balanced by our bill on W & J Brown & Co £ 364.12.0 for which we obtained par, altho first rate [bills] are selling at ½[%] Dist James Carruthers, shipments to W & J B & Co, since the new year amount to $96,000, we believe the principal part of which is Sea Island, by which we hope there will be no loss, We almost offended him by discouraging the shipment of uplands[.] of Sea Islands we did not pretend to give an opinion—

. . . . . . . . . . . . . . . .

## To Messrs Adger & Black (Charleston)

15 February 1820

Our last was dated 9 Inst since which we have recd your esteemed favours 5 & 8th Inst and are pleased to see you have arranged with Mr. Matheson for 50 Bales to go forward to our friends [W & J Brown & Co. of Liverpool] taking his Bill for the advance on our a/c at par, we would be glad if further shipments would offer on same terms—

. . . . . . . . . . . . . . . .

## To Messrs Adger & Black (Charleston)

9 February 1820

Your esteemed favours of 31st. Ulto and 3 Inst are received with Invoices for cotton per Bingham & Fama our proportions of which we placed to your credit, We have letters from W & J B & Co to 1 Jany handing us sales of our Sea Islands per Ceres, that shipment left us about $2000— We have now recd sales of every Bale shipped last year which left us a profit besides the advantage to the Liverpool house of the influencing other property [to be consigned to it for commission sale]

We hope and from present prospects we think it likely this year at least so far will do as well if not better—

. . . . . . . . . . . . . . . .

We learn from JAB & Co [John A Brown & Co] who had got the [ship] Maryland to go to W & J B & Co which is well, We are sorry to hear cotton seems to be creeping up and the quality not so good, We fear it will get too high to operate in, the Quotations of the [ship] Albion['s] uplands 12½ @ 14 [12.5 to 14 cents per pound] being an advance on the last quotations will tend still further to raise it

A B & Co

## To Messrs W & J Brown & Co

BALTIMORE May 16, 1821

GENT.

. . .in Augusta & Savannah, Jno Cumming & Son & Adger & Black in Charleston can give you the best information respecting the standing of your correspondents

. . . . . . . . . . . . . . . .

## To Martin Pleasants & Co (Huntsville)

BALTIMORE 19 January 1836

Since writing you on 7th. inst we are in receipt of your favor of 2nd. and are pleased to find you can avoid drawing on us the drafts you advise will have due honor on presentation but as the French affair [2] is becoming more unpleasant every day we hope you will not draw for any further sums as we would much rather decline all business than have our responsibilities out with such a cloud hanging over our commercial community & further we would rather forego the advantages of consignments to our friends [the Liverpool branch] than come under acceptances for advances as all American property will be liable to capture if war takes place & with the present

[2] This is a reference to a diplomatic dispute with France resulting from outstanding claims against that country for confiscations and damages to American ships and other property during the Napoleonic Wars. France had accepted in a convention of 1831 American claims totalling 23,500,000 francs but the French Chamber of Deputies postponed the appropriation until President Jackson threatened reprisals against French property in his annual message of 1834.—S.B.

difficulties there is no calculating on the Insurance offices taking risks without making exceptions to French molestation and consequently if war grows out of the difficulties the parties making the advance would in all probability have to run the risk. We think it but right to give you these views & unless matters are settled we think your house in Orleans had better decline making advances to keep on the safe side—This being the case we wish to enter into no new engagements that can be avoided until we see what is to be the end of this unpleasant affair[.] we are very sorry to have to take this step but we would rather forego the chance of making money than put any thing at hazzard that can be helped—We consider at the present high price of Cotton in Orleans it would be the height of folly for the Planters to ship to Liverpool & if every thing was settled we would not be willing to advance over ¾ or ⅘ of the present value as all accounts agree that the crop will be about 1350 Bales which will be more than sufficient for the consumption[.] in the meantime if any change take[s] place that will justify our going on as usual you shall be advised—

## To John Cumming & Son (Savannah)

BALTIMORE 11 January 1836

. . .we think the late accounts from Liverpool being so unfavorable for Cotton must put the price down with you

. . . . . . . . . . . . . . .

## To J. C. Magossin, Cashr. (New Orleans)

BALTIMORE 9 January 1836

When Bolton Jackson was here last summer he made an arrangement with us to receive the money for the notes deposited with you for collection as they came round & left it optional with us to take the amount either in New Orleans or this place. We find the first note falls due on 29th. inst which is shortly after you receive this[.] we therefore enclose Mr. Jackson's order to you and as we have no occasion for the funds in New Orleans we will thank you to remit us the same from time to time as they become due the amount we are to place to Mr. Jacksons credit when received and as we presume he left his views with you we have nothing to say as to the mode of remitting whether in check or draft[.] We hold Mr. Jackson's checks on the Bank of Louisianna for the amount but we presume his order to you will be sufficient authority for you to make remittances, . . .

## To Benjamin Story (New Orleans)

BALTIMORE 20 January 1836

. . .As respects Cotton we have made up our minds to do nothing in it this season except to put a few hundred Bales in our own ships to give them a start in freight[.] The state of our affairs with France is such that we do not wish to enter into any new engagements that can be avoided as we are fearful war will yet grow out of the difference. We sent you last year 2 notes of Geo W Phillips & John Rheas[?] $6600 each for collection one of which was paid & we now wish to call your attention to the other which was to be paid in 12 months with interest at the rate of 10% pr annum[.] the time of payment will expire in all March—& we presume the parties will pay it at that time . . .

## To Yeatman Woods & Co (New Orleans)

BALTIMORE 19 January 1836

Your favors of 31 ulto & 2d. inst are received the former enclosing £ 2500 & the latter £ 1000 Sterling for your credit[.] we do not like the position of things with France & we think the sooner you get bills to remit to W & J Brown the better as in case of war it will not be an easy matter to make remittances in such bills as you like & we are not anxious for consignments at any advance as by the time the shipments are made it's uncertain whether Insurance would be effected on the property without molestation by the French being excepted & in case of loss it would not be easy to recover from the shippers. At the present price of Cotton with you we would not advance over ¾ or ⅘ of the cost even if every thing was settled as we think the article far above its value & heavy losses must be the result of shipments at such high rates. We can rely on your remitting to W & J Brown & Co as fast as you can get bills you like & therefore enclose you the certificate No 2 of the notes deposited in the Bank of Louisianna subject to your order on the return of the certificates which we have endorsed to you Exchange on England 9 to 9½ pCt prem[ium]

## To Byrne Hermann & Co (New Orleans)

BALTIMORE 27 April 1836

. . .Our friend R D Shepherd Esq of this place [Baltimore] but formerly of Boston is desirous of employing his ship Orozimbo in the freighting business between New Orleans & Liverpool, the ship to be consigned to you in New Orleans & W & J Brown & Co in Liverpool[.] she is 405 Tons & carrys 1800 Bales of New Orleans Cotton & is now about leaving Liverpool for your address we have assured Mr. Shepherd you will do all in your power to promote his interest & have informed him in case a full freight could not at any time be got, that if you considered Cotton at safe prices we & you would put in Bale for Bale with him not to exceed in the whole 600 Bales[.] should any purchases be made in this way it will be as well in order to keep the account distinct from other transactions for you to draw on us for the exact cost of the shipments & we will reimburse ourselves by drafts on Liverpool requesting W & J Brown & Co to place the profit or loss whatever it may be to the respective accounts that is ½ to Mr. Shepherd ¼ yours & ¼ ours Mr. Shepherds object being freight he does not wish to make shipments on owners account unless it should be absolutely necessary & than as small as possible. He will no doubt give you his instructions in time respecting the ship, the Captn. will find letters on his arrival requesting him to consign the ship to you—. . .

## To Sanford & Cleveland (Mobile)

BALTIMORE 6 April 1837

We wrote to you on 1st. inst returning Robinson Beale & Cos draft on Geo. C. Morton for $5000 with protest for non payment—Mr[?] Morton being anxious to protect a draft of those gentlemen due on 20th. inst for $6000 has applied to us for a further advance of $2800 on the cotton pr Powhatan which would make including the returned draft an advance of $7800—If Messrs Robinson Beale & Co: are respectable which we presume they are & have arranged the business to your satisfaction by sending on the bills of lading filled up to W & J Brown & Co we have no objection to make the further advance required provided you do not consider it too much as in times like the present the advances ought to be kept very low—Please write us by return of the express mail which will be in time to pay him the $2800 on acc[ount] of the draft due on 20th. if you think we are safe in doing so—The price of Cotton having declined so much we expect many of the planters will prefer shipping to selling on this side, you may therefore be able to invest our funds as they come round in making advances on consignments to W & J B & Co but the advances ought to be kept very low & to good persons This would be the safest mode of remitting our funds, as no dependance [sic] can be placed in bills in such times

## To C G Allhusen (New Orleans)

BALTIMORE 4 May 1836

Your favr of 16th. ulto is received We have been enquiring amongst our ship Builders about a vessel of the description you want, but they say no estimate of the cost can be given unless they know what her tonnage is to be, the build of the vessel &c None of our carpenters will contract to furnish the vessel complete they contract for the hull at a certain rate per Ton & all the outfits must be got from the different Mechanics there are two or three Brigs in the trade between this place & New Orleans which we think are of about the class you want & you have no doubt seen them the Hector we mention as one & the Nelson Clark as another the former cost $32 per ton carpenters measurement for the hull & the latter $30 per ton & the outfits will cost about $32 per ton more exclusive of coppering All materials used in ship building are now 20 pCt higher than they were six months ago— The Brig Isaac Franklin of 187 Tons constantly in the trade between Alexandria & New Orleans is a fine vessel built here & is probably of the size you want—The Nelson Clark & Hector are both different models. We know of no Captain here at present that could take command of the vessel but may here [sic] of one with the necessary qualifications who would be willing to take an interest—There is a first rate man here who would superintend the building of the vessel for a commission of 7½ Pct. his superior is not to be found any place, having been acquianted with vessels nearly his whole life & only having left the sea two or three years ago Payments for the vessel would be required as follows

1/5 when the stem & stern are raised
1/5 when the frames are all up
1/5 when the beams are in
1/5 when launched & the balance when

completed—If you will furnish us with a particular description of the tonnage dimensions, & kind of model &c, we could then get an estimate from the builders of the cost . . . .

## To Benjamin Story (New Orleans)

BALTIMORE 6 April 1837

. . .such times have never been experienced before in this country & there is no Knowing where these failures will end. The same wild speculations have not been entered into by the Merchants of this city [Baltimore] who appear to be snug in their own business & failures are not anticipated to any extent—

. . .The price of Cotton having declined so much we expect many Planters will prefer shipping to meeting the markets on this side, we would therefore prefer your using our funds as they come round in making advances on consignments to W & J Brown & Co, the advances to be kept low & to good houses, this would make some good bills & be the safest way of remitting our funds, as no dependance can be placed in bills at present—. . .

## To James Adger & Co (Charleston)

BALTIMORE 10 April 1837

Your favors of 30th ulto & 4th inst are recd We observe you have been making some purchases of sterling bills and advancing on Cotton [consigned] to W & J B & Co—We wrote you on 1st. inst that we were affraid of Cotton bills and would prefer our funds being used in advances to running the risk of bills in such times unless you Knew they would be good under any circumstances. . . .

## To Asa Higgins (Philadelphia)[3]

BALTIMORE 31 March 1837

Your various letters have all been received and we were sorry to hear of your misfortunes on your homeward passage but we are glad they were not worse—In consequence of the scarcity of money & gloom which pervades the mercantile community we find the orders sent out for goods are very small & that the fall importations will be very light, it will therefore be of little or no object to have the ship Grace Brown in Liverpool by any particular time to come out as first fall ship[.] the time of sailing for the first vessel the Importers wish to be fixed on the 1st of June, which is sooner than you could be in Liverpool even if you went to Charleston & received great despatch there We have therefore written to Jas Adger & Co to put letters

[3] Higgins was undoubtedly a supercargo, i.e., a travelling commercial agent who represented the Browns in buying and selling for them, obtaining freights, etc.—S.B.

on board the pilot boats advising you of the rate of freight & prospects both in Savannah & Charleston & if 5/8 to 11/16 can be got in Charleston with despatch we think it will be as well for you to go in, but if this rate cannot be obtained you will proceed either to Mobile or New Orleans—At our last accounts freights were brisk in Mobile at 15/16[?] & 7/8 in New Orleans—Our friends in Mobile are Sanford & Cleveland & in New Orleans Messrs Martin Pleasants & Co which we mention for your government & should you go to either place you can call on them first to ascertain what they can do for you[,] reporting the ship to yourself, so that you may be at liberty to place her in the hands of any house that can give you the best freight & despatch[,] only stipulating that the ship must go consigned to W & J Brown & Co—If you should stop at Charleston & Mr Adger should be full of vessels, we have no doubt he would not object to your going to any other house that could give you a good freight—The foregoing is Captn Grahams views as well as our own which we hope will also meet your approbation—Captn Leeds mentioned to Captn Graham that vessels going to Mobile should always take 2 Bbls of soft soap to be used in stowing the cargo—

### To Benjamin Story (New Orleans)

BALTO 8 April 1837

. . .we are sorry to say that things in New York are in a most deplorable state and it is impossible to say when a change will take place—Cotton having declined so much with you and as it will no doubt go lower it may be more our interest for you to invest our funds in Cotton as they fall into your hands, than to use them in advancing on the article. we however leave it to your judgement, but we wish you to buy no bills of any kind on our account as its impossible to say what bills will be paid and the only safe way we can see of getting our funds remitted is by purchasing or advancing on Cotton, now that it has got so low and we think must be at safe prices—We do not wish to be drawn in until times change and if you purchase Cotton or make advances on consignments it is only to the extent of the funds in your hands

## 2] Augusta, Georgia: Profile of an Inland Cotton Town in the 1820's and 1830's

### a] AUGUSTA'S COTTON TRADE

*Augusta* city and cap[ital], Richmond Co[unty], is the second town for size in the State. The Savannah river here has a large bend, so that the town stands on the S.W. bank, 88 miles E.N.E. Milledgeville, 127 N.N.W. Savannah, 140 N.W. Charleston, 83 W. Columbia, 23 S.S.W. Edgefield, C.

---

SECTIONS 2a–2d are from Adiel Sherwood, *A Gazetteer of the State of Georgia* (Washington City, Ga.: P. Force, 1837), pp. 60, 122–25, 229–30, 237–38, and 340–41.

H., Lat. 33° 33′, Long. 5° 18′.—The town [contains] . . .two Markets, and four Banks.

. . . . . . . . . . . . . . . . . . . .

Augusta is a place of much trade. More than 150,000 bags of cotton are annually deposited here, and thence carried down the river to Savannah and Charleston, for the European and Northern markets. From Oct. 1, 1825, to Oct. 1, 1826, there were 143,633 bags of cotton stored in this place. Here are 20 warehouses, large buildings, from 300 to 500 feet long, and 40 broad, to secure the immense quantities of produce [1] and merchandise [2] brought to town. Broad street, where the greatest part of the produce is sold, is 180 feet wide, and two miles long, passing nearly through the centre of the city.

There are ten to fifteen steamboats on the river, which perform a trip in four or five days, and carry passengers, and from 800 to 1,000 bags of cotton.—Beside these, there are pole boats, which take from 500 to 800. Daily stages are also constantly running between this and Savannah, Columbia, Milledgeville, and to Athens. They go also to Greensboro, Madison, and Louisville.

Augusta supplies all the up-country, east of the Oconee, and a good deal west of it, with merchandise; she also sends many tons into Tennessee, and into N. and S. Carolina. Recently, however, Hamburg, a small town opposite, on the South Carolina side, founded in 1821, has supplied some goods for the Carolinas. A bridge, 400 yards long, connects the two towns.

. . . . . . . . . . . . . . . . . . . .

Cotton received in Augusta and Hamburg for six months, ending in April, were, bags, in 1824, 121,525; 1825, 103,607; 1826, 137,087; 1827, 136,602.

Freights to Savannah are from one dollar to 37½ cents per bag; to Charleston $ 1[.]50 to 75 cents.

. . . . . . . . . . . . . . . . . . . .

There were no ware-houses at this period [1805] for the reception of cotton, but McKinne's was soon built, just above the bridge. Each purchaser of cotton weighed it before his own door, where it remained, piled up between the trees on the side walks, till sent off in boats. Barter was then much in vogue, and the proportion to the amount of goods, which the seller would take, frequently would control the price of the article.

At 3 or 4 gin-houses much of the cotton raised in the vicinity, and in Burke, was cleaned.

. . . . . . . . . . . . . . . . . . . .

[1] The meaning of "produce," almost certainly, is cotton.—S.B.

[2] The meaning of "merchandise," almost certainly, is dry goods, hardware and a variety of similar finished and semifinished goods that planters bought for use on their plantations.—S.B.

## b] Storage and Commission Rates

RATES OF STORAGE AND COMMISSIONS, REVISED AND ADOPTED UNANIMOUSLY BY THE WAREHOUSE KEEPERS, IN THE CITY OF AUGUSTA, JULY 2D, 1832:—

| | | | | |
|---|---|---|---|---|
| Bale Cotton, | 25 cts. | per 1st mo. | & 12½ | each mo. after. |
| Bbls. and qr. casks | 25 | do. | & 12½ | do. |
| Hogsheads, (large) | 75 | do. | & 37½ | do. |
| do. (small) | 50 | do. | & 25 | do. |
| Pipes | 50 | do. | & 25 | do. |
| Tierces, | 37½ | do. | & 18¾ | do. |
| Trunks, | 37½ | do. | & 18¾ | do. |
| Kegs shot or lead | 37½ | do. | & 18¾ | do. |
| do. Nails | 25 | do. | & 12½ | do. |
| Cotton bagging pr ps., | 12½ | do. | & 6¼ | do. |
| Coils Rope, | 12½ | do. | & 6¼ | do. |
| Hides, | 8 | do. | & 4 | do. |
| Bacon, per piece | 2 | do. | & 1 | do. |
| Chairs, | 12½ | do. | & 6¼ | do. |
| Bedsteads | 50 | do. | & 25 | do. |
| Carriages, (4 wheel) | $2 | do. | & $1 | do. |
| do. (2 do.) | $1 | do. | & 50 | do. |
| Jersey & other wagons, | $1 | do. | & 50 | do. |
| Crates (large) | 75 cts. | per 1st mo. | & 37½ | each mo. after. |
| do. (small) | 50 | do. | & 25 | do. |
| Stills, | 50 | do. | & 25 | do. |
| Anvils, | 12½ | do. | & 6¼ | do. |
| Castings, per piece | 4 | do. | & 2 | do. |
| Iron, per bar | 5 | do. | & 2½ | do. |

All small packages,

Boxes and bales merchandise, 25, 50, 75, and $1, according to sizes.

Re-weighing Cotton 12½ cents per bale, and if *re-stored* the owner is subjected to *extra storage.*

Cotton sold by *Factors* not subject to storage until the expiration of 15 days.

Commissions for selling Cotton 50 cents per bale.

do. Acceptances 2½ per cent.

do. Advancing money, in all cases 2½ per ct.

do. Receiving and forwarding goods 50 per cent on the first month's storage

do. Purchases 2½ per cent.

All postages chargeable.

All *storages due* at the time of the delivery of the article

## c] STAGES FROM AUGUSTA

LIST OF STAGES, &C.—JULY, 1837
THE FOLLOWING IS THE BEST THAT CAN BE FURNISHED AT PRESENT.
1. STAGES FROM AUGUSTA

1. To Washington city, daily.
2. To Charleston, on railroad, daily. Fare $6 75
3. To Charleston, in steamers, often Fare $15.
4. To Abbeville, S.C., twice a week.
5. To Savannah, daily—one day on the Georgia, the other on the South Carolina side, via Robertville. Fare $12 Time, about 23 hours.
6. To Milledgeville, Macon, and Columbus, &c., daily. Two or three lines. Fare to M. $10. Time 22 hours.
7. To Florida, Mobile, &c., via Louisville, Hawkinsville, &c., three times a week.
8. To Gainseville, via Washington, Lexington and Athens, three times a week. Fare $13—$5 to Washington, 9 to Athens, and 4 to Gainseville. At times this line extends to some towns in Cherokee.

## d] THE SAVANNAH RIVER

. . . . . . . . . . . . . . . . .

*Savannah River* forms the N.E. boundary of the State, separating it from S. Carolina. The head streams are the Chatuga from the N.E., and Terrora from the N.W., which unite and form the Tugalo. This is joined 55 miles S.E. by the Kiowee from South Carolina, near the S.E. corner of Franklin, and here the united streams take the name of Savannah, 100 miles by the course of the river, above Augusta. The largest vessels come up to *Five Fathom Hole,* within three miles of the city of Savannah, 18 miles from the ocean; large brigs sail to the wharves; steamboats of 150 tons burthen ascend to Augusta, 127 miles by land, and said to be 340 by water; pole-boats, leaving Augusta go up 100 miles, to the junction of the Kiowee and Tugalo, and passing the mouth of the former river, make their way up the Tugalo to Mullen's ford, near the mouth of Toccoa creek, 150 miles by water, 125 by land, above Augusta. So that the Savannah is navigable 490 miles. Boats on the Tugalo carry from 30 to 60 bags of cotton, and return with eight to ten tons merchandise. Tides flow up but 25 miles, and the water is fresh even at Five Fathom Hole. This is a great convenience to vessels taking in water for a voyage. Millions are floated on the surface of this river every year, and at some seasons every month.

This river is 250 yards wide, and 8 feet deep, on the section between Petersburgh and the junction of the Tugalo with the Kiowee. Were it not for the frequent rapids, steamboats might ascend to this junction. It would seem that a little *canalling* and a few locks would render it so navigable that 50 or 100 tons might be floated on it at a time.

I am satisfied now that the distance by water is not more than 250 miles from Augusta to Savannah. Steamboats can *descend* it in 18 or 20 hours, and *ascend* it in 30. The first steamboat navigated this river to Augusta in 1817, and was gone more than three weeks.

. . . . . . . . . . . . . . . .

The delegates from this State to the railroad convention, at Knoxville, Tenn., July, 1836, made the following report, on the resources of Georgia, her inland navigation, &c.:

On Savannah river, 20 steamboats, and 50 towboats.

. . . . . . . . . . . . . . . .

Regular Packets between Savannah and New York, 15. [1837]

# 3] The Business of William Bostwick, Inland Factor at Augusta, Georgia

## a] Relations with New York Merchants

### To Mr James Edmonson

August 1st. 1829

Dear Sir

Your letter of the 29th Ult. was received this morning. We are a little at a loss how to answer it as we do not exactly understand you, if your meaning is that you want us to assist you by letters, we will do So with pleasure, we have Several friends in business in N.Y. who we Know are willing to Sell goods to any Southern man that we will introduce, and to them we can give you Such letters as will enable you to buy your goods on the usual Terms, viz: at Six to nine months for good papers they generally require it payable at Bank So that you will be Compelled to meet it promptly, if you think your money arrangements will be So that you Could not pay to the day, you Can no doubt buy goods for your paper without making it payable at

---

SECTIONS 3a–3c are from William Bostwick Papers (Beinecke Rare Book and Manuscript Library, Yale University). Printed by courtesy of the Yale University Library.

Bank, we are however decidedly of Opinion that every man that goes into the N.Y. market will find it to his interest to put his name on as good footing as any other in the market, if he Cannot do this we doubt if it be his interest to go there to buy goods, we have entire Confidence in the prudence both of yourself and Capt. Morris and if we were Selling goods in N.Y. we Should be pleased to have Such Customers, and this much we are willing to write to our friends there but for us to become responsible for buying goods for you we could not think of doing So—as, the paper would come immediately into our Banks and fill up our ac[coun]ts So that we Could not get the necessary accommodations for our own regular business—

Should you conclude to visit N.Y. you will find our Mr. Baird there, who will leave here Sometime the last of the ensuing week—

We have Liverpl. dates to the 9th June & c

Yrs &c

B & BAIRD

## To Mr James Edmonson

Augt. 8. 1829

DR SIR,

Yours of the 4 Inst. is at hand.—We presume there will be no difficulty in your being able to purchase goods in New York with the references you can make, in your own Credit, and on as good terms, as anyone else in the back Country—Mr. Baird left here yesterday morning in the stage for New York, and by regular Course will arrive there today a week—he will be there untill the 5th to the 10. Sepr.—should one of you determine to go to N.Y. & be there while Mr. B. is there he will introduce you to several houses that will enable you to effect your purchases we presume to your satisfaction—to Customers who they can rely upon as being good they are very glad in New York to sell goods upon their own Credit, and to be liberal in the time they give.—We will render you all the assistance in our power to promote your views which we presume will be ample to accomplish your wishes, but we cannot accept nor indorse paper—as it might find its way into the Bank here, and would interfere with our accomodation in Bank of our regular business—The expense to go to N.Y. would be a trifle less by water but it would take more time, is very uncertain at this season of the year when you would arrive, and there is now some danger of sickness.—We should recommend you to go by Land, the expense would be about $75.—by water it would cost you about $50.—

Yrs. &c.

B. & BAIRD

## To Messrs Reed & Lee (New York)

October 3, 1826

GENT.

I returned 3 or 4 days since from the Country, and am favored with yours of the 31 Augt.—that of the 10th Augt. I recd. before I left here.—I notice your remarks relative to consignments of cotton and doubt not you are very right.—your Grocery business is heavy enough I presume to require all your attention.—

I know not whether I mentioned to you in my last that I have dissolved Copartnership with Mr. Campfield who has withdrawn from the business, and I have Connected myself with Mr John Burton[,] the proprietor of the Ware House[,] under the firm of Burton & Bostwick.—I have been generally among our Customers in the Country and so far from disposed to quit us, they are doing what they can to get others to store with us.—of the large amt. of our advances There is not one but what is good.—I presume we shall realize a considerable part of our advances during the winter.—I shall remit you as soon as practicable.—We shall be prepared to receive Cotton at the new Ware House next week.—Very little new Cotton has come in as yet, price 9 to 9½ Old [cotton] 7½ to 9

Yrs &c.

W. B.

## To Mr. Leeman Reed (New York)

March 4, 1828

. . .I regret that I have not been able before this to make you a remittance.—You are right in supposing that the low price of Cotton makes it very difficult to realize Collections—We however are receiving Considerable this season of our advances [to the planters] made previous to the destruction of the Ware House, and we believe we shall not be disappointed in our expectations of their being nearly all ultimately good—

. . . . . . . . . . . . . . .

W. B.

## To Messrs Reed & Lee (New York)

June 9, 1828

GENT.—

Inclosed I hand you J. Hunter Cashier of the United States Bank Savannah Check, on the United States Bank of your city, dated 5 Inst. No. 21. at 1 days Sight payable to the order of Ketchum & Burroughs and by them indorsed to your order for $2000. say Two Thousand Dollars.—I must request you to receive this remittance on account, and pass the same to my Credit—Please acknowledge receipt of the same.—the Balance I will remit to you in the Course of the next business season.—

Yours &C.

W.B.

## To Mr. Leeman Reed (New York)

August 1. 1829 [sic]

DEAR SIR

I returned two or three days since from the Country and have received yours of the 8 Ulto.—I Know it is desirable that the Balance due you[,] in which you have so much consulted my accomodation should be closed, and I have been anxious to do it before now—but the fact is since the Ware House was destroyed I have been obliged to do as I could, *not as I would.*—

The provision I have made for you is from monies that will be received in the Course of next season from Customers of the Ware House—at what time it will be received will depend upon what time they sell their Cotton —probably not untill towards the spring—whenever it is received I want to remit the Balance due you.—on that account it would be better and I should prefer it that it should just stand as it does without a Note payable at any particular time—so soon as the money is received I will make you the remittance.—

Yours &c
W. B.

## To Mr. Leeman Reed (New York) for the late firm of Reed & Lee

Feb. 18. 1830

DR. SIR

Inclosed I hand you John T.[?] Lloyd Cashier of the Merchants & Planters Bank of this place Check on the Bank of America, your city No. 985. this date by me indorsed to your order for $977.50.—If I am right in the annexed Statement, this is in full for the Balance due you—Please acknowledge receipt hereof per return of mail, and forward my Account—

You are aware of the obligations I feel under to you for your accomodation to me—it will not soon be forgotten, and possibly some time or other I can do something for you—Our Cotton market for some days has been brisk at 8¾ to 9. c[ents] for fair lots—9¼ for good—and 9½ for prime

Yours Truly
W. B.

| | | |
|---|---|---|
| Balance due 17/20 Sep. pr. Your Account | | 1456.53 |
| Deduct paid on 29 June | 500 | |
| Interest on $500 from 29 June to 20 Sep. | 7.98 | |
| M. [Months] D [Days] | | |
| 2 22 | | 507.98 |
| | | 948.55 |
| Interest on $948.55 from 20 Sep. 1829 to 27 Feb. 1830 is M D | | |
| 5· 7·— | | 28.95 |
| | | $ 977.50 |

## To Messrs Thad Phelps & Co. (New York)

Oct. 22, 1835

GENT

Yours of the 12th & 14 Inst. are at hand. Nothing can be done at your limits—our market is firm at 15¼ to 15½ for good to prime[cotton] and all that is offered is readily taken at these prices—the advices of 8th. ultimo have had little or no effect upon us—I regret to say that since my last our river has continued to go lower—it has rarely if ever fallen so much and so rapidly as within the last 10 days—it is almost impossible for Boats of any draft of water to get to our place—I have used the most Vigilant exertions to get your Cotton off but without success[.] none have been willing to engage to take it *at any specified time*[.] the last Freight was half a cent per lb [indecipherable] $2 per Bale under the existing state of things—I thought I should best fulfill your views by insuring your 299 Bales which I did on the 17 Inst. for 15 days for $16,0 [sic] it is all in what we call fire proof Ware Houses except 8 Bales and I got it done at the rate of 1/10 of one per cent per month [which, together with the cost of the] Policy $1—is $9—to your debit—I notice your anxiety to have it go forward and shall continue to use every exertions [sic] to get it off you may rest assured that not a moment shall be lost I notice your remark in relation to Commission and in reply have to state that any thing less than 2½ per cent is not a compensation for the time and labour necessary to do justice to the arduous and difficult task of purchasing Cotton in the market it is[,] believe [it,] the Customary Commission here I know of several who purchase largely that Charges it and I know of no responsible house that does it for less. the expenses of some former purchases for you convinced me that it was impractible to do it for less there is two or [three?] times the labour and time connected with it than there is in effecting sales in your market as it appears however to have been unexpected to you I will Conform to your views on the purchases already effected and make it 1½ per ct. but must State that for any future orders you may think proper to favour you[sic; me] with it will be out of my power to execute them at any thing less than 2½ per Cent the difference of 1 pr Ct on the Invoice of 101 Bales say $65.25 is at your credit . . .

## To Messrs Thaddeus Phelps & Co (New York)

Oct 29, 1835

I wrote you on the 27 Inst handing Invoice of 299 Bales Cotton Since the[n] yours of the 24 Inst is at hand We have no change in our market Sales to day are at 14½ to 14¾ for good to prime there is less coming in and considerable of what is coming in is going in Store on a/c of the Planters—The Rail Road can take but a very inconsiderable portion of the cotton going from this place they have been full for 3 or 4 weeks the Cotton being engaged for a Considerable time ahead there was no possibility of sending yours that way In any of your future orders it may be well to give me authority to send the Cotton that way In the event of great difficulty of shipping it by the River—it may occasionally be got off in small parcels per Rail Road—Above I hand you Check for $4000. with which please pay Mr Howards Acceptance for that Sum due at your office 3/6 Novr [1] erase his signature and enclose the acceptance [to] me

You[r]s Resp[ectfull]y

WB

[1] See the letter of Aug. 1, 1829 to James Edmonson. The acceptance was made payable at a merchant's office on any day between Nov. 3 and Nov. 6. Had it been made payable at a bank a specific date would have been fixed.—S.B.

## To Messrs Chesebrough Saterlee & Co (New York)

March 13, 1833

Annexed I hand you a Small order which please Ship per first Vessell of the Schooner Line if to be had at my limits, Consigned to S. D. Corbitt Savannah.—inclose bill of Lading to him by the Vessell—Send me bill per mail—as the amot. will be Small you need not insure.—

Yr's &c

WB

25 pieces light Gingham Prints if you have them or can procure them Such as I bought 30 pieces of you in September @ 18c not exceeding that price.
30 Pieces plain Pink Buff Blue & brown Ginghams @ not exceeding 24c—
20 Ps. low priced Silk Flag Hhdfs Say @ $—[sic] 20 Flax Thread—Say 5[d] No. 18. 10d No. 22 5[d] No. 25 [5 dozen of number 18 thread, etc.]
20 Gro[ss] Blk[Black] Lasting Buttons—I bot. these in September @ 40c
6 Ps pink & White wide Stripe Gingham (stripe say ¼ to ⅜ inch wide [&] 4[ps.] Blue & White (wide Stripe Gingham (stripe Say ¼ to ⅜ inch wide [the last two items] at not exceeding 26c
24 Doz. net Suspenders same as I had of you in September 4 Doz. each

| #5 | #7 | #10 | #14 | #18 | #70 |
|---|---|---|---|---|---|
| 55c | 57½ | 60. | 67½ | 72½ | 80.— |

## To Mr. George Scott

AUGUSTA 11 Decr 1829

DEAR SIR

We have received from Mess Jno & Wm Kelly New York for Collection Scott & Banks Note @ 12 Mos from 19 Decr 1828. for $2339.53—which we presume will have your timely attention . . .

Yours Respectfully

B & B

## To Messrs J. P. & J. Nesmith (New York)

March 21, 1833—

Please Ship me per first Vessell of the Schr. Line 1 case of, ¾ Bleached Shirtings Same as previously had of you two or three times, Say last on 8 Dec. @ 8¾c provided they are at the Same price—Consign to S. D. Corbitt, Savannah, and inclose bill of Lading to him by the Vessell—Send me the bill per mail—As the amt. will be Small if you prefer it make the same deductions [for cash] as before, and I will Send you the money on receipt of the bill.—

Yr's &c.

W. B.

New York August 17 1836

Bot of Mills & Co 6 Mo

3 ps Blk Gro de Swiss 232 1/2 Yds 69 — 160 43

New York August 17 1836

John Haggerty & Sons 6 Mo

13 ps 4/4 Irish Linen 339 55 186 59

39 — Col'd 3/4 Merino (4 [illegible]) 7.25 283 75

120 Duffle Blankets 54 x 76 (2 [illegible] 1.80) 85 103 80

20 ps 10/4 [illegible] Sheeting 619 1/2 Yds 11 68 15

28 — Carolina Plaid Ginghams 1481 14 1/2 214 75 857 04

Brig Tybee

New York August 18 1836

Robert Smith 6 Mo

10 6 lb Boxes Hyson Tea 60 lb 65 39 00

5 13 do 65 65 42 25

2 10 do 20 75 19 00

5 6 Gunpowder do 30 75 22 50

2 Cases Canisters Gunpowder 1/2 24 [illegible] 48 lb 82 39 36

Bot fr 2 Cartage 25 2 25 164 36

New York August 18 1836

Bot of Masters & Marcoe Cash

30 lb Turkey Red Yarn [illegible] 112 1/2 33 75

de duct 5 pr ct for Cash 1 69 32 06

New York August 18 1836

Bot of Austin Wilmerding & Co 6 Mo

10 Gro Large Ova Coat Pearl Buttons 2/10 23 75

20 ps Jaconet Cambric 400 Yds 28 112 00 135 75

New York August 19 1836

Bot of Chas Grabbe & Victor 7 Mo

5 doz Ladies Wht Cotton Hose 18 15 62

5 " " " " " 240 17 50

5 " " " " " 234 18 75

5 " " " " " 60 19 37

5 " " " " " 60 20 62

5 " " " " " 70 22 50

5 " " " " " 232 25 00

5 " " Brown " " 239 27 75

5 " " " " " 234 25 63

5 Mens " " " 234 23 75

5 " " " " 239 26 25

5 " Brown Cotton Socks 213 8 75

5 " " " " 215 2 — 10 00

5 " " " " 229 11 25 268 74

Brig Tybee

Merchandise (including cotton garments) ordered by Bostwick from New York, August, 1836.

FROM the William Bostwick Papers (Beinecke Rare Book and Manuscript Library, Yale University). Courtesy Yale University Library.

To Messrs Reed & Sturges (New York)

AUGUSTA 16 March 1833

GENT

Above I hand you Draft for Five Hundred dollars which you will please have accepted and place the same to my credit

Yours Respectfully

WM BOSTWICK

To Mr. D. H. Merwin (Westfield, Mass)—

Nov. 21. 1835

DEAR SIR—

The lot of Segars you purchased for me through Messrs E. N and J. Thomson seem to answer very well thus far and to please my customers—and I shall ere long want more of them, when I will send to you to purchase them for me—For the present I want a few more of Such as you Sent me hundred[?] "Pellin"—If you can procure more of the Same quality please Send me 5[5,000]

Send them to E. N. & J. Thomson in New Haven requesting them to Consign them to Havens Suydam[?] & co New York with instructions to Consign them to Chs, [sic] Lippitt Savannah—[who would then forward them to Bostwick at Augusta] Please Send me bill per mail and on receipt of it I will Send you a Check— . . .

WB.

## b] RELATIONS WITH COASTAL FACTORS

To Mr Elias Bliss (Savannah)

21th. [sic] Sept 1829

DEAR SIR

Some goods from New York consigned to you to receive and forward to us, ought to have arrived with you before now, and as we have no advice from you, we supposed you might have sent us Boat Receipts by the mail, which ought to have arrived here on Monday last, and which was lost, If so please forward us Duplicate Receipts. If not shipped, please give them all the despatch possible

Yrs &c

B & BAIRD

To Mr Elias Bliss (Savannah)

AUGUSTA July 23, 1831

. . . In our operations of business we find it necessary to use a friend in Savannah now & then it therefore becomes us to look for one who is in good credit so that if we want to draw a dft on him from time to time they will always go without any trouble to us—and with those that we do our, [sic] receiving & forwarding business it is desirable to do the other— . . .

## To Mr Chas Lippet [sic] (Savannah)

October 17, 1835

DEAR SIR

Yours of the 15.th. Inst. is at hand—so soon as you can ascertain the number of Hdhs. [hogsheads] of Sugar that the Caledonia takes [brings to Savannah for me] you will please give me the earliest advice to enable me to effect insurance—She is the slowest of all Boats and I am fearful she will not deliver her cargo here before Christmas—but is doubtless the best you could do—As the ballance of the Sugar received by you for me will probably lie in Savannah Some little time you will please insure them until Shipped [up river to me at Augusta]—you have sent me no Receipt for a cask (containing Waggon Boxes & Cut Tacks) & 2 Bundles German Steel [which arrived in Savannah for me] per Ship Milledgeville bill of lading dated 27 August nor for the 20 Boxes Tobacco you wrote me you had found per Brig Maddison—and of the 30 Bags Coffee pr Brig Maddison you have sent me Receipt for but 28 Bags—Have you received the lot of Iron pr Ship Oglethorpe[?] I hope you will manage to get the Freight of it up river at a reasonable Freight it does not bear a light [sic!] freight[.] I[f] you could let it lie Safely without expense I would rather it would do so a short time than to pay as high as customary tho there are some of the size I am in want of

Yours Respy

WB.

## To Mr. Charles Lippitt (Savannah)

AUGUSTA Oct. 24, 1836

I have engaged the freight per the Iron Steam Boat Co[mpany] of 299 Bales Cotton belonging to Thad Phelps & Co of New York to whom you will please Ship it immediately[.] this Cotton has been detained here some 10 days or a fortnight for want of an opportunity to ship it and Mess[ers] T Phelps are very anxious that it should reach N York as soon as possible[.] I give you this early advice of the frght being engaged that you may keep it in [river?] and perhaps give it greater dispatch by engaging the freight of the vessell that will be the first off after the cotton arrives at your place[.] 60 Bales of the lot have gone on board to day [sic] that will leave here to morrow [sic] or monday the other 239 bales will probably go on board monday or Tuesday next and leave here by wednesday—please arrange it so as to give all dispatch possible— . . .

## To Mr Charles Lippitt (Savannah)

27 Oct 1835

DEAR SIR

Annexed is rect for 60 Bales Cotton which please ship to Messrs Thad Phelps & Co New York with all the dispatch practible [sic] charging them with expenses—As you receive cheese from N York please ship them [sic] by such boats as you think *will make the most speed* and please use your best exertions to give them every dispatch practicable—

Yrs
W.B

N.B: The remaining 239 Bales went on board yesterday and I presume will leave here to day or Tomorrow

W. B.

To Mr Charles Lippitt (Savannah)

29 Dec 1835

DEAR SIR.—

Please say what is the lowest at which you can buy 50 Bbls Northern Potatoes in good order & the lowest Freight at which you can Send them up at—P.S. If you can lay them down here at $2 Send me 50. Bbls Bbls [sic] in good order.—

Yrs
WB.

To Mr. Chas Lippett (Savannah)

November 21st 1835

DEAR SIR

Above I hand you check for $400 which please place to my Credit—What ever Cheese you may have for me I hope you will take advantage of the present rise of the river to send up at once otherwise there will be great danger in this warm weather of its getting Spoilt—I trust too that my lot [Iron?] will now Come up immediately—I am much in want of it—We have now a fine Steam Boat river it having risen here in 4 or 5 days some 5 feet—I shall be glad if you will occasionally let me know what is doing in your market in Salt—

Yours Respectfully
W BOSTWICK

To Mr. John C. Burkmyer (Charleston)

AUGUSTA 7 Dec 1835

DEAR SIR

Yours of *the 26th Nov* acknowledged receipt of mine of *the 21st Nov* in which you state 'you shall write me fully tomorrow' I have not had the pleasure of hearing from you since *untill to-day* . . . .

the delay is unfortunate as the information I sought for from your Market was intended to govern me in some opperations I had in view here & it was desirable to have had the information by return of Mail My acceptance will have attention in due time

Yours Very Respectfully
WILLIAM BOSTWICK

## To Mr John C. Burkmyer (Charleston)

AUGUSTA 19 December 1838

DEAR SIR

Above I hand you check for $1036.65—which dispose of as at foot. please erase my Signature to my acceptance and enclose the Same to me—as the demand is now over for Bagging and the article every where exceedingly dull (at New Orleans I see it is a drug as also at New York) I doubt not that a proper degree of vigilance in your market for some little time to come will enable you to effect some purchases at very low prices I want 300 to 400 pieces of Heavy bagging weighing 1⅜ to 1½ lb to the Yard 42 inch [sic] [wide]—and say 100 pieces light Hemp weighing 1 to 1⅛ lbs to the Yard 42 to 43 inches wide—I would as soon buy it for cash as any other way—May I have your vigilant attention to this matter for 2 or 3 Months to come if not convenient to you or if not consistent with your other operations please have the goodness to inform me that I may arrange to obtain the services of Some other Correspondent—I trust I shall soon have your advise [sic] of what the prospect is for the sale of Molasses in your in your [sic] market

Yours Respl

WB

PS—do you know if there is any prospect of having a direct mail service to your place

WB

| | |
|---|---|
| pay my acceptance of your Draft due 20/23 Dec payable at either of the Banks in Charleston | $1015.10 |
| pay your a/c of Expences on 28 Bbl Flour [per] Moses | 21.55 |
| | $1036.65 |

## c] RELATIONS WITH PLANTERS

24th Dec 1829

[A CIRCULAR LETTER TO 49 PLANTERS AND STOREKEEPERS]

Advices from Liverpool to the 16 Nov. continue to be favourable for cotton—prices have advanced fully an ⅛d.—Sales of the week previous were 24,600 Bales at 5⅛d to 6½d.[1] These accounts have produced a better demand in our market [Augusta]. and sales of prime lots can be made at an advance of about ¼c—very good to prime lots 8¾ to 9c.—fair to good lots 8¼ to 8½c. The bulk of cotton having come in and been sold, we look for a further improvement after the Holidays.—

Bagging 21 to 23c Sugar 9 to 12c Coffee 14 to 17c
Iron 5½ Salt 55c

1 d = pence. Since Bostwick is quoting prices in the English market he does so in terms of English money.—S.B.

(Circular) Augusta 23 May 1829

The Subscribers having associated themselves together in the Ware House and Commission business will continue the business of Burton & Bostwick from the first of June next, under the firm of Bostwick & Baird —

Our Ware House and Close Stores are the same as those occupied by Burton & Bostwick and are in perfect order for the reception of Cotton and Merchandize — We shall be thankfull for your custom and Patronage and will use our best exertions to give satisfaction in all business you may entrust to our charge —

The last advices from Liverpool to the 16th April are about the same as for some time previously. Sales of Cotton were at 5 1/8d to 6 1/8d Our market is steady at 8 1/2 to 8 3/4c for good to prime lots Choice selections command 9 Cents

Bagging 22 to 26c Sugar 10 to 12 1/2c Coffee 14 to 18c
Iron 5 1/2c Salt 55c

(A)
John Adkins
William Andrews
Milton E. Aycock
Michael L. Andrews
Doct. A. Armstead
Mark Anthony

(B)
John H. Brantly
William Barrow
Elijah Brown
Wm M. Barefield
J. W. Battle
J. N. Bolton
William B. Brewer
James F. Billingslea
W. & J. Billingslea
Blackman Burton
William Barnet
Samuel Blakely
Abraham Beall
Matthew Bronson
Henry Banks
Asa Beall
Samuel N Bailey
Wesley S Bailey

(C)
William Curry
Anderson Comer
George Cook
Turner Chapman
Abraham Cook
Solomon Chapman
D. B. Cade
Abraham Chenault
George W. Carter
Beckley C. Cook
A. A. Carsfiken
Samuel Cole
John Calhoun
Wiley Curry
Jacob Caver
Holman Childers
William Cade
John G Caldwell
Nathaniel Curry
Willis Curry

(D)
L. Q. C. Desampert
D. C. Daniel
James Daniel
William Daniel
John Dupree
Elijah Dobbs
A. L. Dickerson

(E)
David Elder
Bennet H Ely
A. W. Elder
John F Elder
Wilbourn Ely
Robt L Edwards
Isaac O Edwards
Elam Evans
Edmund Elder
James Edmonson

(F)
Benjamin Fleming
[illegible]
Joseph Ferguson
Richard Fortson
Robt Fleming

Announcement of the partnership of Bostwick & Baird (formerly Burton & Bostwick), 1829.

FROM the William Bostwick Papers (Beinecke Rare Book and Manuscript Library, Yale University). Courtesy Yale University Library.

## To Mr James Bell (Elberton)

19 Dec 1835

Dear Sir.—

Yours of the 9 inst is at hand In your purchases and engagements to me I have always been disposed to consult your accomodations as to time and am still disposed to do so—As every thing in this life is reciprocal or ought to be so it is perhaps no more than right that if I consult your accomodation that you should send your orders to me for goods—I am confident that I can execute them as much for your interest and to your satisfaction as can be done in the market—Cotton is selling at 13 to 13½ for good to prime fair quality 12½ to 12¾—inferior 9 to 11

Yours Respectfully
WB

## To Majr. T. Livingston

10th July 1829

Dear Sir

Col. Bowie has Shown us your letter requesting an advance of Four Hundred Dollars until October—Herewith we forward you the amount for which Col. Bowie has given us your note payable 1 Oct next—

The last advices from Liverpool to the 24 May are a little more favorable for cotton than previously—Sales were at 5d to 6½d Our market is very low and dull Choice Selections 8½ to 8¾c good to prime lots 8 to 8¼ fair lots 7½c

With a tender of our Services in the Ware House and Commission business we are

Ys &c
B & Baird

## To Major Wyatt W Starke (Columbia)

Augusta July 27th 1829

D Sir

Your favor of the 24th Inst by Mr Baker was handed us this morning, we are sorry that Mr. B. cannot carry up the Bagging &c ordered we presume however that an oportunity [sic] will offer before you will want the articles, should any of the neighbourhood Waggons be coming down you had perhaps better speak with them, as they may come hear [sic] and leave with out our seeing them, make no positive engagement with them for the freight as we may send it of[f] before they come . . . .

From the tenor of your Letter we infer that you would like to have more money we will reply to that part of your letter by saying that (tho we are not over stocked with the article) any reasonable sum you may want—it will afford us pleasure to accomodate you, and you will please draw on us accordingly.

Respectfully
Bostwick & Baird

## To Major Wyatt W Starke (Columbia)

AUGUSTA 3d Decr 1829

. . . Agreeably to your request we inclose you herein $500, say five Hundred Dollars in bills of the Bank of the State of Georgia. as at foot which please acknowledge receipt of per return of the Mail . . . .

Bk of State of Georgia E No. 84 dated 28 Jany 1826 payable at Greensborough to Chs A Read $100.00 [Bank of State of Georgia E No.] 152 [dated] 26 Augst 1825 [payable at] Milledgeville [to] Geo. R. Clayton [$] 100— . . .

## To Mr Wm Cox

AUGUSTA Nov 20th 1829

DEAR SIR

. . . We have let Mr [Pavy?] have a small bill of dry goods on twelve months and rely on you to see it paid. Mr L Gibson declined selling him his groceries on such long time[.] we introduced him to Mess [Rentren?] & Hill, a very respectable man who let him have them & expects us to see it paid.

Yours Respectfully

BOSTWICK & BAIRD

## To Messrs Johnston & Gwin

AUGUSTA August 3rd 1829

. . . We take the liberty of addressing you this to Say that the note was for Cash advanced to Mr. Griffith more than 3 years ago upon which all we ever got was a Commission of 2½ p Ct.

Yr &c

B & BOSTWICK

## To Mr A. M. Langdon

AUGUSTA 2nd January 1830

DEAR SIR

Agreeable to your request we hand you our account for advances and charges on your Goods, amount two hundred and seventy five 90/100 Dollars, we hope it may be found correct and prove satisfactory. we have accounts from Liverpool to the 24 Nov by way of N York, they are favourable for Cotton, and have had some effects in our market

Yrs

B & B

## To Mr Jacob F Cavin

AUGUSTA January 2nd 1830

DR SIR

Ys of the 31st ultimo is before us. we have sold your cotton at the limit of 8½ cents tho we had pretty hard work to do so, in fact if there had not of [sic] been a little stir in the market yesterday we could not have sold it for that price—above you have account-sales by which you will see that there is in our hands Two Hundred and thirteen dollars sixty nine cents subject to your order

Yrs Respectfully
B & B

## To Mr A T Stokes

AUGUSTA Jany 2nd 1830

DEAR SIR

We hand you above the sales of your Thirteen Bales Cotton at 8¼, we had hard work to get the ¼ but as we had told you we thought it worth that we were determined that you should not be disappointed—Enclosed you have one Hundred and forty three dollars and 18¾ cents being the balance due you after paying the amt of your note & Interest, that we handed to you when you were here We hope all may be found satisfactory and that you may do us the pleasure of favouring us with your future business, in which event you may rely on it that every exertion shall be used to give satisfaction, and we flatter ourselves that there would be no reason for complaint

Yrs Respectfully
BOSTWICK & B

## To Rem Remson Esqr

AUGUSTA 9th January 1830

DEAR SIR

We have sold your 28 Bales cotton agreeably to your instructions, to nett 8⅜ c— . . .

Yrs
B. & B

## To William Jones

20th June 1829

DEAR SIR

We have had another unusually dull week in the cotton market, and prices have again declined. Sales have been at fully ¼ c lower than they were last week—fine lots will not Command over 8 c. and choice Selections 8¼ to 8½ c fair lots are Selling at 9 t[o] 7½ c [sic] We inclose you herein an extract of the last advices from Liverpool to the 9th. May by which you will See that Sales were at about the Same as for some time previously—Say 5 d. to 6 d—

The present extreme depression in our market must be owing in some degree to there being So few buyers, many of whom have left here, and there is little or no Competition in the market—

Under these Circumstances we have Concluded not to Force a Sale of your cotton in Such a State of the Market—until we hear from you—We Shall therefore (unless there should be a little improvement) wait for your further instructions

Yours Respectfully
BOSTWICK & BAIRD

To Col. Wm Carry

AUGUSTA 23rd. Jany. 1830

DEAR SIR

We received for you per McGils Boat 6 Bales, which we have sold agreeably to your instructions, at 8¾ c Account sales are annexed, nett proceeds at your credit $176.83—We have paid Edward Quin your acct in full $36.91 at your Debit. Our cotton market continues without any motion or change [since] you was [sic] here.—it is more dull, but prices are about the same

Yrs

BOSTWICK & BAIRD

To William Jones, Esqr. (Elbert Co)

[December 1835]

. . . . . . . . . . . . . . . .

DEAR SIR

I have Sold your 8 Bales Cotton at 14 cents which was the best I could do as there seems no prospect of the Market being any better for some time to come I thought it would be for your interest to sell—Account Sales are above & enclosed I send you Three hundred forty five Dollars leaving a Balance due you & subject to your order as per Account above of $2.89 Whenever you want articles from Augusta I shall be happy to attend to your orders

Yours Respectfully

WM BOSTWICK

To Mr Wm Greenwood

Oct 19 1829

DEAR SIR

We have sold your 7 Bales cotton on the Waggon. . . . We have purchased the articles ordered and forwarded them by your waggon. . . .

Yrs

BOSTWICK & BAIRD

To Mr Cornelius Robinson

September 19th. 1829

DEAR SIR

. . . . . . . . . . . . . . . .

Several loads of new cotton have come to market and Such as was for sale brought 9 to 9½ cents

Yours &c

B & BAIRD

To Mr R L Edwards

Augt 29th. 1829

DEAR SIR

Yours of the 26 Inst. by Mr Bell is at hand We forwarded the articles ordered by Mr Jones for you by Becks Boat that left here on the 19th Inst.

with directions to leave them at Watkins Landing We now forward you by Mr Bell agreeably to your Request Two Hundred Dollars (say $200—) and Bagging & Salt Bill is annexed—

Ys
B & BAIRD

To Col. Harper

AUGUSTA Jany 8th 1830

DR SIR
We shiped [sic] your Piano by a waggon to the care of Mr John T. Lamar Macon, on the 26th last Month and would have written to you then but that we expected you here the early part of this month, We used some exertion to get the article sent earlier but found it impossible, hope no great inconvenience has been experienced by the delay

Respectfully
BOSTWICK & BAIRD

To Mr Thomas Williams

AUGUSTA 13th Nov. 1829

DEAR SIR
Yours of the 8 Inst is at hand. We regret to hear of the misfortune you have met with from your Gin—We hope this may find you recovering. In reply to your letter we would only observe that we always feel. [sic] a pleasure in doing what we can for the accomodation of our friends and that should you want the sum you mention through the next summer, we will advance it to you agreeably to your request

Yours Respectfully
BOSTWICK & BAIRD

## d] THE ACCOUNTS OF THREE PLANTERS

ISHAM RANEY "PLANTER" OGLETHORPE CO.

| | | | | | | | | | |
|---|---|---|---|---|---|---|---|---|---|
| 1829 | | | | | 1830 | | | | |
| Sept[r] | 25 | To Sundries | 17 | 30.75 | July | 5 | By Cash | 198 | 53.12 |
| Dec | 2 | " " | 66 | 20.50 | | | | | |
| 1830 | | | | | | | | | |
| March | 12 | To Interest | 138 | 1.87 | | | | | |
| | | | | 53.12 | | | | | 53.12 |

FROM Bostwick & Baird Ledger, vol. 1 (June, 1829–May, 1834), pp. 210 and 333 (Beinecke Rare Book and Manuscript Library, Yale University). Printed by courtesy of the Yale University Library.

LEWIS J. DUEPREE "PLANTER" SEN[r] DEKALBE CO G[EORG][ia]

| | | | | | | | | | |
|---|---|---|---|---|---|---|---|---|---|
| 1831 | | | | | 1833 | | | | |
| August | 11 | To Merchs | 320 | 143.12 | Feby | 28 | By Bills Receivable | 538. | 151.21 |
| 1833 | | | | | | | | | |
| Feby | 28 | To Interest | 536 | 8.09 | | | | | |
| | | | | 151.21 | | | | | 151.21 |

DR. EDWARD HUGHES "PLANTER" BURKE COUNTY

| | | | | | | | | | |
|---|---|---|---|---|---|---|---|---|---|
| 1829 | | | | | 1830 | | | | |
| Dec[r] | 21 | To Sundries | 80 | 307.50 | May | 10 | By Produce | 172 | 1009.05 |
| 1830 | | | | | | | | | |
| Jany | 16 | " " | 97 | 572.50 | | | | | |
| May | 14 | " Interest | 174 | 21.94 | | | | | |
| | 14 | " Balance | | 161.11 | | | | | |
| 1830 | | | | 1009.05 | 1830 | | | | 1009.05 |
| May | 19 | " Cash | 177 | 167.11 | May | 14 | By Balance | | 167.11 |
| 1832 | | | | | 1836 | | | | |
| March | 29 | To Merch[s] | 414 | 32.50 | January | 19 | By Cash | 158 | 32.50 |

## e] RELATIONS WITH COUNTRY STOREKEEPERS

### To Mess[rs] Watkins & Speed ([probably] Elberton)

12th September 1829

GENT

Annexed we hand Receipt for 13 Packges Merchandize by John Downers Waggon—This is all we have in Store for you except Such as by your instructions we are to forward by Boat Say 4 Boxes Glass Ware 1 Basket Do and 9 Kegs Nailes the latter if we can forward by waggons at 50 c before any opportunity offers by Boat we shall do so—The agreement made with Mr. Downer for the freight of his Load is that it is to be satisfactory to you—

Yours of the 10th Inst. is at hand the 2 Boxes pr Caledonia are included in Downers Load—

Acts. [accounts] are recd. from Lpool to the 26th July no change in that mark[e]t Sales of Cotton were at 5c to 6¼ c. [sic; should be pence, not cents]

Yrs &c

B & BAIRD

---

FROM William Bostwick Papers (Beinecke Rare Book and Manuscript Library, Yale University). Printed by courtesy of the Yale University Library.

To Messrs Watkins & Speed ([probably] Elberton)

19 Sept 1829

GENT.

Since our last we have recd. from Thomas Butter & Co Receipt pr Steam Boat Cos. Boats for the following goods for you, at Customary freight (viz) 1 Hhd. Sugar 2 barrels 26 Boxes 5 Tierces 1 Bundle Steel 20 ps Bagging 5 Hhds 1 pipe 5 Bales 1 Bag chains and 1 Bundle Scythes—Say 68 packages—as the river is now very low, and Boats have to be lightened a long way down the agent cannot say when they will be here. Probably during next week and the week after

We have now in Store for you 11 Boxes 1 Basket & 1 Bundle Scythes which we Shall forward agreeably to your instructions together with any more that may arrive pr first opportunity

Yrs & c

B & BAIRD

To Messrs T Speed & Co (Elberton)

Oct 10th 1829

GENT

Yours of the 5 Inst is at hand enclosing John Watkins draft on us [in favor of T Speed & Co] for $65.00—which we have placed to your credit—"

. . . . . . . . . . . . . . .

To Messrs A & J Sellers (McDonough)

Dec 12, 1835

GENT,

The purchase of goods made by Mr. [Shiner?] last Spring for you being due I will thank you to write me a line informing me how Soon it will Suit your Convenience to pay it— . . .

Yr's &c

WB.

To Messrs L Bissel & Co

June 15 th. 1829

GENT

Yours of the 6th Inst. is at hand, inclosing Forty Dollars which is at your credit in Burton & Bostwicks Books—Col Scovall had Spoken to us about accepting your draft for $700, and we informed him that it was out of our power to accept Drafts in that way at long time without Produce [cotton] in Store—

The advices from Liverpool to the 1 May Continue much the Same as previously &c

Yrs &c

B & BAIRD

# 4] Relations between Country Storekeepers and Coastal Factors: Some Letters of Andrew Jackson, Storekeeper

## To John Hutchings

KNOXVILLE, March 17, 1804

DEAR JACK.

On yesterday I reached this place from Jonesborough and found your letter of the 13th. Instant in the post office inclosing the price current at new orleans of all kind of groceries, from which I am certain that we will find a great advantage and saving in laying in all our Groceries, nails, and steel at that place, and perhaps Nankeens. I wish you to make the arangement with Mr Davidson, and I think the boat can reach Nashville from Neworleans against the first of July. this plan will enable us always to convert our cash to beneficial purposes in cumberland, and in case the Boat can reach Nashville against the 10th. or 20th of July it will be as early as our goods can reach there from Philadelphia. I therefore think that the better plan to adopt, is to bring our groceries, nails and steele from Neworleans. From the prices of Deer and Bear skins I think it will be well to sell at Neworleans, the small furs in Nashville. Bear skins sells well in Baltimore, but as our object is to get clear of Debt I think it best not to risque much, and to sell at any markett where we can sell to save ourselves.

I am sorry Mr Fisher did not buy the Bear skins, but it may happen that we will receive a better price for them at Neworleans. The iron is delivered at the north fork of Holston, I saw colo. Preston, and also Mr Baker who I had the contract with to carry it to Nashville. he as soon as the iron was delivered declined taking Mr Kings load, in short such was the situation of things I was obliged to agree to receive it, and from Mr Deaderick telling me he would not receive the half I have changed the contract in part, I have agreed to receive five ton of castings in liew of that much iron, the castings at forty pounds pr ton, this in case the castings reaches the north fork before the water rises. Holston is now rising and I expect the Boat to descend the river in a few days—this expence will have to be met some how. I hope Mr Sewal has returned and has brought some cash and that Capt Campbell has remitted the cash on hand, and that the Debt of Thos Mitchel has been recovered, from this source I hope the amount of the freitage of the iron can be raised which will be $375. if it cannot write me immediately and I will remit what I can to that use, it must be had, and be there at the arival of the Boat. I have stated to Mr Deaderick that he may still have half, and requested him to say to you whether he will receive it or not, if he does only half the above sum will be [have] to be paid by us. write me on the

FROM John Spencer Bassett, ed., *Correspondence of Andrew Jackson* (Washington, D.C.: The Carnegie Institution, 1926), vol. I, pp. 96–101. Reprinted by permission of the publisher.

receipt of this letter and inform me whether the sum can be raised or not there and I will in case it cannot send on my certificates for two hundred dollars, and the Ballance in cash. we can make money out of the iron and castings. we must sell for cash if Possible. you will place the money in the hand of Tatam if you can raise it, to whom I have directed Baker to apply. you will have to give Greer a particular charge about the iron to have it all weighed, and get Major Tatam to notify him on its arival. I shall expect you to send me a statement of the amount of cotton shipped to Neworleans by us—as soon as sold send on the Bills to me in Philadelphia, directed to the care of Meeker Denman and Co. I stated to you in case Mr Coffee went on to enclose them to me at Nashville but from your letter I expect he will not, it would be gratefull to me if he could with advantage to all as it is a long and tedious Journey, but I will encounter it. I am sorry I wrote Mr Coffee to come to this place unless he comes on prepared to go on to Philadelphia The Severeites is all quiet, and the old rascal has to father the Blackguard peace himself, altho he wishes to lay it on his son in law *Windel* who can scarcely read english. They are too base a set to speak about. My Dear Jack it is the last letter I will (I expect) write you before you set out. let me Just repeat, write me about the cash to pay the freightage of the iron, whether it can be raised or not, whether D[eadrick] and Tatam takes one half. send me the amount of our cotton, and a memorandom of goods to be Bot. and lastly, send on the Bills as soon as Possible to me at Philadelphia directed as before, and if Possible purchase they Groceries at Neworleans. You must state to me your determination on this subject and May heaven Preserve you farewell.

P S Say to Mr Coffee if he is not started that he need not come on unless he intends [to go] on to Philadelphia. Would it not be well to sell as much of the iron at cost, say seven pence pr lb. as would pay the carriage, even at six pence. if Mr Deaderick does not receive half, I think some of the merchants would buy at this price. the ballance we would then have to raise the original cost out of. if cash can not be commanded in hand for it it will sell at one shilling for cotton by retail and we will have to this time twelve months to make the cash out of the produce we receive. if we can have a general assortment of groceries iron salt and so forth we must make money the ensuing season. resolution and industry with oeconomy will remove mountains. will it not be well to get the Boat to deliver the iron at my landing instruct Greer accordingly. I wish a house prepared to receive the goods either the long room of the new building [?] or a house at the lick as you and Mrs Jackson may conclude.

## John Hutchings to Jackson.

NASHVILLE, March 30, 1804

DEAR SIR:

I this evening retched nashvill on my way to Orleans, after undergoing Some feteague. I had the misfortun of Sinking one of the Boates after being about half loaded, the Boate Sprung aleake in the Bow, and all we Could do She would go to Bottom, there was about Twenty or Twenty five Bales that got Wet, I gave them Two days sun before I put them on Board, I also have plased them on Top of the Boates, I was under the necessaty of taking the publick Boate, and was under the necessaty of Taking off Every plank all Round the gunnels.

The amount of Cotton is as follows [1]

| | |
|---|---|
| Cotton from Hunters Hill | 25,567 |
| Cotton from Gallatin | 16 364 |
| ——— from Lebanon | 14,148 |
| | 56 079 |

I Recd your letter by the last mail, I shew the letter to aunt Jackson, which has Served to gave her mi[n]d Greate ease. She has Taken up an Idia that mr. Coffee was going on Dueling Bisness.

I have Seen Majr. Tatum and named to him Respecting the Iron, he States that they will not Receve any part. I am Vary much affraid that it will be Vary hard to sell as the seasson for selling is past; for my part when every Cash is bought in Que[s]tion, I feele feerful and not[h]ing will Command it. I wish you to reeturn and let mr. Coffee go on, for god only knows how the mony is to be Raist for the Carriges for the Iron. for my part I Cant see how this bisness [is] to be Condu[c]ted in boath our absences. I have nothing more at present. I will let you heare from me at Natcez.

Hea[l]th and Respect

## N. Davidson to Jackson.

NEW ORLEANS, July 14, 1804

DEAR SIR,

Your letter of 24th. June addressed to B D and Co.[2] has been duly received, and as it expresses sentiments pointed to me, I have taken the liberty to address you in my own name. It becomes incumbent on me to state as near as possible the particulars of this business done for your House, and by which you have conceiv'd yourself so much injured; I cannot but suppose it is from misinformation or sentiments of this kind would never have come from you.

When your Mr Hutchings arrived here with the Cotton, it was seen by him that it was impossible to effect a Sale at any thing like a saving price, the nominal price being only 13$ french wt. and this he objected to take, several days elapsed before any thing was done.

I did not concceive that I had any direction whatever of the Cotton, either as to its sale or its destination, Mr H. being on the spot, as partner, and owner of the Cotton, could best judge what might be best for your interest. True it is Sir, that in a conversation with you the last time we met, you stated that the Cotton should be sent on to me to this place, and at the same time expressed a pointed objection to Ship to Europe and requested to

[1] This statement seems to mean that Jackson and Hutchings had been conducting stores at Hunter's Hill, Gallatin, and Lebanon before the triple partnership of 1804 was formed.

[2] Boggs, Davidson, and Co.

sell on the spot. Had the business been left on this footing a sale should have been made here at the best possible price.

But on the 28th. Febry. after you had started from home, and when at Gallatine, I received pr. Mr Anderson your letter wherein you advised me you had concluded to send on Mr Hutchings, *with the Cotton,* that he had sufficient funds in his hands to discharge all the debts, and that he had proper instructions to dispose and apportion the amount, and requesting I would receive our claim at this place. this I conceived paramount to any directions given to me, and as I have before observed when Mr H. arrived, I did *not* conceive myself in any power to act, except by his direction, other, than giving such advice as in my power to do, he might request.

When Mr. Hutchings asked my advice as to the destination, or what had best be done, I gave him such as at the same time I should have done to any one else, and which I thought best for his interest, and *in* which if any inconvenience was suffered we loose our proportion. At the same time observed in the conversation as to the shipment to Liverpool of a part, that to me you had expressed a disapprobation to a foreign shipment, but observed, that I believed it best for your interest, and at the same time, requested that he would write you; and state that it was advice of mine, and not an act, *this he promised to do.*

When Mr H. had made up his mind to ship it, having put it on board *himself, I can pledge my honor* that no agreement was made or even talk'd of as to advance, other than that expressed in the receipt given him, nor would I have made any other.

I will here remark, that you are under mistaken idias as to advantages accruing to the shipping merchant, from Shipments of this kind made, it is of no kind of interest or benefit to us, and we do it purely to accommodate. and we beg you to take it in this light. We only receive the advances which, we ourselves make, and on which we pay interest from the very day it's made, untill the property is sold, and the Consignee in Cash.

As to interest being stopt on Debts due by the shippee, it is more than ever we know, nor do we believe it is the Case, as it respects ourselves we can in truth say we are not in want of such assistance, for as yet we have been able to meet our engagements abroad without ever a charge of the kind, and were it even the Case, this shipment of yours which you have chose to infer we have used for this object, would be but a sorry assistance to us I assure you.

You are also mistaken as to interest charged on the shipments of the last Year. The Enquiry I recollect you made of me when at Nashville. I stated that the interest on ⅔ *d.* should cease on the shipment being made and the other ⅓ when the sales were received, *and on which we loose,* but which I chose to allow in Stothart and Bell's instance as the quarter part was a payment to ourselves.

But Sir to the point. I was totally uninformed as to any agreement being made between Mr Massey and Mr Hutchings. if so, why not Mr H. mention it to me. Mr Massey may have expressed as in his opinion it would neat 17 or 18 Cents. and so did I, or should not have advised a shipment. But does it follow that we should make an advance of price that there is a probability of its neating, in failure of which we should lie for at least one season independent of our debt under a heavy advance to you. No Sir, at the time it was done I conceived we were doing for you even more than could be expected in making an advance on a price much above the Market here, and which appeared perfectly satisfactory to Mr. Hutchings.

As to giving Bills for the amount of the two thirds. it could make no kind of difference to us, and had Mr Hutchings expressed a preference for them he should have reced them. but as a further shipment was to be made, and we supposed you would be in Philada. when the direction for payment would arrive, I conceived nothing further necessary than to direct Mr Boggs what was to be paid on your accot. and you with them could make the destribution, and *this also appeared to be satisfactory to Mr H.* Mr Boggs was by the first opportunity advised of the shipment with direction to appropriate the Sum as you might order, and which there is no doubt but has been done, if you have left the list with you[r] agent.

As to the business transacted with Mess and Cayes both of which were entire strangers to me as to business. The offer of an advance was made by Mr Massey (through me) it was done by a mistaken calculation of his, and they benefited by it. and will inform you that for him I had a great desire to be off the Contract.

As to an offer made you by Messrs. Clifford when at Nashville, I knew of none, nor would it have had any influence with me, or induced any offer from me. The Only benefit we have or need is a common commission here for transacting the business, and it can be of no more interest to us in shipping to an European Port, than an Atlantic one, and in this branch we shall always strive to give satisfaction here. It surprises me that Mr Hutchings when here should appear perfectly satisfied with every thing done by us for him, that he should receive the receipt, which when I delivered read to him, *and which he confessed to be correct,* and then on his return home to state what you relate respecting our Conduct, is truly to me astonishing. I am convinced you must have given this business no reflection or you would not have formed the conclusion you have expressed in your letter.

I have already by direction of your partner when here and shall again, direct G and W. to Close the Sales immediately.

Yours etc

## Jackson and Hutchings to Boggs and Davidson.

HUNTERS HILL, TENNESSEE, July 31, 1804.

GENTLEMEN:

Your letter of the 23rd of June inclosing the acct. of sales of 130 Bales of cotton shipped in the brigg Maria the 19th June 1803 reached us the 24th Inst. We observe from the receipt of your Mr. Davidson that there was recd. 133 Bales of cotton, one of which was injur,d, repacked with other Cotton and sent to Philadelphia, two therefore remains unaccounted for.

We have with due attention viewed the amt. of expence as stated by Mr. Barber which appears exorbitant, some of the Items we do not understand, and one of which we do conceive cannot be consistent with the custom of

Merchants and Justice apply to us, which shall be stated in order. The Items that we do not understand and wish to be explained are first "£ 1560 injured [insured] at 3½ Guineas, etc. and carried out, £62.3.7. What this insurance applies to we are at a loss, whether it is the Cotton, or the sum raised on the sales, therefore before we can say any thing on that subject we wish to know the real charge—second "Guarantee commissions on whole amt. 4 Pr. Ct. £:94.5—we cannot well understand, whether this is a commission on sales or whether it is a charge for guarranteeing the payment of the purchase money. If the latter we would be happy to be advised how and by what law usage or custom, this is introduced and established. Just observing if it is an item customary amongst Merchants, and that others are in the habit of paying, we would not if in our power wish to be exonerated from it therefore wish your explanation on this Item.

The charge which we conceive cannot apply to us in the sum of £124.4 Interest on cash advanced: It will be recollected that the custom is well established in Shipments, that the shipper is entitled to draw for ⅔ of the amt. of the Shipment as soon as the Cotton is on board, last year this was done in every case except ours, and the whole remained in your hands, Messrs. Stothart and Bell advise that they did not draw a cent on that cotton shipped, it follows that we were (or they, which is all one) entitled to receive from you on the shipment ⅔, therefore the expence paid by you were cash we was entituled to and there would be Justice in requiring interest on the Balance of the ⅔ in your hands, but cannot be a shaddow of claim upon us for that Interest as we understand the custom established. Your Mr Davidson well understood the advantage resulting to you by all this Cash remaining in your hands, and for this reason ( as we suppose) did come into an express agreement and declaration that Stothart and Bell should receive a credit for the neet proceeds which should be entered as of the 16th June 1803, and that no Interest should be calculated on their debt to the Amt. of the Neet proceeds from the above debt being the day of the shipment, these observations will apply to the charge of Interest that you have made in the acct. of Watson and Jackson, which we do not conceive we ought to pay for the reason before stated and expect that the Interest in both cases will be struck out and a credit entered for the nett proceeds to Stothart and Bell as of the 16th. of June 1803, agreeable to the promise of your Mr. Davidson.

There is an item in your acct. against Watson and Jackson for "proportion of Postages and other small charges not included in the acct. of Sales". this is a small acct. but not being informed of the Justice of the demand, before we can say we are liable to pay, we wish the Justice of it to be explained, and rest assured as soon as we find it a charge that we are bound or ought to pay or allow it will give us pleasure to do it, but it being of date June 12th. 1804, long after the sales were made, and Cash in hand we are at a loss to know how it can apply to us as the Cotton was shipped for and on your acct. but still it may be Just and agreeable to custom if so as soon as it is shewn to us, we will with pleasure admit it.

The statement by your Mr. Davidson of the time the credit should be entered has been the guide for the settlement between Stothart and Bell and us we therefore wish your answer as early as convenient that we may close those Accts. Some few Posts ago I forwarded to Mr. William Stothart Philadelphia a Bill of Laden of 100 Bales of our cotton shipped in Brig Felicity Capt. Jones, for Liverpool to be presented to you for payment of ⅔ the amt. shipped. This shipment was contrary to expectation. when our Andrew Jackson went on to Philadelphia his directions were different and did not expect it, some circumstances attending the shipment truly unpleasant, And tend to lessen that confidence in your Mr. Davidson that we flattered ourselves were so well placed. As advised by our Mr. Hutchings when he reached New orleans and found Cotton only at 12/100, he applied to Mr. D. to whom he was referred for advise who advised a shipment to Liverpool and did expressly agree to Invoice the Cotton at 14/100 and draw bills for the Amt. Mr. Massey agent for Green and Wainwright being there and on examination of the Cotton stated that to a certainty it would neet from 17 to 18/100. as soon as the Cotton was on board our Mr. H. applied for the Bill of laden and the Bills. When your Mr. Davidson did refuse to Invoice the Cotton at more than 13/100 and would not draw any bills, but detained Mr. H. until the Mail had left the City and then only gave him the Memorandom which no doubt Mr. Stothart has handed you. This Sir is conduct that is unpleasant indeed, but as we have wrote your Mr. Davidson on the subject expecting him to give directions for the payment of ⅔ at 14/100 we shall refrain at present from remarking further on the subject; But we must observe that your Mr. David[s]on was well advised that we had been offered by the Mr. Clifford 14/100 for our Cotton to draw immediately for ⅔—Credit our acct. with part of the other third, and as soon as sales were effected the balance to be subject to our Order. this we refused to accede to from principals of Justice to our Creditors all of which your Mr Davidson was advised off and did applaud, and I cannot refrain from observing that the treatment to our Mr. Hutchings under the banners of promised friendship and services are such that require an explanation from your Mr. Davidson, and I hope he has ordered you to advance the ⅔ at 14/100.

Sales are dull, small quantities of Cotton planted, but at present look promising; our A. Jackson has made sale of his possessions, is to receive ⅔ of the amt. on Christmass day next. this we flatter ourselves will enable us to meet all our debts next spring.

With sentiments of Esteem and respect we are Gentlemen Your Mo. Obt. Servts.

# CONCLUSION

In any historical reconstruction it is necessary to take into account the effects of numerous interacting forces if one wishes to explain the most simple event. The problem of explanation increases with the complexity of the event. And the growth of a national economy—involving intricate interplay between political, social, technological, and psychological factors, as well as economic ones—is indeed a complex "event." It is, however, difficult to apply the methodology required by the philosophy that all things are necessary for the explanation of any one thing. Fortunately, one need not try. Common sense suggests that economic growth, even within the bounds of a single national arena, cannot have occurred everywhere with the same degree of rapidity. What must be explained, therefore, are the causes of divergence—in either direction—from "average" growth.

In the rapidly developing economy before the Civil War, the foreign demand for American cotton set in motion by the English industrial revolution is a factor with an unusually satisfying degree of explanatory power. American earnings from the sale of cotton abroad permitted the importation of capital necessary to sustain the pace of growth, and at the same time helped supply the means by which significantly specializing geographic regions were enabled to exchange their respective surpluses with each other. This tendency to concentrate resources on particular kinds of economic activity—encountered at the occupational as well as the territorial and sectoral levels, since all levels were influenced by widening markets for goods and services—enabled the economy as a whole to function with a higher degree of efficiency and sped the pace of its growth.

# Suggested Readings

(Books and articles from which selections have been reprinted in this volume are not listed below.)

ALBION, ROBERT G., *The Rise of New York Port.* New York, 1939.

———, *Square Riggers on Schedule: The New York Sailing Packets to England, France and the Cotton Ports.* Princeton, 1938.

———, "New York Port and Its Disappointed Rivals, 1815–1860," *Journal of Economic and Business History,* III (1930–31), 602–29.

ANDREANO, RALPH, ed., *New Views on American Economic Development.* Cambridge, Mass., 1965. [See pp. 187–225 for the exchange between Albert Fishlow and Robert W. Fogel.]

ATHERTON, LEWIS, *The Southern Country Store, 1800–1860.* Baton Rouge, La., 1949.

BRUCHEY, STUART, *The Roots of American Economic Growth, 1607–1861.* New York, 1965.

BUCK, NORMAN S., *The Development of Anglo-American Trade, 1800–1850.* New Haven, 1925.

COLE, ARTHUR H., "Cyclical and Sectional Variations in the Sale of Public Lands, 1816–60," *Review of Economics and Statistics,* IX, No. 1 (Jan., 1927), 50 ff.

CONRAD, A. H., and JOHN R. MEYERS, "The Economics of Slavery in the Ante-Bellum South," *Journal of Political Economy,* LXVI, No. 2 (April, 1958), 95–130.

GENOVESE, EUGENE D., *The Political Economy of Slavery.* New York, 1965.

———, "The Significance of the Southern Plantation for American Economic Growth," *Journal of Southern History,* XXVIII (Nov., 1962), 422–37.

HAMMOND, MATTHEW B., *The Cotton Industry: An Essay in American Economic History.* New York, 1897.

HELPER, HINTON R., *The Impending Crisis of the South: How to Meet It.* New York, 1857.

HIDY, RALPH, *The House of Baring in American Trade and Finance.* Cambridge, Mass., 1949.

INGLE, EDWARD, *Southern Sidelights, a Picture of Social and Economic Life in the South a Generation Before the War.* New York, 1896.

JONES, FRED M., *Middlemen in the Domestic and Foreign Commerce of the United States, 1800–1860.* Urbana, Ill., 1937.

KENT, FRANK R., *The Story of Alexander Brown & Sons.* Baltimore, 1925.

KETTELL, THOMAS P., *Southern Wealth and Northern Profits, as Exhibited in Statistical Facts and Official Figures.* New York, 1860.

NORTH, DOUGLASS C., *The Economic Growth of the United States, 1790–1860.* Englewood Cliffs, N.J., 1961.

NORTH, DOUGLASS C., "International Capital Flows and the Development of the American West," *Journal of Economic History,* XVI, No. 4 (Dec. 1956), 493–505.

———, *Growth and Welfare in the American Past: A New Economic History.* Englewood Cliffs, N.J., 1966.

PHILLIPS, ULRICH B., *American Negro Slavery.* New York, 1918.

———, *A History of Transportation in the Eastern Cotton Belt to 1860.* New York, 1908.

SCHMIDT, LOUIS B., "Internal Commerce and the Development of National Economy Before 1860," *Journal of Political Economy,* XLVII (Dec., 1939), 798–822.

———, "The Internal Grain Trade of the United States," *Iowa Journal of History and Politics,* XVIII, No. 1 (Jan., 1920), 103 ff.

SMITH, ALFRED G., *Economic Readjustment of an Old Cotton State: South Carolina, 1820–1860.* Columbia, S.C., 1958.

STAMPP, KENNETH M., *The Peculiar Institution: Slavery in the Ante-Bellum South.* New York, 1958.

STIGLER, GEORGE J., "The Division of Labor is Limited by the Extent of the Market," *Journal of Political Economy,* LIX, No. 3 (June, 1951), 185–93.

TAYLOR, GEORGE R., *The Transportation Revolution, 1815–1860.* New York, 1951.

WENDER, HERBERT, *Southern Commercial Conventions, 1837–1859.* Baltimore, 1930.

WOODMAN, HAROLD D., "Itinerant Cotton Merchants of the Antebellum South," *Agricultural History,* XL (April, 1966), 79–90.